Test Prep

MCSE

Windows NT® Server 4

Second Edition

William J. Anderson
R. Andrew Brice
Bill Matsoukas
Michael Lane Thomas

New Riders

201 West 103rd Street, Indianapolis, Indiana 46290

MCSE TestPrep: Windows NT Server 4, Second Edition

International Standard Book Number: 0-7357-0012-5

Library of Congress Catalog Card Number: 98-88004

Printed in the United States of America

First Printing: December, 1998

00 99 98   4 3 2 1

Trademarks

Warning and Disclaimer

EXECUTIVE EDITOR
Mary Foote

ACQUISITIONS EDITOR
Steve Weiss

DEVELOPMENT EDITOR
Ami Frank

MANAGING EDITOR
Sarah Kearns

PROJECT EDITOR
Clint McCarty

COPY EDITOR
Amy Lepore

INDEXER
Craig Small

TECHNICAL EDITORS
Jeff Peo
John Shaw

PROOFREADER
Maribeth Echard

PRODUCTION
Jeannette McKay

Contents at a Glance

Table of Contents

4 Connectivity   163

5 Monitoring and Optimization   189

About the Authors

William J. Anderson wrote his first computer program in Fortran using key punch cards in the '60s. Bill showed a real knack for the logic required to program, but his real love was golf. He was a member of the golf team at Michigan State University. Upon completing college, he became a professional golfer and earned a living giving lessons. In the late '70s, Bill suffered a career-ending injury and was forced to find something other than golf to make a living. He found computers again in the '80s. He was one of the first to install Novell networks in San Diego. He was also one of the first to provide the training end users needed to operate their workstations on corporate networks. Bill was a Principal Instructor for the San Diego branch of a national training company, earning instructor of the year honors for the years 1992–1995, and still teaches official curriculum as a Microsoft Certified Trainer and Certified Novell Instructor. He is the president of his own consulting firm specializing in Internet and WAN technologies. He hosts over 20 e-commerce websites on his servers. He also holds an MCSE, CNE, and MCP+ Internet. Bill can be contacted at bill@webshare.com.

R. Andrew Brice currently works as a Senior Instructor for Prosoft. His certifications include Novell's CNA and CNE in both 3.x and 4.x, as well as Microsoft's Certified Professional, Microsoft Certified Trainer, and Microsoft Certified Systems Engineer in Windows NT 3.51 and 4.0. He has currently been certified as a Certified Internet Webmaster (CIW) in Security, Administration, and TCP/IP. Since 1991, he has consulted in network design and implementation for small and large organizations including Fortune 1000. Over the last four years, he has included training on both Microsoft and Novell curriculum. He has coauthored and been a technical editor for more than 10 books published by Macmillan, some of which include *MCSE TestPrep: Windows 95* and *MCSE Fast Track: Windows 98*. As a speaker at trade shows such as Internet World '98, he has presented daylong seminars on topics ranging from TCP/IP to Windows NT and UNIX integration. He credits his accomplishments to the love and support provided by both his wife Susan and daughter Katie. He can be reached at andrewb@prosofttraining.com.

Bill Matsoukas is a Principal Consultant for an international firm. He is a Certified NetWare Engineer as well as an MCSE. Bill lives in Westminster, Colorado, with his wife Terrilynn and three children. When not working, he likes to take advantage of living in Colorado by biking, hiking, and snowboarding.

Michael Lane Thomas began his long trek toward epiphany in the early '90s, beginning with his sudden realization that the "hard-seater" from Shanghai to Canton was an optimistic overstatement at best. After spending time working as an English teacher in Japan, moonlighting as a "batboy" at Tokyo Dome's Baseball Café, and living the life of a *gaijin*, Michael got his first taste of the Internet while acting as a business consultant to Global Online Japan, Japan's first commercial provider of Internet access. Not knowing what to do, he took a slow boat to China, detoured through Macao, Hong Kong, and Beijing, only to get lost somewhere in the middle of Ulan Bator, the capital of Mongolia. The sudden realization that this wasn't Kansas anymore represented Michael's second step toward epiphany. After a trans-Siberian trip (via *Monkey Business*), a midnight customs scare sneaking out of Russia, and a run-in with a burly border-crossing guard in Lithuania, Michael's realization that this *definitely* wasn't Kansas anymore made his trip to epiphany nearly complete. Upon returning to Jayhawk Country, Michael met, fell in love with, and married his lovely wife Jennifer. Only then, did he finally understand the meaning of epiphany. Since then, Michael has spent his time earning his A+, MCSE, MCSD, MCT certifications, and becoming the first professional awarded the MCSE+I title. When not writing, speaking, or burning candles at both ends, Michael can be reached at michael@thefastlane.com.

Dedication

From Bill Anderson: I dedicate my work on this project to RaeLynn, for her undying faith and support.

From Andrew Brice: I would like to dedicate this book to my beautiful and loving wife Susan. I love you, kitten! You make my life complete!

From William Matsoukas: My work in this book is by default dedicated to my daughter Kimmy. The earnings from the book are going from the publisher to my bank to Boston University.

From Michael Lane Thomas: I dedicate my efforts to the love and support of my beautiful wife Jennifer, and to the grace and understanding of Jesus Christ.

Acknowledgments

From Bill Anderson: Thanks to Jeff Peo and John Shaw for their fine technical editing.

From Andrew Brice: I would like to thank everyone at Macmillan including Steve Weiss, Nancy Warner, Ami Frank, Nancy Maragioglio, and David Dwyer for their continued patience and guidance. A special thank you goes to Emmett Dulaney for allowing me the opportunity to participate in such a wonderful project. I would be remiss in passing up the opportunity to thank my Mom and Dad for the wonderful guidance they provided me in my youth. Lastly, I would like to thank my wife Susan and daughter Katie for their continued patience and support through the long hours I spent huddled next to my computer. Thank you, girls!

From Bill Matsoukas: The toughest part of writing technical books is the author review, where the technical editors scrutinize your work and note every mistake in your manuscript. Without tech editors, it would be impossible to provide you with a completely reliable source of information. Thanks to Jeff Peo and John Shaw.

From Michael Lane Thomas: Special thanks to the technical editors, Jeff and John, my Acquisitions Editor Steve, and to those whose guidance and patience were indispensable on this project. Extra special thanks to Mark Atkinson, an associate I am honored to call my friend, and to Larry P. Thomas, whose love, patience, and honor make me proud to call him Daddy.

Tell Us What You Think!

As the reader of this book, *you* are our most important critic and commentator. We value your opinion and want to know what we're doing right, what we could do better, what areas you'd like to see us publish in, and any other words of wisdom you're willing to pass our way.

As the Executive Editor for the Certification team at Macmillan Computer Publishing, I welcome your comments. You can fax, email, or write me directly to let me know what you did or didn't like about this book—as well as what we can do to make our books stronger.

Please note that I cannot help you with technical problems related to the topic of this book, and that due to the high volume of mail I receive, I might not be able to reply to every message.

When you write, please be sure to include this book's title and author, as well as your name and phone or fax number. I will carefully review your comments and share them with the author and editors who worked on the book.

Fax: 317-581-4663

Email: certification@mcp.com

Mail: Mary Foote
            Executive Editor
            Certification
            Macmillan Computer Publishing
            201 West 103rd Street
            Indianapolis, IN 46290 USA

Introduction

The MCSE TestPrep series serves as a study aid for people preparing for Microsoft Certification exams. The series is intended to help reinforce and clarify information with which you are already familiar by providing sample questions and tests as well as summary information relevant to each of the exam objectives. Note that this series is not intended to be the only source for your preparation; rather, it is a review of information with a set of practice tests that can be used to increase your familiarity with the exam questions. Using books in this series with the complementary MCSE: Training Guide books can increase your likelihood of success when taking the exam.

WHO SHOULD READ THIS BOOK

The Windows NT Server 4 book in the MCSE TestPrep series is intended specifically for students in the final stages of preparing for Microsoft's Windows NT Server 4 (70–067) exam, which is one of the core exam electives in the MCSE Microsoft Windows NT 4.0 Track program.

HOW THIS BOOK HELPS YOU

This book provides a wealth of review questions that are similar to those you will encounter on the actual exam and are categorized by the exam objectives published by Microsoft. Each answer is explained in detail in the objective's Answers and Explanations section. The Further Review section provides additional information that is crucial for successfully passing the exam. The two full-length practice exams at the end of the book will help you determine whether you have mastered the skills necessary to successfully complete the exam. It also will identify any areas you need to study further before taking the exam.

How to Use This Book

This book is designed to be used during the final stages of exam preparation. When you feel like you're fairly well prepared for the exam, use this book as a test of your knowledge. Each objective is covered by a minimum of 10 questions. Start by using the practice questions as a self-quiz. Circle what you think is the correct answer (or answers), and then check your answers against the Answer Key. Identify which questions you missed and find them in the Answers and Explanations section. Here you will find the question repeated, the correct answer(s), and a thorough explanation. You can use the Further Review section if you missed several questions for one objective. After going through the questions for each objective, you will know where your comprehension is sufficient and what you need to continue to study. This is the best study tool available to help reinforce what you already know and to identify areas that require more work.

After you have taken the practice tests and feel confident in the material, you are ready to schedule your exam. Use this book for a final quick review just before taking the test to make sure all the important concepts are set in your mind. Appendix C, "Fast Facts," summarizes key information you need to know about each objective. This feature provides an excellent last-minute review before you take the exam.

Hardware/Software Recommendations

MCSE TestPrep: Windows NT Server 4 Enterprise, 2nd Edition will help you review concepts with which you already have training and experience. To make the most of the review, you need to have as much background and experience as possible. The best way to do this is to combine studying with working on real networks by using the products on which you will be tested. This section describes the minimum computer requirements you need to build a good practice environment.

- Any computer on the Microsoft Hardware Compatibility List

- 486DX 33 MHz or better (Pentium recommended)

- A minimum of 16MB of RAM (32MB recommended)

- 125MB (or more) of free disk space (160MB for RISC-based systems)

- 3 1/2-inch 1.44MB floppy drive

- VGA (or Super VGA) video adapter

- VGA (or Super VGA) monitor

- Mouse or equivalent pointing device

- Two-speed (or faster) CD-ROM drive

- Presence on an NT Network

- Windows NT Server software

WHAT THE NT SERVER 4 EXAM (#70-067) COVERS

The NT Server 4 exam (#70-067) covers the four main topic areas represented by the conceptual groupings of the test objectives. Each chapter represents one or more of these main topic areas. The exam objectives are listed by topic area in the following sections.

Planning

Plan the disk drive configuration for various requirements. Requirements include the following:

- Choosing a file system
- Choosing a fault-tolerance method

Choose a protocol for various situations. Protocols include the following:

- TCP/IP
- NWLink IPX/SPX-Compatible Transport
- NetBEUI

Installation and Configuration

Install Windows NT Server on Intel-based platforms.

Install Windows NT Server to perform various server roles. Server roles include the following:

- Primary domain controller
- Backup domain controller
- Member server

Install Windows NT Server by using various methods. Installation methods include the following:

- CD-ROM
- Over the network
- Network Client Administrator
- Express versus custom

Configure protocols and protocol bindings. Protocols include the following:

- TCP/IP
- NWLink IPX/SPX-Compatible Transport
- NetBEUI

Configure network adapters. Considerations include the following:

- Changing IRQ, IO base, and memory addresses
- Configuring multiple adapters

Configure Windows NT Server core services. Services include the following:

- Directory Replicator
- License Manager
- Other services

Configure peripherals and devices. Peripherals and devices include the following:

- Communication devices
- SCSI devices
- Tape device drivers
- UPS devices and UPS service
- Mouse drivers, display drivers, and keyboard drivers

Configure hard disks to meet various requirements. Requirements include the following:

- Allocating disk space capacity
- Providing redundancy
- Improving performance
- Providing security
- Formatting

Configure printers. Tasks include the following:

- Adding and configuring a printer
- Implementing a printer pool
- Setting print priorities

Configure a Windows NT Server computer for various types of client computers. Client computer types include the following:

- Windows NT Workstation
- Microsoft Windows 95
- Microsoft MS-DOS–based

Managing Resources

Manage user and group accounts. Considerations include the following:

- Managing Windows NT groups
- Managing Windows NT user rights
- Administering account policies
- Auditing changes to the user account database

Create and manage policies and profiles for various situations. Policies and profiles include the following:

- Local user profiles
- Roaming user profiles
- System policies

Administer remote servers from various types of client computers. Client computer types include the following:

- Windows 95
- Windows NT Workstation

Manage disk resources. Tasks include the following:

- Copying and moving files between file systems
- Creating and sharing resources
- Implementing permissions and security
- Establishing file auditing

Connectivity

Configure Windows NT Server for interoperability with NetWare servers by using various tools. Tools include the following:

- Gateway Services for NetWare
- Migration Tool for NetWare

Install and configure Remote Access Service (RAS). Configuration options include the following:

- Configuring RAS communications
- Configuring RAS protocols
- Configuring RAS security
- Configuring Dial-Up Networking clients

Monitoring and Optimization

Monitor performance of various functions by using Performance Monitor. Functions include the following:

- Processor
- Memory
- Disk
- Network

Identify performance bottlenecks.

Troubleshooting

Choose the appropriate course of action to take to resolve installation failures.

Choose the appropriate course of action to take to resolve boot failures.

Choose the appropriate course of action to take to resolve configuration errors.

Choose the appropriate course of action to take to resolve printer problems.

Choose the appropriate course of action to take to resolve RAS problems.

Choose the appropriate course of action to take to resolve connectivity problems.

Choose the appropriate course of action to take to resolve resource access problems and permission problems.

Choose the appropriate course of action to take to resolve fault-tolerance failures. Fault-tolerance methods include the following:

- Tape backup
- Mirroring
- Stripe set with parity
- Disk duplexing

Good Luck!

As you approach the final stages of exam preparation, New Riders wishes you the best of luck. If you should find, after using this TestPrep tool, that you need further study in a particular area, look into purchasing a second edition New Riders Training Guide, a complete, thorough, and accurate study guide. If you would like to try computerized testing, check out New Riders' Top Score software simulation suite. It includes an exclusive test engine that mimics Microsoft styles and an NT Simulator!

Keep us posted on your success. A registration card is located in the back of the book. Fill it out and fax or send it in. We'd love to hear from you. Good luck on your exam.

NEW RIDERS PUBLISHING

The staff of New Riders Publishing is committed to bringing you the very best in computer reference material. Each New Riders book is the result of months of work by authors and staff who research and refine the information contained within its covers.

As part of this commitment to you, the NRP reader, New Riders invites your input. Please let us know if you enjoy this book, if you have trouble with the information or examples presented, or if you have a suggestion for the next edition.

If you have a question or comment about any New Riders book, you can contact New Riders Publishing in several ways. We will respond to as many readers as we can. Your name, address, or phone number will never become part of a mailing list or be used for any purpose other than to help us continue to bring you the best books possible. You can write to us at the following address:

New Riders Publishing
Attn: Publisher
201 W. 103rd Street
Indianapolis, IN 46290

If you prefer, you can fax New Riders Publishing at (317) 817-7448.

You also can send email to New Riders at the following Internet address:

certification@mcp.com

NRP is an imprint of Macmillan Computer Publishing. To obtain a catalog or information, or to purchase any Macmillan Computer Publishing book, call (800) 428-5331.

Thank you for selecting *MCSE Test Prep: Windows NT Server 4, Second Edition!*

Planning

This chapter will help you study the Planning test objectives for Microsoft's Exam 70-067, Implementing and Supporting Microsoft Windows NT Server 4.0. A successful implementation of Windows NT Server requires informed planning. Informed planning means developing a configuration based on the context of the Windows NT Server installation. The context of the installation includes the physical environment, the logical structure of the existing environment, technical requirements, and business requirements. The context will influence the selection of protocols and the disk drive configuration, which are the two test objectives covered in this chapter.

OBJECTIVES

Microsoft's stated objectives for the Planning category are as follows:

Plan hard disk drive file system and fault tolerance configuration based on system requirements such as performance needs and network security standards.

▶ To effectively plan the installation and configuration of a Windows NT computer, you should understand the configuration options available in terms of mass data storage (hard disk drives). The purpose of this exam objective is to make sure you understand these options and how to select a hard disk drive configuration appropriate to your performance and security goals.

continues

Select the best network protocol(s) based on network design objectives such as capacity, ease of management, and network architecture. Protocols include the following:

> **TCP/IP**
>
> **NWLink IPX/SPX-Compatible Transport**
>
> **NetBEUI**

▶ Windows NT offers a rich set of network protocols and associated administrative, performance, and troubleshooting tools. Choosing the best protocol(s) for a given implementation of Windows NT Server requires a clear understanding of the available protocols and their respective strengths and weaknesses. This exam objective tests your knowledge of the mainstream Windows NT protocols.

PLANNING DISK DRIVE CONFIGURATIONS

1. **You need to install and configure Windows NT Server on a computer equipped with the following:**

   - **Pentium II 233MHz processor**
   - **128MB RAM**
   - **5–9GB SCSI hard disk drives**

   This new computer will be used as a database. The information stored in the database is considered very sensitive. What steps might you take to make sure the data on the new computer is safe from hackers and corporate spies? Select all that apply.

   A. Place the computer in a secure physical environment, such as a locked office with limited public access.

   B. Configure the system partition as a FAT partition.

   C. Enable TCP/IP security on all network cards installed in the computer.

   D. Configure the new computer as a backup domain controller.

   E. Configure the volume that will hold the data as an NTFS volume.

2. **You are administrator for a Windows NT file server that has a single 2GB hard disk drive. The entire hard disk drive is** partitioned as a single FAT volume. The hard disk drive is almost out of free space. You purchase and install a second 9GB hard drive. How do you configure the second drive to minimize the impact on users with data and applications stored on the original 2GB volume? Select the best response.

   A. Simply extend the original FAT partition to include the additional 9GB of disk space.

   B. Convert the original FAT partition to NTFS format and then extend the newly created NTFS volume to include the additional 9GB of free disk space.

   C. Partition and format the entire 9GB on the new hard disk drive as a FAT volume and mirror the two disk drives. Set the 9GB partition as the active partition and reformat the 2GB drive.

   D. Partition and format the new 9GB hard drive as an NTFS volume. Move or reinstall user data and applications to the new drive.

   E. Reinstall Windows NT Server on the computer using the 9GB hard drive as the primary partition. Move or reinstall user data and applications to the new primary partition.

3. **Which file systems does Windows NT 4.0 support? Select the best response.**

   A. NTFS, HPFS, FAT

   B. FAT, CDFS, NTFS

   C. NTFS, FAT

   D. FAT, HPFS

   E. NTFS, CDFS

4. **Which of the following computer configurations meet the minimum hardware requirements for Windows NT Server? Select all that apply.**

   A. Pentium 200, 12MB RAM, 1GB hard disk space available

   B. 486 DX2/66, 16MB RAM, 120MB hard disk space available

   C. Pentium II, 32MB RAM, 200MB hard disk space available

   D. 486 DX33, 16MB RAM, 150MB hard disk space available

   E. Pentium 75, 64MB RAM, 90MB hard disk space available

5. **You are installing a new Windows NT Server computer. The new server will be used for sensitive company information. Money for this new equipment and operating system is limited, so you have only two 6GB hard disk drives in the new computer.**

   Required Results:
   Provide at least 4GB of disk space for user data.

   Maximize security for data on the new computer.

   Optional Results:
   Provide for rapid recovery from a disk-drive failure.

   Maximize disk performance for available resources.

   Proposed Solution:
   When installing Windows NT Server on the new computer, configure the two hard disk drives as mirrored NTFS volumes.

   A. The proposed solution meets both of the required results and neither of the optional results.

   B. The proposed solution meets one of the required results and both of the optional results.

   C. The proposed solution meets both of the required results and both of the optional results.

   D. The proposed solution meets neither of the required results and neither of the optional results.

   E. The proposed solution meets neither of the required results and both of the optional results.

6. **You are installing a new Windows NT server on your company's network. The new server will support a large SQL database that utilizes transaction logging for write operations. The new computer is equipped as follows:**

   • **Dual Pentium II 450 processors**

   • **128MB RAM**

   • **5–9GB SCSI hard drives**

   Required Results:
   Maximize data I/O performance.

   Optimize data recoverability.

Optional Results:

Facilitate optimum security for the data.

Maximize disk space available for the database.

Proposed Solution:

Install Windows NT Server on a disk drive formatted by using the FAT file system. Configure the remaining four disk drives as a striped set. Partition the entire striped set as an extended partition and format the extended partition as a single NTFS volume. Locate the NT page file on the striped set volume. Configure the SQL database so the transaction files are placed on the FAT partition.

   A. The proposed solution meets both of the required results and both of the optional results.

   B. The proposed solution meets one of the required results and both of the optional results.

   C. The proposed solution meets both of the required results and one of the optional results.

   D. The proposed solution meets neither of the required results and neither of the optional results.

   E. The proposed solution meets neither of the required results and both of the optional results.

7. **One of the NT Server computers on your network is equipped as follows:**

   • **Pentium II 433 processor**

   • **64MB RAM**

   • **1–4GB hard disk drive with a single FAT partition**

You purchase a 6GB hard disk drive. How might you configure the disk drives to provide fault tolerance and to improve disk throughput? Select the best response.

   A. Partition 2GB of the new disk drive as the system and boot partition. Configure the remaining 4GB on the new drive and the other 4GB drive as a mirrored set.

   B. Configure all 10GB of disk space as a single stripe set with parity.

   C. Configure all 10GB of disk space as a single stripe set.

   D. Install the new disk drive as a mirror drive, create an extended partition with the remaining 2GB, and place the page file on the extended partition.

   E. Install the new disk drive and then add the new disk space to the existing partition.

8. **You install Windows NT Server on a computer with MS-DOS installed, configuring the computer using the dual-boot option. In addition, you install a second hard disk drive, configuring it as a single extended partition. You create a volume on the new partition, which you format using NTFS and to which you assign drive letter F. When you boot the computer to MS-DOS, you cannot access the F: drive. Why? Select the best response.**

A. Drive F: is larger than 4GB; therefore, MS-DOS cannot access the volume.

B. The partition was not created by using FDISK, so the partition signature is incorrect.

C. The partition table for the disk drive is corrupted.

D. Only Windows NT can access an NTFS volume.

E. Security on the NTFS volume is configured to deny access to the operating system. Because no user is logged on when using MS-DOS, access is denied.

9. **What is the maximum number of non-contiguous areas of free space a logical volume can span?**

   A. 32

   B. 16

   C. 4

   D. 8

   E. Unlimited

10. **One of the Windows NT Server computers on your network has a single 6GB disk drive. The drive is partitioned with a 2GB partition, which serves as both the system and the boot partition. The remaining space is configured as an extended partition assigned to a single NTFS volume. You add fault tolerance to the disk-drive storage for this computer by adding another 6GB drive and then configuring the two drives as a mirrored set. Although the second drive is the**

same size as the original, the sector size on the two drives differs. Which of the following statements is true about this configuration? Select all that apply.

   A. You must use a Windows NT startup disk to restart the system if the original disk drive fails.

   B. Only the extended partition is mirrored.

   C. Only the system partition is mirrored.

   D. Should either disk drive fail, the computer should continue to operate without interruption.

   E. Should either disk drive fail, the computer must be restarted.

11. **One of the Windows NT Server computers on your network is equipped with a single EIDE disk drive. The disk drive is partitioned with a system partition and an extended partition. The system partition also is the boot partition, and Windows NT is installed in a directory named WINNT. Which of the following ARC pathnames is correct for this configuration?**

   A. scsi(0)disk(1)rdisk(0)partition(1)

   B. multi(0)disk(0)rdisk(2)partition(1)

   C. multi(0)disk(0)rdisk(0)partition(1)

   D. multi(0)disk(0)rdisk(0)partition(1)\ WINNT

   E. multi(0)disk(0)rdisk(0)partition(0)\ WINNT

12. **Your Windows NT Server computer is configured to write a memory dump file on a Kernel STOP error. The computer encounters such an error, but the memory dump file is nowhere to be found on the hard disk drive. Why? Select the best response.**

　A. There is insufficient disk space to write the file.

B. The operating system does not have write permission to the system directory.

C. The page file is located on a partition other than the boot partition.

D. The boot partition is FAT.

E. The boot partition is NTFS.

ANSWER KEY

1. A-E	5. C	9. A
2. D	6. E	10. A-D
3. B	7. D	11. D
4. C-D	8. D	12. C

ANSWERS & EXPLANATIONS

PLANNING DISK DRIVE CONFIGURATIONS

1. You need to install and configure Windows NT Server on a computer equipped with the following:

   - **Pentium II 233MHz processor**

   - **128MB RAM**

   - **5–9GB SCSI hard disk drives**

   This new computer will be used as a database. The information stored in the database is considered very sensitive. What steps might you take to make sure the data on the new computer is safe from hackers and corporate spies? Select all that apply.

   A. Place the computer in a secure physical environment, such as a locked office with limited public access.

   E. Configure the volume that will hold the data as an NTFS volume.

1. CORRECT ANSWERS: A-E

Some of the most effective solutions concerning network security also are the simplest solutions. Placing a computer in a locked room is both inexpensive and a highly effective way to protect sensitive data.

NTFS offers sophisticated security at the file, directory, and volume levels. Users and groups can be assigned varying levels of access to data on the volume.

2. You are administrator for a Windows NT file server that has a single 2GB hard disk drive. The entire hard disk drive is partitioned as a single FAT volume. The hard disk drive is almost out of free space. You purchase and install a second 9GB hard drive. How do you configure the second drive to minimize impact on users with data and applications stored on the original 2GB volume? Select the best response.

   D. Partition and format the new 9GB hard drive as an NTFS volume. Move or reinstall user data and applications to the new drive.

2. CORRECT ANSWER: D

There are two keys to discerning the correct answer for this question. First, the primary partition cannot be extended. Second, the maximum size for a FAT partition is around 2GB. These two facts eliminate answers A, B, and C.

Answers D and E both work. Answer D is the best answer because it is less disruptive to add a new partition and to move data and applications than it is to reinstall Windows NT Server.

Answer B would be the best answer if you could extend the system partition. Because the original disk configuration for this server consists of a single partition, that partition has to be both the boot and the system partition. System partitions cannot be extended.

3. Which file systems does Windows NT 4.0 support? Select the best response.

    D. FAT, CDFS, NTFS

Windows NT Server 4 supports File Allocation Table (FAT), CD-ROM File System (CDFS), and NT File System (NTFS). High Performance File System (HPFS) is an OS/2 file system; it is supported by Windows NT Server 3.51 but not Windows NT Server 4.

Keep in mind that many Microsoft exam questions have more than one correct answer. It is up to you to determine the *most* correct answer. In this question, answers C and E are both correct. Answer B, however, is the answer that includes all file systems supported.

4. Which of the following computer configurations meet the minimum hardware requirements for Windows NT Server? Select all that apply.

    C. Pentium II, 32MB RAM, 200MB hard disk space available

    D. 486 DX33, 16MB RAM, 150MB hard disk space available

For x86-based computers, the minimum hardware requirements for NT Server are a 486DX/33 processor, 16MB RAM, and 130MB of disk space.

5. Proposed Solution:
When installing Windows NT Server on the new computer, configure the two hard disk drives as mirrored NTFS volumes.

    C. The proposed solution meets both of the required results and both of the optional results.

For this question, you first need to consider the available options for hard disk configurations. Striping and striping with parity require at least three disk drives; therefore, the available options are disk mirroring and single-disk operation.

Disk mirroring requires a 50-percent redundancy rate. It is clear that the requirement for 2GB of disk space is met, whether or not disk mirroring is selected.

Security always is enhanced when you select the NTFS file system. The FAT file system offers no security, but the NTFS file system has several levels of security for both files and directories.

Disk mirroring facilitates the most rapid recovery from disk failure. In most cases, service is not interrupted, and the failed drive can be replaced during scheduled downtime.

Disk mirroring also meets the optional performance requirements. Disk mirroring allows for simultaneous reads and only a small performance penalty for writes, so the overall performance is optimized over a single-disk configuration.

Note that, for the cost of an additional disk-controller card, disk duplexing would be a better configuration option in terms of both performance and fault tolerance. The question is explicit concerning available resources, however, so disk duplexing is not an option.

6. Proposed Solution:
Install Windows NT Server on a disk drive formatted using the FAT file system. Configure the remaining four disk drives as a striped set. Partition the entire striped set as an extended partition and format the extended partition as a single NTFS volume. Locate the NT page file on the striped set volume. Configure the SQL database so the transaction files are placed on the FAT partition.

   E. The proposed solution meets neither of the required results and both of the optional results.

6. CORRECT ANSWER: E

Although disk striping is the fastest of the available drive configurations, this performance advantage is degraded by placing the page file on the striped set volume. A better solution is to place the page file on the system partition. The best solution is to break the first disk drive into two FAT partitions and then place the page file on the second (nonsystem) partition.

The SQL transaction log is critical for data recovery in a transaction-logging database. Placing the transaction logs on a nonfault-tolerant drive is not a good idea. Placing the transaction log on a FAT volume improves performance because sequential reads and writes are very efficient. A better solution is to use two of the five disk drives as a mirrored set.

Striping without parity is not fault tolerant; therefore, it cannot meet the second required result. In most cases, it probably is better to trade some performance for fault tolerance. This can be accomplished by using disk striping with parity on the NTFS volume.

Striping without parity uses the least amount of disk space overhead while providing good performance. This fulfills the second optional result.

Because NTFS has file- and directory-level security, configuring the database volume with NTFS meets the first optional result.

7. One of the NT Server computers on your network is equipped as follows:

- **Pentium II 433 processor**
- **64MB RAM**
- **1–4GB hard disk drive with a single FAT partition**

You purchase a 6GB hard disk drive. How might you configure the disk drives to provide fault tolerance and to improve disk throughput? Select the best response.

D. Install the new disk drive as a mirror drive, create an extended partition with the remaining 2GB, and place the page file on the extended partition.

Both striping and striping with parity require a minimum of three disk drives; therefore, answers B and C do not work.

Because there is only one partition on the existing system, it must be a system partition. System partitions cannot be extended; therefore, answer does not work either. Additionally, this configuration offers no fault tolerance.

This question requires that two objectives be met: establish fault tolerance and improve disk throughput. Answer D meets both objectives. The configuration suggested in answer A, however, improves disk throughput to a greater degree than the configuration described in answer D. Many exam questions require you to select the best solution for a given problem, even though there might be more than one valid solution.

8. You install Windows NT Server on a computer with MS-DOS installed, configuring the computer using the dual-boot option. In addition, you install a second hard disk drive, configuring it as a single extended partition. You create a volume on the new partition, which you format using NTFS and to which you assign drive letter F. When you boot the computer to MS-DOS, you cannot access the F: drive. Why? Select the best response.

D. Only Windows NT can access an NTFS volume.

A disadvantage of using NTFS on a dual-boot computer is that only the Windows NT operating system can access an NTFS volume. Note, however, that Windows NT clients can access data stored on a shared NTFS volume.

9. What is the maximum number of noncontiguous areas of free space a logical volume can span?

A. 32

A single Windows NT volume can consist of space on as many as 32 physical disk drives. Using Disk Administrator, you can select the free space on all drives by holding down the Control key and clicking on each area. After the area is selected, choose the Create Volume Set option from the Partition menu. After the volume set has been created and the change has been committed, the volume set must be formatted. Note also that a volume set requires a minimum of two noncontiguous areas.

10. One of the Windows NT Server computers on your network has a single
6GB disk drive. The drive is partitioned
with a 2GB partition, which serves as
both the system and the boot partition.
The remaining space is configured as
an extended partition assigned to a
single NTFS volume. You add fault tolerance to the disk-drive storage for this
computer by adding another 6GB drive
then configuring the two drives as a
mirrored set. Although the second drive
is the same size as the original, the
sector size on the two drives differs.
Which of the following statements is
true about this configuration? Select
all that apply.

   A. You must use a Windows NT startup
   disk to restart the system if the
   original disk drive fails.

   D. Should either disk drive fail, the computer should continue to operate
   without interruption.

10. CORRECT ANSWERS: A-D

If disk drives that do not have identical geometries are mirrored, the second disk installed (the shadow disk) cannot be
used to boot the Windows NT computer without the aid of a
Windows NT startup disk. Normal operation of the computer
usually is not interrupted.

The startup disk is used to boot the Windows NT computer
from the shadow disk drive. This disk has a boot sector as well
as the necessary hardware startup files required to boot
Windows NT. The ARC pathname in the BOOT.INI file points
to the system partition on the shadow disk drive.

A Windows NT startup disk must be created manually. You
can use the following steps:

1. Format a floppy disk using Windows NT Explorer.
   Formatting with Explorer places a boot record on the
   floppy; formatting a disk from the command line does
   not.

2. Copy the following files to the newly formatted disk:

   NTLDR

   BOOT.INI

   NTDETECT.COM

   BOOTSECT.DOS (If you want to dual boot from the
   startup disk)

   NTBOOTDD.SYS (If you are using SCSI disk drives)

Note that, by default, all these files are marked as System and
Hidden files.

3. Edit the ARC pathname in the BOOT.INI if necessary.

11. One of the Windows NT Server computers on your network is equipped with a single EIDE disk drive. The disk drive is partitioned with a system partition and an extended partition. The system partition also is the boot partition, and Windows NT is installed in a directory named WINNT. Which of the following ARC pathnames is correct for this configuration?

    D. multi(0)disk(0)rdisk(0)partition(1)\
       WINNT

Here is how this ARC pathname is read:

multi(0)	The disk drive controller number, beginning with 0.
disk(0)	The SCSI ID for the disk, beginning with 0. Not used with multi.
rdisk(0)	Ordinal disk number for the controller, beginning with 0.
partition(1)	Partition number on the target disk, beginning with 1.
\WINNT	Pathname for the system directory.

12. Your Windows NT Server computer is configured to write a memory dump file on a Kernel STOP error. The computer encounters such an error, but the memory dump file is nowhere to be found on the hard disk drive. Why? Select the best response.

    C. The page file is located on a partition other than the boot partition.

Although placing the page file on a partition other than the boot partition can improve disk I/O performance, it also disables the memory dump option for Kernel STOP errors.

PLANNING DISK DRIVE CONFIGURATION

When studying how to plan disk drive configuration, make sure you firmly understand the following concepts: partition types, managing partitions, minimum hardware requirements, and ARC pathnames. The following sections briefly discuss each of these concepts.

Windows NT Hard Disk Partition Types

Table 1.1 shows and describes the possible contents of the System ID field in the partition table for a disk drive installed on a Windows NT computer.

TABLE 1.1   VALID VALUES FOR THE SYSTEM ID FIELD

System ID	Description
0x01	12-bit FAT partition or logical drive. This value is assigned to volumes with fewer than 32,680 sectors.
0x01	16-bit FAT partition or logical drive. 16-bit FAT partitions have more than 32,680 sectors but fewer than 65,535.
0x05	Extended partition.
0x06	BIGDOS (FAT32) partition or logical drive. Windows NT cannot access a FAT32 partition.
0x07	NTFS partition or logical drive.

Minimum Hardware Requirements

The following are the minimum hardware requirements for installing Windows NT Server on an x86 computer:

- Intel 486/33 or better processor
- 16MB RAM
- 130MB free disk space

ARC Pathnames

Advanced RISC Computing (ARC) pathnames are used in the Windows NT boot process. ARC pathnames point to the location of each instance of Windows NT installed on a computer. The following is the format of an ARC pathname:

multi(controller num)disk(scsi id)rdisk(disk num)partition(partition num)

or

scsi(controller num)disk(scsi id)rdisk(disk num)partition(partition num)

Multi(controller num) describes the ordinal controller number, beginning with 0. The value of controller num for multi()always should be 0. For SCSI controllers, the syntax is scsi(controller num).

Disk(scsi id) is the SCSI ID of the physical disk. This parameter always is 0 when used with multi().

Rdisk(disk num) represents the ordinal disk

number, starting with 0, when used with multi(). When used with scsi(), disk num represents the logical unit number (LUN) of the disk drive.

Partition(partition num) points to the ordinal partition number, beginning with 1.

You might encounter a question on the exam that asks you to identify one of the components in an ARC pathname, such as the following:

scsi(0)disk(1)rdisk(1)partition(2)

You should know that this ARC pathname points to a SCSI disk drive on controller number 0. The disk drive's SCSI ID number is physical disk number 1. The system partition is on partition number 2, which is the second partition on the drive.

CHOOSING A WINDOWS NT NETWORK PROTOCOL

1. You are installing a network for a client. The single-segment network consists of one Windows NT Server computer, three Windows 98 workstations, and a laser printer connected to one of the workstations. Your client has limited resources and therefore requires a network that is easy to manage. Which protocol should you use on this network?

   A. NetBEUI

   B. TCP/IP and NWLink

   C. NWLink

   D. DLC and TCP/IP

   E. NetBIOS

2. What Windows NT Server service facilitates IP address assignment for network nodes?

   A. DNS

   B. DHCP

   C. NDS

   D. NDIS

   E. WINS

3. You are installing a Windows NT Server computer on a network that has both UNIX hosts and NetWare 4.x file servers. What protocol(s) are required to communicate with UNIX and NetWare computers? Select all that apply.

   A. TCP/IP

   B. NetBEUI

   C. DLC

   D. NWLink

   E. NetBIOS

4. Using the network described in question 3, what service must be installed on the Windows NT Server computer to allow Windows NT clients to access shared files on the NetWare servers?

   A. NetWare Directory Service

   B. Client Service for NetWare

   C. Gateway Service for NetWare

   D. NWLink File Service

   E. Print Services for NetWare

5. Using the network described in question 3, what service must be installed to facilitate printing to UNIX printers from Windows NT clients?

   A. Client Services for UNIX

   B. Microsoft TCP/IP Printing

   C. UNIX Services for Microsoft NT

   D. LPR

   E. NDS

6. When might you install the Data Link Control (DLC) protocol on a Windows NT computer? Select all that apply.

A. When connecting to IBM mainframe equipment

B. When connecting to Novell print services

C. When connecting to Hewlett-Packard network-connected printers

D. When connecting to Macintosh computers

E. When using UNIX print services

7. **Which layer of the OSI model is responsible for making sure information is transmitted over the network in the correct order and without loss or duplication of data?**

A. Network

B. LLC

C. Session

D. Transport

E. Application

8. **Which protocol in the TCP/IP suite is used for optimum performance over varying network bandwidth conditions?**

A. IP

B. TCP

C. ICMP

D. SNMP

E. UDP

9. **You are installing Internet Information Server on a Windows NT Server computer that will be connected to the Internet through an ISDN modem. Which protocol must be installed on this computer to communicate across the Internet?**

A. TCP/IP

B. DNS

C. NWLink

D. IPX/SPX

E. NetBEUI

10. **Which Windows NT Server service is used to map IP addresses to NetBIOS names?**

A. DNS

B. NDS

C. DSN

D. WINS

E. DHCP

ANSWER KEY

1. A	5. B	8. B
2. B	6. A-C	9. A
3. A-D	7. D	10. D
4. C		

ANSWERS & EXPLANATIONS

CHOOSING A WINDOWS NT NETWORK PROTOCOL

1. You are installing a network for a client. The single-segment network consists of one Windows NT Server computer, three Windows 98 workstations, and a laser printer connected to one of the workstations. Your client has limited resources and therefore requires a network that is easy to manage. Which protocol should you use on this network?

   A. NetBEUI

1. CORRECT ANSWER: A

NetBEUI is a simple, fast, reliable protocol. It should be used in situations in which simplicity and ease of management are important.

Note that, in the scenario for this question, the network is single segment. This is important because NetBEUI is not a routable protocol and should not be used on a routed network.

2. What Windows NT Server service facilitates IP address assignment for network nodes?

   B. DHCP

2. CORRECT ANSWER: B

The Dynamic Host Configuration Protocol not only handles assignment of IP addresses to network nodes, it also can be used to configure a number of IP parameters for network nodes, including default gateways and node types.

3. You are installing a Windows NT Server computer on a network that has both UNIX hosts and NetWare 4.x file servers. What protocol(s) are required to communicate with UNIX and NetWare computers? Select all that apply.

   A. TCP/IP
   D. NWLink

3. CORRECT ANSWERS: A - D

TCP/IP is the protocol used by UNIX computers. NWLink is Microsoft's implementation of IPX. IPX is the native protocol for NetWare Servers.

Note that Novell's newest server product, NetWare 5.0, can use TCP/IP as its native protocol. This is why the question specifies NetWare 4.x servers.

4. Using the network described in question 3, what service must be installed on the Windows NT Server computer to allow Windows NT clients to access shared files on the NetWare servers?

   C. Client Service for NetWare

4. CORRECT ANSWER: C

Gateway Service for NetWare enables a Windows NT Server to log on to a NetWare server and provide Windows NT clients with access to shared files and printers.

Client Service for NetWare enables Windows NT Workstation and Windows 9x clients to log on to NetWare servers.

NetWare Directory Service (NDS) is Novell's directory services. NWLink File Service and Print Services for NetWare do not exist.

5. Using the network described in question 3, what service must be installed to facilitate printing to UNIX printers from Windows NT clients?

B. Microsoft TCP/IP Printing

5. CORRECT ANSWER: B

The Microsoft TCP/IP Printing Service enables a Windows NT Server to send TCP/IP print jobs to a UNIX-hosted printer. The service is associated with one or more printers on the Windows NT server, and these printers are shared.

6. When might you install the Data Link Control (DLC) protocol on a Windows NT computer? Select all that apply.

A. When connecting to IBM mainframe equipment

C. When connecting to Hewlett-Packard network-connected printers

6. CORRECT ANSWERS: A - C

The Data Link Control (DLC) protocol is a limited-use, nonroutable protocol shipped with Windows NT. As its name implies, DLC provides applications with direct access to the data link layer.

DLC is one of the protocols built into many Hewlett-Packard DirectJet network interface cards. DLC also is used to communicate with computers running a DLC protocol stack, usually IBM mainframes and other SNA hosts.

7. Which layer of the OSI model is responsible for making sure information is transmitted over the network in the correct order and without loss or duplication of data?

D. Transport

7. CORRECT ANSWER: D

A complete description of the OSI layers can be found in the following section, "Further Review: Choosing a Windows NT Network Protocol."

8. Which protocol in the TCP/IP suite is used for optimum performance over varying network bandwidth conditions?

B. TCP

8. CORRECT ANSWER: B

Transport Control Protocol (TCP) provides connection-oriented, reliable data transmission over the network. It optimizes performance under varying network conditions through receive windows sizing, delayed acknowledgments, PMTU discovery, and dead gateway detection.

9. You are installing Internet Information Server on a Windows NT Server computer that will be connected to the Internet through an ISDN modem. Which protocol must be installed on this computer to communicate across the Internet?

   A. TCP/IP

10. Which Windows NT Server service is used to map IP addresses to NetBIOS names?

   D. WINS

9. CORRECT ANSWER: A

TCP/IP is the protocol of the Internet. Other protocols can be transmitted over the Internet, but they are tunneled through TCP/IP. *Tunneling* means the foreign protocol packets are wrapped in TCP/IP packets for Internet transport. In the world of the Internet, TCP/IP is king. This is a basic concept with which you should be well-acquainted well before you attempt to pass the exam.

10. CORRECT ANSWER: D

The Windows Internet Naming Service (WINS) enables applications that use NetBIOS names to communicate with computers on a TCP/IP network.

CHOOSING A WINDOWS NT NETWORK PROTOCOL

One of the most useful tools for understanding and evaluating network protocols is the OSI model. All protocols can be mapped, or compared, to the OSI model. This enables you to recognize the functionality and structure of a given protocol in relation to other protocols. It is a good idea not only to memorize but to understand the OSI model.

The OSI Model Layers

Table 1.2 identifies and describes the function of each Open Systems Interconnect (OSI) model layer.

TABLE 1.2 THE SEVEN LAYERS OF THE OSI PROTOCOL MODEL

Layer	Description
Application	Facilitates access to the network by user-level applications. Functions provided include resource sharing, RPC support, directory services, and electronic messaging.
Presentation	Performs data translation. The presentation layer accepts data from the application layer, translates it to a common format, and then sends this data to the session layer. Conversely, the presentation layer also accepts data from the session layer in a common format, translates the data, and then sends it to the application layer.
Session	Manages communication between processes running on different computers. This includes data buffer management and message delimiting.
Transport	Manages message delivery. The transport layer ensures that data is delivered without loss or duplication and in the correct order.
Network	Delivers and receives data across the network. The network layer fragments messages from the transport layer into protocol-defined data packets and delivers them to the data link layer. The process of creating these packets includes addressing the packets.
Data Link	Facilitates reliable delivery of data across the network. The data link layer fragments data packets into frames, which are passed to the physical layer. Frames are the final data format and are placed on the wire.
Physical	The physical layer is a bit-stream-oriented structure that controls the physical transmission of data.

CHAPTER SUMMARY

A majority of the planning for a server installation is related to the disk drive and the network protocol configuration. Decisions made in these two areas can dramatically impact the quality of the Windows NT Server installation. Microsoft reflects this in the questions on the Windows NT Server exam. The following are some areas you should know for these objectives:

- **General disk drive and protocol configuration:** When you take the Microsoft exam, you likely will encounter at least one scenario question for disk drive configuration and one scenario question about network protocol selection and configuration.

- **ARC pathnames:** It is a simple matter to make sure you understand ARC pathnames. Be sure you understand how to read an ARC pathname and how to associate it with a particular configuration.

- **Windows NT file systems:** Know the file systems available and their respective strengths and weaknesses.

- **Windows NT fault tolerance:** You likely will be expected to know what RAID levels are represented as well as their strengths and weaknesses.

- **OSI model:** Memorize the OSI models and their general functionality. I use a mnemonic device to represent the layers in top-to-bottom order. "All People Seem To Need Data Processing" represents Application, Presentation, Session, Transport, Network, Data Link, and Physical.

- **NetWare:** You probably will be asked about integrating Windows NT Server into a NetWare environment.

- **TCP/IP and TCP/IP support services:** There will be questions about TCP/IP configuration and TCP/IP support services such as DNS, WINS, and DHCP.

This chapter will help you study the Installation and Configuration test objectives for Microsoft's exam 70-067, Implementing and Supporting Microsoft Windows NT Server 4.0. You will be tested on your understanding of all aspects of installing Windows NT computers in general and Windows NT Server computers in particular. The areas covered on the exam are presented in this chapter; however, expect the exam to emphasize fault-tolerance configuration, protocol configuration, disk partitions, printer configuration, and server roles.

Installation and Configuration

OBJECTIVES

The following Microsoft test objectives are covered in this chapter:

Install Windows NT on Intel-based platforms.

▶ Although Windows NT is available for the RISC platform, the primary focus for the test is Intel-based computers. You should know the flow of the installation process. You also should know the important operations performed during the installation process:

- Start a Windows NT installation and use the command-line switches

- Choose the correct installation option

- Install network components

- Create an emergency repair disk

continues

Install Windows NT Server to perform various server roles. Server roles include PDC, BDC, and member server.

▶ The purpose of this test objective is to make sure the candidate understands how a server role is selected, when a given role can be used, and what differences exist between roles.

Install Windows NT Server using various methods. Various methods include CD-ROM, over-the-network, Network Client Administrator, and express versus custom.

▶ This test objective measures your understanding of the different ways Windows NT can be installed as well as the advantages and disadvantages of each method.

Configure Protocols and protocol bindings. Protocols include TCP/IP, NWLink IPX/SPX-Compatible Transport, and NetBEUI.

▶ Windows NT ships with several network protocols. This test objective measures your understanding of these protocols—the mechanics of installing and configuring them, selecting the appropriate protocol for a given situation, binding protocols, and setting binding order. You should be familiar with the following network protocols:

- NetBEUI
- NWLink
- TCP/IP
- DLC
- AppleTalk

Configure Network Adapters. Considerations include changing IRQ, IOBase and memory addresses, and configuring multiple adapters.

▶ Although most network adapters are PC cards and require no configuration, many systems still use ISA standard network adapters. ISA cards often require manual configuration of I/O address space, interrupts, and buffer memory addresses to avoid conflicts with other devices installed on the server.

Windows NT Server often is installed with more than one network adapter to service multiple subnets (multihomed computers). You must understand the unique protocol, network traffic management, and routing issues presented when setting up a multihomed Windows NT computer.

Configure Windows NT Core services. Services include Directory Replicator, License Manager, and other services.

▶ Windows NT services are background processes that perform primarily system-level functions. Windows NT services support the operation of Windows NT Server.

Configure peripherals and devices. Peripherals and devices include communication devices, SCSI devices, tape device drivers, UPS devices and UPS service, mouse drivers, display drivers, and keyboard drivers.

▶ Windows NT ships with drivers for several standard devices such as keyboards, video adapters, SCSI interface cards, and uninterruptible power supplies (UPS). One exam objective is to make sure you understand how to configure standard devices and their associated drivers.

It also is important that you know how to access the configuration settings for devices and understand the meaning of those settings.

Configure hard disks to meet various requirements. Requirements include allocating disk space capacity, providing redundancy, improving performance, providing security, and formatting.

▶ One of the more important duties of a Windows NT Server administrator is managing hard disk drive storage. It is important to understand how to perform various installation and maintenance operations by using Disk Administrator. After completing this section, you should be able to install and configure hard disk drives. The exam will require you to know this procedure.

Configure printers. Tasks include adding and configuring a printer, implementing a printer pool, and setting print priorities.

▶ The Microsoft exam will test your knowledge of printer installation and configuration. To pass this exam objective, you should know the various methods available for adding a printer share to a client, creating and configuring a printer on a Windows NT computer, configuring printer pools, setting printer permissions, and configuring the print spooler.

Configure a Windows NT server computer for various types of client computers. Client computer types include Windows NT Workstation, Windows 95, and MS-DOS based.

▶ The primary purpose of Windows NT Server is to provide resources to other computers on the network (clients). The Microsoft exam covers connecting and configuring clients to a Windows NT server such as Windows NT workstations and Windows 9x computers. Both MS-DOS computers and Macintosh machines are covered to a small degree, although neither is noted on the official Microsoft objectives list.

PRACTICE QUESTIONS

INSTALLING WINDOWS NT SERVER ON INTEL-BASED PLATFORMS

1. You have installed Windows NT 4.0 Server on a computer by using the Typical option. The computer has an ISA Plug and Play sound card installed; however, Windows NT cannot seem to find the card when the computer boots. What should you do to add Plug and Play support to this installation of Windows NT? Select the best response.

   A. Reinstall Windows NT by using the Custom option and then select the Plug and Play Support option.

   B. Install a Plug and Play support driver, which is shipped with Windows NT.

   C. Plug and Play support, by default, is disabled when you install Windows NT. Enable it by using the Plug and Play applet in the Control Panel.

   D. Start the Plug and Play service by using the Services applet in the Control Panel and then disable the service when the installation is complete.

   E. None of the above. Windows NT does not support ISA Plug and Play.

2. You installed a Windows NT Server 4.0 on your company's network as a member server. The licensing for this computer is per seat. Your company subsequently consummates a per-server licensing agreement with Microsoft. What must you do to change Windows NT Server to per-server licensing mode? Select the best response.

   A. Change the licensing mode from per seat to per server by using the License Manager utility.

   B. Reinstall Windows NT Server to change the licensing mode.

   C. Remove the computer from the domain, change the licensing mode, and then rejoin the domain.

   D. Change the licensing mode on a Windows NT Server computer by modifying the Registry.

   E. After the licensing mode is set to per seat, it cannot be changed. You must reinstall Windows NT Server.

3. Which of the following is the program used to install Windows NT?

   A. SETUP.EXE

   B. WINNT.EXE

   C. Installation Manager

   D. Active Setup

   E. WINCOM

4. **Someone in the office has misplaced the Windows NT setup floppy disks. How do you replace them? Select the best response.**

   A. These disks are serialized. Order a new set from Microsoft.

   B. Disk images of the disks are stored on the Windows NT CD-ROM. Use the DISKLIB program to write the images to a set of formatted floppy disks.

   C. Required files for the startup disks are stored on the Windows NT CD-ROM. Copy these files to a set of formatted floppy disks.

   D. From the Windows NT CD-ROM, run WINNT.EXE by using the /OX switch.

   E. Run WINNT32.EXE from your computer's System directory by using the /C switch.

5. **You are installing Windows NT 4.0 on a computer that already has Windows NT 3.51 installed. You want to configure the computer as a dual-boot machine. Assuming the Windows NT installation used default settings, what must you do to make sure you can run either Windows NT 4.0 or 3.51 on the computer? Select the best response.**

   A. The computer cannot be configured as a dual-boot machine. When the Windows NT 4.0 installation program detects an instance of Windows NT 3.x, it forces an upgrade.

   B. If the current file system in the boot partition is FAT, you must convert it to NTFS.

   C. You must manually edit the BOOT.INI file to include Windows NT 4.0 in the Start menu. This is done after the installation is complete.

   D. You must install Windows NT 4.0 on a partition other than the partition on which Windows NT 3.51 is installed.

   E. You must install Windows NT 4.0 in a directory other than \WINNT in the boot partition.

6. **You are installing Windows NT Server, and you would like to take advantage of NTFS for security. Your supervisor is concerned about compatibility of NT with other operating systems on the network. Is this a valid concern? Select the best response.**

   A. Yes, because NTFS is not compatible with any other operating system.

   B. No, because NTFS is compatible with all other operating systems.

   C. No, because the only time NTFS partitions cannot be accessed by other operating systems is when those operating systems are running on the same computer.

   D. Yes, because NTFS supports long filenames; other operating systems might not.

   E. Yes, because other operating systems can bypass NTFS security.

7. **You have successfully completed an installation of Windows NT Server. You have installed some applications and have added several local groups and users. How would you create an emergency repair disk to help protect your installation and configuration? Select the best response.**

    A. Run `\WINNT\SYSTEM32\RDISK.EXE` by using Windows NT Explorer.

    B. Run `MAKEEDR.EXE` by using the Run option in the Start menu.

    C. Run `\WINNT\SYSTEM32\RDISK.EXE` by using My Computer.

    D. Copy `BOOT.INI`, `NTLDR`, and `NDETECT` from the system partition to a formatted floppy disk.

    E. Run `RDISK.EXE /S` by using the Run option in the Start menu.

8. **You are installing Windows NT. Setup cannot detect the network interface card installed on the computer. The network card you are using is not listed on the HCL. How do you configure the network card? Select the best response.**

    A. Check the instructions that came with the network card for information about installing the card on a Windows NT computer. If there is no information, check the software shipped with the card (if any) for Windows NT drivers. If no drivers were shipped, check with the manufacturer.

    B. Use the Standard NIC option from the Available Drivers list during setup.

    C. The card was not detected because it is a Plug and Play device. Windows NT does not support Plug and Play. Disable Plug and Play on the card and restart the installation.

    D. The card was not detected because its interrupt or I/O memory settings conflict with another device installed on the computer. Verify and correct these settings and restart the installation.

    E. You must use a different card. If a device is not listed on the HCL, it does not work with Windows NT.

9. **You want to change a Windows NT 4.0 member server to a backup domain controller, so you must reinstall Windows NT Server. You want to run the installation from the Windows NT Server CD-ROM, but you do not want to create a set of startup disks. What program should you run?**

    A. `SETUP /F`

    B. `WINNT32 /UDF`

    C. `WINNT /b`

    D. `SETUP /NS`

    E. If you initiate installation from the CD-ROM, you must create the startup disks during installation. To install Windows NT without creating the startup disk set, you must use the original startup disks.

10. **You want to upgrade your Windows NT Server 3.51 computer to Windows NT Server 4.0 without losing current settings. How can you accomplish this? Select the best response.**

    A. Run `WINNT.EXE` from within Windows NT 3.51.

    B. Boot the computer by using an MS-DOS disk and then run `WINNT32.EXE` from an MS-DOS command prompt.

    C. Run `WINNT.EXE` `/U` by using the Run option in the Start menu.

    D. Run `WINNT32.EXE` from within Windows NT 3.51.

    E. You cannot upgrade a Windows NT 3.51 installation to Windows NT 4.0 because of differences in the Registry structures.

ANSWER KEY

1. B	5. E	8. A
2. A	6. C	9. C
3. B	7. E	10. D
4. D		

ANSWERS & EXPLANATIONS

INSTALLING WINDOWS NT SERVER ON INTEL-BASED PLATFORMS

1. You have installed Windows NT 4.0 Server on a computer using the Typical option. The computer has an ISA Plug and Play sound card installed; however, Windows NT cannot seem to find the card when the computer boots. What should you do to add Plug and Play support to this installation of Windows NT? Select the best response.

   B. Install a Plug and Play support driver, which is shipped with Windows NT.

1. CORRECT ANSWER: B

Windows NT supports Plug and Play on a limited basis. You must install a driver, ISAPNP.SYS, which is shipped with Windows NT. After this driver is installed, it can be disabled or enabled by using the Drivers applet in the Control Panel.

2. You installed a Windows NT Server 4.0 on your company's network as a member server. The licensing for this computer is per seat. Your company subsequently consummates a per server licensing agreement with Microsoft. What must you do to change Windows NT Server to per-server licensing mode? Select the best response.

   A. Change the licensing mode from per seat to per server by using the License Manager utility.

2. CORRECT ANSWER: A

The licensing mode can be changed from per seat to per server on a Windows NT Server, but it cannot be changed from per server to per seat.

Per-server licensing can be managed by a single Master Server on the network, which then keeps track of all concurrent connections to each server. When using a master server to track connections, violations are written to the applications log of the Master Server; otherwise, the violation is written to the applications log of the local server.

3. Which of the following is the program used to install Windows NT?

   B. WINNT.EXE

3. CORRECT ANSWER: B

There are actually two correct answers to this question, only one of which is offered here. WINNT.EXE is a 16-bit installation program; WINNT32.EXE is a 32-bit program that runs only under Windows NT. WINNT32.EXE can be used to install additional instances of Windows NT on a Windows NT computer; however, it usually is used to upgrade existing Windows NT installations.

4. **Someone in the office has misplaced the Windows NT setup floppy disks. How do you replace them? Select the best response.**

   D. From the Windows NT CD-ROM, run WINNT.EXE by using the /OX switch.

The startup floppy disks can be created by using WINNT.EXE on a computer running MS-DOS, Windows 3.x, Windows 9x, or Windows NT, as long as the computer has a CD-ROM available.

5. **You are installing Windows NT 4.0 on a computer that already has Windows NT 3.51 installed. You want to configure the computer as a dual-boot machine. Assuming the Windows NT installation used default settings, what must you do to make sure you can run either Windows NT 4.0 or 3.51 on the computer? Select the best response.**

   E. You must install Windows NT 4.0 in a directory other than \WINNT in the boot partition.

The key to this question is that Windows NT 3.51 was installed using the default settings. This means it is located in the \WINNT directory on the boot partition. To create a dual boot, Windows NT 4.0 must be installed in a different directory, either on another partition or on the same partition as Windows NT 3.51.

6. **You are installing Windows NT Server, and you would like to take advantage of NTFS for security. Your supervisor is concerned about compatibility of NT with other operating systems on the network. Is this a valid concern? Select the best response.**

   C. No, because NTFS partitions are not accessible by other operating systems only if those operating systems are running on the same computer.

When a Windows NT computer is connected to the network, its resources (including disk storage) are shared with other machines in a fashion that is compatible with many other operating systems including MS-DOS, Windows 3.x, Windows 9x, and Windows NT. The fact that a Windows NT computer uses NTFS does not impact its accessibility to other machines on the network.

7. **You have successfully completed an installation of Windows NT Server. You have installed some applications and have added several local groups and users. How would you create an emergency repair disk to help protect your installation and configuration? Select the best response.**

   E. Run RDISK.EXE /S from the Start\Run... menu.

RDISK.EXE is the program that creates the emergency repair disk. To update the Default, Sam, and security files, RDISK.EXE must be run with the command-line switch /S.

8. You are installing Windows NT. Setup cannot detect the network interface card installed on the computer. The network card you are using is not listed on the HCL. How do you configure the network card? Select the best response.

   A. Check the instructions that came with the network card for information about installing the card on a Windows NT computer. If there is no information, check the software shipped with the card (if any) for Windows NT drivers. If no drivers were shipped, check with the manufacturer.

The Hardware Compatibility List (HCL) is a fairly comprehensive list of hardware that has been tested and reported to be compatible with Windows NT. It is by no means a complete list. Many products on the market will work with Windows NT, and most are shipped with Windows NT drivers.

9. You want to change a Windows NT 4.0 member server to a backup domain controller, so you must reinstall Windows NT Server. You want to run the installation from the Windows NT Server CD-ROM, but you do not want to create a set of startup disks. What program should you run?

   C. WINNT /b

Because a 32-bit operating system already is installed on the computer, you also can use the WINNT32 /b command.

10. You want to upgrade your Windows NT Server 3.51 computer to Windows NT Server 4.0 without losing current settings. How can you accomplish this? Select the best response.

    D. Run WINNT32.EXE from within Windows NT 3.51.

WINNT32.EXE is a 32-bit application commonly used to upgrade from previous versions of Windows NT. It also can be used to install an additional instance of Windows NT on a computer already running Windows NT. WINNT32.EXE runs only in the Windows NT environment.

INSTALLING WINDOWS NT SERVER ON INTEL-BASED PLATFORMS

One of the more rudimentary bits of knowledge you likely will be tested on is your knowledge of the minimum requirements to both install and use Windows NT Server or the Windows NT Option Pack. The following two sections detail these requirements. It is a good idea to memorize them.

Minimum Hardware Requirements for Windows NT Server 4.0

To install Windows NT Server on an Intel-based computer, you must have the following hardware (as a minimum):

- 80486/33 processor
- 16MB RAM
- 125MB available hard disk space
- VGA video card and monitor
- CD-ROM drive or a network card

▼ **NOTE**

The requirements for a RISC-based computer are the same, except that 130MB of available disk space is required.

The retail (off-the-shelf) version of Windows NT Server 4.0 supports up to four processors. Many hardware vendors offer drivers that enable Windows NT 4.0 to support up to 32 processors.

Minimum Hardware Requirements for Windows NT 4.0 Option Pack

The primary component of the Windows NT 4.0 Option Pack is Internet Information Server (IIS). The requirements to run IIS on an Intel platform are as follows:

- Windows NT Server 4.0 (or Windows NT Workstation 4.0 with Service Pack 3 and Microsoft Internet Explorer 4.01 installed)
- 486/66 processor
- 32MB RAM
- 50MB available hard disk space (Windows NT Server 4.0)
- 40MB available hard disk space (Windows NT Workstation 4.0)

▼ **NOTE**

The requirements to run IIS on a RISC platform are the same, except that a minimum of a 150MHz Alpha processor is required.

WINDOWS NT SERVER 4.0 SERVER ROLES

1. You are about to replace the primary domain controller on your company's single-domain network with a newer, faster computer. The PDC is used for logon services only and is one of five domain controllers on your company's network. In addition, you must meet the following criteria:

   The new computer will be used as the PDC.

   The name of the PDC should remain the same.

   This operation should not interrupt network operations.

   Which of the following scenarios can accomplish all these goals? Select the best response.

   A. Install the new computer on the network as a backup domain controller, promote it to PDC, and then remove the old PDC from the network.

   B. Remove the PDC from the network and install the new computer as a PDC.

   C. Promote one of the other domain controllers on the network to PDC, remove the old PDC from the network, install the new computer as a BDC, and then promote it to PDC.

   D. You cannot add the new computer to the network with the same name as the old PDC because it will have a different security ID (SID).

   E. Install the new computer on the network as a backup domain controller with a different name than the existing PDC, promote it to a PDC, remove the old PDC, and then rename the new PDC.

2. Your company's network has two domains, SALES and ADMIN. Each domain has three domain controllers. A new sales office opens. It is decided that the new office should have a local domain controller. A limited budget means you must use one of the ADMIN BDCs to add a new BDC to the SALES domain. How do you accomplish this? Select the best response.

   A. Move the server to the new location, connect to the network, and then change the domain assignment to SALES by using the Network applet in Control Panel.

   B. Move the server to the new location and then reinstall Windows NT Server, configuring the computer as a BDC for the SALES domain.

   C. Move the server to the new location and then reinstall Windows NT Server, configuring the computer as a member server. After the computer has joined the domain, promote it to a BDC.

D. Move the server to the new location, connect to the network, and then change the computer name and domain assignment by using the Properties option in Network Neighborhood.

E. Reinstall Windows NT Server on the computer offline. Configure it as a BDC for the SALES domain and then move the server to the new location.

3. **Your company's network has two locations, Dallas and Houston. A full T1 line connects the locations. You are installing a new single-domain Windows NT network that includes two new servers to be used as domain controllers. Your plan is to locate the PDC in Dallas and the BDC in Houston. As it turns out, the new computer is shipped to Houston, and the computer earmarked for Dallas is backordered for six weeks. Time constraints require you to get the network up and running within a week. How can you set up the network now, add the new computer when it comes in, and still end up with the PDC in Dallas? Select the best response.**

A. Install the computer in Houston as a member server belonging to a workgroup with the same name as the proposed domain. When the Dallas computer arrives, install it as a PDC and then promote the Houston server to a PDC.

B. Install the Houston computer as a BDC. When the Dallas computer arrives, install it as a PDC.

C. Install the computer in Houston as a member server. When the Dallas server arrives, install it as a PDC and then reinstall the Houston server as a BDC.

D. Install the Houston computer as a PDC. When the Dallas computer arrives, install it as a BDC and then promote it to PDC.

E. Tell your boss that he just has to wait until the Dallas computer arrives. Then you can install the Dallas computer as a PDC and the Houston computer as a BDC.

4. **You must move a member server to a new domain. How do you accomplish this task? Select the best response.**

A. Create a computer account for the server on the new domain. Join the domain by changing the domain name using the Network applet in Control Panel on the member server.

B. Create a computer account for the server on the new domain by using a different name for the server. Change the name of the member server to the name specified when the new domain account was created. Join the domain by using the Network applet in Control Panel.

C. Move the domain account from the old domain to the new domain by using Server Manager. Change the domain assignment on the member server to the new domain by using the Network applet in Control Panel.

D. Reinstall Windows NT Server on the computer. Configure it as a member server and join the new domain.

E. Change the domain membership of the computer by using the NET DOMAIN /UPDATE command.

5. **Which of the following tools is used to force synchronization of the user account database among domain controllers? Select the best response.**

   A. Domain Manager

   B. Server Administrator

   C. User Manager for Domains

   D. Server Manager

   E. WINNT32.EXE

6. **Where is the user account database for a domain stored? Select the best response.**

   A. Only on the PDC.

   B. On BDCs and the PDC.

   C. On BDCs, PDCs, and member servers.

   D. The master copy is stored on the PDC. Backup copies are stored on Windows NT servers that have been configured using the Replication Manager for backup storage.

   E. The domain user account database is a distributed database stored on all domain controllers in a domain.

7. **You are installing a new BDC on a new segment of a routed, TCP/IP network. This network is small and therefore does not utilize WINS name resolution. What must you do to make sure the new server can communicate with the PDC? Select the best response.**

   A. You must install a DNS server on the segment, either on the new BDC or on another Windows NT Server computer.

   B. You must configure the Default Gateway parameter for TCP/IP to point to a WINS server.

   C. You must add an entry to the LMHOSTS file on the new BDC, that specifies the name and IP address of the PDC, and then configure the BDC to resolve NetBIOS names using LMHOSTS.

   D. You must configure the Domain Server parameter for TCP/IP to point to the PDC.

   E. You must specify the location of the PDC during installation by running WINNT.EXE using the /P<ipaddress> command-line option.

8. **You are installing a small network for a company (30 users). The budget for this new network allows for a single Windows NT Server computer with more than enough hardware resources to serve as a print applications server.**

Required Results:

User accounts must be centrally managed.

Workstation accounts must be centrally managed.

Optional Results:

The single printer in the budget must be available to all users.

The network should be designed so it is easy to add more Windows NT Server computers as well as Windows 98 client computers.

Proposed solution:

Install the Windows NT Server computer as a PDC, install Windows 98 on the workstations, and then connect them to the server using the Microsoft network client. Connect a printer to the server and then share it on the network, assigning print rights to the group Everyone.

  A. The proposed solution meets both of the required results and both of the optional results.

  B. The proposed solution meets both of the required results and one of the optional results.

  C. The proposed solution meets one of the required results and both of the optional results.

  D. The proposed solution meets one of the required results and one of the optional results.

  E. The proposed solution meets neither of the required results but both of the optional results.

9. **Your company has just purchased a RISC-based computer with four processors, two 4GB hard drives, and 128MB of RAM. Your domain, named MIS, currently has a less attractive Windows NT 3.51 server acting as the PDC for MIS. It is your intention to make your new RISC machine your PDC. What is the correct procedure to accomplish this task? Select the best response.**

  A. Take the Windows NT 3.51 server offline, install Windows NT Server 4.0 on the RISC computer, and mark it as a PDC. Then bring the Windows NT 3.51 server back online and demote it to a BDC.

  B. Install NT Server 4.0 on the RISC computer, configuring it as a BDC in the MIS domain. Promote the RISC computer to a PDC. The Windows NT Server 3.51 automatically is demoted to a BDC when another computer is promoted. Remove the Windows NT Server 3.51 computer from the network.

  C. Upgrade the Windows NT 3.51 server to Windows NT Server 4.0, keeping it configured as a PDC. Install NT Server 4.0 on the RISC computer, configuring it as a BDC in the MIS domain. Promote the RISC computer to a PDC.

  D. Install Windows NT 4.0 Server on the RISC computer, configuring it as a BDC for MIS. Take the Windows NT 3.51 server offline and install Windows NT 4.0 Server, configuring it as a PDC. Move the PDC back online and then promote the RISC computer to a PDC.

E. This cannot be done. RISC-based computers cannot be configured as domain controllers.

10. **Which of the following are attributes of a member server? Select all that apply.**

    A. A member server can be a file and print server.

    B. A member server can belong to a domain and a workgroup at the same time.

    C. A member server can validate logon requests from clients.

    D. A member server can be a RAS server.

    E. A member server can be a master browser.

11. **You are installing a Windows NT Server computer, configuring it as a BDC. A DHCP server is available on the network.**

How do you configure this computer to obtain its IP address from the DHCP server? Select the best response.

A. This is impossible. Windows NT Server computers must have a static IP address.

B. You must edit the IPCONFIG.INI file, adding the statement "DHCP=1".

C. During the IP configuration part of the installation, choose to participate in DHCP.

D. After installation, change the computer's IP address in the LMHOSTS file to 0.0.0.0.

E. After the installation, use the Network applet in the Control Panel to change the TCP/IP configuration to use DHCP. Then add the computer name to the leasing database on the DHCP server.

ANSWER KEY		
1. C	5. D	9. B
2. B	6. B	10. A-D-E
3. D	7. C	11. C
4. A	8. C	

WINDOWS NT SERVER 4.0 SERVER ROLES

1. You are about to replace the primary domain controller on your company's single-domain network with a newer, faster computer. The PDC is used for logon services only and is one of five domain controllers on your company's network. In addition, you must meet the following criteria:

The new computer will be used as the PDC.

The name of the PDC should remain the same.

This operation should not interrupt network operations.

Which of the following scenarios can accomplish all these goals? Select the best response.

C. Promote one of the other domain controllers on the network to PDC, remove the old PDC from the network, install the new computer as a BDC, and then promote it to PDC.

1. CORRECT ANSWER: C

First, look at what is wrong with the other answers. Answer A does not let you use the same name as the old PDC because the two would be online at the same time. You cannot install a computer on the network as a PDC when there is an existing domain, so answer B is incorrect. You can, however, add a Windows NT computer to the network using the same name as a previous Windows NT computer, as long as you delete the account for the old computer and then create a new one.

When you promote a domain controller to PDC, the existing PDC is demoted to BDC. This enables the old PDC to be shut down and removed from the network in a graceful fashion. As long as you delete the account for the old PDC, you can add a new BDC with the same name and then promote it to a PDC.

2. Your company's network has two domains, SALES and ADMIN. Each domain has three domain controllers. A new sales office opens. It is decided that the new office should have a local domain controller. A limited budget means you must use one of the ADMIN BDCs to add a new BDC to the SALES domain. How do you accomplish this? Select the best response.

B. Move the server to the new location and then reinstall Windows NT Server, configuring the computer as a BDC for the SALES domain.

2. CORRECT ANSWER: B

Knowing the following keys to this question can earn you at least one correct answer on the exam:

1. There is no way to promote a member server to a domain controller. You must reinstall Windows NT Server.

2. There is no way to move a domain controller to another domain. You must reinstall Windows NT Server.

3. Your company's network has two locations, Dallas and Houston. A full T1 line connects the locations. You are installing a new single-domain Windows NT network that includes two new servers to be used as domain controllers. Your plan is to locate the PDC in Dallas and the BDC in Houston. As it turns out, the new computer is shipped to Houston, and the computer earmarked for Dallas is backordered for six weeks. Time constraints require you to get the network up and running within a week. How can you set up the network now, add the new computer when it comes in, and still end up with the PDC in Dallas? Select the best response.

   D. Install the Houston computer as a PDC. When the Dallas computer arrives, install it as a BDC and then promote it to PDC.

3. CORRECT ANSWER: D

This answer is correct because the first Windows NT computer installed on a domain must be a PDC. The solution works; however, users logging on in Dallas will be authenticated over the T1 connection until the new computer is installed in Dallas.

4. You must move a member server to a new domain. How do you accomplish this task? Select the best response.

   A. Create a computer account for the server on the new domain. Join the domain by changing the domain name using the Network applet in Control Panel on the member server.

4. CORRECT ANSWER: A

Changing a member server's domain is a simple process because the server does not interact with the domain controllers in terms of domain user authentication and security. Moving a member server to a different domain can be complicated, however, in terms of its resources, which might be used by other computers and applications in the current domain.

5. Which of the following tools is used to force synchronization of the user account database among domain controllers? Select the best response.

   D. Server Manager

5. CORRECT ANSWER: D

Server Manager can be run from any domain controller to manage other computers on the network. One of its options is to force an update of the user account database among all the domain controllers.

6. Where is the user account database for a domain stored? Select the best response.

   B. On BDCs and the PDC.

6. CORRECT ANSWER: B

A master copy of the domain user account database is stored on the PDC and is replicated to all domain controllers in the domain. This replication is set up automatically when you install BDCs on the network.

7. You are installing a new BDC on a new segment of a routed, TCP/IP network. This network is small and therefore does not utilize WINS name resolution. What must you do to make sure the new server can communicate with the PDC? Select the best response.

C. You must add an entry to the LMHOSTS file on the new BDC, which specifies the name and IP address of the PDC, and then configure the BDC to resolve NetBIOS names using LMHOSTS.

7. CORRECT ANSWER: C

The LMHOSTS file is used to resolve NetBIOS names to IP addresses on networks where WINS is not available. It also can be used as a backup against WINS server failures.

8. Proposed solution:
Install the Windows NT Server computer as a PDC, install Windows 98 on the workstations, and then connect them to the server by using the Microsoft network client. Connect a printer to the server and then share it on the network, assigning print rights to the group Everyone.

C The proposed solution meets one of the required results and both of the optional results.

8. CORRECT ANSWER: C

Configuring the Windows NT Server computer as a PDC means you are implementing a domain. One of the advantages of a domain is that user accounts can be centrally managed.

Only Windows NT computers (both Windows NT Server and Windows NT Workstation) can be members of a domain. When a Windows NT workstation joins a domain, it establishes a secure communication channel with Windows NT member servers and domain controllers in the domain. This enables Windows NT workstations to be remotely managed. Windows 98 computers only can be client computers in the domain.

Sharing the printer on any of the computers on this network would make it a network resource. Sharing it on a computer that is (presumably) on all the time increases availability.

9. Your company has just purchased a RISC-based computer with four processors, two 4GB hard drives, and 128MB of RAM. Your domain, named MIS, currently has a less attractive Windows NT 3.51 server acting as the PDC for MIS. It is your intention to make your new RISC machine your PDC. What is the correct procedure to accomplish this task? Select the best response.

9. CORRECT ANSWER: B

Windows NT 3.51 domain controllers are compatible with Windows NT 4.0 domain controllers. This task, therefore, is a simple process of installing Windows NT 4.0 Server and then changing server roles for two computers.

B. Install NT Server 4.0 on the RISC computer, configuring it as a BDC in the MIS domain. Promote the RISC computer to a PDC. The Windows NT Server 3.51 automatically is demoted to a BDC when another computer is promoted. Remove the Windows NT Server 3.51 computer from the network.

10. Which of the following are attributes of a member server? Select all that apply.

    A. A member server can be a file and print server.

    D. A member server can be a RAS server.

    E. A member server can be a master browser.

10. CORRECT ANSWERS: A-D-E

Only domain controllers can validate user logon requests. Windows NT computers (both Windows NT Server and Windows NT Workstation) can belong to a domain or a workgroup but not simultaneously. Windows 9x computers can belong to both at the same time.

11. You are installing a Windows NT Server computer, configuring it as a BDC. A DHCP server is available on the network. How do you configure this computer to obtain its IP address from the DHCP server? Select the best response.

    C. During the IP configuration part of the installation, choose to participate in DHCP.

11. CORRECT ANSWER: C

Setting up a Windows NT computer as a DHCP client is simple. A check box in the TCP/IP settings sets the computer as a DHCP client. No other configuration is required.

Although Windows NT Server computers can be configured as DHCP clients, it generally is not a good idea to do so. A Windows NT server can communicate with other TCP/IP devices that know the server only by its IP address.

FURTHER REVIEW

WINDOWS NT SERVER ROLES

Table 2.1 describes the three possible roles served on a network by a Windows NT Server computer. Understanding these roles and their inherent implications in terms of functionality, interoperation with other Windows NT servers, and configuration paths is essential to achieving the server roles' test objective.

Windows NT Role Synopsis

There likely will be several exam questions about the functions and characteristics of the following server roles. Table 2.1 provides a brief description of each.

TABLE 2.1 THE THREE PRIMARY ROLES A SERVER CAN BE CONFIGURED TO PERFORM ON A MICROSOFT NETWORK

Role	Description
Primary domain controller (PDC)	Maintains the master copy of the user account database. Authenticates domain logon requests. Maintains trust relationships between domains. Every domain must have exactly one PDC. Can perform other duties, such as WINS, DHCP, and DNS server. Also can be used as a print, file, and application server. Other duties performed depend on the networking environment. It must be the first computer installed in a domain, but it can be demoted to a BDC after another domain controller is installed in the domain.
Backup domain controller (BDC)	Maintains a copy of the user account database, which periodically is updated by the PDC. Authenticates domain logon requests. Maintains trust relationships between domains. Domains can have any number of BDCs. Can perform other duties, such as WINS, DHCP, and DNS server. Also can be used as a print, file, and application server. Other duties performed depend on the networking environment. Can be promoted to a PDC.
Member server	Plays no part in domain user account and security management. Used primarily as a file, print, and applications server. Can perform other duties such as WINS, DHCP, and DNS server. Can belong to a workgroup or a domain but not simultaneously. Cannot be promoted to a BDC or PDC. To change a member server to a domain controller, Windows NT Server must be reinstalled.

WINDOWS NT INSTALLATION METHODS

1. **You are installing a Windows NT server that has limited disk-space availability. How can you reduce the size of the installation? Select the best response.**

   A. Install Windows NT Server by using the Typical installation option.

   B. Install Windows NT Server by using the Portable installation option.

   C. Install Windows NT Server by using the Compact installation option.

   D. Install Windows NT Server by using the Custom installation option.

   E. Install Windows NT Server and configure the hard disk drive as an NTFS partition.

2. **You have some MS-DOS computers at your site that must be connected to the Windows NT 4.0 network. Network connections are not yet available for these computers, but you have time to configure them now. How can you get the bulk of the work out of the way before the network connections are available? Select the best response.**

   A. Use Client Administrator on a Windows NT server to create a set of installation disks for Microsoft Network Client for MS-DOS. Install network cards on the computers and then install and configure the client software by using the installation disks.

   B. Use Client Administrator on a Windows NT server to create a network startup disk for Microsoft Network Client for MS-DOS. Install network cards on the computers and then install and configure the client software by using the startup disk.

   C. Purchase a copy of Microsoft Client for MS-DOS for each computer. Install network cards on the computers and then install the client software you purchased.

   D. This cannot be done. Windows NT Server 4.0 does not support MS-DOS clients.

   E. Microsoft Client for MS-DOS can be installed only over the network. You can install only the network cards and wait for the network connections.

3. **Which is the best way to improve the performance of an over-the-network installation of Windows NT Server?**

   A. Buy a faster CD-ROM drive and install it in the source Windows NT server.

   B. Copy the contents of the Windows NT Server CD-ROM to a hard disk drive on the server, share the directory, and use it as the installation source rather than sharing the source server's CD-ROM drive.

C. Copy the contents of the shared CD-ROM drive on the source server to the local hard disk on the target computer. Start the installation from the local drive.

D. Increase the network frame size for the source Windows NT server by using the TCP/IP applet in Control Panel. This enables the server to send the data to the target computer in larger, more efficient frames.

E. For the source server, use the Windows NT server with the fastest processor.

4. **Which of the following network operations can a client using Microsoft Client for MS-DOS perform? Select the best response.**

   A. Participate in server announcements

   B. Receive Exchange mail

   C. Obtain an IP address via DHCP

   D. Participate in directory synchronization

   E. Act as a browser computer

5. **Which command runs an unattended installation by using an answer file?**

   A. `SETUP /u: <answer file>`

   B `WINNT /f: <answer file>`

   C. `WINNT32 /u: <answer file>`

   D. `WINNT /u: <answer file> /s: <install location>`

   E. `SETUP /u: <answer file> /s: <install location>`

6. **You are assigned the task of installing Windows NT on more than 100 computers. These computers are not all identical; three different network cards and two different video cards are installed on them. You decide to install over the network by using the unattended mode of `WINNT.EXE`. Considering the hardware differences on the target computers, how can you install Windows NT in unattended mode? Select the best response.**

   A. Create a batch file that runs the SysDiff utility and then executes `WINNT` with the `/S` switch.

   B. Using the SysDiff utility, create a Uniqueness Database File for each target computer. Append the data to the answer file.

   C. Using a text editor, create a Uniqueness Database File that represents the different configurations of the target computers. Include the UDF in the setup process by using the `/UDF` command-line switch with `WINNT`.

   D. Create a separate answer file for each configuration. Specify the answer file to use at install time by using the `/A` switch with `WINNT`.

E. Create a separate answer file for each configuration. Specify the answer file to use at install time by using the /A switch with WINNT32.

7. **You are configuring an automated setup of several Windows NT computers. You have several files you want to execute as part of the setup. How do you run these programs during a Windows NT installation? Select the best response.**

A. Create a directory named Runonce at the root of the install distribution point and then copy the executables into that directory.

B. Create a directory named OEM at the root of the install distribution point. Copy the executables into OEM and then specify the files to run in CMDLINES.TXT. Place CMDLINES.TXT in the OEM directory.

C. Start the installation from a batch file that includes commands to execute the additional files.

D. Create a text file named CMDLINES.BAT that contains the command to run the additional files. Put CMDLINES.BAT in the root directory of the distribution point.

E. Place the commands to run the additional commands in the AUTOEXEC.BAT file. Set the installation script to reboot when the installation is complete.

8. **What are three ways you can improve over-the-network speed for a new Windows NT installation?**

A. Use the NetBEUI protocol when the distribution point is on the same segment as the target.

B. Use HIMEM.SYS, EMM386.EXE, and SMARTDRV.EXE for the text-mode portion of the installation.

C. Disable HIMEM.SYS, EMM386.EXE, and SMARTDRV.EXE for the text-mode portion of the installation.

D. Use the /N switch with WINNT.

E. Do not copy the DRVLIB.NIC directory to the target.

9. **Which tool is used to create automated installation of Windows NT applications when performing unattended installs?**

A. APPIMAGE.EXE

B. SYSIMG.EXE

C. SYSDIFF.EXE

D. REGEDIT32.EXE

E. SMSPKG.EXE

10. **How do you configure a Windows NT unattended installation to reboot the computer without prompting? Select the best response.**

A. Add a REBOOT command to the appropriate answer file.

B. Run REGEDIT and add a reboot command to the RUNONCE key during installation.

C. Add the REBOOT command to the AUTOEXEC.BAT file, which is copied over during installation.

D. Run RUNDLL32.EXE and call SETUPAPI.DLL referencing the appropriate function call and INF file on the command line.

E. Run WINNT using the /R switch.

ANSWER KEY

1. D	5. D	8. A-B-E
2. A	6. C	9. C
3. B	7. B	10. D
4. C		

ANSWERS & EXPLANATIONS

WINDOWS NT INSTALLATION METHODS

1. **You are installing Windows NT server that has limited disk space availability. How can you reduce the size of the installation? Select the best response.**

   D. **Install Windows NT Server by using the Custom installation option.**

1. CORRECT ANSWER: D

There is only one correct answer for this question because the only option available for Windows NT Server is Custom. Custom installation enables you to add or eliminate some components from the installation. You can, for example, opt not to install games, RAS, or accessibility options to save disk space. The other installation options listed are valid but only for Windows NT Workstation. NTFS uses more disk resources than a FAT partition.

2. **You have some MS-DOS computers at your site that must be connected to the Windows NT 4.0 network. Network connections are not yet available for these computers, but you have time to configure them now. How can you get the bulk of the work out of the way before the network connections are available? Select the best response.**

   A. **Use Client Administrator on a Windows NT server to create a set of installation disks for Microsoft Network Client for MS-DOS. Install network cards on the computers and then install and configure the client software by using the installation disks.**

2. CORRECT ANSWER: A

There are two options for creating a Client for MS-DOS setup. You can create a network startup disk, which boots the computer, connects to the server, and then installs the client by using the installation files on a server share. When you create the installation disks, the installation files are written to floppy disks. The installation is done by using the floppy files—no connection to the network is required.

3. **Which is the best way to improve the performance of an over-the-network installation of Windows NT Server?**

   B. **Copy the contents of the Windows NT Server CD-ROM to a hard disk drive on the server, share the directory, and use it as the installation source rather than sharing the source server's CD-ROM drive.**

3. CORRECT ANSWER: B

At this time, a hard disk drive is faster than a CD-ROM drive and will facilitate a faster over-the-network installation. After the installation files are moved to a hard disk drive, the slowest part of the installation is the network transport. Increasing the speed of the microprocessor does not help much because the bottleneck is the network connection.

4. Which of the following network operations can a client using Microsoft Client for MS-DOS perform? Select the best response.

  C. Obtain an IP address via DHCP

The MS-DOS client is very limited. In addition to being able to utilize a DHCP server, Microsoft Client for MS-DOS can map to disk drive share points and to shared printers.

5. What command runs an unattended installation by using an answer file?

  D. `WINNT /u: <answer file> /s: <install location>`

Unattended installations are useful for deploying Windows NT over the network to a large number of computers. Note that `WINNT32` also supports unattended installations and uses the same command-line parameters.

The answer file is a text file containing keywords and values that represent Windows NT configuration options. Syntax for the answer file can be found in Table 2.2 in the following section, "Further Review: Installation Methods."

EXAM TIP

Memorize the command-line switches for `WINNT.EXE`. You will be asked which command is used to perform a given installation procedure. The correct answer will be `WINNT.EXE` with one or more of the switches listed in Table 2.2 in the following section, "For Further Review: Installation Methods."

6. You are assigned the task of installing Windows NT on more than 100 computers. These computers are not all identical; three different network cards and two different video cards are installed on them. You decide to install over the network by using the unattended mode of `WINNT.EXE`. Considering the hardware differences on the target computers, how can you install Windows NT in unattended mode? Select the best response.

  C. Using a text editor, create a Uniqueness Database File that represents the different configurations of the target computers. Include the UDF in the setup process by using the `/UDF` command-line switch with `WINNT`.

The purpose of a Uniqueness Database File (UDF) is to enable you to install Windows NT on computers with different configurations without creating a different setup script for each unique configuration. A UDF comprises sections in install script format (`UNATTEND.TXT`) that reflect differences in target computer hardware configurations. These sections are indexed by machine ID. To install Windows NT on a computer using a UDF, the `WINNT` command is issued using the parameter `/UDF:<id>,[<filename>]`. The `<id>` is the index ID for the sections in the UDF' `<filename>` is the MS-DOS format name of the UDF.

Although you can create an answer file for each different configuration, it is much simpler and more manageable to use a UDF file. Consider how much easier it is to change a common configuration when you have only one answer file.

7. You are configuring an automated setup of several Windows NT computers. You have several files you want to execute as part of the setup. How do you run these programs during a Windows NT installation? Select the best response.

   B. Create a directory named OEM at the root of the install distribution point. Copy the executables into OEM and then specify the files to run in CMDLINES.TXT. Place CMD-LINES.TXT in the OEM directory.

7. CORRECT ANSWER: B

The OEM directory can be used to execute additional programs, either during or after the Windows NT installation. It also is used to copy additional files of any type to the new installation, to provide OEM drivers for text mode setup, and to provide OEM drivers for Windows NT.

8. What are three ways you can improve over-the-network speed for a new Windows NT installation?

   A. Use the NetBEUI protocol when the distribution point is on the same segment as the target.

   B. Use HIMEM.SYS, EMM386.EXE, and SMARTDRV.EXE for the text-mode portion of the installation.

   E. Do not copy the DRVLIB.NIC directory to the target computer during the text mode installation stage.

8. CORRECT ANSWERS: A–B-E

NetBEUI is a compact, fast, and easy-to-configure protocol. It is ideal for over-the-network installations. One drawback of NetBEUI is that it is not routable; therefore, both the source and target computers must be on the same network segment.

The text mode of the Windows NT installation runs under (16-bit) MS-DOS. Much of the work done in the text mode is file copies. Enabling high memory using HIMEM.SYS and EMM386.EXE and then caching disk drive I/O with SMARTDRV.EXE improves the file copy performance substantially.

The DRVLIB.NIC directory contains driver software for more than 80 different network adapters and totals approximately 20MB of disk storage. This directory is copied to the target computer during the text mode of a Windows NT installation. All that is necessary for most installations is one of these directories, which can be accessed from the original CD-ROM or from another file when needed by the GUI portion of the Windows NT installation.

9. Which tool is used to create auto-mated installation of Windows NT applications when performing unattended installs?

C. SYSDIFF.EXE

Using SYSDIFF to automatically install applications is a three-step process, as follows:

1. Build a fresh installation of Windows NT from the distribution server. Use SYSDIFF in the SNAP mode to create a snapshot image of the installation.

2. Install and configure the application(s) and then run SYSDIFF in DIFF mode. SYSDIFF creates a file that contains all changes.

3. Add the application to your unattended installation by running SYSDIFF in INF mode. This creates an OEM directory in the root of the install distribution point (if necessary) and copies the required files to OEM.

10. How do you configure a Windows NT unattended installation to reboot the computer without prompting? Select the best response.

D. Run RUNDLL32.EXE and call SETUPAPI.DLL referencing the appropriate function call and INF file on the command line.

SETUPAPI.DLL is an installation engine that can be used to customize Windows NT installations. SETUPAPI can be used to copy files, to update the Registry, to modify files, and to reboot the computer. SETUPAPI.DLL is called from an Install section of a Windows 95–style .INF file by the CMDLINES.TXT file. To reboot the target computer during Windows NT installation, add the following line to any Install section of the .INF file:

```
RUNDLL32 SETUPAPI.DLL,InstallHinfSection <section>
<reboot-mode> <inf-name>
```

where

<section> is an Install section in the .INF file.

<reboot-mode> determines which of five reboot modes should be used.

<inf-name> is the INF filename.

The following are the reboot modes:

Never Reboot—0 or 128. The target computer will not reboot. The client must decide whether the target computer should be rebooted. If there is a file

`C:\WINDOWS\WININIT.INI` that is at least 1 byte in size, the target computer will reboot.

Always Silent Reboot—1 or 129. The computer reboots without prompting the user.

Always Prompt Reboot—2 or 130. The target computer always prompts the user to begin the reboot sequence.

Silent Reboot—3 or 131. Setup decides whether the target computer should reboot. User is not notified or prompted.

Prompt Reboot—4 or 132. Setup decides whether the target computer should be rebooted; user is prompted.

FURTHER REVIEW

WINDOWS NT INSTALLATION METHODS

Installing Windows NT is a flexible process, in part because of the flexibility of WINNT.EXE. WINNT.EXE provides the command-line options that empower you to execute custom tools and scripts, which enable you to perform Windows NT installations pretty much any way you like. It is important to know how to use the WINNT.EXE command-line switches to invoke scripts and tools as well as to control the behavior of WINNT.EXE in some other ways. Table 2.2 describes the command-line switches for WINNT.EXE.

Command Line Switches for WINNT.EXE

Several command-line switches are available when you execute WINNT.EXE. Expect to see exam questions in which you must select the correct command-line switch or switches to accomplish a task. Table 2.2 defines the switches for WINNT.EXE.

TABLE 2.2 WINNT.EXE SWITCH DEFINITIONS

Switch	Description
/S[:]sourcepath	Location of Windows NT files to be copied during installation prep. Usually used when performing an over-the-network installation.
/T[:]tempdrive	Target drive for Windows NT files copied during installation prep. If not specified, WINNT finds a target drive (usually C).
/I[:]inffile	Filename of setup information file. DOSNET.INF is the default file.
/B	Execute installation without creating floppy installation disks (requires /s).
/U	Install in unattended mode using optional script file (/s).
/R:[sourcepath]	Optional directory to be installed.
/RX	Optional directory to be copied.
/E:	Command to be run when the GUI setup completes.
/W	Only for starting WINNT.EXE from within Windows 3.x or Windows 95. When /W is used, the /B switch is disabled.

PRACTICE QUESTIONS

CONFIGURING PROTOCOLS ON WINDOWS NT SERVER

1. **You have just installed a second network card on a Windows NT server and have configured the card with TCP/IP. Both network cards on the computer are configured with TCP/IP. Computers on each segment attached to the Windows NT server can communicate with the server, but they cannot "see" computers connected to the other segment. Which of the following is likely the problem?**

   A. Windows NT Server does not support internal routing. You must connect the two segments with a router.

   B. IP routing is not enabled on the server. You must enable IP routing by using the IPCONFIG tool.

   C. The IP addresses for the two network cards have different subnet masks. You must reconfigure one or both of the cards so the subnet masks are the same.

   D. The Address Resolution Protocol is not configured. You must install it by using the ARP utility.

   E. IP routing is not enabled on the server. You must enable IP routing by using the Network applet in Control Panel.

2. **You are responsible for integrating Windows NT Server and NetWare servers**

on your company's network. You successfully install Windows NT Server and connect it to the network; however, the new server cannot access any of the NetWare servers. What is likely the problem? Select all that apply.

   A. The NetWare servers are version 3.x and are not compatible with Windows NT Server 4.0.

   B. The native protocol for the NetWare servers is IPX/SPX. You must add the NWLink protocol to Windows NT Server 4.0.

   C. You must install Gateway Services for NetWare to manage communication between Windows NT Server and NetWare.

   D. You must install NetWare Client 32 on the new server to manage communication between Windows NT Server and NetWare.

   E. You must install NetBEUI on the new server to facilitate NetBIOS name resolution.

3. **You have NetWare 4.x and 3.x servers on the network that use different frame types. How do you configure Windows NT Server to facilitate communicating with all the NetWare servers? Select the best response.**

A. Use the `IPXROUTE CONFIG` command-line utility to assign additional frame types to the network card.

B. Use the `IPCONFIG` command-line utility to assign additional frame types to the network card.

C. You must edit the Registry to assign additional frame types to the network card.

D. You must add another network card to the server. You can have only one frame type per protocol bound to a network card. You can bind a protocol to a network card only once.

E. Add frame types using the Network applet in Control Panel.

4. Which LMHOSTS file directive instructs Windows NT Server to load the specified NetBIOS name and IP address into the name cache?

A. #PRE

B. #MEM

C. #CACHE

D. #DOM

E. None of the above. All names automatically are loaded into name cache when Windows NT Server is booted.

5. What protocol facilitates secure remote access to a Windows NT network over the Internet?

A. FTP

B. PTP

C. PPTP

D. RAS

E. SLIP

6. Which two encryption algorithms does PPTP use?

A. RSA RC4 with a 40-bit session key

B. DOD 128-bit key

C. Password Authentication Protocol

D. RFC1001

E. Challenge Handshake Authentication Protocol

7. Microsoft Remote Access Service (RAS) supports which protocols? Select all that apply.

A. TCP/IP

B. Serial Line IP (SLIP)

C. PPTP

D. Point-to-Point Protocol (PPP)

E. Microsoft RAS Protocol

8. You have installed a new Windows NT Server computer on a network that contains primarily TCP/IP hosts. A small portion of the user community uses either IPX or NetBEUI. You install all three protocols. When configuring these protocols on the new server, what might you do to improve the server's performance? Select the best response.

A. Make sure the packet type for all protocols is 802.2.

B. Make sure you use a different packet type for each protocol.

C. Set the binding order so TCP/IP is first for all network cards.

D. Set the MTU to maximum size (9,182 bytes).

E. Do nothing. Microsoft protocols are self-tuning.

9. **How many IP hosts can be connected to a single segment on a class C network?**

   A. 256

   B. 255

   C. 1,024

   D. 4,096

   E. 254

10. **You are installing a second network card on a Windows NT Server computer. The computer is connected to a TCP/IP network. You must enable IP routing on this server; however, the network manager has instructed you NOT to use the RIP routing protocol. How do you make sure IP traffic is routed through this computer correctly? Select the best response.**

   A. Add the IP addresses for the network cards to the default gateway lists on all other routers on the network.

   B. Add the IP addresses for the network cards to the default gateway lists on all other routers connected to the same segments as the network cards.

   C. Add a second IP address to each card so they belong to both network segments.

   D. Configure the LMHOSTS file to point to default gateways on both network segments.

   E. Configure a persistent static routing table on the computer by using the ROUTE command-line utility.

ANSWER KEY

1. E	5. C	8. C
2. B-C	6. C-E	9. E
3. E	7. B-C-D-E	10. E
4. A		

CONFIGURING PROTOCOLS ON WINDOWS NT SERVER

1. You have just installed a second network card on a Windows NT server and have configured the card with TCP/IP. Both network cards on the computer are configured with TCP/IP. Computers on each segment attached to the Windows NT server can communicate with the server, but they cannot "see" computers connected to the other segment. Which of the following is likely the problem?

   E. IP routing is not enabled on the server. You must enable IP routing by using the Network applet in Control Panel.

1. CORRECT ANSWER: E

Multihomed Windows NT Server computers can act as a TCP/IP router. After all the network cards on the computer have TCP/IP bound to them, a check box in the TCP/IP configuration dialog box enables IP routing.

2. You are responsible for integrating Windows NT Server and NetWare servers on your company's network. You successfully install Windows NT Server and connect it to the network; however, the new server cannot access any of the NetWare servers. What is likely the problem? Select all that apply.

   B. The native protocol for the NetWare servers is IPX/SPX. You must add the NWLink protocol to the Windows NT Server 4.0.

   C. You must install Gateway Services for NetWare to manage communication between Windows NT Server and NetWare.

2. CORRECT ANSWERS: B-C

Although you can use NetWare Client 32 to communicate with NetWare servers, Gateway Service for NetWare is more appropriate for this situation.

3. You have NetWare 4.x and 3.x servers on the network that use different frame types. How do you configure Windows NT Server to facilitate communicating with all the NetWare servers? Select the best response.

   E. Add frame types using the Network applet in Control Panel.

3. CORRECT ANSWER: E

Windows NT Server enables you to add frame types through Control Panel; however, Windows NT Workstation requires you to edit the Registry to add frame types.

4. Which LMHOSTS file directive instructs Windows NT Server to load the specified NetBIOS name and IP address into the name cache?

A. #PRE

4. CORRECT ANSWER: A

When a Windows NT computer is configured to use the LMHOSTS file for NetBIOS name resolution, NetBIOS names and their associated IP addresses that are preceded by the #PRE (PREload) directive are loaded into the name cache when Windows NT is started. This is useful for names of frequently accessed computers.

EXAM TIP

You probably can expect at least one question about LMHOSTS file configuration or NetBIOS node types on the exam. See the next section, "For Further Review: Configuring Protocols on Windows NT Server," for a description of LMHOSTS file directives and definitions of NetBIOS node types.

5. What protocol facilitates secure remote access to a Windows NT network over the Internet?

C. PPTP

5. CORRECT ANSWER: C

The Point-to-Point Tunneling Protocol (PPTP) was introduced with Windows NT version 4.0. Remote access is accomplished using a RAS connection. You can bet the farm you will be asked about PPTP on the exam.

6. Which two encryption algorithms does PPTP use?

C. Password Authentication Protocol

E. Challenge Handshake Authentication Protocol

6. CORRECT ANSWERS: C - E

You should memorize this answer. RSA RC4 with a 40-bit session key encryption is the bulk data encryption used for PPP connections between RAS clients and servers.

7. Microsoft Remote Access Service (RAS) supports which protocols? Select all that apply.

B. Serial Line IP (SLIP)

C. PPTP

D. Point-to-Point Protocol (PPP)

E. Microsoft RAS Protocol

7. CORRECT ANSWERS: B – C – D - E

Microsoft RAS uses PPTP protocol for over-the-Internet secure connections. Microsoft RAS Protocol also is called asynchronous NetBEUI.

When a remote client connects using NetBEUI, the RAS server uses a service called NetBIOS Gateway to translate the packets to IPX or TCP/IP (unless the LAN is using NetBEUI). Such a connection enables the RAS client to access the network; however, the RAS client cannot run applications that depend on IPX or TCP/IP at the client level.

8. You have installed a new Windows NT Server computer on a network that contains primarily TCP/IP hosts. A small portion of the user community uses either IPX or NetBEUI. You install all three protocols. When configuring these protocols on the new server, what might you do to improve the server's performance? Select the best response.

    C. Set the binding order so TCP/IP is first for all network cards.

8. CORRECT ANSWER: C

The binding order is the order in which the computer finds information on the network. If TCP/IP is the first protocol in the binding sequence, access to a network that is mostly TCP/IP is optimized.

9. How many IP hosts can be connected to a single segment on a class C network?

    E. 254

9. CORRECT ANSWER: E

The subnet mask for a class C network is 255.255.255.0. This means one octet is available for host numbers. Host addresses are 0–255 (256 host numbers). Host number 0 is reserved for the network number, however, and 255 is reserved for broadcasts. Therefore, 254 host numbers actually are available.

IP addressing is based on a four-byte (or octet) number, which is expressed in decimal form and separated by dots. An example of an IP address is 192.123.78.4. Although the IP address usually is expressed in decimal notation, it is important to keep in mind that machines see this address in binary form.

IP addresses define the network number and the host number for a given network device. A subnet mask defines the boundary between the network and host portions of an IP address. A subnet mask is a four-octet number formatted in the same fashion as an IP address. To obtain the network portion of an IP address, you can perform a bitwise AND with the address and the subnet mask. For example, the network address for IP address 192.123.17.121 with a subnet mask of 255.255.255.0 is 192.123.17.0.

192.123.17.121
in binary form: 11000000.11101100.00010001.00111001

255.255.255.0
in binary form: 11111111.11111111.11111111.00000000

Bitwise AND
result: 11000000.11101100.00010001.00000000

Result in decimal format: 192.123.17.0

Conversely, to obtain the host portion of an IP address, you can perform a bitwise AND on the IP address by using the bitwise NOT of the subnet mask.

192.123.17.121 in
binary form: 11000000.11101100.00010001.00111001

NOT 255.255.255.0
in binary form: 00000000.00000000.00000000.11111111

Bitwise AND result:
00000000.00000000.00000000.00111001

Result in decimal format: 0.0.0.121

Note that the host portion of an IP address cannot be all 0s or all 1s in binary notation.

By RFC standards, IP addresses are divided into classes based on the octet boundary combined with the value of the first octet. The three primary classes are as follows:

Class	Subnet Mask	First Octet Range
A	255.0.0.0	0–126
B	255.255.0.0	127–191
C	255.255.255.0	192–223

Although the standard classes define the most commonly used subnet masks, remember that subnet masks do not necessarily define octet boundaries. When they do not, calculating network and host addresses can be tricky because the octets for network addresses expressed in decimal format are not necessarily contiguous. Consider the class B IP address 190.228.0.0. Valid network addresses for subnet mask 255.255.192.0 include the following:

190.228.0.0
190.228.64.0

190.228.128.0

190.228.192.0

In addition, hosts that belong to the same network can look like they are connected to different networks. Using the preceding example, note that the following IP addresses belong to the same network (190.228.192.0):

190.228.192.18

190.228.254.134

190.228.213.209

For the exam, you must be able to determine network addresses when given a full IP address and a subnet mask. You also should know how to determine how many networks can be derived from a standard class IP address and a nonstandard subnet mask.

---

10. You are installing a second network card on a Windows NT Server computer. The computer is connected to a TCP/IP network. You must enable the IP routing on this server; however, the network manager has instructed you NOT to use the RIP routing protocol. How do you make sure IP traffic is routed through this computer correctly? Select the best response.

    E. Configure a persistent static routing table on the computer by using the ROUTE command-line utility.

10. CORRECT ANSWER: E

When you create a static routing table on a Windows NT computer, it automatically is persistent. That is, the routing information is not lost when the computer is restarted.

FURTHER REVIEW

CONFIGURING PROTOCOLS ON WINDOWS NT SERVER

One of the most common issues when configuring a network is name resolution. On a Windows NT network, name resolution is provided by WINS (NetBIOS names) and DNS (TCP/IP domain names). A connected host can resolve a name in several ways. Table 2.4 defines the actions taken to resolve names by different node types on a network. One way that some nodes resolve names is by reading the LMHOSTS file. Table 2.3 describes the syntax used in the Windows NT LMHOSTS files.

LMHOSTS File Directives

Windows NT provides several directives that enable you to customize and better manage LMHOSTS files. The LMHOSTS file helps provide compatibility with older LAN Manager machines and supports Microsoft network name resolution. Table 2.3 defines the LMHOSTS file directives.

TABLE 2.3 **LMHOSTS FILE DIRECTIVES**

Directive	Description
#DOM:<domain>	Domain specifier. This directive indicates that the NetBIOS name and IP address that follow represent a domain controller belonging to <domain>. The #DOM: directive usually is used in conjunction with #PRE.
#PRE	The #PRE directive instructs Windows NT to read the specified NetBIOS name and IP address into name cache memory.
#INCLUDE<filename>	#INCLUDE is used to read and parse another LMHOSTS-format file. The file specified by <filename> can be local or can be stored on another network host. #INCLUDE files on other network hosts are referenced by UNC name.
#BEGIN_ALTERNATE	Marks the beginning of an #INCLUDE block. An #INCLUDE block is a group of #INCLUDE statements that specify identical files in different locations. After the file is successfully read, the rest of the #INCLUDE statements are ignored.
#END_ALTERNATE	Marks the end of an #INCLUDE block.
#MH	Indicates that the specified NetBIOS name has multiple IP addresses. The limit for one name is 25 IP addresses.
\0xnn	Used to represent a nonprinting character in a NetBIOS name, where nn is a hexadecimal number.
#SG	Obscure directive that enables you to define IP groups for browsing and broadcasts.

NetBIOS Node Types

A computer's node type defines the procedure it uses to register and resolve NetBIOS names. A Windows NT computer can register its NetBIOS name by broadcasting or by contacting a WINS server directly. Name resolution can be accomplished by checking its internal name cache, by broadcasting to locate a name server, by reading an LMHOSTS file, or by contacting a WINS server directly. Note that all Windows NT node types check their local name cache before taking any other action. DHCP can be configured to set the node type for clients when assigning an IP address (see Table 2.4).

TABLE 2.4 NetBIOS Node Types for Windows NT Computers

Node Type	Description
b-node	Uses only broadcasts for both name resolution and registration. Windows NT b-nodes are enhanced to also check the LMHOSTS file if the broadcasts fail.
p-node	Uses only NetBIOS name server (a WINS server in the Windows NT environment) for both name resolution and registration.
m-node	Uses broadcasts for NetBIOS name registration and resolution. If a name cannot be resolved using broadcasts, an m-node becomes a p-node. In other words, it looks for a WINS server.
h-node	Uses a WINS server for name resolution and registration. If the node cannot locate a WINS server, it becomes b-node. While in b-node mode, the computer continues to look for a WINS server. If a WINS server subsequently is located, the computer becomes an h-node.

▼ **NOTE**

Windows NT computers will first query a DNS server (when available) when the NetBIOS name has a period in it.

PRACTICE QUESTIONS

CONFIGURE NETWORK ADAPTERS

1. You have installed a Windows NT Server computer to act as a router between Network 1 and Network 2. The two network adapters are installed on the computer with IP addresses configured as follows:

Adapter	IP Address	Subnet Mask
Adapter 1:	181.96.219.17	255.255.192.0
Adapter 2:	181.96.193.134	255.255.192.0

   Computers on Network 1 are not able to see Network 2 and vice versa. What might the problem be? Select the best response.

   A. Routing is not enabled on the Windows NT server.

   B. Both network adapters have the same subnet address.

   C. Static routing tables have not been created on the Windows NT server.

   D. Both network adapters do not have the same subnet address.

   E. Default gateways are not configured on both network adapters.

2. You have just installed a network adapter on your Windows NT computer by using drivers provided by the manufacturer. When you restart the computer, the following message appears:

   At least one service or driver failed during system startup. Use Event Viewer to examine the event log for details.

   The event log contains the following message:

   Event ID: 7000
   The <*your network adapter*> Driver service failed to start due to the following error: A device attached to the system is not functioning.

   What might you do to track down this problem? Select all that apply.

   A. Check the interrupt on the network adapter and make sure it does not conflict with another device.

   B. If the network adapter is an ISA card, move it to a PCI slot in the computer.

   C. If the network adapter is a PCI card, move it to the enhanced PCI slot.

   D. Check the DMA channel-number setting on the card and confirm that it does not conflict with existing devices.

   E. Uninstall the adapter drivers and then manually remove any settings for the card in the Registry. Reinstall the drivers.

3. You have installed Windows NT Server on a multihomed computer that will serve as a gateway to several NetWare servers by using the IPX protocol, as well

as a print server for Microsoft network clients using the TCP/IP protocol. The traffic load from the NetWare servers is quite heavy, so you want to isolate the NetWare traffic on the server from the Microsoft client traffic. How should you configure the network adapters for this computer? Select the best response.

A. Install both NWLink and TCP/IP on both network adapters. Configure the network cost value for each adapter such that one adapter is biased toward NWLink traffic and the other toward TCP/IP.

B. Install NWLink on both adapters and TCP/IP on only one adapter. Then enable IPX routing on the computer.

C. Install TCP/IP on both adapters and NWLink on only one adapter. Then enable TCP/IP routing on the computer.

D. Install TCP/IP on one adapter and NWLink on the other.

E. None of the above. Only one network adapter can be concurrently attached to a network when using a multi-homed Windows NT computer.

4. **When installing Windows NT, what settings are available to view or to configure from setup's Adapter Card Setup dialog box? Select the best response.**

A. IRQ, DMA channel, I/O address.

B. Bus type, IRQ, I/O address.

C. Slot number, Bus type.

D. IRQ, slot number, DMA channel.

E. It depends on the network adapter.

5. **You are asked to configure a Windows NT Server computer to act as a Point-to-Point Tunneling Protocol (PPTP) server so clients connected to the local network can connect to the Internet. What are the minimum hardware requirements for this computer? Select the best response.**

A. The same requirements as for Windows NT Server 4.0 and a network adapter that supports PPTP

B. The same requirements as for Windows NT Server 4.0 and two network adapters, or a network adapter and a modem or an ISDN device

C. The same requirements as for Windows NT Server 4.0 and a network adapter

D. The same requirements as for Windows NT Server 4.0, a PCI network adapter, and a modem or an ISDN device

E. The same requirements as for Windows NT Server plus 50MB free disk space, a network adapter, and a modem or ISDN device

6. **To enhance performance, you add a network card to your company's Windows NT Server computer and connect the card to the same network as the existing card. The cards are configured with TCP/IP and NetBEUI. When you restart the computer, you get**

a duplicate name error and the server service does not start. Why did the computer encounter this error, and how do you correct the problem? Select the best response.

A. TCP/IP must have a different IP domain name assigned to each network adapter. Add the new address to the network DNS server or to the computer's LMHOSTS file.

B. WINS must have a unique NetBIOS name for each network adapter connected to the network. Create a static entry for the second network adapter in the WINS database.

C. NetBEUI cannot be running on two network cards connected to the same segment on a multihomed computer. Remove NetBEUI from one of the network adapters.

D. TCP/IP did not bind to the new network adapter; it was added to the existing one. Unbind the second instance of TCP/IP from the first network adapter and bind it to the second.

E. NetBEUI did not bind to the new network adapter; it was added to the existing one. Unbind one instance of NetBEUI from the first adapter and bind it to the second.

7. Which of the following features can enhance network adapter performance? Select all that apply.

A. Direct Memory Access (DMA)

B. Protocol caching

C. Bus mastering

D. Shared-adapter memory

E. Write-ahead buffering

8. You have a multihomed Windows NT computer connected to two TCP/IP networks. You have just installed an HP JetDirect-equipped printer on each network. You install the DLC protocol on both cards; however, you cannot connect to the new printer on one of the networks. What is the problem and how can you correct it? Select the best response.

A. DLC can be bound to only one network adapter on a multihomed Windows NT computer. You can use TCP/IP to connect to one of the printers.

B. The HP print monitor can manage only one network adapter per Windows NT computer. You can use TCP/IP to connect to one of the printers.

C. DLC routing is enabled. Disable DLC routing.

D. DLC routing is disabled. Enable DLC routing.

E. JetDirect devices cannot be used by Windows NT Server. You can connect to the printers directly from the workstations by using IP printing.

9. Your company's TCP/IP network consists of two physical segments connected by a multihomed Windows NT Server

computer with routing enabled. The Windows NT server is the PDC for both segments and also is a WINS server. Everything works properly on the network except clients on one of the segments cannot browse across the segment boundary even though the Windows NT server can see the devices on both segments. How can you correct this problem? Select the best response.

A. Enable IP routing.

B. Configure the Windows NT server so it is not the master browser. Configure a computer on each segment to serve as a master browser.

C. Add a static entry for each network adapter on the Windows NT server.

D. Configure the Windows NT server so it is always the domain master browser.

E. Change the Registry so the Windows NT server provides browser information to both segments.

10. What command is used to determine the IP address, subnet mask, and default gateway of a Windows NT computer?

A. `NET VIEW`

B. `ROUTE /ALL`

C. `NET IP /ALL`

D. `IPCONFIG /ALL`

E. `WINIPCFG /ALL`

ANSWER KEY

1. B	5. B	8. B
2. A-D-E	6. C	9. E
3. D	7. A-C-D	10. D
4. E		

CONFIGURE NETWORK ADAPTERS

1. You have installed a Windows NT Server computer to act as a router between Network 1 and Network 2. The two network adapters are installed on the computer with IP addresses configured as follows:

Adapter	*IP Address*	*Subnet Mask*
Adapter 1:	181.96.219.17	255.255.192.0
Adapter 2:	181.96.193.134	255.255.192.0

   Computers on Network 1 are not able to see Network 2 and vice versa. What might the problem be? Select the best response.

   B. Both network adapters have the same subnet address.

1. CORRECT ANSWER: B

Although the first octet of the IP addresses for the two network adapters indicates class B addresses, the subnet mask, which is the same for both adapters, uses the first two bits of the third octet as part of the network address. The third octet for each network adapter IP address starts with 11 in binary format. Both adapters have the same subnet address. As with any other IP router, a multihomed Windows NT computer used as a router must route between two different networks.

2. You have just installed a network adapter on your Windows NT computer by using drivers provided by the manufacturer. When you restart the computer, the following message appears:

   At least one service or driver failed during system startup. Use Event Viewer to examine the event log for details.

   The event log contains the following message:

   Event ID: 7000
   The *<your network adapter>* Driver service failed to start due to the following error: A device attached to the system is not functioning.

   What might you do to track down this problem? Select all that apply.

   A. Check the interrupt on the network adapter and make sure it does not conflict with another device.

2. CORRECT ANSWERS: A - D - E

The error messages indicate that the drivers failed to recognize or initialize the network adapter. The most likely cause of this type of failure is a conflict with another device on the network. The conflict can be with the interrupt address, DMA channel, or the I/O address. Check these settings on the network adapter and then check settings for existing devices under the Resources tab in Windows NT Diagnostics.

If you fail to find a hardware conflict, you should attempt to reinstall the driver. Before attempting to reinstall the driver, uninstall the driver by using the Adapters tab in Control Panel's Network applet. You also should make sure all traces of the adapter are removed from the Registry. Remove the following Registry keys:

```
HKEY_LOCAL_MACHINE\SOFTWARE\<adapter name>

HKEY_LOCAL_MACHINE\SOFTWARE\Microsoft\WindowsNT\
➡CurrentVersion\NetworkCards\<adapter number>
```

D. Check the DMA channel-number setting on the card and confirm that it does not conflict with existing devices.

E. Uninstall the adapter drivers and then manually remove any settings for the card in the Registry. Reinstall the drivers.

```
HKEY_LOCAL_MACHINE\SYSTEM\CurrentControlSet\Services
➥\<adapter name>
```

3. You have installed Windows NT Server on a multihomed computer that will serve as a gateway to several NetWare servers by using the IPX protocol, as well as a print server for Microsoft network clients using the TCP/IP protocol. The traffic load from the NetWare servers is quite heavy, so you want to isolate the NetWare traffic on the server from the Microsoft client traffic. How should you configure the network adapters for this computer? Select the best response.

   D. Install TCP/IP on one adapter and NWLink on the other.

3. CORRECT ANSWER: D

Server network traffic congestion can be managed by adding more network adapters to a Windows NT server and attaching them to the same network. In this case, different protocols on each network adapter forces the traffic to be segregated.

4. When installing Windows NT, what settings are available to view or to configure from setup's Adapter Card Setup dialog box? Select the best response.

   E. It depends on the network adapter.

4. CORRECT ANSWER: E

During network-adapter configuration, setup checks the network-adapter driver for a configuration segment. If one is found, setup runs this code. Any user-configurable parameters are presented by a program provided by the manufacturer. This also applies to devices other than network adapters such as sound cards and hard-drive controllers.

5. You are asked to configure a Windows NT Server computer to act as a Point-to-Point Tunneling Protocol (PPTP) server so clients connected to the local network can connect to the Internet. What are the minimum hardware requirements for this computer? Select the best response.

   B. The same requirements as for Windows NT Server 4.0 and two network adapters, or a network adapter and a modem or an ISDN device

5. CORRECT ANSWER: B

PPTP protocol primarily is used to provide a secure connection over a public network (such as the Internet). A PPTP server accepts packets from a connected client, wraps the packets in PPTP, and then sends them out a different port. PPTP servers also accept PPTP traffic, unwrap the packets, and send them to the target client. Note that PPTP servers are protocol-independent in terms of the client communication.

Because a PPTP server, by definition, moves data between two or more ports, a network adapter and a device that connects to the Internet are necessary to meet the requirements of question 5. (Remember that a network card can be used to connect to the Internet.)

6. To enhance performance, you add a network card to your company's Windows NT Server computer and connect the card to the same network as the existing card. The cards are configured with TCP/IP and NetBEUI. When you restart the computer, you get a duplicate name error and the server service does not start. Why did the computer encounter this error, and how do you correct the problem? Select the best response.

   C. NetBEUI cannot be running on two network cards connected to the same segment on a multihomed computer. Remove NetBEUI from one of the network adapters.

6. CORRECT ANSWER: C

NetBEUI binds to all network adapters installed on a Windows NT computer. NetBEUI cannot be bound to more than one network adapter per network per Windows NT computer. You must unbind NetBEUI from one of the adapters by using the Bindings tab in Control Panel's Network applet.

7. Which of the following features can enhance network adapter performance? Select all that apply.

   A. Direct Memory Access (DMA)
   C. Bus mastering
   D. Shared-adapter memory

7. CORRECT ANSWERS: A – C - D

A network adapter (or any device) that has DMA can write data to and read data from the computer directly without using the CPU.

Bus mastering also bypasses the CPU and writes and reads data directly. A bus-mastering device takes control of the computer's bus for short periods of time, further freeing the CPU to concentrate on other tasks.

Shared-adapter memory is onboard I/O RAM that the computer sees as part of its memory. This eliminates the need to move the memory to the computer's RAM.

8. You have a multihomed Windows NT computer connected to two TCP/IP networks. You have just installed an HP JetDirect-equipped printer on each network. You install DLC protocol on both cards; however, you cannot connect to the new printer on one of the networks. What is the problem and how to you correct it? Select the best response.

B. The HP print monitor can manage only one network adapter per Windows NT computer. You can use TCP/IP to connect to one of the printers.

The Data-Link Control (DLC) protocol is used to connect JetDirect-enabled devices to a Windows NT computer so that the printers look like they are directly attached to the computer. This usually is done so that a Windows NT server acts as a print server to spool jobs and to provide security for the network-connected printers.

Although DLC can be bound to more than one card on a single Windows NT computer, the HP print monitor (HPMON.DLL) can manage only one network adapter per computer. Under the circumstances of this question, you can allow the clients to connect to one of the JetDirect printers directly or to connect the server to one of the printers using another protocol.

9. Your company's TCP/IP network consists of two physical segments connected by a multihomed Windows NT Server computer with routing enabled. The Windows NT server is the PDC for both segments and also is a WINS server. Everything works properly on the network except clients cannot browse across the segment boundary even though the Windows NT server can see the devices on both segments. How do you correct this problem? Select the best response.

E. Change the Registry so the Windows NT server provides browser information to both segments.

Versions of Windows NT Server 4.0 provide a comprehensive browser list to exactly one network adapter on a multihomed PDC running WINS. Windows NT Server 4.0 has the same characteristic by default, but Windows NT Server 4.0 can be configured to provide browser lists to all connected segments. To enable browsing for both segments, locate the following Registry key:

SYSTEM\CurrentControlSet\Services\Browser\Parameters\

Add a value named UnboundBindings of REG_MULTI_SZ type to the key. Add the name of the driver for each network adapter not providing browser lists to the value.

10. What command is used to determine the IP address, subnet mask, and default gateway of a Windows NT computer?

D. IPCONFIG /ALL

In addition to the basic IP information mentioned in this question, IPCONFIG also is used to show DNS and WINS configuration data and to renew and release DHCP leases. Table 2.5 in the next section, "For Further Review: Configure Network Adapters," describes the command-line switches for IPCONFIG.

CONFIGURE NETWORK ADAPTERS

Because of their UNIX roots, command-line utilities often are used to configure and troubleshoot TCP/IP. Tables 2.5, 2.6, and 2.7 briefly describe three of the most-used IP utilities: IPCONFIG, ROUTE, and NBTSTAT.

The IPCONFIG Utility

Windows NT ships with a number of command-line utilities that are used to troubleshoot and configure TCP/IP. One of the tools used most often is IPCONFIG. Table 2.5 describes the command-line switches used with IPCONFIG.

TABLE 2.5 THE IPCONFIG UTILITY

Switch	Description
/ALL	Displays detailed information about the TCP/IP configuration, including the following: Network adapter description string Physical (MAC) address of the network adapter DHCP-enabled flag IP address Subnet mask Default gateway DHCP Server IP address Primary WINS Server IP address Secondary WINS Server IP address Date DHCP IP address lease obtained Date DHCP IP address lease expires
/RENEW	Renews a DHCP IP address lease
/RELEASE	Releases a DHCP IP address lease

The ROUTE Utility

The ROUTE utility is used to configure Windows NT computers and to troubleshoot. It can be used to add, change, or delete entries in the IP routing table and to view the current entries. The syntax for the ROUTE utility is as follows:

ROUTE [-f¦-p] <command> <destination> [MASK <netmask>] <gateway> METRIC <number>

Table 2.6 describes the command-line switches and parameters.

TABLE 2.6 THE WINDOWS NT ROUTE UTILITY

Switch/Parameter	Description
-f	Clears the routing table. This switch can be used in conjunction with other commands. Must be the first switch.
-p	Sets the command that follows as persistent. Any parameters changed will return after the computer is restarted.
<command>	
print	Prints or displays a route.
add	Adds a route to a routing table.
delete	Removes the specified route from the routing table.
change	Modifies an existing route in the routing table.
<destination>	IP address of the target computer for the command.
MASK <netmask>	Subnet mask to be used for route entry. Default is 255.255.255.255.
<gateway>	Default gateway for route entry.
METRIC <number>	Route entry metric, or cost in number of router hops.

The NBTSTAT Utility

NBTSTAT is used to work with NetBIOS over TCP/IP connections. This utility accesses such information by using the NetBIOS name cache. The syntax for the NBTSTAT utility is as follows:

NBTSTAT [**-a** <remotename>] [**-A** <IP_address>] [**-c**] [**-n**] [**-R**] [**-r**] [**-S**] [**-s**] [<interval>]

Table 2.7 describes the switches and parameters used with NBTSTAT.

TABLE 2.7   THE WINDOWS NT NBTSTAT COMMAND

Switch/Parameter	Description
-a <remotename>	Displays the name cache for <remotename>.
-A <IP address>	Displays the name cache for the host identified by <IP address>.
-c	Displays the name and associated IP address in the cache.
-n	Displays the local NetBIOS names and whether each name has been registered.
-R	Purges the name cache and reloads the LMHOSTS file.
-r	Displays resolution statistics (success rate)
-S	Displays workstation and server session name cache by IP address only.
-s	Displays workstation and server session name cache, attempts to convert IP addresses to names using the LMHOSTS file.
<interval>	Continuous displays of statistics are refreshed every <interval> seconds.

CONFIGURING WINDOWS NT SERVER CORE SERVICES

1. You are the administrator for a small (200-user) routed TCP/IP network. The network comprises several segments with at least one Windows NT server connected to each segment. You are implementing DHCP.

   You want to manage all the IP addresses for the network in a single address pool on a single server. How might you accomplish this? Select all that apply.

   A. It cannot be done. TCP/IP host devices depend on broadcasts to obtain their IP addresses. You must place a DHCP server on each segment of the network.

   B. Install the DHCP service on one Windows NT server. Configure at least one Windows NT server on every other segment as a DHCP relay agent.

   C. Enter the IP address of the DHCP server in the network adapter's TCP/IP configuration for each workstation on the network that uses DHCP.

   D. Configure all the DHCP-enabled computers on the network to point to the DHCP server using an entry in the LMHOSTS file.

   E. Configure the routers on the network to act as DHCP (BOOTP) relay agents.

2. What does the interval setting for directory replication define? Select the best response.

   A. How often import servers check export servers for updates

   B. How often import servers notify export servers of updates

   C. How often an import server checks for updates in the export directory

   D. How often an export server checks for updates in the export directory

   E. How often an export server sends update notices to associated import servers

3. The PDC computer on your network is configured for high availability (UPS, self-correcting memory, RAID ARRAY, dual power supplies, and so on). You also want this computer to serve as the Domain Master Browser for your network. How can you make sure the PDC always is the Domain Master Browser? Select the best response.

   A. You must set the environment variable ISMASTERBROWSER to the value 1.

   B. You must edit the Registry and set the parameter IsDomainMasterBrowser to TRUE.

C. You must define the PDC as a master browser using the Browser applet in the Control Panel.

D. You must define the PDC as a master browser when installing Windows NT Server. Reinstall Windows NT Server using WINNT32.

E. A PDC cannot serve as any kind of browser.

4. **You have just finished installing Windows NT Server and configuring Windows Backup. What must you do to schedule regular, unattended backups? Select the best response.**

A. Start Windows Backup and then set the backup schedule by using the Schedule option in the File menu.

B. Set the backup schedule by using the AT command.

C. Set the backup schedule by using the Windows NT Scheduler service.

D. Create a server script that executes an unattended backup and then schedule execution of the script by using the AT command.

E. Start the Windows NT Scheduler service, create a command file (*.CMD) that executes an unattended backup, and then schedule the execution of the command file using the AT command.

5. **Which of the following is required to implement replication service on a default installation of Windows NT Server? Select all that apply.**

A. You must create a service account.

B. You must start the Replication Service.

C. You must place an entry in the LMHOSTS file for each target import server.

D. You must place a static entry in the WINS database for each target import server.

E. You must specify all export directories using Server Manager.

6. **Your company's routed TCP/IP network has several b-node computers. There is at least one Windows NT Workstation computer on each segment but not necessarily a Windows NT server. The network supports name resolution with DNS and WINS. What might you do to facilitate name resolution for the b-node computers? Select the best response.**

A. Configure the b-node computers to use the DNS service on one or more of the Windows NT workstations on each segment.

B. Configure one Windows NT workstation on each segment to act as a WINS relay agent.

C. Configure all routers to act as WINS relay agents.

D. Configure one Windows NT workstation on each segment to act as a WINS Proxy Agent.

E. Configure one Windows NT computer on each segment to act as a DNS Proxy Agent.

7. **How do you configure the Server Service on a Windows NT computer? Select all that apply.**

    A. Use the Server/Server Services menu item in Server Manager.

    B. Use the NET CONFIG SERVER command.

    C. Edit the Registry.

    D. Use the Services applet in Control Panel.

    E. The Server Service is self-tuning and cannot be configured.

8. **You have installed a Windows NT server on a routed network. All other computers connected to the same segment are Windows 9x computers. How do you configure the new server so it does not act as a browser? Select the best response.**

    A. Uncheck the Potential Browser option in the Services tab of Control Panel's Network applet.

    B. Set the value of the MaintainServerList key in the Registry to No.

    C. Set the value of the environment variable BROWSER to 1.

    D. Uncheck the Browser option in the Properties page for the server.

    E. You cannot disqualify a Windows NT server computer from acting as a browser when it is the only Windows NT server on a network segment.

9. **Which Windows NT service initiates connections to other servers? Select the best response.**

    A. Server

    B. Workstation

    C. Multiple Universal Naming Convention Provider (MUP)

    D. Redirector

    E. Network

10. **What process facilitates the resolution of a TCP/IP address to a name?**

    A. Reverse Address Resolution Protocol (Reverse ARP).

    B. Reverse Windows Internet Naming Service (Reverse WINS).

    C. Reverse Domain Naming System (Reverse DNS).

    D. DNS Reverse Lookup.

    E. You must add the appropriate entries to the LMHOSTS file for the source and target computers.

ANSWER KEY

1. B-E	5. A-B-E	8. A
2. C-D-E	6. D	9. B
3. B	7. A-B-C	10. D
4. E		

ANSWERS & EXPLANATIONS

CONFIGURING WINDOWS NT SERVER CORE SERVICES

1. You are the administrator for a small (200-user) routed TCP/IP network. The network comprises several segments with at least one Windows NT server connected to each segment. You are implementing DHCP.

You want to manage all the IP addresses for the network in a single address pool on a single server. How might you accomplish this? Select all that apply.

B. Install the DHCP service on one Windows NT server. Configure at least one Windows NT server on every other segment as a DHCP relay agent.

E. Configure the routers on the network to act as DHCP (BOOTP) relay agents.

1. CORRECT ANSWERS: B - E

Note that the description of the network does not tell you all the hosts are Windows NT computers. Answers C and D make this assumption. Even if all the hosts on the network are Windows NT computers, however, these answers are incorrect.

The Dynamic Host Configuration Protocol (DHCP) is used primarily to manage allocation of IP addresses for network hosts. Hosts configured as DHCP clients issue a request to DHCP servers for an IP address. The DHCP server is configured to assigned an IP address from a range of IP addresses allocated for that host's network segment. When the DHCP server assigns an IP address, the address belongs to the client only for a predetermined "lease" period. At the end of the lease period, the client must request a new IP address from the DHCP server.

In addition to assigning IP addresses, a DHCP server can be configured to assign a number of other parameters to the DHCP client, such as node type, default gateways, and DNS server addresses.

DHCP is a TCP/IP standard. The DHCP standard includes a definition of a DHCP relay agent. The DHCP relay server accepts DHCP request broadcasts and passes them directly to a DHCP server. Answer E is correct because the vast majority of TCP/IP routers support the BOOTP relay agent function.

2. What does the interval setting for directory replication define? Select the best response.

C. How often an import server checks for updates in the export directory

D. How often an export server checks for updates in the export directory

E. How often an export server sends update notices to associated import servers

2. CORRECT ANSWERS: C – D - E

The interval setting for an export server range is 1 to 60 minutes, with the default being 5 minutes. Adjust this setting depending on the volume of updates, user requirements, and available network bandwidth.

When the interval timer expires, the export server checks the files and folders in the export directory. If any have changed since the last update, the export server notifies associated import servers. The import computer then copies any changed files and folders into its import directory.

The structure of the export directory's contents is maintained on all associated import directories. If a new folder is created in the export directory, it is created on all the import directories at replication time.

3. **The PDC computer on your network is configured for high availability (UPS, self-correcting memory, RAID ARRAY, dual power supplies, and so on). You also want this computer to serve as the Domain Master Browser for your network. How can you ensure the PDC always is the Domain Master Browser? Select the best response.**

   B. **You must edit the Registry and set the parameter IsDomainMasterBrowser to TRUE.**

3. CORRECT ANSWER: B

On a Microsoft network, connected computers select browser roles by holding an election. This election is forced when a Master Browser is disconnected from the network or when a Windows NT server is restarted and it served as a master browser.

The browser election is a weighted election. Different workstation operating systems and configurations have different election biases. A Windows NT Server computer, for example, is elected before a Windows NT Workstation computer.

4. **You have just finished installing Windows NT Server and configuring Windows Backup. What must you do to schedule regular, unattended backups. Select the best response.**

   E. **Start the Windows NT Scheduler service, create a command file (*.CMD) that executes an unattended backup, and then schedule the execution of the command file by using the AT command.**

4. CORRECT ANSWER: E

When you install Windows NT Server, the Schedule service is installed but is not set to start automatically. In addition, the AT command does not run, nor will previously scheduled jobs if the Scheduler service is not started. Therefore, it is essential to set the Scheduler to Automatic by using the Services applet in Control Panel.

▼ **NOTE**

A GUI version of AT.EXE, called WinAt, is available in the Windows NT Server Resource Kit.

5. **Which of the following is required to implement replication service on a default installation of Windows NT Server? Select all that apply.**

  A. You must create a service account.

  B. You must start the replication service.

  E. You must specify all export directories using Server Manager.

The Windows NT replication service requires a service account. A service account is a user account with permission to log on as a service. This account usually is created to support a specific service and is not used for any other purpose.

The WINS database is used to resolve NetBIOS names to IP addresses. When replication is configured, the servers involved already have IP addresses for one another. An entry in the WINS database, whether static or dynamic, has no impact on replication. Likewise, the LMHOSTS file is used to resolve IP domain names to IP addresses and has no bearing on replication.

To create a typical service account, use either User Manager for a local user, or User Manager for Domains for a global user. For a service account used strictly on one computer, a local user is recommended. For a service account used on more than one computer in the domain, create a global user.

In addition to assigning permission to log on as a service, the service account should have a password that never expires. This is because a service account logs on automatically when the service starts (usually when the server is restarted). An expired password not only is an administrative nuisance, it prevents a service from starting at boot time.

The replication service is installed but is not set to automatically start at boot time in a default Windows NT Server installation. You must start the replication service and set the Startup Type attribute to Automatic. Remember that you must create the service account first because the replication service will not start without one.

Although you specify the root import and export directories when configuring the replication service startup (the default is %winroot%\System32\Rpl\<import><export>), you still must specify subdirectories within the import and export directories. Assigning import and export directories can be done using Server Manager.

The WINS database is used to resolve NetBIOS names to IP addresses. When replication is configured, the servers involved already have IP addresses for one another. An entry in the WINS database, whether static or dynamic, has no impact on replication. Likewise, the LMHOSTS file is used to resolve IP domain names to IP addresses and has no bearing on replication.

6. Your company's routed TCP/IP network has several b-node computers. There is at least one Windows NT Workstation computer on each segment but not necessarily a Windows NT server. The network supports name resolution with DNS and WINS. What might you do to facilitate name resolution for the b-node computers? Select the best response.

D. Configure one Windows NT workstation on each segment to act as a WINS Proxy Agent.

6. CORRECT ANSWER: D

A b-node computer uses only broadcasts for name resolution. This means it cannot access DNS or WINS servers across routers. Because there is not a Windows NT server on each segment and the b-node computers are not WINS-enabled, you must devise a way to respond to b-node broadcasts on each network segment.

WINS-enabled Windows NT computers (both servers and workstations) can be configured as WINS Proxy Agents. When a b-node client attempts to resolve a name to an IP address by issuing a broadcast, the WINS Proxy Agent (on the same segment) attempts to resolve the name on behalf of the b-node computer. If the name is not found in the proxy agent's own cache, the agent queries the WINS server. If the WINS server resolves the name and returns a response to the proxy agent, the proxy agent stores the name in its cache and waits for the b-node computer to broadcast another query for that name. If the WINS server cannot resolve the name, the b-node computer receives no response and presumably times out.

▼ NOTE

You should use no more than two WINS Proxy Agent computers on a segment. More than two can result in multiple queries and responses for a single b-node broadcast.

7. How do you configure the Server Service on a Windows NT computer? Select all that apply.

   A. Use the Server/Server Services menu item in Server Manager.

   B. Use the NET CONFIG SERVER command.

   C. Edit the Registry.

7. CORRECT ANSWERS: A - B - C

The Windows NT Server Service is self-tuning. It adjusts its autodisconnect time and memory usage according to connection demands. Other than manually editing the Registry, there is no single utility that can set all Server Service's parameters.

The server service can be configured by using the NET CONFIG command. The following parameters can be set:

AUTODISCONNECT	Time period in minutes that a connection can remain inactive before the server service disconnects the session. The default value is 15.
SERVCOMMENT	A text comment can be assigned to the server. The comment is displayed in the browser, Server Manager, the Server applet, and the NET VIEW command description field. The default value is an empty string (blank).
HIDDEN	Determines whether network browsers can see the server. The default value is OFF (0).

▼ **NOTE**

If you use the NET CONFIG SERVER command to set any of the preceding parameters, the server service's self-tuning capability is disabled.

The Services tab in Control Panel's Network applet is used to set the balance of memory used between throughput for network applications and file sharing. The following performance options are available:

Minimize memory used.

Balance memory used.

Maximize memory for file sharing.

Maximize memory for network applications.

Server Manager and the Server applet in Control Panel can be used to modify the Server Service's comment field.

8. You have installed a Windows NT server on a routed network. All other computers connected to the same segment are Windows 9x computers. How do you configure the new server so it does not act as a browser? Select the best response.

   B. Set the value of the MaintainServerList key in the Registry to No.

8. CORRECT ANSWER: B

If you remember that editing the Registry is the only way to configure the browser service, you probably will get similar questions on the exam right.

Browser service parameter keys are located at `\HKEY_LOCAL_MACHINE\System\CurrentControlSet\Services\` `➥Browser\Parameters`.

9. Which Windows NT service initiates connections to other servers? Select the best response.

   B. Workstation

9. CORRECT ANSWER: B

The Workstation service is the redirector that accepts user-mode input and that passes the data to the Transport Driver Interface (TDI). Note that the Server Service is used to accept connection requests and to make connections to other servers, but it does not initiate connections.

10. What process facilitates the resolution of a TCP/IP address to a name? Select the best response.

    D. DNS reverse lookup

10. CORRECT ANSWER: D

Reverse lookup is defined in RFC 1035. The reverse name database is stored in a special DNS domain. Records in this database are pointer (PTR) records. PTR records are static entries on the DNS server that map to IP domain names for IP addresses. The IP address is resolved by making a query to the DNS server, specifying the IP address and the special domain name in-addr.arpa in the following format:

```
<address>.in-addr.arpa
```

A client computer, for example, needs the name of a computer with the IP address of 192.112.100.43. The client computer will query address as follows:

```
192.112.100.43.in-addr.arpa
```

The client's DNS server will recognize the lookup.com domain and will either resolve the address to a name or pass the query to the appropriate DNS server.

CONFIGURING PERIPHERALS AND DEVICES ON WINDOWS NT SERVER

1. You have just installed a compatible smart UPS on a default installation of a Windows NT computer. What must you do to configure the new device? Select the best response.

   A. Start the UPS service by using the Services applet in Control Panel and then configure it by using the UPS applet in Control Panel.

   B. Start the UPS service by using the Devices applet in Control Panel and then configure it by using Device Manager.

   C. Start the UPS service by using Device Manager and then configure it by using the UPS applet in Control Panel.

   D. Configure the UPS by using the UPS applet in Control Panel and then start the UPS service with the Services applet in Control Panel.

   E. Configure the UPS by using the UPS applet in Control Panel and then start the UPS service with the Devices applet in Control Panel.

2. You are installing Windows NT on several identical computers. You decide to use an unattended installation. The computers are equipped with sound cards.

   How do you install and configure the sound card drivers by using the unattended install? Select the best response.

   A. Configure one of the computers completely and then use SysDiff to create the unattended installation script.

   B. Add a command to the installation script that executes the manufacturer's installation application.

   C. You cannot install a sound card by using unattended install. Run the Multimedia applet from Control Panel after the installation is complete.

   D. Configure the Multimedia applet to execute the first time a user logs on by using the runonce Registry key. Force the Multimedia applet to autoinstall the sound card by using the /u:<driver name> command-line option.

   E. Add the sound card driver to the DRIVERS.INF file used by UNATTENDED.TXT.

3. What likely will happen if you install the wrong video display driver on a Windows NT computer? Select the best response.

   A. You will encounter the Blue Screen of Death.

B. NTLDR will prompt you to use the Last Known Good configuration.

C. Windows NT will load, but you will have no video output.

D. Windows NT will not load. You must reboot the computer to MS-DOS and then manually install the correct driver.

E. Windows NT will load in standard VGA mode, and an error message will be issued.

4. **You must install a modem on your Windows NT Server computer to support RAS connections. The modem is not listed in the most recent Windows NT HCL. What might you do to install this modem? Select three answers.**

A. Attempt to install the modem as Hayes compatible.

B. Add the modem's configuration parameters to the DRIVERS.INF file and then install the modem.

C. Locate and obtain Windows NT drivers or a MODEM.INF file from the modem's manufacturer, if available.

D. Use Windows NT's Detect feature to inspect the modem and then create an INSTALL.INF file for it.

E. Edit the MODEM.INF file shipped with Windows NT by adding a new section for the modem.

5. **You are upgrading a Windows NT Server 3.51 computer to Windows NT Server 4.0. The target computer has the following equipment:**

Pentium 166 processor

128MB RAM

6GB IDE hard disk

CD-ROM

PCI bus

Standard SVGA video display adapter

After completing the installation and executing the final reboot, an error message states that one or more drivers failed to load. When you look at the details in the Event Viewer, you discover the driver that did not load is the IDE disk driver ATDISK. The computer's disk drive is still working. Why did this happen and what should you do about the error? Select the best response.

A. ATDISK is from the Windows NT 3.51 installation and is not compatible with Windows NT 4.0. Install ATDISK from the Windows NT 4.0 CD-ROM.

B. ATDISK is not being used by Windows NT 4.0. Disable the driver by using the Devices applet in Control Panel.

C. The ATAPI driver (for the CD-ROM) is conflicting with ATDISK. Remove both drivers. Reinstall the drivers, installing ATDISK first.

D. There is a conflict with the IDE controller card and the PCI bus. Change the interrupt setting on the IDE controller card.

E. Windows NT autodetect failed to recognize the IDE controller card at install time. Reinstall ATDISK.

6. **You are installing an IDE-type CD-ROM drive on a Windows NT computer, replacing a SCSI CD-ROM. How do you install and configure the drivers for this device? Select the best response.**

A. Use the Devices applet in Control Panel.

B. Use the Services applet in Control Panel.

C. Use the SCSI Devices applet in Control Panel.

D. The manufacturer must provide a setup program.

E. Windows NT will automatically detect and install the new device.

7. **To run Windows Backup on a Windows NT computer, what must you first do? Select the best response.**

A. Install a mass-storage device by using the Devices applet in Control Panel.

B. Install a tape drive by using the Devices applet in Control Panel.

C. Install a mass-storage device by using the Tape Devices applet in Control Panel.

D. Install a tape drive by using the Tape Devices applet in Control Panel.

E. Nothing. Windows Backup will run without a special storage device. It can be configured to back up to a shared or local disk drive.

8. **You are installing a serial device on your Windows NT computer that requires software flow control. What flow control setting should you choose in the Port Configuration dialog box?**

A. XON/XOFF

B. Software

C. IIEE

D. SW/HS

E. DSR

9. **Which of the following examines Windows NT computer hardware (including all hardware-device interfaces) at boot time? Select the best response.**

A. NDETECT.EXE

B. NTLDR.COM

C. NTDETECT.COM

D. NTLDR.EXE

E. HAL.COM

10. **You are installing Windows NT on a computer equipped with a SCSI hard disk drive. What must you do to use the SCSI hard disk drive as the boot drive? Select the best response.**

    A. You must manually add its ARC address to the BOOT.INI file.

    B. You must format the drive as NTFS.

    C. You must format the drive as FAT.

    D. You must disable the BIOS on the host SCSI interface card.

    E. You must enable the BIOS on the host SCSI interface card.

ANSWER KEY

1. D	5. B	8. A
2. C	6. C	9. C
3. E	7. D	10. E
4. A-C-E		

CONFIGURING PERIPHERALS AND DEVICES ON WINDOWS NT SERVER

1. **You have just installed a compatible smart UPS on a default installation of a Windows NT computer. What must you do to configure the new device? Select the best response.**

   D. Configure the UPS by using the UPS applet in Control Panel and then start the UPS service with the Services applet in Control Panel.

1. CORRECT ANSWER: D

You must at least check the Uninterruptible Power Supply Is Installed check box in the UPS applet before the UPS service will start. When the check box is marked and you've clicked OK to close the UPS Configuration dialog box, configuration keys are created in the Registry. The UPS service will not start unless these keys exist in the Registry. An error message is issued when you attempt to start the service.

2. **You are installing Windows NT on several identical computers. You decide to use an unattended installation. The computers are equipped with sound cards. How do you install and configure the sound card drivers using the unattended install? Select the best response.**

   C. You cannot install a sound card by using unattended install. Run the Multimedia applet from Control Panel after the installation is complete.

2. CORRECT ANSWER: C

Two pieces of information can be gleaned from this question. First, sound cards cannot be installed by using an unattended installation. Second, you can configure the unattended install to execute a Control Panel applet at the first logon for the new system. It probably is most useful to use this applet autostart feature under the stated circumstances.

3. **What likely will happen if you install the wrong video display driver on a Windows NT computer? Select the best response.**

   E. Windows NT will load in standard VGA mode, and an error message will be issued.

3. CORRECT ANSWER: E

Windows NT usually can recognize when an incorrect video display driver is installed. It reverts to the standard VGA mode to allow you to correct the problem. If you simply have attempted to update the existing driver, the probable solution is to use the Last Known Good Configuration option presented at boot time.

4. You must install a modem on your Windows NT Server computer to support RAS connections. The modem is not listed in the most recent Windows NT HCL. What might you do to install this modem? Select three answers.

   A. Attempt to install the modem as Hayes compatible.

   C. Locate and obtain Windows NT drivers or a MODEM.INF file form the modem's manufacturer, if available.

   E. Edit the MODEM.INF file shipped with Windows NT by adding a new section for the modem.

4. CORRECT ANSWERS: A – C - E

Because the Hayes AT modem language set is a de facto standard for many brands of modems, you should try using the Hayes driver that best fits the speed and features of your modem.

Modem manufacturers often have a Windows NT driver or MODEM.INF file that was not shipped with the modem. It is a good idea to check.

You can create an entry in the MODEM.INF file for your modem. Create a new section. Using a section for another modem as a template, edit the entries. Reference the modem command language specified in the instructions shipped with the modem.

5. You are upgrading a Windows NT Server 3.51 computer to Windows NT Server 4.0. The target computer has the following equipment:

   Pentium 166 processor

   128MB RAM

   6GB IDE hard disk

   CD-ROM

   PCI bus

   Standard SVGA video display adapter

   After completing the installation and executing the final reboot, an error message states that one or more drivers failed to load. When you look at the details in the Event Viewer, you discover the driver that did not load is the IDE disk driver ATDISK. The computer's disk drive is still working. Why did this happen and what should you do about the error? Select the best response.

   B. ATDISK is not being used by Windows NT 4.0. Disable the driver by using the Devices applet in Control Panel.

5. CORRECT ANSWER: B

In Windows NT 4.0, the ATAPI driver controls IDE disk drives if the computer has a PCI bus. The ATDISK driver no longer is required.

6. You are installing an IDE-type CD-ROM drive on a Windows NT computer, replacing a SCSI CD-ROM. How do you install and configure the drivers for this device? Select the best response.

   C. Use the SCSI Devices applet in Control Panel.

6. CORRECT ANSWER: C

This is not a readily apparent place to install IDE devices and CD-ROM drives with nonstandard drivers; however, the SCSI Devices configuration applet is used for configuring IDE devices. The standard IDE driver, ATAPI.SYS, is listed as a SCSI device when you click the Add button in the Drivers tab of the SCSI Devices applet.

7. To run Windows Backup on a Windows NT computer, what must you first do? Select the best response.

   D. Install a tape drive using the Tape Devices applet in Control Panel.

7. CORRECT ANSWER: D

Windows Backup is designed to work only with tape drives. If you attempt to run the program without a tape drive installed and correctly configured, Windows Backup issues an error message and quits.

8. You are installing a serial device on your Windows NT computer that requires software flow control. What flow control setting should you choose in the Port Configuration dialog box?

   A. XON/XOFF

8. CORRECT ANSWER: A

XON/XOFF is seldom used. Serial ports commonly use hardware flow control. Serial port settings are found in the Ports applet in Control Panel.

9. Which of the following examines Windows NT computer hardware (including all hardware-device interfaces) at boot time? Select the best response.

   C. NTDETECT.COM

9. CORRECT ANSWER: C

Assuming Windows NT is selected at the boot option screen, the Intel boot sequence for Windows NT is as follows:

1. POST. When the computer is powered on, it begins execution in real mode at a predetermined address (0xfffe:0000). This is the start of the Power On Self Test (POST) BIOS routine. POST determines the amount of memory the computer has and checks for required peripheral devices such as the keyboard.

2. Int 19h. When POST completes, it instructs the computer to execute the routine at hardware interrupt 19h. This is the computer reboot interrupt. (This routine is also called for soft reboots.) The reboot routine looks for a boot device. The boot device is determined on the hard disk drive by reading the Master Boot Record (MBR).

3. `BOOTSECT.DOS`. A program contained in the MBR executes. This program searches the boot drive's partition table looking for a partition flagged as "active." When the active partition is located, the boot record (`BOOTSECT.DOS`) for that partition is loaded into memory and is executed.

4. `NTLDR`. The boot record loads `NTLDR`. `NTLDR` switches the computer to unprotected mode, reads `BOOT.INI`, displays operating system options, loads the appropriate operating system, and runs `NTDETECT.COM`.

5. `NTDETECT.COM`. This program inspects the computer hardware for certain devices and then returns the information to `NTLDR`.

6. `NTOSKRNL.EXE`. After `NTDETECT` returns control to `NTLDR`, `NTLDR` executes `NTOSKRNL.EXE`. This program loads the Hardware Abstraction Layer (`HAL.DLL`) and initializes Windows NT.

---

10. You are installing Windows NT on a computer equipped with a SCSI hard disk drive. What must you do to use the SCSI hard disk drive as the boot drive? Select the best response.

   E. You must enable the BIOS on the host SCSI interface card.

10. CORRECT ANSWER: E

When the POST routine completes, or when the computer reboots using interrupt 19h (computer reboot), control is turned over to the BIOS on the host SCSI adapter, which handles the hardware boot process.

▼ **NOTE**

If two SCSI host adapters are installed when you duplex SCSI hard disk drives, you must disable the BIOS on the second card.

CONFIGURING PERIPHERALS AND DEVICES ON WINDOWS NT SERVER

The following devices are detected by NDETECT.COM. The information is returned to NTLDR, which writes the information to the Registry.

- Machine ID/Type
- Bus/Adapter Type
- Video Adapter Type
- Keyboard
- Communication Port
- Parallel Port
- Floppy
- Mouse

CONFIGURING HARD DISKS WITH DISK ADMINISTRATOR

1. **What is a disk signature? Select the best response.**

   A. A 32-bit value that tells Disk Administrator and FDISK the file system in use on a given hard disk drive

   B. A 32-bit value that tells Disk Administrator and FDISK the file system in use on a given disk partition

   C. A 32-bit value that tells Disk Administrator and FDISK the file system in use and a given logical drive

   D. A 32-bit value that marks a physical drive, and is used to identify the drive to Disk Administrator and FDISK

   E. A 32-bit value that marks a physical drive, and is used to identify the drive to Disk Administrator

2. **Upon rebooting a Windows NT computer, you receive an error message that the driver for your SCSI hard drive is corrupted. The system partition for this computer is FAT. How might you replace the bad driver software? Select the best response.**

   A. Because you cannot boot the computer to Windows NT, you must reinstall Windows NT.

   B. Obtain another copy of the driver, boot the computer in MS-DOS, and then copy the driver to `%winroot%\winnt\system32`.

   C. Obtain another copy of the driver, boot the computer in MS-DOS, and then copy the driver to the root directory of the boot partition.

   D. Obtain another copy of the driver, boot the computer in MS-DOS, copy the file to the root directory of the system partition, and then rename the file according to the name specified in `BOOT.INI`.

   E. Obtain another copy of the driver, boot the computer in MS-DOS, copy the file to the root directory of the system partition, and then rename the driver `NTBOOTDD.SYS`.

3. **You are using Disk Administrator to create a mirrored drive set. When you select the shadow partition and then open the Fault Tolerance menu, the Establish Mirror option is not available. (It is grayed out.) Which of the following conditions might be true? Select all that apply.**

   A. You are attempting to mirror two physical (whole) drives, and they do not have the same number of cylinders, heads, and sectors.

B. A partition exists on the shadow drive. You must delete the partition and commit the changes before you can use the drive as a shadow drive.

C. You are attempting to mirror two drives that have nonconsecutive SCSI ID numbers.

D. You are attempting to mirror two drives that are connected to different controller cards.

E. There is less space available on the shadow drive than on the partition you are mirroring on the primary drive.

4. **You are certain there is irreversible corruption on the system partition of your Windows NT Server computer. You want to clean up the system partition and then restore the boot and system files from tape backup. How might you accomplish this task? Select the best response.**

A. Use Disk Administrator's Format command with the Copy System Files and Verify options set. Restore the system files and directories from tape.

B. Use the command-line FORMAT utility with the /S and /V options set. Restore the system files from tape.

C. Use Disk Administrator to delete the system partition. Create a new partition and format. Commit the changes and then restore the system files from tape.

D. Use Windows NT Setup to reformat and verify the partition. If successful, reinstall Windows NT and then restore as required from tape.

E. Use Disk Administrator to create another partition, either on another drive or on the same drive (as long as it is at least the same size as the original partition). Use Disk Administrator to move the system partition to the new location and mark it as the active partition.

5. **You are installing Windows NT on a computer that has a single 9GB hard disk drive. One of your supervisor's requirements for this installation is that all partitions must be FAT format. The other requirement is that the drive must be divided into logical drives C–G. How might you configure this computer? Select the best response.**

A. Create a 2GB system partition at install time. Use Disk Administrator to create the additional partitions and to assign the drive letters.

B. Create a 2GB system partition at install time. Use Disk Administrator to create an extended partition in the remaining free disk space and then create the required additional logical drives in the extended partition.

C. You are limited to two FAT partitions per physical disk. Any additional partitions must be NTFS.

D. You are limited to four partitions per physical disk. At least one of the partitions must be an NTFS extended partition with two logical drives.

E. You are limited to four drive-letter assignments per physical disk. You cannot meet the requirement for logical drives.

6. **Which of the following disk-drive configurations are fault tolerant? Select all that apply.**

   A. RAID 0

   B. Disk duplexing

   C. Disk striping with parity

   D. Disk striping

   E. Disk mirroring

7. **What is the name of the system that manages Windows NT's disk fault tolerance?**

   A. NTFT

   B. NTFS

   C. FTDISK

   D. Hot sparing

   E. FTNT

8. **You are asked to configure a Windows NT Server computer for disk fault tolerance. The computer has four identical disk drives installed. Disk space is at a premium, taking precedence over performance and recovery time. What fault tolerance configuration should you use? Select the best response.**

A. Disk mirroring

B. Disk duplexing

C. Disk striping

D. Disk striping with parity

E. Hot sparing

9. **Which of the following is not a function of Disk Administrator? Select all that apply.**

   A. Create and delete volume sets

   B. Extend system partitions

   C. Create and delete logical volumes in extended partitions

   D. Regenerate lost data for a stripe set with parity

   E. Format extended partitions

10. **You are installing Windows NT Server 4.0 on a computer that has Windows NT Workstation 4.0 installed. You want to maintain both instances of Windows NT on the computer. The disk drives on this computer have a stripe set and several volume sets configured. Once installed, you see that you can access only the system partition with Windows NT Server. What must you do to access the stripe set and volumes set from Windows NT Server? Select the best response.**

   A. Reboot the computer. Windows NT Server recognizes the same disk drive configurations as Windows NT Workstation.

B. Disk Administrator in Windows NT Server will recognize the configuration except for the drive letter assignments. You must reassign the drive letters.

C. You must run the `Read Configuration` command from Disk Administrator in Windows NT Server.

D. Save the disk configuration by using Disk Administrator in Windows NT Workstation. You must use Disk Administrator to find the Windows NT Workstation configuration and then to restore it to the Windows NT Server configuration.

E. Disk configuration information is not compatible between Windows NT Server and Windows NT Workstation.

ANSWER KEY

1. E	5. D	8. D
2. E	6. B-C-E	9. B
3. A-B-E	7. A	10. D
4. D		

ANSWERS & EXPLANATIONS

CONFIGURING HARD DISKS WITH DISK ADMINISTRATOR

1. What is a disk signature? Select the best response.

    E. A 32-bit value that marks a physical drive, and is used to identify the drive to Disk Administrator.

1. CORRECT ANSWER: E

When Disk Administrator is started, it checks installed hard disk drives for a signature. If a signature is not found, you are prompted to enable Disk Administrator to write a signature.

2. Upon rebooting a Windows NT computer, you receive an error message that the driver for your SCSI hard drive is corrupted. The system partition for this computer is FAT. How might you replace the bad driver software? Select the best response.

    E. Obtain another copy of the driver, boot the computer in MS-DOS, copy the file to the root directory of the system partition, and then rename the driver NTBOOTDD.SYS.

2. CORRECT ANSWER: E

When Windows NT is installed on a SCSI disk drive, the SCSI device driver always is named NTBOOTDD.SYS. Remember the difference between the boot partition and the system partitions—their names are contradictory.

3. You are using Disk Administrator to create a mirrored drive set. When you select the shadow partition and then open the Fault Tolerance menu, the Establish Mirror option is not available. (It is grayed out.) Which of the following conditions might be true? Select all that apply.

    A. You are attempting to mirror two physical (whole) drives, and they do not have the same number of cylinders, heads, and sectors.

    B. A partition exists on the shadow drive. You must delete the partition and commit the changes before you can use the drive as a shadow drive.

    E. There is less space available on the shadow drive than on the partition you are mirroring on the primary drive.

3. CORRECT ANSWERS: A – B – E

The three correct answers are the most common reasons Disk Administrator will not let you establish mirroring. Answer D is disk duplexing. Windows NT supports disk duplexing. For the cost of an additional controller card, you can protect the computer against controller-card failure and disk failure.

4. You are certain there is irreversible corruption on the system partition of your Windows NT Server computer. You want to clean up the system partition and then restore the boot and system files from tape backup. How might you accomplish this task? Select the best response.

   D. Use Windows NT Setup to reformat and verify the partition. If successful, reinstall Windows NT and then restore as required from tape.

4. CORRECT ANSWER: D

Disk Administrator will not allow you to delete, format, or move a system partition. The command-line FORMAT utility cannot write system files (the /S parameter).

If the system partition becomes corrupted beyond repair, the only option is to reinstall Windows NT.

5. You are installing Windows NT on a computer that has a single 9GB hard disk drive. One of your supervisor's requirements for this installation is that all partitions must be FAT format. The other requirement is that the drive must be divided into logical drives C–G. How might you configure this computer? Select the best response.

   D. You are limited to four partitions per physical disk. At least one of the partitions must be an NTFS extended partition with two logical drives.

5. CORRECT ANSWER: D

The only way you can achieve five drives (in this case, C through G) on a single physical disk drive is to have one NTFS extended partition. There are only four partition entries available in the partition table on a disk drive. FAT partitions require that the entire partition space be a single logical drive. The stated requirements for this question cannot be met.

6. Which of the following disk-drive configurations are fault tolerant? Select all that apply.

   B. Disk duplexing
   C. Disk striping with parity
   E. Disk mirroring

6. CORRECT ANSWERS: B – C - E

Disk mirroring means a redundant copy of a given partition is maintained on another physical disk drive. Disk duplexing is identical to disk mirroring except the disk drives are connected to different controller cards.

Disk striping spreads data across three or more partitions; disk striping with parity spreads data across three or more physical drives. This includes recovery information that facilitates data being recovered should one of the drives fail.

RAID 0 simply is disk striping. See the section "For Further Review: Configuring Disk Drives" for a description of RAID levels.

7. What is the name of the system that manages Windows NT's disk fault tolerance?

A. NTFT

The fault-tolerance system is NT Fault Tolerance (NTFT), which is managed by a driver named FTDISK.SYS. When fault tolerance is configured by using Disk Manager, FTDISK.SYS is installed and loaded.

FTDISK manages disk I/O to fault-tolerant devices by creating FTDISK objects and attaching them to a fault-tolerant object such as a disk mirror partition. When the file system requests a file operation, FTDISK intercepts the request and passes the I/O request to associated FTDISK objects. If you mirror partition 2 on disk 0 with partition 3 on disk 1, for example, FTDISK attaches an FTDISK object to partition 3 on disk 1. When an I/O request is received for partition 2 on disk 0, FTDISK executes the operation for partition 2 on disk 0 and also sends a copy of the request to the FTDISK object for partition 3 on disk 1. The duplicated request is executed by this FTDISK object.

8. You are asked to configure a Windows NT Server computer for disk fault tolerance. The computer has four identical disk drives installed. Disk space is at a premium, taking precedence over performance and recovery time. What fault tolerance configuration should you use? Select the best response.

D. Disk striping with parity

Disk-shadowing fault tolerance (mirroring and duplexing) is the least efficient configuration. The disk-space loss is 50 percent. Disk striping with parity uses parity data to facilitate data recovery instead of maintaining an exact copy of the data. Disk striping offers no fault tolerance; hot sparing provides bad sector recovery and no disk-failure protection.

9. Which of the following is not a function of Disk Administrator? Select all that apply.

B. Extend system partitions

Disk Administrators cannot extend system partitions because a system partition cannot be extended. When a partition size is selected at install time for the system partition, you are stuck with it unless you want to reinstall Windows NT.

10. You are installing Windows NT Server 4.0 on a computer that has Windows NT Workstation 4.0 installed. You want to maintain both instances of Windows NT on the computer. The disk drives on this computer have a stripe set and several volume sets configured. Once installed, you see that you can access only the system partition with Windows NT Server. What must you do to access the stripe set and volumes set from Windows NT Server? Select the best response.

   D. Save the disk configuration by using Disk Administrator in Windows NT Workstation. You must use Disk Administrator to find the Windows NT Workstation configuration and then restore it to the Windows NT Server configuration.

10. CORRECT ANSWER: D

Usually only the Windows NT installation that created a volume set stripe set without parity, a mirror set, or a stripe set with parity can use that set. Another instance of Windows NT can be configured to use the set. You must use Disk Administrator to save the disk configuration information in one Windows NT instance and to recover it in the other.

Note that any changes to the disk configuration in one instance of Windows NT must be propagated to the other instance.

CONFIGURING HARD DISKS WITH DISK ADMINISTRATOR

Disk Administrator is used to configure many aspects of hard disk drives on a Windows NT computer, including fault-tolerance configuration. For the exam, be prepared to identify the RAID levels and know which are supported by Windows NT. Windows NT supports RAID Levels 0, 1, and 5.

RAID Levels

Few servers of any type are installed today without the benefit of some form of disk drive fault tolerance. Disk drive fault tolerance has come to be known as a Redundant Array of Inexpensive Disks (RAID). Different RAID configurations are known as levels. Table 2.8 describes the six RAID levels.

TABLE 2.8   RAID LEVEL CONFIGURATIONS

RAID Level	Description
RAID 0:	Disk striping. Data is stored across three or more drives. Provides fast data I/O, but no fault tolerance is provided.
RAID 1:	Disk mirroring. Identical data is written to both a drive and a shadow drive. Can be configured by using separate disk drive controllers, known as disk duplexing. Mirroring improves data reads, but writes tend to be slightly slower.
RAID 2:	Disk striping across drives. Also maintains error-correction data. The error-correction scheme for RAID protects against single- and double-bit errors. This requires additional disks for the check bits. RAID 2 is efficient for high-speed writes of data in large blocks and is impractical for small systems.
RAID 3:	Same as level 2 except the error-correction information is stored as parity information on one drive, known as the parity drive. RAID 2 and 3 both use bit striping.
RAID 4:	Disk striping. Data is stored in blocks in a format known as block striping. Parity data is kept on one drive.
RAID 5:	Same as level 4 striping except parity information is spread across the drives, which improves performance.

CONFIGURING PRINTERS ON WINDOWS NT SERVER

1. **Two departments, Accounting and Sales, have identical laser printers in a common area of the office. Both printers are connected to the Windows NT network using an interface card, and both use print spooling on a Windows NT server. The sales printer seldom is used, and the Accounting printer always seems to be congested with print jobs. Many of the print jobs sent to the accounting printer are critical financial and payroll reports.**

Required Results
Provide both departments with access to both printers.

Make sure accounting print jobs are printed as soon as possible.

Optional Results
Maximize all printer throughput.

Facilitate printing to both printers from several UNIX computers in the accounting department.

Proposed Solution
Create a new printer on the Windows NT server, enable print pooling, and then assign the ports for the two laser printers to the new printer. Assign print rights to the users in the accounting department. Set the priority for this printer to 10.

Create another printer on the Windows NT server, enable print pooling, and then assign the ports for the two laser printers to the new printer. Assign print rights to the users in the sales department. Set the priority level for this printer to 1.

Make sure the Microsoft TCP/IP Printing service is installed and is running on the Windows NT server.

Connect all the users in both departments to their respective printers and then delete the original printers on the Windows NT server.

   A. The proposed solution meets both of the required results and both of the optional results.

   B. The proposed solution meets both of the required results and one of the optional results.

   C. The proposed solution meets both of the required results and neither of the optional results.

   D. The proposed solution meets one of the required results and both of the optional results.

   E. The proposed solution meets one of the required results and one of the optional results.

2. **Using the scenario from question 1, how would you configure a UNIX computer to send print jobs to either of the laser printers on a DNS-supported network? Select the best response.**

   A. Configure LPD on the UNIX computer by using the IP name of the Windows NT server as the hostname and using the Windows NT printer name for the accounting department printer as the printer.

B. Configure LPD on the UNIX computer by using the IP name of the Windows NT server as the host name and using the Windows NT printer share name for the accounting department printer as the printer.

C. Configure LPR on the UNIX computer by using the IP name of the Windows NT server as the host name and using the Windows NT printer for the accounting department printer as the printer.

D. Configure LPR on the UNIX computer by using the IP name of the Windows NT server as the host name and using the Windows NT printer share name for the accounting department printer as the printer.

E. Configure LPD on the UNIX computer by using the IP address of the Windows NT server as the host name and using the Windows NT printer share name for the accounting department printer as the printer.

3. **Your Windows NT network is a mix of Windows NT workstations and Windows 95 clients. You install a new print device driver on the Windows NT server that shares a printer to some of these clients. How do you update the print drivers on these clients? Select the best response.**

A. You must use SMS to install the new drivers on all the clients.

B. Updated drivers automatically are installed on all the clients the next time they send a print job.

C. Updated drivers automatically are downloaded to the Windows 95 clients the next time they send a print job. You must install the new drivers on the Windows NT workstations.

D. Updated drivers automatically are downloaded to the Windows NT workstations the next time they send a print job. You must install the new driver on the Windows 95 computers.

E. You must reinstall the new drivers on both Windows NT workstations and Windows 95 clients by deleting the current connection on each workstation and then reconnecting by double-clicking the printer share in Network Neighborhood.

4. **Because of the size and number of print jobs on a particular Windows NT server, you must move the print spool file to a larger disk drive. You set up a print spool file on an NTFS volume. Users report they no longer are able to print. Why? Select the best response.**

A. Print spool files must be on a FAT partition.

B. The printer must be deleted and re-created on the Windows NT server.

C. The users do not have the correct permissions for the new print spool file directory.

D. The client computers must be rebooted so the correct configuration is downloaded from the Windows NT server.

E. You did not create a new print spool file in the new directory. You must create a zero-length file named SPOOL.DAT in the print spool directory.

5. **How can a Windows NT Workstation or a Windows 9x client connect to a printer share on a Windows NT network? Select all that apply.**

   A. Use the Add New Printer wizard, which can be found in the Printers system folder of My Computer.

   B. Use the Add New Printer wizard in the Printers system folder. The Printers system folder can be accessed by using the Start menu.

   C. Use the Print Manager applet in Control Panel.

   D. Use the LPR command-line utility.

   E. Double-click on a print share displayed in Network Neighborhood or drag the Shared Printer icon to your Printers folder.

6. **Your users are experiencing printer errors on overnight print jobs. You suspect the print jobs in question are failing because the host Windows NT server is running out of disk space. How can you confirm this and document it for your boss? Select the best response.**

   A. Enable printer event logging for the host computer. Review all printer events in the Event Viewer's Printer log.

   B. Install the Windows NT Print Monitor service on the host server.

Configure the print monitor service to log all printer events.

   C. Disable print spooling. This forces the client computers to spool locally. If there are no print errors, insufficient disk space is the problem.

   D. Set the print file type to RAW to reduce the size of the print spool. If there are no print errors, insufficient disk space is the problem.

   E. Enable printer event logging for the host computer. Review all printer events in the Event Viewer's System log.

7. **You are installing a "smart" plotter on your network. A smart print device is one that supports bidirectional communication. (That is, the host computer and the device are able to talk to each other.) What software must be installed on a Windows NT host to use the plotter in smart mode? Select the best response.**

   A. A language monitor.

   B. A port monitor.

   C. The print driver for the plotter must support the bidirectional communication.

   D. Windows NT does not support bidirectional communication for print devices.

   E. Windows NT does not support bidirectional communication for network-attached print devices. You must connect the plotter directly to the server's printer port.

8. You want to enable a user to send print jobs and to change printjob status for a particular printer. What permissions should you assign to this user? Select the best response.

   A. Change

   B. Manage Documents

   C. Print

   D. Manage Jobs

   E. Queue Manager

9. What are the two default formats for Windows NT print spool files?

   A. RAW

   B. Winprint

   C. WinntPrint

   D. EPS

   E. EMF

10. You are the administrator for a network that is a mix of Windows NT and Novell servers. The Windows NT servers and clients use TCP/IP; the Novell servers and clients use IPX/SPX. What must you do to enable Novell client computers to print to printers shared by Windows NT servers?

   A. Install TCP/IP on the Novell client(s) and then connect to the Windows NT printer(s) by using the CAPTURE command.

   B. Install TCP/IP on the Novell client(s) and then connect to the Windows NT printer(s) by using the ATTACH command.

   C. Install the NWLink protocol on the Windows NT server that shares the target printer and then connect the Novell client to the printer by using the CAPTURE command.

   D. Install File and Print Services for NetWare on the Windows NT server that shares the target server and then connect the Novell server to the target printer. Connect the Novell client to the target printer through the Novell server.

   E. Install File and Print Services for NetWare on the Windows NT server that shares the target server and then connect the Novell client to the target printer.

ANSWER KEY

1. A	5. A-B-E	8. B
2. C	6. E	9. A-E
3. D	7. A	10. E
4. C		

CONFIGURING PRINTERS ON WINDOWS NT SERVER

1. Proposed Solution

Create a new printer on the Windows NT server, enable print pooling, and then assign the ports for the two laser printers to the new printer. Assign print rights to the users in the accounting department. Set the priority for this printer to 10.

Create another printer on the Windows NT server, enable print pooling, and then assign the ports for the two laser printers to the new printer. Assign print rights to the users in the sales department. Set the priority level for this printer to 1.

Make sure the Microsoft TCP/IP Printing service is installed and is running on the Windows NT server.

Connect all the users in both departments to their respective printers and then delete the original printers on the Windows NT server.

A. The proposed solution meets both of the required results and both of the optional results.

2. Using the scenario from question 1, how would you configure a UNIX computer to send print jobs to either of the laser printers on a DNS-supported network? Select the best response.

C. Configure LPR on the UNIX computer by using the IP name of the Windows NT server as the host name and using the Windows NT printer for the accounting department printer as the printer.

1. CORRECT ANSWER: A

Windows NT printing configuration options are very flexible. You can have multiple printers assigned to a single print device, multiple print devices assigned to a single printer (print pooling), or multiple print devices assigned to multiple printers.

Pooling and prioritizing the print devices in this scenario maximizes throughput.

Printers can be assigned a priority in the Scheduling tab of the printer's Properties page. Higher numbers mean higher priorities.

You do not have to do anything special to support UNIX print jobs other than making sure the Microsoft TCP/IP Printing service is installed and running.

▼ **NOTE**

In the Windows NT world, a *printer* is a logical device, and a *print device* is a physical piece of output hardware. The printer is the configurable object shared by the Windows NT computers; the print device is the hardware to which the printer sends data for output.

2. CORRECT ANSWER: C

LPR is the commonly used remote print utility for UNIX computers. When configuring LPR, you must specify a host name or address and a printer name known to the host. Windows NT Server uses the printer name, not the printer share name, as the TCP/IP printer name.

3. Your Windows NT network is a mix of Windows NT workstations and Windows 95 clients. You install a new print device driver on the Windows NT server that shares a printer to some of these clients. How do you update the print drivers on these clients? Select the best response.

   D. Updated drivers automatically are downloaded to the Windows NT workstations the next time they send a print job. You must install the new driver on the Windows 95 computers.

Windows NT Workstation checks versions. If a newer version is on the server, it is downloaded. Windows 95 clients must have the new drivers installed manually, either using SMS or by another means. Note that this is for driver updates. When a Windows 95 client connects to a new printer type on the network, the driver is downloaded.

4. Because of the size and number of print jobs on a particular Windows NT server, you must move the print spool file to a larger disk drive. You set up a print spool file on an NTFS volume. Users report they are no longer able to print. Why? Select the best response.

   C. The users do not have the correct permissions for the new print spool file directory.

All users that access a printer on a Windows NT server must be able to read, write, and create files. If the print spool directory is on a FAT partition, this is not a problem. If the print spool directory is on an NTFS partition, the users must have Change permissions for the spool directory.

5. How can a Windows NT Workstation or a Windows 9x client connect to a printer share on a Windows NT network? Select all that apply.

   A. Use the Add New Printer wizard, which can be found in the Printers system folder of My Computer.

   B. Use the Add New Printer wizard in the Printers system folder. The Printers system folder can be accessed by using the Start menu.

   E. Double-click on a print share displayed in Network Neighborhood or drag the shared printer icon to your Printers folder.

These answers provide three ways to locate a printer share. Another way to connect to a shared printer is to use the NET USE command. This method is useful for logon scripts when you want to force a printer connection each time a user logs on.

6. Your users are experiencing printer errors on overnight print jobs. You suspect the print jobs in question are failing because the host Windows NT server is running out of disk space. How can you confirm this and document it for your boss? Select the best response.

E. Enable printer event logging for the host computer. Review all printer events in the Event Viewer's System log.

Enabling printer event logging collects information about printer traffic, disk space, and other information and stores it in the System log. Printer event logging is enabled at the server level; all print jobs for all printers spooled on that server are logged.

7. You are installing a "smart" plotter on your network. A smart print device is one that supports bidirectional communication. (That is, the host computer and the device are able to talk to each other.) What software must be installed on a Windows NT host to use the plotter in smart mode? Select the best response.

A. A language monitor.

The Print Job Language (PJL) language monitor ships with Windows NT. The printer must be compliant to Printer Job Language (PJL), or the manufacturer must provide its own language monitor.

A language monitor can report printer status and can add data to the print stream. This enables the print driver to configure and check the status of the printer. It also enables administrators to configure printers over the wire and to monitor printer status.

A port monitor is used to control I/O on physical ports, to which print devices are attached. In most cases, these are serial and parallel ports.

8. You want to enable a user to send print jobs and to change printjob status for a particular printer. What permissions should you assign to this user? Select the best response.

B. Manage Documents

The permissions for printers are described in Table 2.9. Most users are assigned Print permissions, which are the default access rights to printers. You might want to assign other permissions to some users so they can manage documents without changing printer configurations. It also sometimes is desirable to restrict access to a printer, such as when the printer is an expensive resource. Printer permissions are set on a printer's Properties page.

TABLE 2.9 THE FOUR LEVELS OF PERMISSIONS FOR WINDOWS NT PRINTERS

Permission	*Description*
Full Control	User/group has complete access and administrative control.
Manage Documents	User/group can send print jobs to this printer and can change the status of any print job sent by any user. User/group has no control over the printer status.
Print	User/group can submit print jobs and can pause, resume, or delete their own print jobs.
No Access	Denies access to a printer for User/Group.

9. What are the two default formats for Windows NT print spool files?

   A. RAW

   E. EMF

9. CORRECT ANSWERS: A - E

Enhanced metafile (EMF) format is the standard file format spooled on the Windows NT server when the print device is a PCL printer. EMF files can be printed on any print device; they are not hardware-specific. They also tend to be smaller that a print-device specific (RAW) print file because of the way they manage graphic images. Instead of embedded bit-level graphics or graphics-control language in the file, an EMF file contains function calls to the Windows GDI interface. These calls generate the appropriate graphics images at print time.

Most other print devices use the RAW file format. This is a device-dependent print image format.

10. You are the administrator for a network that is a mix of Windows NT and Novell servers. The Windows NT servers and clients use TCP/IP; the Novell servers and clients use IPX/SPX. What must you do to allow Novell client computers to print to printers shared by Windows NT servers?

   E. Install File and Print Services for NetWare on the Windows NT server that shares the target server and then connect the Novell client to the target printer.

10. CORRECT ANSWER: E

File and Print Services for NetWare make shared directories and printers on the Windows NT server look like Novell resources to Novell client.

CONFIGURING PRINTERS ON WINDOWS NT SERVER

Some areas covered by the printer objective of the Microsoft exam are print spooling, printer pools, permissions, and printer driver installation. You should understand print spool configuration as well as the different formats for print jobs. Table 2.10 in the following section describes the available print spool file formats.

Windows NT Spool File Formats

Although EMF and RAW are the most commonly used print spool file formats, other formats also are available. Table 2.10 defines the file formats available in Windows NT.

TABLE 2.10   FILE FORMATS AVAILABLE IN WINDOWS NT

File Format	Description
EMF	Enhance metafile format. This is a compact, portable format. It is not print device-dependent.
RAW	Print image format. RAW files are print device-dependent.
RAW[FF APPEND]	Same as a RAW file except a form feed character is appended to the end of the print job.
RAW[FF AUTO]	Same as a RAW file except the spooler checks for a form feed character at the end of a print job. If the form feed is not present, the spooler appends one.
TEXT	ANSI text format. This format commonly is used for PostScript print devices.
PSCRIPT1	This format is used for Macintosh clients. It enables a Macintosh client to send a PostScript format print job to a non-PostScript print device.

INSTALLING AND CONFIGURING WINDOWS NT SERVER FOR CLIENTS

1. **How should you add a Windows 3.1 client to a TCP/IP-based Windows NT network? Select the best response.**

   A. You cannot connect a Windows 3.1 computer to a TCP/IP network. You must use the NetBEUI protocol.

   B. Windows 3.1 clients must connect to Windows NT Server through Windows NT's NetBIOS interface. Install NetBIOS on the Windows 3.1 client by using the Network applet in Control Panel.

   C. You must use MS-DOS drivers on a Windows 3.1 Workstation. Use Disk Administrator to create a network startup disk and then install the MS-DOS client over the network.

   D. You cannot connect a Windows 3.1 computer to a TCP/IP network. You must upgrade to at least Windows 3.11 (Windows for Workgroups).

   E. You cannot connect a Windows 3.x computer to a TCP/IP network. You must upgrade to at least Windows 95.

2. **You are the administrator of a TCP/IP-based Windows NT network that includes several NetWare 3.x servers. Microsoft client computers can access NetWare resources by using Gateway Services for NetWare, which is installed** on all the Windows NT Server computers. None of the Microsoft network users have a NetWare User ID. How many user IDs are required on each NetWare server to support Microsoft client access? Select the best response.

   A. None. Gateway Services for NetWare manages the NetWare resources through RPC calls. A formal user connection is not required for RPC communications.

   B. One for each Microsoft client concurrently connected to a given NetWare server. Gateway Services for NetWare connects to the NetWare server with system-generated user IDs. Each Microsoft client attempting to access a NetWare resource causes the gateway service to create a new ID on the NetWare server and then connect. When the connection is closed, the user ID is deleted.

   C. One for each Microsoft client and Windows NT server on the network that ever will access any NetWare resources. The Gateway Services for NetWare service must connect to the NetWare server as a supervisor account. Each client that accesses NetWare resources must connect to the NetWare server with a secure connection based on the MAC address of the client computer.

D. One connection. All that is necessary for Gateway Services for NetWare to share NetWare resources with Microsoft clients is a single connection to a single NetWare server. Resources on other NetWare servers are accessed through the connected NetWare server's resource cache.

E. One. Gateway Services for NetWare connects to the Novell server as a user. This single connection is used to share the Novell resources with Microsoft clients connected to the Windows NT server.

3. **Using the scenario from question 2, what software must be installed on the Microsoft client computers? Select the best response.**

A. You must install NWLink on each client workstation. Because the NetWare servers are version 3.x, IPX/SPX is the only native protocol they support.

B. You must install Microsoft Client for NetWare on each client workstation. The Microsoft client software cannot recognize the data format on NetWare resources.

C. You must install both NWLink protocol and Microsoft Client for NetWare on the client computers because Microsoft Client for NetWare requires NWLink.

D. You do not have to install any additional software on a Microsoft client computer to access NetWare resources

through Gateway Services for NetWare.

E. You must install the NetBIOS interface on each Microsoft client computer. Gateway Services for NetWare communicates with the workstation by using the NetBIOS interface.

4. **Which of the following Windows NT Server administration software can be installed and used by a Windows NT Workstation client? Select all that apply.**

A. User Manager for Domains

B. Disk Administrator

C. Remoteboot Manager

D. User Profile Editor

E. Services for Macintosh Manager

5. **Which of the following are required to create a network setup disk for a Windows 95 client using Network Client Administrator? Select all that apply.**

A. An MS-DOS system disk

B. A Windows 95 CD-ROM

C. A Windows 95 system disk

D. A network share for the Windows 95 install directory

E. A local user on the Windows NT server with access to the Windows 95 install directory

6. **You suspect an unauthorized user is trying to log on to your network overnight when the offices are empty.**

What is the most efficient way to confirm this? Select the best response.

A. Use Event Viewer to check the System log for your domain's PDC each morning.

B. Enable logon error-event tracking and review Event Viewer's System log each day.

C. Use Event Viewer to check the Security log for your domain's PDC each day.

D. Enable logon error-event tracking and review the Security log for all domain controllers each day.

E. Use Event Viewer to check the Security log for all domain controllers each morning.

7. **Which of the following components automatically are installed when Services for Macintosh is installed on a Windows NT Server computer? Select all that apply.**

A. File Server for Macintosh

B. Gateway Services for Macintosh

C. AppleTalk

D. Print Server for Macintosh

E. Macintosh Share Service

8. **You are installing Windows NT workstations on your Windows NT network for the customer service department. There is not a one-to-one relationship between computers and users in customer service because all three shifts use the computers.**

Required Results

All the new workstations are configured identically and are "locked" so users cannot change the desktop.

Any customer service user can log on to any of the new computers.

Optional Results

New customer service users logging on for the first time get the standard desktop.

Non-customer service users cannot log on to these workstations.

Proposed Solution

Install and configure one of the Windows NT workstations. Create a mandatory profile and place it on a shared network drive. Set the permissions on the shared network drive so customer service users have read-only access to the drive and all other users have no access permissions. Configure all customer service users to use the mandatory profile.

A. The proposed solution meets both of the required results and both of the optional results.

B. The proposed solution meets both of the required results and one of the optional results.

C. The proposed solution meets one of the required results and both of the optional results.

D. The proposed solution meets one of the required results and one of the optional results.

E. The proposed solution meets neither of the required results but both of the optional results.

9. **Review the scenario in question 8. You find that some users are copying games to the computers and then running them from a command prompt or from the Run option in the Start menu. What should you do to eliminate this problem? Select the best response.**

   A. Disable access to `CMD.EXE` in the mandatory profile.

   B. Remove the Run command from the Start menu in the mandatory profile and remove the command prompt icon from the Programs section of the Start menu.

   C. Delete `CMD.EXE`.

   D. Remove the Run command from the Start menu and set the Run Only Allowed Windows Applications restriction using a system policy file. Configure the system so users have access to required applications but specifically not `CMD.EXE`.

   E. Remove the Run command from the Start menu and delete `CMD.EXE`.

10. **A user on your network keeps changing her roaming profile to a local profile. It is company policy to maintain roaming profiles for all users. What can you do to restrict her from changing the profile? Select the best response.**

    A. Mark the profile in the shared network drive as Read Only.

    B. Delete the System (`SYSDM.CPL`) applet.

    C. Set the Registry key for profile type to Read Only.

    D. Restrict users from changing the profile type using system policies.

    E. Restrict users from changing the profile type in the profile configuration.

ANSWER KEY

1. C	5. A-D	8. B
2. E	6. D	9. D
3. D	7. A-C-D	10. B
4. A-C-D-E		

INSTALLING AND CONFIGURING WINDOWS NT CLIENTS

1. **How should you add a Windows 3.1 client to a TCP/IP-based Windows NT network? Select the best response.**

   C. You must use MS-DOS drivers on a Windows 3.1 workstation. Use Disk Administrator to create a network startup disk and then install the MS-DOS client over the network.

1. CORRECT ANSWER: C

Windows 3.1 has very limited "network awareness" and does not support native network communication. As Windows 3.1 "sits on top" of MS-DOS, network communications are maintained and resources are provided by the underlying MS-DOS operating system.

Windows for Workgroups offers integrated network communications. In addition, many of the network components are 32-bit applications.

Microsoft Client for MS-DOS, Windows for Workgroups, Windows 9x, and Windows NT Workstation all support IPX (NWLink), NetBEUI, and TCP/IP protocols. Windows NT Server does not support NetBIOS. It provides a NetBIOS interface for applications, and NetBIOS communication is tunneled through TCP/IP.

2. **You are the administrator of a TCP/IP-based Windows NT network that includes several NetWare 3.x servers. Microsoft client computers can access NetWare resources using Gateway Services for NetWare, which is installed on all the Windows NT Server computers. None of the Microsoft network users have a NetWare User ID. How many user IDs are required on each NetWare server to support Microsoft client access? Select the best response.**

   E. One. Gateway Services for NetWare connects to the Novell server as a user. This single connection is used to share the Novell resources with Microsoft clients connected to the Windows NT server.

2. CORRECT ANSWER: E

To connect Gateway Services for NetWare to the NetWare server, create a user account on the NetWare server with supervisor permissions. Gateway Services for NetWare logs on to the NetWare server and uses the connection to provide NetWare resource access for the Microsoft clients. As far as the NetWare server is concerned, the single GWSN user is accessing all the resources, which in reality are being used by the Microsoft clients. Because NetWare users can be configured to have more than one concurrent connection to a server, the single user can provide access to all Windows NT servers that require a connection.

3. Using the scenario from question 2, what software must be installed on the Microsoft client computers? Select the best response.

D. You do not have to install any additional software on a Microsoft client computer to access NetWare resources through Gateway Services for NetWare.

3. CORRECT ANSWER: D

A gateway, by definition, is used to facilitate communication between disparate devices. If you have to install the native NetWare protocol or the NetWare client, what is the point of the gateway?

4. Which of the following Windows NT Server administration software can be installed and used by a Windows NT Workstation client? Select all that apply.

A. User Manager for Domains

C. Remoteboot Manager

D. User Profile Editor

E. Services for Macintosh Manager

4. CORRECT ANSWERS: A - C - D - E

Windows NT Server ships with the following client-based administration software for Windows NT Workstation:

DHCP Manager

Remote Access Administrator

Remoteboot Manager

Server Manager

Services for Macintosh Manager

User Manager for Domains

WINS Manager

User Profile Editor

5. Which of the following are required to create a network setup disk for a Windows 95 client using Network Client Administrator? Select all that apply.

A. An MS-DOS system disk

D. A network share for the Windows 95 install directory

5. CORRECT ANSWERS: A - D

In theory, a Windows 95 system disk will work. The Windows 95 files are so large, however, that there is not enough room on the disk for all the network setup files.

6. You suspect an unauthorized user is trying to log on to your network overnight when the offices are empty. What is the most efficient way to confirm this? Select the best response.

D. Enable logon error-event tracking and review the Security log for all domain controllers each day.

6. CORRECT ANSWER: D

When logon error tracking is enabled, one of the errors tracked is failed logon attempts. Logon error tracking is off by default when Windows NT Server is installed. It must be enabled using the Audit feature in User Manager for Domains before failed logon attempts are written to the Security log.

7. Which of the following components automatically are installed when Services for Macintosh is installed on a Windows NT Server computer? Select all that apply.

A. File Server for Macintosh

C. AppleTalk

D. Print Server for Macintosh

---

7. CORRECT ANSWERS: A - C - D

After Services for Macintosh is installed on the server, Macintosh computers on the network require no additional software to access the Windows NT server.

When you install Services for Macintosh, an icon is created in the Windows NT server's Control Panel. This applet gives the administrator the same server administration capabilities as the MacFile menu except for volume management. The MacFile menu is added to Windows NT Explorer.

---

8. Proposed Solution

Install and configure one of the Windows NT workstations. Create a mandatory profile and place it on a shared network drive. Set the permissions on the shared network drive so customer service users have read-only access to the drive and all other users have no access permissions. Configure all customer service users to use the mandatory profile.

B. The proposed solution meets both of the required results and one of the optional results.

---

8. CORRECT ANSWER: B

A mandatory profile is a profile that cannot be changed by the user. Users can modify the desktop during a session, but the changes are not saved.

Because the profile is identical for all the computers in customer service, they all can use the same profile on a shared network drive. The profile, therefore, is accessible to the users from any of the computers (a roaming profile).

A standard installation of Windows NT Workstation, as described in this scenario, does not preclude any user with a valid network or local logon name and password from logging on to one of the customer service computers. You can limit a user's access to up to eight computers (by name) in his user configuration, but this was not explicitly stated in the scenario.

---

9. Review the scenario in question 8. You find that some users are copying games to the computers and then running them from a command prompt or from the Run option in the Start menu. What should you do to eliminate this problem? Select the best response.

D. Remove the Run command from the Start menu and set the Run Only Allowed Windows Applications restriction using a system policy file. Configure the system so users have access to required applications but specifically not CMD.EXE.

---

9. CORRECT ANSWER: D

Although deleting CMD.EXE (the Windows NT command-line shell) might work in some cases, you would have to assume that Windows-based programs are not being used. Therefore, deleting CMD.EXE not only is questionable for technical reasons, it might not solve the problem.

System policies control many aspects of Windows NT and Windows 9x clients. You can remove items from the Start menu (such as the Run command), and you can specify which Windows applications are allowed to execute.

10. A user on your network keeps changing her roaming profile to a local profile. It is company policy to maintain roaming profiles for all users. What can you do to restrict her from changing the profile? Select the best response.

   B. Delete the System (SYSDM.CPL) applet.

User profile settings are stored in the Registry under the following:

HKEY_LOCAL_MACHINE\Software\Microsoft\ WindowsNT\CurrentVersion\ProfileList

Every user that ever logged on to a particular Windows NT 4.0 computer has a subkey in the preceding Registry hive. The subkey is named with the user's security ID (SID). The user profile type is stored in the State key. You can set this key by using system policies, but it does not prevent the user from changing it by using the System applet in Control Panel.

If the drive where SYSTEM.CPL lives is NTFS, you can remove her read permission. If the drive is FAT, you must delete or move the applet.

INSTALLING AND CONFIGURING CLIENTS FOR WINDOWS NT SERVER

You likely will encounter at least one question on the Microsoft exam that tests your knowledge of user profiles and system policies. You should know how to configure local, roaming, and mandatory profiles. You also should know how to implement system policies. You should know the primary areas affected or controlled by each of these administration tools. Table 2.11 defines the key concepts for user profiles and system policies.

TABLE 2.11   UNDERSTANDING POLICIES AND PROFILES

Key Term	Description
Local Profile	A computer-specific profile stored on the local hard drive. A local profile is available to a user only when he logs on to the specific computer.
Mandatory Profile	A mandatory profile is a profile the user cannot modify. Mandatory profiles usually are assigned to a person or group that requires a standard interface. A mandatory profile always is a roaming profile.
Roaming Profile	A roaming profile is stored on a shared network drive and is available to any computer. A user can log on to any computer that can use a particular profile. Windows NT and Windows 9x use differently formatted profile files that are not compatible across platforms.
Roaming User	A user that logs on to different computers on the network and that uses a roaming profile.
System Policy	A System Policy defines resources available to a group or to a single user. It primarily is used to enforce organizational policy and computer configuration. System Policy is implemented through Registry settings.

CHAPTER SUMMARY

The installation and configuration portion of the Microsoft exam is one of the toughest. Much of the knowledge required to pass this section is based on brute memorization rather than logical induction and deduction. Of all the information presented in this chapter, you should memorize the following information cold. It can be a substantial part of your grade.

- Minimum hardware requirements for Windows NT Server 4.0
- WINNT command-line switches
- Installing, promoting, demoting, adding, and removing domain controllers
- Creating network startup disks
- IP subnet masking and subnet classes
- DHCP, WINS, and DNS functionality
- Browser configuration
- Replication configuration
- Configuring fault-tolerant disk drives
- Partitions, volumes, volume sets
- The difference between a system partition and a boot partition
- Printer pooling
- Print queue permissions
- Macintosh requirements
- The difference between per-seat and per-server licensing

CHAPTER 3

Managing Resources

There is a difference between knowing how to administrate a Windows NT server and *knowing* Windows NT Server. The difference is in the depth of your knowledge about Windows NT Server functionality. It is not knowing what function a Windows NT server can perform but knowing *how* it accomplishes that function. An in-depth understanding of Windows NT Server resources is an advantage when taking the exam as well as when working in the real world. Many solutions can be deduced based on an understanding of Windows NT capabilities and internals.

Many of the practice questions in this chapter test your in-depth knowledge of Windows NT resource management, and answers often must be deduced. When a practice question tests your understanding of the mechanics of performing a task, the explanation of the solution usually goes into the details of the process or procedures. This ensures that you know not only the correct answer but why that answer is correct.

Microsoft's stated objectives for the Managing Resources category are as follows:

Manage user and group accounts.

▶ Effective management of resources and security on a Windows NT server demands a thorough understanding of user and group management. To successfully manage user and group accounts, you should understand the following:

- Administering Windows NT users and groups

- Managing Windows NT user rights

- Administering account policies

- Auditing changes to the user account database

Create and manage profiles and policies.

▶ User account policies and profiles are useful management tools both in the network environment and on a local Windows NT computer. To effectively manage profiles, you should understand the following:

continues

- Creating, managing, and removing local user profiles

- Creating, managing, and removing roaming user profiles

- Implementing and managing system policies

- User accounts and policies

Remote administration of Windows NT servers from Windows 95 and Windows NT clients.

▶ Several functional areas of Windows NT Server can be managed from client computers, including the following:

- Windows NT DNS and WINS servers

- Replication services

- License Manager

- Print services

• The Microsoft exam at least touches on these areas to determine your understanding of when and how these tools can be used.

Manage disk resources.

▶ One of the primary purposes of a file server is to provide disk storage for network clients. Managing disk storage on a Windows NT server requires that you understand:

- Copying and moving files

- Creating and sharing disk-drive resources

- Administering disk-drive security

- Auditing disk file activity

MANAGING USER AND GROUP ACCOUNTS

1. **You have just added a new Windows NT server to your network. The server has been correctly configured as a member server and has successfully joined the WWFCorp domain. WWFCorp is the only domain on the network. What is the best way to grant the group Domain Admins administrative rights to the new computer? Select the best response.**

    A. Add Domain Admins to the local group Administrators on the new computer.

    B. Global groups cannot be members of a local group, so add each member of Domain Admins to the local Administrators group on the new computer.

    C. Global groups cannot be members of a local group, so add the local Administrators group to the global Domain Admins group.

    D. The permissions for Domain Admins are assigned automatically; no configuration is required.

    E. Create local users on the new computer with the same user IDs and passwords as the users in the Domain Admins group. Add the new local users to the local Administrators group.

2. **Users in the sales department require read-only access to a shared folder on a Windows NT Server member computer. The computer belongs to the same domain as the users. The member server's data volume is NTFS. How should you structure permission assignment for the sales department users? Select the best response.**

    A. Create a global group and add the sales department users to the new group. Create a local group on the member server and add the global group to the local group. Assign the read-only permissions for the share and the disk directory to the local group.

    B. Create a global group and add the sales department users to the new group. Assign the appropriate permissions for the share and the disk directory to the global group.

    C. Create a local group and add the sales department users to the new group. Assign the appropriate permissions for the share and the disk directory to the local group.

    D. Assign the appropriate permissions for the share and the disk directory to each sales department user.

E. Create a local user and assign the appropriate permissions to the share and the disk directory for the new local user. Inform the sales department users of the user ID and the password for that local user. When sales department users attempt to connect to the shared directory, they are prompted to log on. Users can access the shared folder by logging on as the local user.

3. **Your company's network includes two wide-area connections. To expedite user authentication, you install a BDC at both the remote sites. To facilitate local management, you add a selected user at each site to the local Administrator's group on their respective BDC. What permissions do these users have? Select the best response.**

A. They have Administrator rights on their respective BDCs.

B. They have Administrator rights on any of the domain controllers for the domain.

C. They have Administrator rights on any Windows NT computer that belongs to the domain.

D. They have Administrator rights on their respective BDCs and have Power User rights on all other domain controllers.

E. They have Administrator rights on their respective BDCs and have Power User rights on all other Windows NT computers that belong to the domain.

4. **You want to grant Becky permission to configure, view, and clear the security logs on a Windows NT member server. To which of the following built-in groups can you add her user account to accomplish this?**

A. Server Operators

B. Administrators

C. Power Users

D. Account Operators

E. Domain Operators

5. **You suspect that one of the administrators in your Windows NT network is assigning advanced rights to some global users without authorization. How can you monitor such activity?**

A. Enable security alerts by using Event View and then periodically check the System Log.

B. Disable advanced rights for all members of the Domain Users group by using the Policies settings in User Manager for Domains. Periodically check the system log for attempted changes to any members of Domain Users.

C. Enable security auditing on all Windows NT servers by using Server Manager and then periodically check the Security Log by using Event Viewer.

D. Enable auditing for Security Policy Changes by using the Policies/ Auditing menu in User Manager for

Domains. Periodically check the Security Log by using Event Viewer.

E. Enable auditing for Object Access by using the Policies/Auditing menu in Event Viewer and then periodically check the Security Log by using Event Viewer.

6. **Which of the following user account policy settings are available by default on Windows NT computers? Select all that apply.**

    A. Minimum password length

    B. Require numeric characters

    C. Case sensitivity

    D. Lockout duration

    E. Password history

7. **Which user right is assigned to a service account?**

    A. Interact with the desktop

    B. Log on as a process

    C. Log on as a service

    D. Install and remove device drivers

    E. Log on as a process thread

8. **You are the administrator of a small (75-user), single-domain Windows NT network that has two Windows NT Server computers connected. Both servers are domain controllers. You add a third Windows NT Server computer to the network, configuring it as a member server. The new server is successfully added to the domain.**

One global user account, BAKUP, belongs to the Backup Operators group on the PDC. You log on to the domain from the new member server and attempt to perform a backup of the member server's hard drive, but you get an access-denied error. Why? Select the best response.

    A. The global group Backup Operators can back up and restore files only on domain controllers.

    B. The global group Backup Operators should have been, but was not, automatically added to the local group Backup Operators when the member server joined the domain.

    C. The local group Backup Operators on the domain controllers has permission to back up and restore files only on the local computer.

    D. The local group Backup Operators on the domain controllers has permission to back up and restore files only on the domain controllers.

    E. Only local users can back up and restore files on a Windows NT computer.

9. **Using the scenario from question 8, what might you do to remedy the problem? Select the best response.**

    A. Add the local group Backup Operators to the global group Backup Operators on that server.

    B. Add the global group Backup Operators to the local group Backup Operators on that server.

C. Add the local group Backup Operators on the domain controllers to the local group Backup Operators on the member server.

D. Explicitly assign rights to user BAKUP to back up and restore files on that computer.

E. Create a global group for backup operators, add that group to the Backup Operators group on the member server, and add BAKUP to the global group for backup operators.

10. **What role or local built-in group might you assign a user to if you want that user** to create new global users, but not add those users to the Administrators or Domain Admins group? Select the best response.

A. Power Users on a member server

B. Power Users on a member server or on a domain controller

C. Power Users on any Windows NT computer that belongs to the domain

D. Account Operators on a domain controller

E. Account Operators on any Windows NT Server computer

ANSWER KEY

1. D	5. D	8. D
2. A	6. A-D-E	9. E
3. B	7. C	10. D
4. B		

MANAGING USER AND GROUP ACCOUNTS

1. You have just added a new Windows NT server to your network. The server has been correctly configured as a member server and has successfully joined the WWFCorp domain. WWFCorp is the only domain on the network. What is the best way to grant the group Domain Admins administrative rights to the new computer? Select the best response.

   D. The permissions for Domain Admins are assigned automatically; no configuration is required.

1. CORRECT ANSWER: D

The key to this question is that the computer successfully joined the WWFCorp domain. When a Windows NT computer joins a domain, the Domain Admins and Domain Users groups automatically are added to the local Administrators and Users groups, respectively.

Note also that answer B can be eliminated if you know the differences between local and global groups. Local groups can have global groups as members; global groups cannot have local groups as members.

2. Users in the sales department require read-only access to a shared folder on a Windows NT Server member computer. The computer belongs to the same domain as the users. The member server's data volume is NTFS. How should you structure permission assignment for the sales department users? Select the best response.

   A. Create a global group and add the sales department users to the new group. Create a local group on the member server and add the global group to the local group. Assign the read-only permissions for the share and the disk directory to the local group.

2. CORRECT ANSWER: A

This question is interesting because all the answers work. The objective of the question is to determine whether you know the *best* way to structure permissions according to Microsoft.

According to Microsoft, the recommended chain of assignment is AGLP—Account, Global, Local, Permissions. User accounts belong to global groups, global groups belong to local groups, and local groups are assigned permissions.

From an administrator's perspective, this is a reasonable structure for assigning permissions because users are assigned specific access rights based on the global groups to which they belong.

3. Your company's network includes two wide-area connections. To expedite user authentication, you install a BDC at both the remote sites. To facilitate local management, you add a selected user at each site to the local Administrator's group on their respective BDC. What permissions do these users have? Select the best response.

3. CORRECT ANSWER: B

The local security database is handled differently on domain controllers than on member servers. Domain controllers use the same local security database; therefore, when you add a user or group to a local security database on a domain controller, you have added it to all the domain controllers.

B. They have Administrator rights on any of the domain controllers for the domain.

4. You want to grant Becky permission to configure, view, and clear the security logs on a Windows NT member server. To which of the following built-in groups can you add her user account to accomplish this? Select all that apply.

   B. Administrators

4. CORRECT ANSWER: B

The Administrators group is the only group that, by default, has permission to access, modify, and configure security logs. This right, however, can be explicitly assigned to another group or to a user. The Domain Admins group has this permission by default because it is a member of the local Administrators group on member servers.

5. You suspect that one of the administrators in your Windows NT network is assigning advanced rights to some global users without authorization. How can you monitor such activity?

   D. Enable auditing for Security Policy Changes using the Policies/Auditing menu in User Manager for Domains. Periodically check the Security Log using Event Viewer.

5. CORRECT ANSWER: D

Security auditing can be enabled using the Policies menu in User Manager for Domains. This also is where security rights are assigned to users and groups; more precisely, it is where users and groups are added to security rights lists. All auditing configured on a Windows NT computer is written to event logs and can be accessed using Event Viewer.

6. Which of the following user account policy settings are available by default on Windows NT computers? Select all that apply.

   A. Minimum password length
   D. Lockout duration
   E. Password history

6. CORRECT ANSWERS: A-D-E

Global user account polices are configured with User Manager for Domains. The same account policies can be configured for local users using User Manager.

7. Which user right is assigned to a service account?

   C. Log on as a service

7. CORRECT ANSWER: C

Service accounts often are used on Windows NT servers and workstations. The common definition of a service account is a user account that has the right to log on as a service. Service accounts usually have a password that never expires because they are expected to log on when their associated service starts.

8. You are the administrator of a small (75-user), single-domain Windows NT network that has two Windows NT Server computers connected. Both servers are domain controllers. You add a third Windows NT Server computer to the network, configuring it as a member server. The new server is successfully added to the domain.

One global user account, BAKUP, belongs to the Backup Operators group on the PDC. You log on to the domain from the new member server and attempt to perform a backup of the member server's hard drive, but you get an access-denied error. Why? Select the best response.

   D. The local group Backup Operators on the domain controllers has permission to back up and restore files only on the domain controllers.

8. CORRECT ANSWER: D

The domain controllers for a given domain share the domain account database. This account database includes local groups and users. A local group or a local user created on one domain controller automatically becomes a local group or a local user on all domain controllers. This is not true of member servers, however. The built-in local group Backup Operators on the member server is distinct from the local group of the same name on the domain controllers.

9. Using the scenario from question 8, what might you do to remedy the problem? Select the best response.

   E. Create a global group for backup operators, add that group to the Backup Operators group on the member server, and add BAKUP to the global group for backup operators.

9. CORRECT ANSWER: E

The answer to this question can be deduced by applying the AGLP rule (Account, Global, Local, Permissions). Microsoft says you should use the AGLP chain to assign permissions in a domain environment. The correct way to assign backup and restore permissions to user account(s) is to add the account(s) to a global group belonging to a local group that has backup and restore permissions to the target Windows NT computer.

10. What role or local built-in group might you assign a user to if you want that user to create new global users but not add those users to the Administrators or Domain Admins group? Select the best response.

   D. Account Operators on a domain controller

10. CORRECT ANSWER: D

Rights related to global users must be addressed by using domain controllers. Members of Account Operators can create and manage global user accounts. Members of Power Users on a member server can create and manage only local users.

MANAGING USER AND GROUP ACCOUNTS

When Windows NT is installed, certain users and groups automatically are created. Different groups are created, depending on whether the computer you are installing is a domain controller. Tables 3.1 through 3.4 describe these users and groups.

EXAM TIP

Expect that at least one question on the exam will test your knowledge of built-in groups.

Built-in Windows NT Server Global Groups for Domain Controllers

When a Windows NT computer is installed as a domain controller, certain global groups automatically are created. Table 3.1 describes these groups.

TABLE 3.1   BUILT-IN GLOBAL GROUPS FOR DOMAIN CONTROLLERS

Group	Default Members	Description
Domain Admins	Administrator	Has administrative rights to all domain controllers. Has administrative rights to all Windows NT computers that join the domain. Administrators or any member of the Domain Admins group can modify this group.
Domain Users	Administrator	Is a member of the local Users group on domain controllers and is added to the local Users group when Windows NT member servers and workstations join the domain. This group has ordinary user rights. Administrators and Account Operators can modify this group.
Domain Guests	Guest	Members of this group have limited permissions on the network. This group is a member of the local Guests group on domain controllers and can be modified by Administrators and Account Operators.

Built-in Windows NT Server Local Groups for Domain Controllers

In addition to the built-in global groups described in Table 3.1, Windows NT domain controllers have a set of built-in local groups. Table 3.2 describes these local groups.

TABLE 3.2 **BUILT-IN LOCAL GROUPS FOR DOMAIN CONTROLLERS**

Group	Default Members	Description
Administrators	Administrator, Domain Admins	Members of this group can perform any and all operations on the computer and on all other domain controllers belonging to the same domain.
Server Operators	(none)	Members can log on locally, change the system time, shut down the computer either locally or remotely, back up and restore files, enable and disable server shares, and lock the console.
Account Operators	(none)	Members can log on locally, add computer accounts to the domain, shut down the system, manage user accounts, manage local groups, and manage global groups. Account Operators cannot manage accounts for any members of Domain Admins or Administrators, nor can they manage domain Admins, Administrators, Server Operators, Account Operators, Print Operators, Backup Operators, or any global group that is a member of these groups.
Backup Operators	(none)	Members can log on locally, back up and restore files, and shut down the computer (locally).
Print Operators	(none)	Members can log on locally, shut down the computer (locally), and manage server printer shares.
Users	Administrator	Members can manage local groups and can access the computer from the network.
Everyone	Administrator	Members can access the computer from the network. This group contains any account connected to the network.
Guests	(none)	Guests have no rights on the computer.
Replicator	(none)	Members can log on to the computer and all other domain controllers for this domain as a service.

Built-in Windows NT Local Groups for Workstations and Member Servers

Windows NT Server computers that are installed as member servers and Windows NT Workstation computers have a set of built-in local groups that differ from domain controllers. Table 3.3 describes these local groups.

TABLE 3.3   **BUILT-IN LOCAL GROUPS FOR WINDOWS NT SERVER AND WINDOWS NT WORKSTATION COMPUTERS**

Group	Default Members	Description
Administrators	Administrator, Domain Admins	Members can perform any and all operations on the computer.
Power Users	(none)	Members can log on locally, access the computer from the network, shut down the computer locally or remotely, manage user accounts, manage local groups, lock the console, and manage server shares. Power Users cannot manage Administrators or Backup Operators. Power Users can manage only user accounts and groups they create as well as Power Users, Users, and Guests.
Backup Operators	(none)	Members can log on locally, shut down the computer locally, back up files, and restore files.
Users	Administrator	Users can log on locally, shut down the computer locally, and manage local groups they create.
Everyone	Administrator	Members can log on locally, shut down the computer locally, lock the console, and access the computer from the network.
Guests	(none)	Members have no rights on the computer.
Replicator	(none)	Members can log on to the computer as a service.

It is important to note that these rights are explicit rights and that some groups also have implicit rights. Members of the Users group, for example, can access the computer from the network because Users are, by default, members of Everyone.

Built-in User Accounts on Windows NT Server and Windows NT Workstation Computers

Both Windows NT Server and Windows NT Workstation computers have the same two built-in user accounts. Table 3.4 describes these accounts.

TABLE 3.4   **BUILT-IN USER ACCOUNTS ON WINDOWS NT COMPUTERS**

User Account	Default Group Membership
Administrator	Administrators, Users, Everyone
Guest	Guests

MANAGING USER PROFILES AND SYSTEM POLICIES

1. You have just installed several Windows NT Workstation computers on your network. They are configured for local profiles. When users attempt to log on to the computers, the error message `Cannot access this folder: the path is too long` is issued, the desktop is blank, and the users' only option is to log off. What is the problem? Select the best response.

   A. The file system on the workstation is FAT, which is limited to 64 characters. The default profiles are stored in a path longer than 64 characters.

   B. The file system on the workstation is NTFS, which is limited to 128 characters. The default profiles are stored in a path longer than 128 characters.

   C. The file system on the workstation is FAT. Permissions for the `%systemroot%` directory are incorrect.

   D. The file system on the workstation is NTFS. Permissions for the `%systemroot%` directory are incorrect.

   E. Either A or B.

2. You have created user profiles for all the Windows NT Workstation users on your network. The profiles are roaming, non-mandatory profiles, and are stored on a Windows NT member server. What happens when you take the member server down for maintenance, Windows NT users attempt to log on, and their user profiles are not accessible? Select the best response.

   A. The Windows NT workstation uses the local user profile for Default User.

   B. The Windows NT workstation uses the local user profile for All Users.

   C. The Windows NT workstation issues an error message and prompts for a path to the required profile.

   D. The Windows NT workstation uses a profile cached from the current user's last logon.

   E. The Windows NT workstation creates a new profile by using the profile transaction log, `Ntuser.dat.log`.

3. By using the scenario in question 2, what happens if the user successfully logs on to the network, quits, and then logs on again after the member server containing the user profiles is operational? Select the best response.

   A. The Windows NT workstation issues a warning then prompts the user to load either the local profile or the global profile.

   B. The Windows NT workstation automatically loads the local profile.

   C. The Windows NT workstation automatically loads the roaming profile.

D. The Windows NT workstation creates a new profile by using the remote transaction log, `Ntuser.dat.log`.

E. The Windows NT workstation creates a new profile by using the local transaction log, `Ntuser.dat.log`.

4. **How do you delete a mandatory user profile? Select the best response.**

A. Delete the profile by using the Profiles tab of the System applet in Control Panel on any Windows NT workstation or server in the domain.

B. Delete the profile by using the Profiles tab of the System applet in Control Panel on any Windows NT computer the user has logged on.

C. Delete the profile stored on the remote computer.

D. Delete the profile by using the Profiles tab of the System applet in Control Panel on any Windows NT computer the user has logged on or on a domain controller. Remove the user profile path from the user's account with User Manager for Domains.

E. Delete the profile by using the Profiles tab of the System applet in Control Panel on any Windows NT computer the user has logged on or a domain controller. Delete all local profiles on any Windows NT computer the user has logged on and delete the profile path from the user's account with User Manager for Domains.

5. **Assuming you have a Windows NT Server network with only Windows NT workstations attached, how do you create a default user profile for all users in a domain? Select the best response.**

A. Create and save a profile named Default on the PDC for the domain.

B. Create and save a profile on any workstation and log on to that workstation as a Domain Admin. Using the Profiles tab in Control Panel's System applet, copy the profile to the PDCs `Netlogon` directory in a folder named `Default User`.

C. Create and save a profile on any workstation and log on to that workstation as a Domain Admin. Using the Profiles tab in Control Panel's System applet, copy the profile to the PDC's `Netlogon` directory and rename the profile `Default User`.

D. Create and save a profile on any workstation and log on to that workstation as a Domain Admin. Using the Profiles tab in Control Panel's System applet, copy the profile to the PDCs `Netlogon` directory and rename the profile `Default User`. Assign the profile path to Default User to all user accounts.

E. Create and save a profile on any workstation and log on to that workstation as a Domain Admin. Using the Profiles tab in Control Panel's System applet, copy the profile to the PDCs `Netlogon` directory in a folder named `Default User`. Assign the profile path to all users' accounts.

6. **How is a system policy for a domain created? Select the best response.**

    A. Use RegEdit32 to configure the desired settings in the HKEY_LOCAL_MACHINE key of the Registry. Export HKEY_LOCAL_MACHINE to a file named `System.Reg`. Store `System.Reg` in the `Netlogon` directory of the PDC in a subdirectory named `Default Policy`.

    B. Use RegEdit32 to configure the desired settings in the HKEY_LOCAL_USER key of the Registry. Export HKEY_LOCAL_USER to a file named `System.Reg`. Store `System.Reg` in the `Netlogon` directory of the PDC in a subdirectory named `Default Policy`.

    C. Use System Policy Editor to configure the desired settings. Save the settings to a file named `NTConfig.Pol` and store it in the domain PDCs `Netlogon` directory.

    D. Use System Policy Editor to configure the desired settings. Save the settings to a file named `NTConfig.Pol` and store it in the domain PDCs `Netlogon` directory in a subdirectory named `Default Policy`.

    E. Use System Policy Editor to configure the desired settings. Save the settings to a file named `NTConfig.Pol`. Distribute `NTConfig.Pol` to the `%systemroot%` directory on all Windows NT computers in the domain.

7. **Which keys in the Windows NT Registry does a System Policy file impact when it is loaded? Select all that apply.**

    A. HKEY_LOCAL_USER

    B. HKEY_LOCAL_MACHINE

    C. HKEY_CURRENT_USER

    D. HKEY_CURRENT_MACHINE

    E. HKEY_CURRENT_CONFIG

8. **Your company's Windows NT network employs system policies for two of the four domains. Several Windows NT workstations in the accounting department require special handling in terms of computer and user security for those machines. The accounting department computers belong to a domain that employs system policies. How do you configure the system policies to accommodate the security requirements for the computers and users in the Accounting department without impacting any other computers on the network?**

    A. Create a new domain for the accounting department and assign the modified system policies to the new domain.

    B. Modify a copy of the system policies and place the policies file on the domain controller used by accounting department users for authentication.

    C. Remove the accounting department computers and users from the domain and create a workgroup for the accounting department. Place a copy of the modified system policies on each Windows NT workstation in the accounting department.

D. Create a workgroup for the users in the accounting department and assign them to a modified system policies file by specifying a path to system policies in their user accounts.

E. Create a group for accounting department users. Modify the system policies to implement different settings for the accounting department users and their Windows NT computers.

9. **You have several Windows NT workstation computers on your network with different video cards and monitors that are capable of different resolutions and color palettes. How do you create a roaming profile that will work correctly for all users on all Windows NT workstations? Select the best response.**

A. Use Profile Editor to specify the video display type for each Windows NT workstation in `NTUser.Dat`.

B. Create a profile for each user for each computer. Use a logon script to determine the combination of computer and user logging on and to select the appropriate profile.

C. Change the color palette settings on all Windows NT workstations so they're identical. Windows NT adjusts the video resolution automatically.

D. Change the video resolution so it's identical on all Windows NT workstations. Windows NT adjusts the color palette settings automatically.

E. Roaming profiles are not a viable option in this scenario.

10. **Roaming profiles are not used on your company's network. You are installing a Windows NT computer in the shipping department that will be used exclusively to track outgoing shipments. This computer will be used by an indeterminate number of users, but never for anything other than the single application that tracks outgoing shipments. You want this application to execute at logon time, and you want to remove all unnecessary icons and menu items from the desktop. How do you modify the default user profile to accomplish this task? Select the best response.**

A. Create the desired desktop configuration and copy it to the `Default User` directory by using the Profiles tab in Control Panel's System applet.

B. Create the desired desktop configuration and copy it to the `%systemroot%` directory in a folder named `Default Profile` by using the Profiles tab in Control Panel's System applet.

C. Create the desired desktop configuration and copy it to the `%systemroot%` directory by using the Profiles tab in Control Panel's System applet.

D. Configure the Windows NT computer with a common local user. Log on as that user and configure the desktop as required. Ask all users to log on to this computer with the local user ID.

E. Create the desired desktop configuration and save it on the local hard drive. Configure all users that use the workstation to use the local profile by specifying its path in their user accounts.

ANSWER KEY

1. D	5. B	8. E
2. D	6. C	9. E
3. A	7. B-C	10. A
4. D		

MANAGING USER PROFILES AND SYSTEM POLICIES

1. You have just installed several Windows NT Workstation computers on your network. They are configured for local profiles. When users attempt to log on to the computers, the error message `Cannot access this folder: the path is too long` is issued, the desktop is blank, and the users' only option is to log off. What is the problem? Select the best response.

   D. The file system on the workstation is NTFS. Permissions for the `%systemroot%` directory are incorrect.

1. CORRECT ANSWER: D

If a local user profile (including the default profile, which is used the first time a user logs on) is stored on an NTFS partition, the user must have at least Read permission to the `%systemroot%` directory (usually `C:\WINNT`). There is no security on a FAT partition; therefore, all users have full rights to `%systemroot%`.

2. You have created user profiles for all the Windows NT Workstation users on your network. The profiles are roaming, nonmandatory profiles and are stored on a Windows NT member server. What happens when you take the member server down for maintenance, Windows NT users attempt to log on, and their user profiles are not accessible? Select the best response.

   D. The Windows NT workstation uses a profile cached from the current user's last logon.

2. CORRECT ANSWER: D

When a user logs off from a Windows NT computer, a user profile is saved in the local Profiles folder. If the user is assigned a roaming profile, another copy of the profile is saved on the remote computer. When a user assigned a roaming profile logs on to a Windows NT computer, the computer checks the remote computer for the roaming profile. If it is not found, the local copy of the profile is loaded.

3. Using the scenario in question 2, what happens if the user successfully logs on to the network, quits, and then logs on again after the member server containing the user profiles is operational? Select the best response.

   A. The Windows NT workstation issues a warning and then prompts the user to load either the local profile or the global profile.

3. CORRECT ANSWER: A

When a user with a roaming profile logs off after using the local profile because a roaming profile was not found, a copy of the current setting is saved as a local profile. When the same user subsequently logs on to the same Windows NT computer, the workstation recognizes that the local profile is newer than the remote roaming profile. The computer then prompts the user to select which profile to use. When the user logs off, the profile is saved to both the local and remote locations. The profiles are now back in sync.

4. How do you delete a mandatory user profile? Select the best response.

    D. Delete the profile by using the Profiles tab of the System applet in Control Panel on any Windows NT computer the user has logged on or on a domain controller. Remove the user profile path from the user's account with User Manager for Domains.

Deleting a mandatory profile requires two operations: deleting the profile data from the remote location and removing the profile path from the user's account information. You can manually delete the profile data from the remote server, but using the Profiles tab is much simpler. User Manager for Domains is used to modify user account configurations. Answer E assumes that a local copy of the mandatory profile is stored on local Windows NT computers; this is not the case.

5. Assuming you have a Windows NT Server network with only Windows NT workstations attached, how do you create a default user profile for all users in a domain? Select the best response.

    B. Create and save a profile on any workstation and log on to that workstation as a Domain Admin. Using the Profiles tab in Control Panel's System applet, copy the profile to the PDCs `Netlogon` directory in a folder named `Default User`.

When a profile is stored in a folder named `Default User` in a domain PDCs `Netlogon` directory, Windows NT recognizes it as a default profile for all domain users. Note that this folder and profile must be replicated to domain BDCs as well.

6. How is a system policy for a domain created? Select the best response.

    C. Use System Policy Editor to configure the desired settings. Save the settings to a file named `NTConfig.Pol` and store it in the domain PDCs `Netlogon` directory.

When a user logs on to the network using a Windows NT computer, the computer checks for a file named `NTConfig.Pol` in the `Netlogon` directory. If `NTConfig.Pol` is found, the settings overwrite current settings on the Windows NT computer. Note that `NTConfig.Pol` must be replicated to all domain controllers.

Replication is a Windows NT Server service that facilitates automatic duplication of directory structures and files on two or more Window NT Server computers. Although the `Netlogon` directory is a default replication directory, replication is not automatically activated when Windows NT Server is installed. You must start the Replication service on each participating computer and configure the replication process using Server Manager.

7. Which keys in the Windows NT Registry does a System Policy file impact when it is loaded? Select all that apply.

  B. HKEY_LOCAL_MACHINE

  C. HKEY_CURRENT_USER

7. CORRECT ANSWERS: B-C

Using the System Policy Editor, the Default User and Default Computer settings correspond to the HKEY_CURRENT_USER and HKEY_LOCAL_MACHINE keys, respectively. The system policies file consists of Registry settings that overwrite the local computer settings when the file is loaded.

8. Your company's Windows NT network employs system policies for two of the four domains. Several Windows NT workstations in the accounting department require special handling in terms of computer and user security for those machines. The accounting department computers belong to a domain that employs system policies. How do you configure the system policies to accommodate the security requirements for the computers and users in the accounting department without impacting any other computers on the network?

  E. Create a group for accounting department users. Modify the system policies to implement different settings for the accounting department users and their Windows NT computers.

8. CORRECT ANSWER: E

Although answer A looks like a viable solution, it does not work completely. If an accounting department user logs on to the accounting department's domain by using a Windows NT computer belonging to a different domain that does not use system policies, the user policies for the accounting department user will be enforced on the local computer. When another user subsequently logs on to that computer, the computer will not find a system policy. The previous user policies will be used.

The System Policy Editor enables you to assign policy settings to specific users, groups, and Windows NT computers.

9. You have several Windows NT workstation computers on your network with different video cards and monitors that are capable of different resolutions and color palettes. How do you create a roaming profile that will work correctly for all users on all Windows NT workstations? Select the best response.

  E. Roaming profiles are not a viable option in this scenario.

9. CORRECT ANSWER: E

User profiles do not work correctly when used on Windows NT computers that have dissimilar video adapters or sound cards. In this scenario, it probably is best to use local profiles. The users have a profile on each workstation they use, although the desktop might differ from computer to computer.

10. Roaming profiles are not used on your company's network. You are installing a Windows NT computer in the shipping department that will be used exclusively to track outgoing shipments. This computer will be used by an indeterminate number of users but never for anything other than the single application that tracks outgoing shipments. You want this application to execute at logon time, and you want to remove all unnecessary icons and menu items from the desktop. How do you modify the default user profile to accomplish this task? Select the best response.

   A. Create the desired desktop configuration and copy it to the `Default User` directory by using the Profiles tab in Control Panel's System applet.

10. CORRECT ANSWER: A

Answer A is the simplest solution to a simple challenge. Every installation of Windows NT has a `Default User` folder within the `Profiles` folder. The contents of this folder are used to automatically create a local profile when a new user logs on to the computer. When a new user logs on, Windows NT checks the user account configuration to determine whether the account is assigned a default user profile. If no user profile is specified, Windows NT copies the user profile stored in the local `Default User` folder to the new user's folder.

MANAGING USER PROFILES AND SYSTEM POLICIES

Windows NT user profiles record the state of a user's desktop so it can be recalled when that user logs on again. Table 3.5 describes the information saved in a Windows NT user profile.

TABLE 3.5 INFORMATION IN WINDOWS NT USER PROFILES

User Profile Setting Group	Description
Windows NT Explorer	Contains all the configuration settings for Windows NT Explorer that a given user is permitted to modify.
Taskbar	Contains personal program groups (information stored in a user's personal menu structure) and associated properties, program items and associated properties, and taskbar configuration settings the user is allowed to change.
Printers settings	Maintains persistent network printer connections.
Control Panel	Contains all the settings in Control Panel that users can modify.
Accessories	Contains all user application settings affecting the Windows NT environment including Calculator, Clock, Notepad, Paint, and HyperTerminal.
Windows applications	Many Win32 applications are designed to track application settings for each user. Information for these applications is saved in the user profile.
Online Help bookmarks	Windows NT Help bookmarks are saved in the user profile.

REMOTE ADMINISTRATION OF WINDOWS NT SERVERS FROM WINDOWS NT AND WINDOWS 9x CLIENTS

1. **Your company's network consists of three networks connected by full T1 lines. A single Windows NT Server computer is installed at each site. You use a Windows NT Workstation computer to perform most of your network administration tasks. How do you configure these servers to notify you of any system errors? Select the best response.**

    A. Configure the Alerter service on each server to send any administrative alerts to all servers on the network.

    B. Configure the Messaging service on each server to send any administrative error messages to all servers in the domain.

    C. For each server, enable the Messaging service. Using the Services applet in Control Panel, configure the computer to send alerts to your Windows NT workstation. Configure the Alerter service to send alerts to your user account. Enable messaging on your workstation and on any other network computer you use.

    D. On the primary domain controller, enable the Messaging service. Configure the Alerter service to send alerts to your user account. Enable

messaging on your workstation and on any other network computer you use.

    E. Configure Windows Messaging on each server to send you any and all alerts through email. Configure your email client to notify you of new mail from any of the servers.

2. **For security reasons, you want to disable remote access to the Registry on several Windows NT Server computers, even for users with administrative permissions. How do you accomplish this? Select the best response.**

    A. You cannot restrict administrators from remotely accessing the Registry on a Windows NT computer.

    B. You can disable remote access to the Registry; however, this means print spooling and replication must be disabled.

    C. Disable remote access to the Registry by creating certain Registry keys and assigning them the appropriate values.

    D. Disable remote access to the Registry by using Policy Editor.

    E. Disable remote access to the Registry by using Profile Editor.

3. Which tool is used on a Windows NT computer to monitor user connections and resource-utilization information on other Windows NT computers?

   A. User Manager for Domains

   B. Server Manager

   C. Resource Manager for Domains

   D. NET.EXE

   E. SMS Remote

4. Which of the following remote tools for Windows 9x clients are shipped with Windows NT Server? Select all that apply.

   A. DHCP Manager

   B. Server Manager

   C. User Manager for Domains

   D. Event Viewer

   E. WINS Manager

5. Your company's network has several multihomed Windows NT Server computers that serve as Remote Access Server routers. Which of the following remote tools might you use to manage routing on these computers? Select all that apply.

   A. Server Manager

   B. NET.EXE

   C. RNET.EXE

   D. ROUTMON.EXE

   E. Routing and Remote Access Server Administrator

6. Your Windows NT network consists of a mix of Windows NT, Windows 9x, and UNIX computers. Both WINS and DHCP are implemented on this network. How do you facilitate NetBIOS name resolution for the UNIX computers? Select the best response.

   A. Install WINS Client for UNIX on each of the UNIX computers.

   B. Install WINS Server for UNIX on at least one of the UNIX computers and install WINS Client for UNIX on the remaining UNIX computers.

   C. Change all the hosts on the network to static IP addresses and distribute an updated HOSTS file to all UNIX clients.

   D. Implement dynamic DNS/WINS integration.

   E. The TCP/IP for UNIX computers resolves NetBIOS names as a b-node host; therefore, you must have a WINS server or a WINS relay agent connected to every segment of the network.

7. What is the maximum length of a NetBIOS name?

   A. 32 characters

   B. 64 characters

   C. 255 characters

   D. 15 characters

   E. 16 characters

8. **Three Windows NT servers on your network are running DNS servers, which are configured to perform dynamic WINS lookups. You suspect one of the servers has a much slower response time than the others because of an excessive request load. What might you do to test your theory? Select all that apply.**

   A. Compare input and output statistics for all the DNS servers using DNS Manager.

   B. Configure Event Viewer to audit DNS errors for each computer running DNS server and then review the Application logs.

   C. Calculate the number of requests per second processed by each DNS server. Check the time and the date each DNS server was started using Event Viewer and then divide the number of requests processed by the amount of time each DNS server has been running. The number of requests processed can be found by using DNS Manager.

   D. Monitor processor and memory for the instance "DNS" on each computer running DNS server. You can monitor this information by using Performance Monitor.

   E. Test the response time of each computer running DNS server by using the PING utility.

9. **The single-segment Windows NT network environment you administer uses DHCP for most of its clients,** employing a single DHCP server. The network clients include a substantial number of laptops used by the sales department. The laptop users tend to be out of the office more often than they are in, and they usually are gone for several weeks at a time. How should you configure DHCP to best manage your limited IP addresses and to compensate for the logon patterns of these laptops? Select the best response.

   A. Use DHCP Manager to extend the lease time for clients.

   B. Use DHCP Manager to shorten the lease time for clients.

   C. Use DHCP Manager to automatically adjust the lease time for optimum utilization of IP address leases.

   D. Use DHCP Manager to create a range of IP addresses reserved for the laptop computers.

   E. Configure the laptops with static IP addresses.

10. **How should you install and configure a printer connected to a remote Windows NT server that belongs to a trusting domain? Select the best response.**

    A. Connect to the remote domain PDC by using an interprocess communications share and use Find to locate the target computer name. Open the target computer and launch the Add Printer wizard in remote installation mode.

B. Browse the remote domain and locate the remote computer. Add the printer by using the New/Printer option in the Properties page for the computer.

C. Run the Add Printer wizard on your local computer. Choose the Network Printer option and then browse to the target computer. Add the printer by using the New/Printer option in the Properties page for that printer.

D. Use the Computer/Add Resource menu option in Server Manager to launch the Add Printer wizard in remote installation mode.

E. Install and configure the printer drivers on a local Windows NT computer. Copy the profile to the remote computer by using the Profiles tab of Control Panel's System applet.

ANSWER KEY

1. C	5. D-E	8. C-D
2. C	6. D	9. B
3. B	7. E	10. A
4. B-C-D		

REMOTE ADMINISTRATION OF WINDOWS NT SERVERS FROM WINDOWS NT AND WINDOWS 95 CLIENTS

1. **Your company's network consists of three networks connected by full T1 lines. A single Windows NT Server computer is installed at each site. You use a Windows NT Workstation computer to perform most of your network administration tasks. How do you configure these servers to notify you of any system errors? Select the best response.**

   C. For each server, enable the Messaging service. Using the Services applet in Control Panel, configure the computer to send alerts to your Windows NT workstation. Configure the Alerter service to send alerts to your user account. Enable messaging on your workstation and on any other network computer you use.

1. CORRECT ANSWER: C

The Windows NT Alerter service can be configured to send administrative alerts to user accounts. If you are logged on to the network and the computer you are using has Windows Messaging enabled, you will receive administrative alerts. Windows NT servers also can be configured to send the same administrative alerts to one or more Windows Messaging–enabled computers on the network.

2. **For security reasons, you want to disable remote access to the Registry on several Windows NT Server computers, even for users with administrative permissions. How do you accomplish this? Select the best response.**

   C. Disable remote access to the Registry by creating certain Registry keys and assigning them the appropriate values.

2. CORRECT ANSWER: C

To disable remote access to the Registry for a Windows NT computer, create the string value Registry key HKEY_LOCAL_MACHINE\SYSTEM\CurrentControlSet\Control\SecurePipeServers\winreg, assign it the value Registry Server, and then clear all users' permissions for that key.

To enable remote access to selected keys in the Registry by other computers, create the multistring Registry key HKEY_LOCAL_MACHINE\SYSTEM\CurrentControlSet\Control\SecurePipeServers\winreg\AllowedPaths\Machine. Assign this key a list of Registry keys that can be accessed.

To enable remote access to selected keys in the Registry by users, create the multistring Registry key HKEY_LOCAL_ MACHINE\SYSTEM\CurrentControlSet\Control\SecurePipe Servers\winreg\AllowedPaths\Users. Assign this key a list of Registry keys that can be accessed by user accounts.

3. **Which tool is used on a Windows NT computer to monitor user connections and resource-utilization information on other Windows NT computers?**

   B. Server Manager

3. CORRECT ANSWER: B

In addition to listing the shared resources on a remote Windows NT computer, Server Manager reports the resource name, the number of users connected to the resource, and the resource path. When the resource is selected, any users currently connected to the resource are displayed as well as the elapsed time since each user connected to the resource and the number of files opened by each user.

4. **Which of the following remote tools for Windows 9x clients are shipped with Windows NT Server? Select all that apply.**

   B. Server Manager
   C. User Manager for Domains
   D. Event Viewer

4. CORRECT ANSWERS: B-C-D

Windows NT Server ships with the following remote tools for managing Windows NT servers from a Windows 9x client:

- User Manager for Domains

- Server Manager

- Event Viewer

- Windows Explorer extensions that enable Explorer to manage NTFS permissions, printer permissions, and auditing

- Operating extensions that enable management of drives on Windows NT servers running File and Print Services for NetWare

5. **Your company's network has several multihomed Windows NT Server computers that serve as Remote Access Server routers. Which of the following remote tools might you use to manage routing on these computers? Select all that apply.**

   D. ROUTMON.EXE
   E. Routing and Remote Access Server Administrator

5. CORRECT ANSWERS: D-E

ROUTMON.EXE is a command-line utility used to modify the target Windows NT computers and to retrieve information about the RAS routing configuration. Routing and Remote Access Server Administrator is a GUI application that serves the same general purpose as ROUTMON.EXE, although there are some differences.

6. Your Windows NT network consists of a mix of Windows NT, Windows 9x, and UNIX computers. Both WINS and DHCP are implemented on this network. How do you facilitate NetBIOS name resolution for the UNIX computers? Select the best response.

   D. Implement dynamic DNS/WINS integration.

6. CORRECT ANSWER: D

Beginning with Windows NT Server 4.0, DNS can be configured to interact dynamically with WINS. When a UNIX computer attempts to resolve a name, it queries the DNS server. If the DNS server cannot resolve the name, it queries the WINS server. If the name in question is in the WINS database, the corresponding IP address is returned to the DNS server. The DNS server responds to the UNIX workstation as if the IP address is in the DNS database. Dynamic DNS/WINS integration is a powerful tool because it provides DNS name resolution for hosts with dynamic IP addresses.

7. What is the maximum length of a NetBIOS name?

   E. 16 characters

7. CORRECT ANSWER: E

This is sort of a trick question because Windows NT only allows you to use up to 15 characters for a NetBIOS name. This is because Windows NT uses the last byte of the NetBIOS name to indicate the type of object the name is associated with. If you open WINS Manager, select a server, and view the database, you will notice a hexadecimal representation of the last character of each NetBIOS name, delimited by brackets. Table 3.6 in the following section, "For Further Review: Remote Administration of Windows NT Servers for Windows NT and Windows 9x Clients," defines the different hexadecimal values used by Windows NT.

8. Three Windows NT servers on your network are running DNS servers, which are configured to perform dynamic WINS lookups. You suspect one of the servers has a much slower response time than the others because of an excessive request load. What might you do to test your theory? Select all that apply.

   C. Calculate the number of requests per second processed by each DNS server. Check the time and the date each DNS server was started using Event Viewer and then divide the number of requests processed by the

8. CORRECT ANSWERS: C-D

DNS Manager does track and display DNS server input and output statistics. These statistics are a cumulative record from the time the DNS server was started. Simply comparing the raw values reveals nothing unless all DNS servers being compared were started at the same time. Dividing input and output statistics by time tells you whether one of the DNS servers is working harder than the others.

Performance Monitor can watch and log resources used by the DNS server instance running on each computer. You also might want to look at the computers' physical disk activity and network congestion for their respective segments.

amount of time each DNS server has been running. The number of requests processed can be found using DNS Manager.

D. Monitor processor and memory for the instance "DNS" on each computer running DNS server. You can monitor this information using Performance Monitor.

9. The single-segment Windows NT network environment you administer uses DHCP for most of its clients, employing a single DHCP server. The network clients include a substantial number of laptops used by the sales department. The laptop users tend to be out of the office more often than they are in, and they usually are gone for several weeks at a time. How should you configure DHCP to best manage your limited IP addresses and to compensate for the logon patterns of these laptops? Select the best response.

B. Use DHCP Manager to shorten the lease time for clients.

9. CORRECT ANSWER: B

The last thing you want to do in this situation is tie up scarce IP addresses that might not be fully utilized. This is likely to happen if you extend the IP address lease time or use static IP addresses.

You cannot assign a range of IP addresses to a specific client or clients. Even if you could, you would still be tying up addresses that very likely would be underutilized.

Of these choices, your best option is to trade off some additional network traffic to shorten the IP address lease time.

10. How should you install and configure a printer connected to a remote Windows NT server that belongs to a trusting domain? Select the best response.

A. Connect to the remote domain PDC by using an interprocess communications share and use Find to locate the target computer name. Open the target computer and launch the Add Printer wizard in remote installation mode.

10. CORRECT ANSWER: A

Assuming you have the appropriate rights, you can connect to another domain by using IPC and can remotely install a printer by using the Add Printer wizard, as follows:

1. Connect to the remote domain's PDC by using the following command:

```
NET USE \\computername\IPC$ /USER:accountname
password
```

2. Use Find Computer to locate the remote machine and double-click on its icon in the found list.

   or

   Chose Run from the Start menu and enter the computer name.

In either case, a window for the computer opens. One of the items in the window should be a Printers icon.

3. Double-click on the Printers icon. You will see the Add Printer icon.

4. Double-click on the Add Printer icon to start the Add Printer wizard in remote installation mode.

REMOTE ADMINISTRATION OF WINDOWS NT SERVERS FROM WINDOWS NT AND WINDOWS 95 CLIENTS

Each NetBIOS name on a Microsoft network must be at least 2 and can be as many as 16 characters in length. The last character in the NetBIOS name is appended by the system. This character is a hexadecimal value that identifies the type of object the NetBIOS name represents. A Windows NT NetBIOS name might look like the following

in the WINS administrator database listing:

\\SERVER1[03H]

Many times, several different objects belonging to the same host, such as Workstation service and Server service, register with the WINS server. Table 3.6 describes the object types used and their associated ID number.

TABLE 3.6 DESCRIPTIONS OF NETBIOS NAME IDS

Name[Hexadecimal ID]	Description
computer name[00h]	Workstation Service.
computer name[03h]	Messenger Service.
computer name[06h]	Remote Access Service (RAS). Is registered with the WINS server only when this service is started on a RAS server.
computer name[1Fh]	Network Dynamic Data Exchange (NetDDE).
computer name[20h]	Server Service.
computer name[21h]	RAS Client Service.
computer name[BEh]	Network Monitoring Agent Service. Name is right-padded with + if the name is fewer than 15 characters.
computer name[BFh]	Network Monitoring Utility. Name is right-padded with + if the name is fewer than 15 characters.
username[03h]	Currently logged on users. The name is used by the Server service to process "send to" commands.
domain name[1Bh]	The Primary Domain Controller (PDC) running as the Domain Master Browser. Is used to facilitate remote browsing of domains.
domain name[1D]	Master Browser.
domain name[00h]	(Group Name) Workstation Service. Enables Windows NT computers to receive browser broadcasts from LAN Manager computers.
domain name[1Ch]	Domain controllers within the domain. This name can have as many as 25 IP addresses. One IP address is the PDC; the others are IP addresses of BDCs.
domain name[1Eh]	Used for browsing. The WINS server returns the broadcast address for the segment to which the requesting WINS client belongs.
__MSBROWSE__[01h]	The Master Browser for each subnet. The WINS server returns the broadcast address for the segment to which the requesting WINS client belongs.

MANAGING DISK RESOURCES

Assume you have a typical user on your network who goes by the handle TSMITH. Use the following table of permissions assigned to TSMITH for disk volumes, directories, and files to answer questions 1-6.

Volume Name	Volume Type	Directory Name	Directory Permissions	Filename	File Permissions
System1	FAT	UTILS	N/A	CLEAR.EXE ERASE.COM MOVE.EXE	N/A N/A N/A
Apps1	NTFS	MICRO	Read	LEAD.EXE	Read
				TRAIL.EXE	Read
				MID.EXE	Read
		INTRA	Change	LEAD.MDB	Add & Change
				TRAIL.MDB	Add
				MID.MDB	Change
Data1	NTFS	LOGS	Change	MIPS.LOG	Add
				PIF.LOG	Change
				PERF.LOG	Full Control

1. If you copy CLEAR.EXE to the LOGS directory, what permissions does TSMITH have for CLEAR.EXE?

   A. No Access

   B. R

   C. RWXD

   D. R

   E. RW

2. If you move directory INTRA into the directory MICRO, what permissions are assigned to TSMITH for INTRA?

   A. No Access

   B. Read

   C. Change

   D. Add

   E. Add & Change

3. If you copy MIPS.LOG to MICRO, what permissions does TSMITH have for MIPS.LOG?

   A. No Access

   B. Full Control

   C. Add & Change

D. Read

E. Add

4. **If you move `Trail.mdb` to `MICRO`, what permissions does TSMITH have for `Trail.mdb`?**

   A. No Access

   B. Full Control

   C. Add & Change

   D. Read

   E. Add

5. **If you copy directory `MICRO` into directory `INTRA`, what permissions does TSMITH have for `MICRO` in the new location?**

   A. No Access

   B. Change

   C. Add & Change

   D. Read

   E. Read & Change

6. **If you copy directory `MICRO` into directory `LOGS`, what permissions does TSMITH have for `MICRO` in the new location?**

   A. No Access

   B. Change

   C. Add & Change

   D. Read

   E. Read & Change

7. **User MIKEG belongs to two local groups on a Windows NT server: Sales and Accounting. Sales is assigned Read permissions to the directory `QUOTA`;**

Accounting is assigned Change permissions to the same directory. What effective permissions does MIKEG have for the `QUOTA` directory?

   A. Change

   B. Read

   C. Read & Change

   D. Add & Change

   E. No Access

8. **Global group AcctMgrs is assigned Full Access permissions for directory share Invoices. AcctMgrs also belongs to a local group on the Windows NT server that has Read permissions for the directory shared by Invoices. What effective permissions do members of AcctMgrs have for the Invoices share?**

   A. No Access

   B. Read

   C. Read & Change

   D. Full Access

   E. Add & Read

9. **Global group AdminMgrs has Full Access permissions for file share Personnel. Global group ProdMgrs has Read permissions for file share Personnel. User BENGI is a member of both AdminMgrs and ProdMgrs. What effective permissions does user BENGI have for the Personnel file share?**

   A. No Access

   B. Read

C. Full Access

D. Change

E. Add & Change

10. User TOMF has Full Control permissions for the file COUNTS.MDB stored in directory DATA on an NTFS volume. TOMF is assigned Read permissions for the directory DATA. Which of the following operations can TOMF perform on file COUNTS.MDB? Select all that apply.

   A. Copy COUNTS.MDB to a FAT volume on the same Windows NT computer.

   B. Move COUNTS.MDB to a FAT volume on the same Windows NT computer.

   C. Delete COUNTS.MDB.

   D. Make a copy of COUNTS.MDB named COUNTS.BAK in the same directory (DATA).

   E. Rename COUNTS.MDB to COUNTS2.MDB.

11. User JIMK has RXO permissions for the file PARTS.DAT. Jim needs to change the permissions for this file to Add & Change. What can JIMK do to effect this change? Select the best response.

   A. Because JIMK owns the file, he can change the permissions by using the command-line ATTRIB.EXE utility.

   B. Because JIMK owns the file, he can change the permissions by using Windows NT Explorer or the CACLS.EXE command-line utility.

   C. Take ownership of the file by using Windows NT Explorer and then change the permissions by using the command-line utility ATTRIB.EXE.

   D. Take ownership of the file by using Windows NT Explorer and then change the permissions by using the command-line utility CACLS.EXE.

   E. JIMK cannot change the permissions. He must contact an administrator.

ANSWER KEY

1. C	5. B	9. C
2. C	6. B	10. A-B-C-E
3. D	7. A	11. D
4. E	8. B	

ANSWERS & EXPLANATIONS

MANAGING DISK RESOURCES

1. If you copy CLEAR.EXE to the LOGS directory, what permissions does TSMITH have for CLEAR.EXE?

   C. RWXD

1. CORRECT ANSWER: C

RWXD is the individual permission set that comprises the Change standard permission. When a file is created in a directory, the file inherits the directory's permissions. When a file is copied or moved from a FAT or an NTFS volume, it effectively is being created in the new location. User TSMITH has permission to read, write, execute, and delete the file in question.

2. If you move directory INTRA into the directory MICRO, what permissions are assigned to TSMITH for INTRA?

   C. Change

2. CORRECT ANSWER: C

When files are moved to a different directory on the same NTFS volume, the directory retains its permissions. This is because the directory is not physically moved or created in a new location; its logical location on the volume is changed by NTFS.

3. If you copy MIPS.LOG to MICRO, what permissions does TSMITH have for MIPS.LOG in the new location?

   D. Read

3. CORRECT ANSWER: D

When a file is created on an NTFS volume, it inherits permissions from the directory. Copying a file across volume boundaries means the source file effectively is created in the new location on the NTFS volume. Therefore, it inherits permissions from the target directory.

4. If you move TRAIL.MDB to MICRO, what permissions does TSMITH have for TRAIL.MDB?

   E. Add

4. CORRECT ANSWER: E

When files are moved to a different directory on the same NTFS volume, the files retain their permissions. This is because the file is not physically moved or created in the new location; it is assigned the new logical location by NTFS.

5. If you copy directory MICRO into directory INTRA, what permissions does TSMITH have for MICRO in the new location?

   B. Change

5. CORRECT ANSWER: B

When you create a new directory on an NTFS volume, that directory inherits its permissions from its parent directory. When you execute a directory copy, you effectively are creating a new directory in the new location.

6. If you copy directory MICRO into directory LOGS, what permissions does TSMITH have for MICRO in the new location?

   B. Change

6. CORRECT ANSWER: B

When a directory is created on an NTFS volume, it inherits permissions from its parent directory. When directories are copied, they effectively are being created at the target location.

7. User MIKEG belongs to two local groups on a Windows NT server: Sales and Accounting. Sales is assigned Read permissions to the directory QUOTA; Accounting is assigned Change permissions to the same directory. What effective permissions does MIKEG have for the QUOTA directory?

   A. Change

7. CORRECT ANSWER: A

NTFS file and directory permissions are cumulative. If a user or another object has different permissions for a file or directory from different sources, the effective permissions are the sum of all permissions assigned. Note that No Access overrides all file and directory permissions.

8. Global group AcctMgrs is assigned Full Access permissions for directory share Invoices. AcctMgrs also belongs to a local group on the Windows NT server that has Read permissions for the NTFS directory shared by Invoices. What effective permission do members of AcctMgrs have for the Invoices share?

   B. Read

8. CORRECT ANSWER: B

When combining the permissions of a share and the associated NTFS directory, the most restrictive permissions apply. If a share is created with Read access for a given user, for example, and that user has Full Control permissions for the associated NTFS directory, the user has only Read permissions when connecting to the share over the network.

Shares created for NTFS directories usually are configured with Full Access permissions, and the NTFS directory is configured with the necessary restrictions. This is because NTFS permissions are much more flexible than share permissions, and NTFS permissions apply even when a user logs on to the server locally.

Conversely, shares for FAT directories are configured with the required permissions because there is no security on the associated directory. The share permissions apply only when the user connects to the share over the network.

9. Global group AdminMgrs has Full Access permissions for file share Personnel. Global group ProdMgrs has Read permissions for file share Personnel. User BENGI is a member of both AdminMgrs and ProdMgrs. What effective permissions does user BENGI have for the Personnel file share?

   C. Full Access

9. CORRECT ANSWER: C

When a user has different permissions for a directory share from two different sources, the least restrictive permission is applied.

10. User TOMF has Full Control permissions for the file COUNTS.MDB stored in directory DATA on an NTFS volume. TOMF is assigned Read permissions for the directory DATA. Which of the following operations can TOMF perform on file COUNTS.MDB? Select all that apply.

   A. Copy COUNTS.MDB to a FAT volume on the same Windows NT computer.

   B. Move COUNTS.MDB to a FAT volume on the same Windows NT computer.

   C. Delete COUNTS.MDB.

   E. Rename COUNTS.MDB to COUNTS2.MDB.

10. CORRECT ANSWERS: A-B-C-E

File permissions override directory permissions on an NTFS volume; therefore, the only operation listed that user TOMF cannot perform is copying the file. This is because the copy operation requires write permissions for the directory.

11. User JIMK has RXO permissions for the file PARTS.DAT. Jim needs to change the permissions for this file to Add & Change. What can JIMK do to effect this change? Select the best response.

   D. Take ownership of the file by using Windows NT Explorer and then change the permissions using the command-line utility CACLS.EXE.

11. CORRECT ANSWER: D

The "O" permission means a user has the right to take ownership of a file or directory. Owners have the right to change any of the permissions for the file or directory. Note that you can change permissions by using Windows NT Explorer.

MANAGING DISK RESOURCES

Permissions are a big part of managing Windows NT resources. The primary areas in which permissions are granted are files, directories, shares, and printers. The next four sections describe the details of these permissions, which you should know for the exam.

NTFS Individual Permissions

When setting security on an NTFS volume, a set of standard permissions can be applied to files or directories. These standard permissions are combinations of the individual file and directory permissions. Table 3.7 describes the NTFS individual permissions. You also can use the Special option

when assigning NTFS permissions. The Special option enables you to use any combination of the individual permissions.

NTFS Standard Permissions

Certain named combinations of individual NTFS permissions, called standard permissions, are available when assigning security to an NTFS file or directory. Table 3.8 describes the standard NTFS permissions.

TABLE 3.7   NTFS INDIVIDUAL PERMISSIONS

Permission Flag	File Permission	Directory Permission
R (Read)	Read files	Read file and directory listings
W (Write)	Modify file contents	Create files and directories
X (eXecute)	Run executable files	Change directories
D (Delete)	Delete files	Delete directories
P (Permissions)	Modify file permissions	Modify directory permissions
O (Ownership)	Take ownership of a file	Take ownership of a directory

TABLE 3.8 STANDARD FILE PERMISSIONS

Standard Permission	Individual Permissions for Files	Individual Permissions for Directories
No Access	No permissions	No permissions
List	N/A	R (Read)
Read	R (Read) X (eXecute)	R (Read) X (eXecute)
Add	N/A	W (Write) X (eXecute)
Add & Read	R (Read) W (Write) X (eXecute)	R (Read) X (eXecute)
Change	R (Read) W (Write) X (eXecute) D (Delete)	R (Read) W (Write) X (eXecute) D (Delete)
Full Control	R (Read) W (Write) X (eXecute) D (Delete) P (Permissions) O (Ownership)	R (Read) W (Write) X (eXecute) D (Delete) P (Permissions) O (Ownership)

Directory and File Share Permissions

In addition to the security capability of NTFS, file and directory shares also can be assigned permissions. File and directory share permissions are useful for controlling access to FAT volumes, which have no local security. Table 3.9 describes file and directory share permissions.

TABLE 3.9 FILE AND DIRECTORY SHARE PERMISSIONS

Permission	Description
No Access	Permits the user to connect to the share; however, the associated files and directories cannot be accessed or listed. Note that this permission overrides all other permissions a

Permission	Description
	user might be assigned from other sources such as individual assignment or membership in another group with assigned permissions to the same share.
Read	Allows users to list directories and files, to view the files and their attributes, to run executable files, and to navigate subdirectories.
Change	In addition to Read access, the user can create subdirectories, create files, modify files, modify file attributes, delete files, and delete subdirectories.
Full Access	In addition to all Change permissions, the user can take ownership (assuming the user has as well as allows Take Ownership).

Printer Permissions

Users can be assigned permissions other than the default Print permissions for the special group Everyone, which is assigned when the printer is created. Table 3.10 describes the printer permissions for Windows NT and Windows 9x computers.

TABLE 3.10 PRINTER PERMISSIONS

Printer Permission	Description
No Access	As with the No Access permissions for NTFS objects and file shares, this permission overrides any other permissions assigned to a user from a different source.
Print	The user has permission to send print jobs. All users can pause, resume, and delete their own print jobs.
Manage Documents	The user can pause, resume, delete, and control output settings for print jobs.
Full Access	In addition to permissions assigned for Print and Manage Documents, users with Full Access permissions can pause, resume, and purge the print queue(s) for the printer, can configure and delete the printer, and can assign permissions.

CHAPTER SUMMARY

Managing resources is a skill required for almost any installation, implementation, or maintenance task you might perform on a Windows NT Server computer. As such, the Microsoft exam will certainly test at a detailed level for this objective. To successfully complete the Managing Resources objective, you should know the following:

- The relationship between local groups, global groups, and users. Know the rules of membership for groups.

- The AGLP rule.

- The effect of creating local users and groups on a domain controller.

- Audit configuration.

- Built-in users and groups.

- The difference between roaming, mandatory, and local profiles.

- Implementing system policies for a domain.

- Which remote tools for Windows 9x clients are shipped with Windows NT Server.

- The impact on NTFS permissions when files and directories are moved or copied.

- The relationship between directory permissions and member file permissions in terms of effective permissions.

- The relationship between directory and file permissions and directory share permissions in terms of effective permissions.

- Effective permissions for users belonging to two groups that have different permissions to the same object.

CHAPTER 4

Connectivity

The questions in this chapter address the two major components of NetWare network connectivity in a Windows NT server environment—Gateway Services for NetWare and Migration Tool for NetWare. You will examine the configuration of a Windows NT server for interoperability with NetWare servers, and you will review how to install and configure Remote Access Service to allow connectivity in LAN, WAN, or dial-in situations. You also will review how RAS can be installed on a Windows NT machine to enable a remote client to call in and access that machine and its network. Dial-Up Networking (DUN), incorporated in a Windows NT RAS server, enables the remote Windows NT client to access a RAS server. This is similar to how you utilize Dial-Up Networking on a Windows 95 client to access an Internet service provider.

OBJECTIVES

This chapter helps prepare you for the exam by covering the following objectives:

Configure Windows NT Server for interoperability with NetWare servers by using various tools. The tools include

- **Gateway Services for NetWare**

- **Migration Tool for NetWare**

▶ While configuring Windows NT for interoperability with NetWare servers, we will examine the elements and steps involved in allowing Microsoft clients to seamlessly integrate with NetWare resources. We also will examine the Migration Tool for NetWare as a resource for incorporating NetWare servers into a Windows NT domain.

continues

Install and configure Remote Access Service (RAS). Configuration options include

- **Configuring RAS communications**
- **Configuring RAS protocols**
- **Configuring RAS security**
- **Configuring Dial-Up Networking clients**

▶ Installing and configuring Remote Access Service encompasses the steps toward allowing a client to remotely access an organization's network. By examining the communications, protocols, and security involved, we can gain a better understanding of the steps involved in properly configuring and maintaining remote clients.

CONFIGURING WINDOWS NT SERVER FOR INTEROPERABILITY WITH NETWARE SERVERS

1. **When configuring Gateway Service for NetWare, what steps must be completed on the NetWare server to allow connectivity? Select all that apply.**

    A. Install Gateway Service for NetWare.

    B. Create a group called NTGATEWAY.

    C. Install Client for Microsoft Networks.

    D. Create a standard user.

    E. Place the standard user in the NTGATEWAY group.

2. **What is required for a Windows NT server to access resources on a NetWare server? Select all that apply.**

    A. NWLink IPX/SPX-compatible transport

    B. Client for NetWare Networks

    C. Gateway Service for NetWare

    D. Client Service for NetWare

    E. Client for Microsoft Networks

3. **How many user connections are required on a NetWare server for 35 Windows clients to access NetWare resources through one Windows NT server configured as a gateway?**

    A. 36

    B. 35

    C. 0

    D. 1

    E. 37

4. **What protocol is installed with Gateway Services for NetWare?**

    A. HTTP

    B. FTP

    C. NWLink IPX/SPX-compatible transport

    D. TCP/IP

    E. NetBEUI

5. **How do you install Gateway Service for NetWare? Select the best response.**

    A. Select Start, Run and type `NWCONV.exe`.

    B. Select the GSNW icon in Control Panel.

    C. Install Gateway Service for NetWare from the Services tab in the Network control panel.

    D. Select the CSNW icon in Control Panel.

    E. Install Gateway Service for NetWare from the Protocols tab in the Network control panel.

6. **What program is used to facilitate the NetWare to Windows NT migration?**

    A. NWRDR.SYS

    B. NWCONV.EXE

    C. NWCONFIG.DLL

    D. NWSCRIPT.EXE

    E. NW16.EXE

7. **When migrating NetWare users to a Windows NT domain, what options are available for configuring passwords? Select all that apply.**

    A. All migrated users can have the same password.

    B. All migrated users can have blank passwords.

    C. All passwords can be retained.

    D. All passwords can be assigned from a mapping file.

    E. All passwords can be the same as the username.

8. **What options can be migrated from a NetWare server to a Windows NT domain? Select all that apply.**

    A. Users

    B. Groups

    C. Printers and print queues

    D. Files

    E. NDS partitions to NTFS partitions

9. **Which of the following statements is true when migrating files from a NetWare**

server to a Windows NT domain? Select the best response.

    A. All files and directories inherit the rights of the NTFS parent directory or drive.

    B. All files and directories have the default NTFS permission Everyone-Full Control.

    C. By default, no NetWare volumes are transferred.

    D. The Create "C" and File Scan "F" rights are ignored when directories are transferred.

    E. To retain NetWare file system security, files must be migrated to an NTFS partition.

10. **What steps are necessary prior to performing a NetWare server migration? Select all that apply.**

    A. Obtain Supervisor and Administrative security equivalence on both the NetWare and Windows NT servers.

    B. Create Windows NT printers to match the NetWare print queues.

    C. Perform several trial migrations.

    D. Prepare the Mapping file for enhanced file security.

    E. Create available free space on the NTFS partition for the file transfers.

11. **Your company is closing its office on the West Coast. It is your responsibility to add the NetWare 3.x servers to the CORP domain on the East Coast. Currently, the**

CORP domain consists of two Windows NT servers that share both files and printers. There are 50 Windows 95 client machines on the CORP domain. All the Windows 95 clients must have access to files and printers on the Windows NT server and the NetWare 3.x servers. What steps must be taken to accomplish this? Select the best response.

A. Install and configure Client Services for NetWare on all the Windows 95 client machines.

B. Install and configure Gateway Services for NetWare on all the 3.x servers.

C. Install and configure Client Services for NetWare on all the 3.x servers.

D. Install and configure Gateway Services for NetWare on all the Windows NT servers.

ANSWER KEY

1. B-D-E	5. C	9. E
2. C	6. B	10. A-C-E
3. D	7. A-B-D-E	11. D
4. C	8. A-B-D	

ANSWERS & EXPLANATIONS

CONFIGURING WINDOWS NT SERVER FOR INTEROPERABILITY WITH NETWARE SERVERS

1. When configuring Gateway Service for NetWare, what steps must be completed on the NetWare server to allow connectivity? Select all that apply.

   B. Create a group called NTGATEWAY.

   D. Create a standard user.

   E. Place the standard user in the NTGATEWAY group.

1. CORRECT ANSWERS: B-D-E

When configuring Gateway Services for NetWare on a Windows NT server, three steps must be completed prior to its use. On the NetWare server, you must create a standard user, create a group named NTGATEWAY, and make the newly created user a member of that group. The standard user you create on the NetWare server also must exist in the Windows NT domain. Answer C, Install Client for Microsoft Networks, is available only on Windows 95 and Windows 98 clients. For more information, see Gateway Service for NetWare.

2. What is required for a Windows NT server to access resources on a NetWare server? Select all that apply.

   A. NWLink IPX/SPX-compatible transport

   C. Gateway Service for NetWare

2. CORRECT ANSWERS: A-C

Gateway Service for NetWare is the main configuration option necessary to access resources on a NetWare server. During the installation of Gateway Service for NetWare, two additional components automatically are installed along with the service. The first component is Client Service for NetWare, the same service found in Windows NT Workstation. The second component is NWLink IPX/SPX-compatible transport. Unless previously installed, the NWLink protocol is added for network communication with the NetWare default protocol. Both Client for NetWare Networks and Client for Microsoft Networks are available only on Windows 95 and Windows 98 clients.

3. How many user connections are required on a NetWare server for 35 Windows clients to access NetWare resources through one Windows NT server configured as a gateway?

   D. 1

3. CORRECT ANSWER: D

Gateway Service for NetWare utilizes only one NetWare connection. This can be both good and bad. It can be good because the number of NetWare user licenses does not need to be increased. It can be bad because of the potential bottleneck. The more simultaneous users connect from the Windows NT side, the bigger the bottleneck.

4. What protocol is installed along with Gateway Services for NetWare?

   C. NWLink IPX/SPX-compatible transport

4. CORRECT ANSWER: C

Unless previously installed, the NWLink protocol is added for network communication with the NetWare default protocol. Both HTTP and FTP are added components of TCP/IP, which is installed independently of Gateway Service for NetWare. NetBEUI is the default protocol for Windows for Workgroups and Microsoft LanManager.

5. How do you install Gateway Services for NetWare? Select the best response.

   C. Install Gateway Service for NetWare from the Services tab in the Network control panel.

5. CORRECT ANSWER: C

The installation of Gateway Service for NetWare can be accomplished through the Services tab in the Network dialog box. Typing `NWCONV.exe` executes the Migration Tool for NetWare. The GSNW icon doesn't appear in the control panel until after the service is installed. The CSNW icon is available only with Windows NT Workstation.

Gateway Service for NetWare

The explanation in this section supports questions 1–5.

Gateway Services for NetWare (GSNW) is available only with Windows NT Server. GSNW performs the following functions:

- It enables Windows NT Server systems to access NetWare file and print resources directly.

- It enables a Windows NT Server to act as a gateway to NetWare resources. Non-NetWare clients on a Windows NT network then can access NetWare resources through the gateway as if they were accessing Windows NT resources. There is no need for NetWare client licensing.

GSNW is a practical solution for occasional NetWare access, but it is not designed to serve as a high-volume solution for a busy network. Because all Windows NT clients must reach the NetWare server through a single connection, there is great potential for a bottleneck. In addition, performance diminishes considerably with increased traffic.

Network clients with operating systems that use Server Message Block (SMB)—Windows NT, Windows 95, and Windows for Workgroups—can access a share through a GSNW gateway. GSNW supports both NDS-based and bindery-based NetWare systems.

▼ **NOTE**

NetWare Directory Service (NDS) is a distributed database of network resources primarily associated with NetWare 4.x systems. Bindery-based NetWare networks primarily are associated with NetWare 3.x.

To install GSNW, you must be logged on the Windows NT server as an Administrator. Before installing GSNW, you must remove any NetWare redirectors presently on your system (such as Novell NetWare Services for Windows NT), and you must reboot the Server. GSNW is a network service; it is installed using the Services tab of Control Panel's Network applet. You can install GSNW using the following steps:

1. Choose Start, Settings, Control Panel. Double-click on the Control Panel's Network icon.

2. In the Network dialog box, select the Services tab. Click on the Add button to open the Select Network Services dialog box.

3. Select Gateway (and Client) Services for NetWare in the Network Service list. Click on OK.

4. Windows NT prompts you for the location of the files (typically, the installation CD-ROM).

5. Windows NT asks whether you want to restart your system. You must restart the system to enable the new service.

To configure GSNW to act as a gateway to NetWare resources, you must have supervisor equivalence on the NetWare server and perform the following steps:

1. Using NetWare's Syscon utility, create a group called NTGATEWAY on the NetWare server.

2. Using NetWare's Syscon utility, create a user account on the NetWare server for the gateway. Add the gateway user account to the NTGATEWAY group.

3. Double-click on the GSNW icon in the Control Panel. The Gateway Service for NetWare dialog box opens. The Preferred Server, Default Tree and Context, Print Options, and Login Script Options frames are discussed in the following section.

4. To configure Windows NT to act as a gateway, click on the Gateway button. The Configure Gateway dialog box opens.

5. Select the Enable Gateway check box. In the Gateway Account text box, enter the name of the account you created on the NetWare server. Below the account name, enter the password for the account and retype the password in the Confirm Password text box.

GSNW essentially enables you to create a Windows NT share for a resource on a NetWare server. Microsoft network machines that use Server Message Block (SMB), such as Windows NT, Windows 95, and Windows for Workgroups, then can access the share even if they don't have NetWare client software. NetWare directories and volumes presently shared through a gateway appear in the Share Name list at the bottom of the Configure Gateway dialog box.

To create a new share for a NetWare directory or volume, click on the Add button in the Configure Gateway dialog box. You are asked to enter a share name and a network path to the NetWare resource. You then can enter a drive letter for the share. The share appears to Windows NT, Windows 95, and Windows for Workgroups machines as a network drive on the gateway machine.

The Remove button in the Configure Gateway dialog box removes a gateway share. The Permissions button enables you to set permissions for the share.

Client Services for NetWare (CSNW) enables a Windows NT workstation to access file and print services on a NetWare server. CSNW is incorporated into Windows NT Server's GSNW. GSNW and CSNW both support NDS-based and bindery-based NetWare servers. GSNW and CSNW also support Novell's NetWare Core Protocol (NCP) and Large Internet Protocol (LIP).

CSNW, like GSNW, is a network service; you install it using the Services tab of the Control Panel's Network applet. If you're running Windows NT Server, CSNW functions are installed automatically when you install GSNW.

The first time you log on after you install CSNW or GSNW, Windows NT prompts you to enter a preferred server and attempts to validate your credentials for the NetWare network.

The Select Preferred Server for NetWare dialog box shows the name of the user attempting to log on and a drop-down list of available NetWare servers. As implied by the username parameter, this is a per-user configuration parameter. The selected server is stored in HKEY_CURRENT_USER, not HKEY_LOCAL_MACHINE.

Choose <None> in the Select Preferred Server for NetWare dialog box if you don't want a preferred server to authenticate your logon request. Choosing the Cancel button just defers the decision until the next time you log on.

After you select a preferred server, Windows NT always tries to have that server authenticate the user. If the server is unavailable, the user is prompted to select a new preferred server. A user can change his preferred server at any time using the new CSNW icon in Control Panel. (This icon was added during installation of CSNW.)

Double-clicking on the GSNW icon in Control Panel opens the Gateway Service for NetWare dialog box, which enables you to select a preferred server and a default tree and context for the NetWare network.

6. What program is used to facilitate the NetWare to Windows NT migration?

    B. NWCONV.EXE

6. CORRECT ANSWER: B

To execute the Migration Tool for NetWare, you can go to Start, Run and type **NWCONV**. This starts the Migration Tool for NetWare utility. Clicking on Migration Tool for NetWare under Programs, Administrative Tools also can activate the utility.

7. When migrating NetWare users to a Windows NT domain, what options are available for configuring passwords? Select all that apply.

    A. All migrated users can have the same password.

    B. All migrated users can have blank passwords.

    D. All passwords can be assigned from a mapping file.

    E. All passwords can be the same as the username.

7. CORRECT ANSWERS: A-B-D-E

During the migration of a NetWare environment, all the options except All Passwords Will Be Retained are available. The option to retain all passwords is unavailable because of the security issues surrounding such an event. If the Migration Tool for NetWare had the capability to read all the users' passwords, just think of the security implications. For more information, see Migration Tool for NetWare.

8. What options can be migrated from a NetWare server to a Windows NT domain? Select all that apply.

    A. Users

    B. Groups

    D. Files

8. CORRECT ANSWERS: A-B-D

Migrating a NetWare server's information to a Windows NT domain can be useful in converting to a Windows NT domain model. The types of information capable of migration are users, groups, and files. Printers and print queues, along with NDS partitions and NTFS partitions, have different infrastructures and are not capable of being migrated.

9. Which of the following statements is true when migrating files from a NetWare server to a Windows NT domain? Select the best response.

    E. To retain NetWare file system security, they must be migrated to an NTFS partition.

9. CORRECT ANSWER: E

When migrating files to a Windows NT Server with NTFS, all file system properties are retained. The specific rights are transferred from the NetWare server to the Windows NT server and are converted to the Microsoft equivalent of the NetWare rights.

10. What steps are necessary prior to performing a real NetWare server
migration? Select all that apply.

    A. Obtain Supervisor and Administrative
security equivalence on both the
NetWare and Windows NT servers.

    C. Perform several trial migrations.

    E. Create available free space on the
NTFS partition for the file transfers.

10. CORRECT ANSWERS: A-C-E

After installing Gateway Service for NetWare, you can configure your Migration Tool for NetWare to transfer (migrate)
users, groups, and files. To efficiently and effectively perform
the migration, you must obtain Supervisor and Administrative
security equivalence. It also is recommended that you run
several trial migrations to simulate the actual migration of
users and data. Because printers and print queues are not
capable of migration (they can be discarded, however, for the
migration of files), you must have an available NTFS partition
with enough free hard disk space.

11. Your company is closing its office on
the West Coast. It is your responsibility
to add the NetWare 3.*x* servers to the
CORP domain on the East Coast.
Currently, the CORP domain consists of
two Windows NT servers that share
both files and printers. There are 50
Windows 95 client machines on the
CORP domain. All the Windows 95
clients must have access to files and
printers on the Windows NT server and
the NetWare 3.*x* servers. What steps
must be taken to accomplish this?
Select the best response.

    D. Install and configure Gateway
Services for NetWare on all the
Windows NT servers.

11. CORRECT ANSWER: D

The best answer in this scenario is to install Gateway Services
for NetWare so no additional configuration is necessary on the
Windows 95 clients in the CORP domain. Installing Client
for NetWare Networks on all the Windows clients would
enable them to access the NetWare 3.*x* servers, but administration would be an issue. Installing Gateway or Client
Services for NetWare on the NetWare server is not an available
option. These services are available only on Windows NT
machines.

Migration Tool for NetWare

The explanation in this section supports questions 6–10.

To ease the transition from NetWare to NT Server, Microsoft
provides a tool to automate the migration process. The
Migration Tool for NetWare transfers file and directory information and user and group account information from a
NetWare server to a Windows NT domain controller. The
Migration Tool for NetWare also preserves logon scripts and
directory- and file-effective rights. You have the option to
indicate which accounts, files, or directories you want
migrated. If the Migration Tool were allowed to access the
NetWare bindery and to extract the usernames along with
their current passwords, security on a NetWare server would

be breached. This would be a serious issue for NetWare administrators. Because of the security involved, the Migration Tool for NetWare cannot preserve the original NetWare passwords, but it does provide the capability to set up new passwords.

The Migration Tool for NetWare can migrate NetWare resources to the domain controller on which it is running, or it can execute from a separate NT server or workstation and migrate the NetWare resources to a domain controller elsewhere on the network. NWLink and Gateway Services for NetWare must be running both on the computer running Migration Tool for NetWare and on the domain controller receiving the migration.

To run the Migration Tool for NetWare, choose Start, Run and type **nwconv** in the Run dialog box.

The Migration Tool for NetWare provides a number of options for transferring file and account information. Always migrate files and directories to an NTFS partition if possible. NTFS file and directory permissions provide the equivalent of the trustee rights specified for these resources in the NetWare environment.

INSTALLING AND CONFIGURING REMOTE ACCESS SERVICE (RAS)

1. **What steps must you take to enable the logging features provided by the RAS server? Select the best response.**

   A. Through the RAS Administrator program, enable the PPP and Device logs. The logs then can be viewed in the `\winnt\system32\logs\ras` directory.

   B. The Registry must be edited manually using `Regedt32.exe`. After the appropriate changes are made, logging begins when the RAS server is restarted.

   C. From the Policies menu in User Manager for Domains, select the Audit option. From there, you can enable PPP and Device logs if you have installed the RAS server. All log entries can then be viewed from the Event Viewer.

   D. RAS logging can be accomplished only through third-party software.

   E. Through the Performance Monitor.

2. **What methods can be used to grant users the capability to dial in to a RAS server? Select all that apply.**

   A. In User Manager for Domains, select a user and click on the Dialin button to grant access.

   B. Through the RAS Administrator program.

   C. Through RAS Server services in the Services tab in the Network Control Panel.

   D. After RAS is installed, all newly created users automatically are given the Dialin permission.

   E. When the user creates a new phonebook entry, NT prompts the user to use the RAS server.

3. **Which of the following network protocols are available to RAS clients through the RAS server? Select all that apply.**

   A. NWLink IPX/SPX-compatible transport

   B. NetBEUI

   C. TCP/IP

   D. AppleTalk

   E. DLC

4. **Which of the following are valid security measures offered by RAS? Select all that apply.**

   A. Callback security

   B. MS/CHAP

C. PPP

D. PPTP

E. SLIP

5. **How many simultaneous connections can the RAS server support in Windows NT Server?**

    A. 2

    B. 16

    C. 64

    D. 256

    E. Unlimited

6. **What types of remote servers can a DUN client dial in to? Select all that apply.**

    A. SLIP server

    B. PPTP server

    C. PPP server

    D. Windows NT 3.1/WFW RAS servers

    E. Site server

7. **What protocol can RAS use to ensure private communications across a public line?**

    A. PPP

    B. SSL

    C. SMIME

    D. PPTP

    E. SLIP

8. **Which devices can a client use to dial in to a RAS server by default? Select all that apply.**

    A. Modem

    B. X.25 device

    C. ISDN modem

    D. PAD device

    E. Router

9. **Which methods of security enable remote users to save money on long-distance phone calls? Select all that apply.**

    A. No Callback security

    B. Callback security

    C. Callback security at a predetermined number

    D. NT challenge/response

    E. Clear text

10. **Which type of application protocol can be routed through a RAS server using different networking protocols?**

    A. Mailslots

    B. Named Pipes

    C. RPCs

    D. NetBIOS

    E. HTTP

11. **Which protocols are supported by PPP? Select all that apply.**

    A. NWLink IPX/SPX-compatible transport

    B. NetBEUI

    C. TCP/IP

    D. AppleTalk

    E. DLC

12. **Which protocol does SLIP support?**

    A. NWLink IPX/SPX-compatible transport

    B. NetBEUI

    C. TCP/IP

    D. AppleTalk

    E. DLC

13. **Which of the following settings are valid when determining client access? Select all that apply.**

    A. This Computer Only

    B. This Workgroup Only

    C. This Domain Only

    D. Any Trusted Domain

    E. Entire Network

14. **What must be installed to enable a Windows 95 client to utilize PPTP? Select the best response.**

    A. A PPTP-compatible modem.

    B. User authentication.

    C. Dial-Up Networking version 1.2.

    D. A PPTP-compatible network interface card.

    E. Nothing. Windows 95 supports PPTP with no additional configuration.

15. **You are the network administrator of a small company. You recently installed** RAS Server on an NT server to provide your remote users with network access when they are traveling. All your clients use Windows 95 and use TCP/IP as their primary protocol. After instructing all the RAS clients how to use the service, several clients report that they are unable to connect. After further investigation, you discover the clients are connecting to the server but cannot get past the logon prompt. What is the most likely cause of the problem? Select the best response.

    A. The clients have NWLink IPX/SPX installed.

    B. The clients and RAS server have different encryption settings.

    C. The clients are configured to dial in to a SLIP server.

    D. Callback security is enabled at the RAS Server.

    E. The clients have the wrong modem installed.

16. **What methods can be used to allocate IP addresses to dial-up clients? Select all that apply.**

    A. The RAS server can allocate IP addresses from a preconfigured static pool configured on the RAS server.

    B. The client can request that his own IP address be used.

    C. From a BootP server.

    D. From a DHCP server.

    E. From a SLIP Server.

17. **What feature of RAS enables clients to use multiple modems to establish a single link to a RAS server?**

    A. Multiconnect

    B. Multilink

    C. Multiplexing

    D. Multiline

    E. RAS Multitasking

ANSWER KEY

1. B	7. D	13. A-E
2. A-B	8. A-B-C	14. C
3. A-B-C	9. B-C	15. B
4. A-B-D	10. D	16. A-B-D
5. D	11. A-B-C	17. B
6. A-C-D	12. C	

INSTALLING AND CONFIGURING REMOTE ACCESS SERVICE (RAS)

1. What steps must you take to enable the logging features provided by the RAS server? Select the best response.

   B. The Registry must be edited manually using Regedt32.exe. **After the appropriate changes are made, logging begins when the RAS server is restarted.**

1. CORRECT ANSWER: B

Windows NT Remote Access Service has the capability to log information about connectivity. The logging, however, must be configured manually in the Registry.

The following steps outline the manual configuration necessary to enable RAS logging:

1. Click Start, Run and enter the Registry Editor (**REGEDT32.EXE**).

2. From the HKEY_LOCAL_MACHINE subtree, go to the following key:

   SYSTEM\CurrentControlSet\Services\RasMan\ Parameters

3. Change the value of the Logging parameter to 1, as follows:

   Logging:REG_DWORD:0x1

4. All changes made with the Registry Editor are immediate.

To activate the logging, stop and restart the Remote Access Server service. It is not necessary to shut down and restart Windows NT.

2. What methods can be used to grant users the capability to dial in to a RAS server? Select all that apply.

   A. In User Manager for Domains, select a user and click on the Dialin button to grant access.

   B. Through the RAS Administrator program.

2. CORRECT ANSWERS: A-B

After the installation of Remote Access Server is complete, you still must grant users the capability to dial in. Dial-in permission is not given to any users by default as an added layer of security. This can be accomplished through the Remote Access Server Administrator program or through User Manager. The modem and network properties are configurable through RAS properties on the Services tab in Network Properties. Phone Book entries do not relate to security in the form of Dial-in permissions.

3. Which of the following network protocols are available to RAS clients through the RAS server? Select all that apply.

   A. NWlink IPX/SPX-compatible transport
   B. NetBEUI
   C. TCP/IP

3. CORRECT ANSWERS: A-B-C

By default, RAS makes the NWLink, NetBEUI, and TCP/IP protocols available to clients. This is configurable through Network Properties on the Services tab. Although AppleTalk and DLC are supported by Windows NT, the RAS server does not extend that support. For more information, see the Further Review section that covers RAS.

4. Which of the following are valid security measures offered by RAS? Select all that apply.

   A. Callback security
   B. MS/CHAP
   D. PPTP

4. CORRECT ANSWERS: A-B-D

RAS is designed for security. Some security features include auditing, callback, encryption, security hosts, and PPTP filtering. MS/CHAP is the authentication/encryption algorithm used to authenticate MS clients. It sends the user account in encrypted format and can be used to encrypt all data. PPTP is for VPNs. PPP and SLIP are incorrect answers because they are nothing more than line protocols and provide no type of security. For more information, see the Further Review section that covers RAS.

5. How many simultaneous connections can the RAS server support in Windows NT Server?

   D. 256

5. CORRECT ANSWER: D

RAS supports up to 256 simultaneous connections. Microsoft has stated that it is possible to go beyond this limit; however, they only have tested the RAS capabilities to the point of 256 simultaneous connections.

6. What types of remote servers can a DUN client dial in to? Select all that apply.

   A. SLIP server
   C. PPP server
   D. Windows NT 3.1/WFW RAS servers

6. CORRECT ANSWERS: A-C-D

As a client, RAS can dial in to and access any Remote Access Server accepting Serial Line Internet Protocol (SLIP) or Point-to-Point Protocol (PPP). This includes UNIX systems as well as Windows NT, Windows 95, and WFW RAS servers.

7. What protocol can RAS use to ensure private communications across a public line?

D. PPTP

The Point-to-Point Tunneling Protocol enables encrypted packets to travel over a publicly accessible network such as the Internet. The Point-to-Point Tunneling Protocol (PPTP) is related to PPP, but PPTP is a protocol that enables you to transmit PPP packets over a TCP/IP network securely. Because the Internet is a TCP/IP network, PPTP provides highly private network links over the otherwise highly public Internet. PPTP connections are encrypted, making them nearly impenetrable to virtual voyeurs.

In fact, PPTP is part of an emerging technology called virtual private networks (VPNs). The point of VPNs is to provide corporate networks with the same (or close to the same) security over the Internet as they would have over a direct connection.

Another exciting advantage of PPTP (and another reason it fits nicely into the scheme of virtual private networks) is that it doesn't discriminate among protocols. Because PPP supports NetBEUI, IPX, and other network protocols and because PPTP operates on PPP packets, PPTP enables you to transmit non-TCP/IP protocols over the Internet.

Because PPTP provides intranet privacy over the open Internet, it can reduce costs significantly in some situations. Networks that once would have depended on extravagant direct connections now can hook up using a local Internet service provider.

EXAM TIP

It is important to be comfortable with the types of protocols used as well as their advantages and disadvantages. The Point-to-Point Tunneling Protocol might be touched on, but the concept is still new enough that there might not be many questions about it.

8. Which devices can a client use to dial in to a RAS server by default? Select all that apply.

A. Modem

B. X.25 device

C. ISDN modem

RAS supports PSTN, X.25, null-modem and ISDN modems. Because PSTN is supported, modems that access a phone line also are included for dial in. PAD devices and routers are used only in a dedicated-line environment and are not compatible with RAS. For more information, see the Further Review section that covers RAS.

9. Which methods of security enable remote users to save money on long-distance phone calls? Select all that apply.

B. Callback security

C. Callback security at a predetermined number

9. CORRECT ANSWERS: B-C

With the enhanced callback security feature, the RAS server can call a user back at a predefined number or at a new number to save the user money on long-distance charges. Employees who travel or telecommute, for example, might have the option only to access RAS using a long-distance connection. With callback security, the RAS server can call the user back for security purposes as well as to take on the long-distance costs.

10. Which type of application protocol can be routed through a RAS server using different networking protocols?

D. NetBIOS

10. CORRECT ANSWER: D

If a client dials in using only IPX, he can access a server on the network that only runs IP. In this scenario, RAS can act as a NetBIOS router. The RAS server requires that both IPX and IP be installed, and it can route all NetBIOS applications between the two endpoints. It cannot, however, route any of the other Application layer protocols listed (Mail Slots, Named Pipes, RPCs, HTTP).

11. Which protocols are supported by PPP? Select all that apply.

A. NWLink IPX/SPX-compatible transport

B. NetBEUI

C. TCP/IP

D. AppleTalk

11. CORRECT ANSWERS: A-B-C-D

The Point-to-Point Protocol (PPP) originally was conceived as a deluxe version of SLIP. Like SLIP, PPP is an industry standard for point-to-point communications, but PPP offers several advantages over SLIP. Most notably, PPP isn't limited to TCP/IP. PPP also supports IPX, NetBEUI, and several other network protocols such as AppleTalk and DECnet.

Because PPP supports so many protocols, it provides much more flexibility in configuring network communications. Windows NT automatically binds RAS to TCP/IP, NetBEUI, and IPX if those protocols are installed at the same time as RAS.

12. Which protocol does SLIP support?

    C. TCP/IP

The Serial Line Internet Protocol (SLIP) is a standard protocol for serial line connections over TCP/IP networks. Each node in a SLIP connection must have a static IP address; that is, you can't use Windows NT features such as DHCP and WINS. Unlike PPP, SLIP does not support NetBEUI or IPX; you must use TCP/IP with SLIP.

13. Which of the following settings are valid when determining client access? Select all that apply.

    A. This Computer Only

    E. Entire Network

RAS servers have the capability to limit a remote user to This Computer Only or to the Entire Network. This setting is configured through the Network Properties Services tab under RAS properties. For more information, see the Further Review section that covers RAS.

14. What must be installed to enable a Windows 95 client to utilize PPTP? Select the best response.

    C. Dial-Up Networking version 1.2

Windows 95, by default, doesn't have the capability to utilize PPTP. To enable this feature, the client must install the DUN 1.2 upgrade. Currently, the Windows 95 OSR2 version that ships with most OEM computer systems includes the DUN 1.2 upgrade. Although User Authentication can be a component of PPTP, the DUN 1.2 upgrade is necessary to reach that step. Any standard modem or network interface card will work.

15. You are the network administrator of a small company. You recently installed RAS Server on an NT server to provide your remote users with network access when they are traveling. All your clients use Windows 95 and use TCP/IP as their primary protocol. After instructing all the RAS clients how to use the service, several clients report that they are unable to connect. After further investigation, you discover the clients are connecting to the server but cannot get past the logon prompt. What is the most likely cause of the problem? Select the best response.

When troubleshooting RAS connectivity, one area of concern is the encryption level. The client and the server must be on the same settings to work properly. Microsoft states that if you are having problems with remote users logging in, you should enable plain-text passwords. From there, you can begin to upgrade the authentication/encryption options (MS/CHAP and so on). The goal in every exam question is to select the best answer. The question is worded "After further investigation, you discover the clients are connecting to the server but cannot get past the logon prompt." If the clients had IPX

B. The clients and RAS server have different encryption settings

or the wrong modem configured, they never would have connected. Even if the students were configured to dial in to a SLIP server, RAS cannot act as a SLIP server. If callback security was enabled, the problem would not surface until after they had successfully logged in to the server.

16. **What methods can be used to allocate IP addresses to dial-up clients? Select all that apply.**

A. The RAS server can allocate IP addresses from a preconfigured static pool configured on the RAS server.

B. The client can request that his own IP address be used.

D. From a DHCP server.

16. CORRECT ANSWERS: A-B-D

During the configuration of the RAS server, you are allowed to set up the network properties to allocate IP addresses from a predefined static pool configured on the RAS server itself. This is a separate pool from any DHCP server on the network. The clients also can request that their own IP address be used. Some ISPs, for example, issue static IP addresses to clients with registered fully qualified domain names. The simplest method is to incorporate the RAS server with the DHCP server (provided you have a DHCP server on the network). RAS servers don't support BootP, nor can they be installed as a SLIP server.

17. **What feature of RAS enables clients to use multiple modems to establish a single link to a RAS server?**

B. Multilink

17. CORRECT ANSWER: B

Multilink is a new feature found in Windows 95, Windows 98, and Windows NT clients. Using Multilink, a Windows NT client computer can establish a RAS connection using more than one physical modem and phone line. One Multilink connection, for example, can use two modems at once (or one modem line and one ISDN line) to form a single logical link. For more information, see the Further Review section that covers RAS.

INSTALLING AND CONFIGURING REMOTE ACCESS SERVICE (RAS)

Windows NT Remote Access Service (RAS) provides the technology to permit an NT-based computer to connect to a remote network using a dial-up connection and to fully participate as a network client. RAS also enables your Windows NT computer to receive dial-up connections from remote computers.

RAS supports SLIP and PPP line protocols and NetBEUI, TCP/IP, and IPX network protocols. Because so many Internet users access their service providers using a phone line, RAS often serves as an Internet interface.

The Dial-Up Networking application (in the Accessories program group) enables you to create phonebook entries, which are preconfigured dial-up connections to specific sites. The Telephony application in the Control Panel enables the remote user to preconfigure dialing properties for different dialing locations.

Connecting to RAS

RAS can connect to a remote computer using any of the following media:

- Public-Switched Telephone Network (PSTN). (Also known as the phone company.) RAS can connect using a modem through an ordinary phone line.

- X.25. A packet-switched network. Computers access the network using a Packet Assembler Disassembler device (PAD). X.25 supports dial-up or direct connections.

- Null modem cable. A cable that connects two computers directly. The computers then communicate using their serial ports (rather than their network adapter cards).

- ISDN. A digital line that provides faster communication and more bandwidth than a regular phone line. (It also costs more—that's why not everybody has it.) A computer must have a special ISDN card to access an ISDN line.

Windows NT 4 also includes a new feature called Multilink. Using Multilink, a Windows NT computer can form a RAS connection using more than one physical pathway. One Multilink connection, for example, can use two modems at once (or one modem line and one ISDN line) to form a single logical link. By using multiple pathways for one connection, Multilink can greatly increase bandwidth. Of course, the computer has to have access to more than one pathway (that is, it must have two modems installed) or you can't use it.

RAS and Security

Like everything else in Windows NT, RAS is designed for security. The following are some of RAS' security features:

- Auditing. RAS can leave an audit trail, enabling you to see who logged on when and what authentication was provided.

- Callback security. You can enable RAS server to use callback security, in which the server hangs up all incoming calls and phones the caller back. You also can limit callback numbers to prearranged sites you know are safe.

- Encryption. RAS can encrypt logon information, or it can encrypt all data crossing the connection.

- Security hosts. In case Windows NT isn't safe enough, you can add an extra dose of security by using a third-party intermediary security host—a computer that stands between the RAS client and the RAS server

and that requires an extra round of authentication.

- PPTP filtering. You can tell Windows NT to filter out all packets except ultra-safe PPTP packets (described in the section "PPTP").

Protocols Supported by RAS

RAS supports the following line protocols:

- SLIP

- PPP

- PPTP

Another advantage of RAS is that it supports encrypted passwords.

CHAPTER SUMMARY

Windows NT provides several tools to help transform a Novell NetWare network into a Microsoft Windows NT domain. By providing Gateway Services for NetWare, an administrator can ease the migration process a little bit at a time. Microsoft emphasizes the importance of knowing what can and cannot migrate from a NetWare server, in particular, usernames with passwords.

In the RAS environment, Microsoft challenges the test subjects by placing them in different scenarios. Some scenarios focus on the capability of the client to access resources given that a particular protocol has been installed. Others focus their attention on the RAS server and the configuration elements involved.

CHAPTER 5

Monitoring and Optimization

This chapter's questions address the issue of monitoring and optimizing system performance on a computer running Windows NT Server 4. Although Windows NT Server 4, once installed, can perform in a mostly self-tuned manner, tweaking the performance of NT Server can yield significant benefits. Certainly, to achieve optimum performance, minor adjustments can be made, requiring a degree of system monitoring to determine baselines and to document system behavior and performance over a statistically meaningful time frame.

OBJECTIVES

The questions and explanations in this chapter help prepare you for the exam by covering the following objectives:

Monitor performance of various functions by using Performance Monitor. Functions include the following:

- **Processor**

- **Memory**

- **Disk**

- **Network**

▶ Microsoft provides a standard administrative tool called Performance Monitor, which ships, installs, and is highly integrated with Windows NT Server 4. Performance Monitor, often referred to as PerfMon, exposes most system components as objects. More accurately, real-time statistical performance information is

continues

reported in Performance Monitor. The information is exposed to the user through elements within PerfMon known as objects, with further division of the information into a large number of object counters. Performance Monitor also provides the user with several views to increase the flexibility and options for viewing this statistical performance information.

Identify performance bottlenecks.

▶ An important goal of monitoring a Windows NT Server system is to identify potential or existing performance bottlenecks in a system. A *bottleneck* occurs when the maximum processing capability of a system component is below the capability of all other related system components. By the very nature or definition of a bottleneck, it is impossible to eliminate a bottleneck that currently exists in some functional system capacity. The goal is to identify and eliminate any significant or consistent bottlenecks within a system.

MONITORING PERFORMANCE OF VARIOUS FUNCTIONS USING PERFORMANCE MONITOR

1. **In Windows NT Server 4.0, the Server service can be configured for a number of different intended uses. The configuration of the Server service can affect virtual memory behavior. One of these optional settings, Maximize Throughput for File Sharing, typically is used in what environment? Select the best response.**

   A. When the NT Server is part of an NT domain model that follows the Master Domain model and consists of only one domain controller

   B. When the primary function of the NT Server is as an application server

   C. When the total number of users is expected to exceed 64 users and a large file cache is desired

   D. When the total number of users is expected to exceed the current setting for licenses in the license pool, as set in Control Panel's License Manager

   E. When the total number of users is expected to exceed 64 concurrent users

2. **When configuring the functional behavior of the Server service, one option is to optimize the system functionality to Minimize Memory Used. Under what expected usage scenario would you want to use this setting? Select the best response.**

   A. When the expected number of users will continuously hover between 20–40 users

   B. When a multiple-resource domain backup domain controller is the primary function of the server

   C. When the total number of users is expected to be fewer than 10 users

   D. When the expected number of users occasionally drops to fewer than 10 users

   E. When a primary domain controller is configured in a domain using at least one backup domain controller for every 2,000 users

3. **In Windows NT Server, where can a user modify the Virtual Memory settings for the system? Select the best response.**

   A. Click on the Virtual Memory button in the Performance tab of the System Properties dialog box.

   B. Click on the Advanced Memory command in the default property page of the System Properties dialog box, which is accessible from the System applet in Control Panel.

C. Choose Virtual Memory from the System applet in Control Panel.

D. Choose the 386 enhanced icon in the Control Panel.

E. None of the above.

4. **When the amount of available physical RAM is insufficient to meet the immediate needs of the applications and operating system components currently in memory, the operating system component that controls the process of relocating data from memory to disk is known as which of the following?**

A. Swap File Manager

B. Virtual Device Manager

C. Virtual Memory Mapper

D. Virtual Memory Manager

E. Virtual Mapping Manager

5. **The use of virtual memory involves replacing a faster form of storage, in terms of retrieval times, with a much slower form (hard disk). What steps can be taken to improve the efficiency of system virtual memory usage? Select all that apply.**

A. Move the pagefile to the boot partition.

B. Establish paging file segments on multiple hard drives.

C. Consolidate the pagefile into a single, centralized pagefile.

D. Relocate to another drive any pagefile segment that exists on the same drive

where the Windows NT System files are located.

E. Set the minimum size of the paging file to a value that will safely exceed the maximum expected pagefile usage during peak usage.

6. **When tweaking the behavior of the Server service in terms of memory allocation, an NT Server can be configured to Maximize Throughput for Network Applications. Under what scenario would this setting best be employed? Select the best response.**

A. When the server is expected to have up to 64 concurrent users

B. When the server is a member server in a workgroup

C. When network throughput is critical

D. When the Server is going to function as a file and print server

E. When an NT Server is designed to function as an application server or as part of a domain with just one domain controller

7. **Which of the following counters are associated with the memory object in the Performance Monitor utility? Select all that apply.**

A. % Processor Time

B. Available Bytes

C. Pages/sec

D. Bytes Total/sec

E. Committed Bytes

8. **Which of the following are valid processor object counters? Select all that apply.**

    A. Pages/sec

    B. % Processing Time

    C. % Processor Time

    D. Processor Queue Length

    E. Interrupts/sec

9. **A review of the Performance Monitor log reveals that unusual behavior has been occurring on your system. Which of the following Interrupts/sec profiles is an indication of a potential problem? Select all that apply.**

    A. Consistently around 700, with spikes up to 1800

    B. Consistently around 1200, with spikes up to 1800

    C. Consistently around 600, with spikes up to 1200

    D. Consistently around 900, with spikes up to 2300

    E. Consistently around 1000, with spikes up to 1200

10. **You are deciding how to implement fault tolerance on your NT Server. You've heard that using hardware fault tolerance is better than using NT's software fault tolerance. Why is one better than the other? Select the best response.**

    A. NT's built-in fault tolerance works only with SCSI.

    B. Software fault tolerance is more reliable than hardware.

    C. Hardware fault tolerance takes the parity calculation load off the processor.

    D. Hardware fault tolerance does not work with NT because of the HAL.

11. **Which Performance Monitor object and counter measure the amount of time the processor is busy? Select the best response.**

    A. Processor: % Busy Time

    B. Processor: % Processor Time

    C. System: % Processor Time

    D. System: TotalProcessorUsage

12. **While monitoring system performance in Performance Monitor, you notice that the Interrupts/sec value has doubled. You haven't increased the number of users or added any new applications to the server. What does this sudden increase imply? Select the best response.**

    A. Nothing. This counter naturally increases over time.

    B. It could mean you have a potential hardware problem—a piece of hardware is generating many more interrupts than normal.

    C. It indicates that the network card is the bottleneck in the system and should be replaced.

    D. It indicates that the CPU is the bottleneck in the system and should be replaced or upgraded.

13. **You're trying to explain the System: Processor Queue Length counter in Performance Monitor to a coworker. Which statement below best describes the purpose of this counter?**

    A. It measures the amount of activity on the processor.

    B. It indicates the number of threads waiting for processor time.

    C. It indicates the number of users waiting to log on to the domain.

    D. It indicates the total CPU usage across all CPUs in the system. You see a number for this counter only if your computer has more than one CPU.

14. **For the past several months, you have been monitoring the disk-related counters on an intermittent basis. You suspect the current hard drive in your system could use a little performance boost. You have decided to add two more disk drives to your system, and you are trying to determine the relative merits, in terms of disk efficiency, of using a stripe set on the additional drives. Which of the following are disk efficiency benefits of using stripe sets?**

    A. Stripe sets provide redundant storage capabilities, thereby reducing retrieval times.

    B. Stripe sets enable Windows NT to perform simultaneous writes, thereby decreasing wait times while writing large amounts of data to a disk drive.

    C. Stripes enable parity information to be written simultaneously with the actual data.

    D. Stripe sets enable data to be written in contiguous locations on the hard disk for every write.

15. **While installing NT Server on a new system with a large hard drive, you come to the part of the installation when you are asked to decide what file system you want. You are interested in file system allocation efficiency. Which file system should you use for the larger partitions? Select the best response.**

    A. NTFS

    B. FAT

    C. FAT32

    D. HPFS

    E. None of the above

16. **You decide to perform some system analysis on the new hard drive you just added to the system. You read that you need to use the `diskperf` command-line utility to enable the disk counters. You enter a `diskperf` command at the command prompt, but upon starting Performance Monitor, you still see no activity in the disk-related counters. What additional steps must you take? Select all that apply.**

    A. Start Performance Monitor.

    B. Rerun the `diskperf` command with the `-y` parameter.

    C. Start Network Monitor.

D. Restart the server.

E. Start the Disk Administrator and choose Commit changes.

17. **What hardware implementations should you use to improve data-transfer performance? Select all that apply.**

A. Use only SCSI host adapters.

B. Use host adapters capable of asynchronous I/O.

C. Implement stripe sets with parity through either NT's Disk Administrator or hardware RAID solutions.

D. Distribute data across several servers to accomplish load balancing.

18. **To optimize the network components in an NT Workstation or Server, which one of the following should you do?**

A. You do not need to do anything. NT automatically optimizes the network components.

B. You should not remove unused adapter cards and protocols.

C. You should always have TCP/IP, NetBEUI, and NWLink installed, even if your computers are using only one protocol. This leaves more paths open in case one protocol becomes unusable.

D. You should disable the server service for a workstation and disable the workstation service for a server.

19. **Which of the following are considerations with regard to optimizing NT with network cards? Select all that apply.**

A. Get a network card with the widest data bus available.

B. Always use NetBEUI when available.

C. Never use NetBEUI.

D. Divide your network into multiple networks, attaching the server to each network with a different adapter.

20. **You have a server that is receiving requests from users running only IPX/SPX, yet you have TCP/IP installed so you can browse IP resources from this machine. How can you configure bindings to improve performance on this server? Select the best response.**

A. Remove TCP/IP.

B. Unbind IPX/SPX from the Workstation service and unbind TCP/IP from the server service.

C. Unbind TCP/IP from the Workstation service and unbind IPX/SPX from the server service.

D. You cannot change the protocol binding on services.

21. **What does the counter Network: Bytes Total/sec measure?**

A. Bytes sent to the network

B. Bytes sent from the network

C. Bytes sent to and from the network

D. Bytes discarded from the network

22. You are monitoring the counter Network: Bytes Total/sec in Performance Monitor. On each server, you tally the total amount; you realize that this amount is nearly the total amount of maximum throughput for your network medium. What does this mean you need to do to increase productivity?

A. You need to install faster network adapters.

B. You need to segment the network.

C. You need to add more memory.

D. You need to upgrade to NDIS 4.0 drivers.

ANSWER KEY

1. C	9. B-D	16. B-D
2. C	10. C	17. A-B-C-D
3. C	11. B	18. D
4. D	12. B	19. A-D
5. B-D-E	13. B	20. B
6. E	14. B	21. C
7. B-C-E	15. A	22. B
8. C-D-E		

MONITORING PERFORMANCE OF VARIOUS FUNCTIONS USING PERFORMANCE MONITOR

1. In Windows NT Server 4.0, the Server service can be configured for a number of different intended uses. The configuration of the Server service can affect virtual memory behavior. One of these optional settings, Maximize Throughput for File Sharing, typically is used in what environment? Select the best response.

    C. When the total number of users is expected to exceed 64 users and a large file cache is desired

1. CORRECT ANSWER: C

When the expected user access count is greater than 64 and a large file cache is desired (as for file and print servers), configuring the Server service to maximize the effective throughput for file sharing generally produces a better overall level of performance.

A server that is not explicitly expected to have more than 64 users or to function as an application server should probably be set to use Balance. User access that is expected to exceed currently available Client Access Licenses does not have any direct effect on server performance, but it does violate Microsoft licensing agreements.

2. When configuring the functional behavior of the Server service, one option is to optimize the system functionality to Minimize Memory Used. Under what expected usage scenario would you want to use this setting? Select the best response.

    C. When the total number of users is expected to be fewer than 10 users

2. CORRECT ANSWER: C

When an NT Server is not expected to be accessed by more than 10 users at a time, Server performance can be optimized greatly by configuring the Server service to minimize memory used for supporting server service functionality.

An expected user access count of 20–40 users requires server resources for use by the Server service that generally exceed those reserved when the Minimize Memory Used setting is in use. In this situation, Balance should be used. A server functioning as a backup domain controller should use the Maximize Throughput for Network Applications setting. Even if the number of users accessing a server occasionally falls below 10 users, it still is best to use the Balance setting. The impact of the number of backup domain controllers in use is moot, considering the number of users will still be much higher, as will the total resource requirements of a server acting as a primary domain controller.

3. **In Windows NT Server, where can a user modify the Virtual Memory settings for the system? Select the best response.**

   C. Choose Virtual Memory from the System applet in Control Panel.

The System applet is the correct location for accessing Virtual Memory configuration settings in Windows NT. The 386 enhanced icon in Control Panel is used in Windows 3.x, and the Performance tab of the System Properties dialog box is used in Windows 95.

Modification of the Virtual Memory settings for a system can result in better performance. If a user knows that the usage pattern of a system results in periodic increases in the size of the pagefile, changing the minimum or initial size ahead of time results in successfully avoiding the overhead of automatic increases in size. The user also averts the receipt of an error dialog box indicating that insufficient memory is available as a result of the need for an increase in pagefile size.

4. **When the amount of available physical RAM is insufficient to meet the immediate needs of the applications and operating system components currently in memory, the operating system component that controls the process of relocating data from memory to disk is known as which of the following?**

   D. Virtual Memory Manager

The Virtual Memory Manager is the portion of the NT kernel that deals with the process of trafficking data in and out of memory and the hard drive real estate reserved for the pagefile.

The Swap File Manager, Virtual Device Manager, Virtual Memory Mapper, and Virtual Mapping Manager do not exist.

5. **The use of virtual memory involves replacing a faster form of storage, in terms of retrieval times, with a much slower form (hard disk). What steps can be taken to improve the efficiency of system virtual memory usage? Select all that apply.**

   B. Establish paging file segments on multiple hard drives.

   D. Relocate to another drive any pagefile segment that exists on the same drive where the Windows NT System files are located.

   E. Set the minimum size of the paging file to a value that will safely exceed the maximum expected pagefile usage during peak usage.

Spreading available pagefile segments across multiple hard drives enables Windows NT to engage multiple drive mechanisms for writing the pages to the disk. Furthermore, relocating a pagefile from a boot partition results in increased read/write times because the process of swapping to disk does not have to compete with the core operating system files that are loading and unloading from the boot partition. If analysis of the pagefile size over time reveals a maximum size under peak conditions, setting the minimum swap file size should effectively eliminate any need to dynamically increase the size of the swap file to accommodate the situational increase in memory requirements. This reduces the overhead incurred when increasing the swap file.

Moving the pagefile to a boot partition actually incurs additional contention for system resources, effectively decreasing performance. Consolidating several pagefile segments into one, centralized pagefile actually decreases pagefile efficiency because of the funneling of all page swapping processes through one hard drive controller.

6. **When tweaking the behavior of the Server service in terms of memory allocation, an NT Server can be configured to Maximize Throughput for Network Applications. Under what scenario would this setting best be employed? Select the best response.**

    E. **When an NT Server is designed to function as an application server or as part of a domain with just one domain controller**

6. CORRECT ANSWER: E

When a Server is destined to perform the functions of a primary domain controller or to act as an application server, requesting the Server service to retain enough memory resources to effectively and efficiently serve the numerous user logon requests, application file requests, and so on, can improve server performance. In addition, this setting should be used for servers functioning as a backup domain controller (in a multidomain controller environment).

A server that expects no more than 64 users should be configured with the Balance setting. Being a member of a workgroup has no direct impact on the expected type of usage. Without explicit indications of user count, the server should be set to Balance. Generic network throughput is not directly related to the server setting of Maximize Throughput for Network Applications. A server expected to function as a file and print server should be set to Maximize Throughput for File Sharing.

7. **Which of the following counters are associated with the memory object in the Performance Monitor utility? Select all that apply.**

    B. **Available Bytes**

    C. **Pages/sec**

    E. **Committed Bytes**

7. CORRECT ANSWERS: B - C - E

Available Bytes, Pages/sec, and Committed Bytes are certainly not the only counters associated with the Memory object. They are, however, the most prevalent in terms of monitoring. For more information see the following section, "Memory."

% Processor Time is a Processor object counter not a Memory object. The Bytes Total/sec is a Server object counter.

Memory

This explanation supports questions 1–7.

When considering optimizing a system, by far the most important factor requiring attention is the amount of memory in a system and whether that amount is sufficient for the common functions the server is being asked to perform. For this reason, two highly visible procedures are monitoring memory usage and adding more RAM.

When considering optimization procedures involving memory, the following two key considerations should be addressed:

- You can never have too much RAM. Having adequate RAM, in some cases, is directly related to reducing the need for paging memory to and from the hard disk, a much slower medium.

- Shadowing the ROM BIOS in RAM does not improve performance in Windows NT. Disabling this feature, therefore, can make more memory available to the system.

EXAM TIP

The exam focuses on Performance Monitor-related questions when testing your knowledge of memory optimization and system monitoring concepts. For this reason, you should be familiar with the following three primary memory counters:

- Pages/sec. This counter measures the number of times a memory page had to be paged in to memory or out to the disk. In essence, this counter measures the overall activity of page swapping.

- Available Bytes. This counter measures the amount of physical memory available for use by the system. When this value falls below 4MB, you are getting excessive paging. In essence, this counter indicates the amount of memory available in RAM.

- Committed Bytes. This counter measures the amount of virtual memory committed to physical RAM or to pagefile space. If the amount of committed bytes exceeds the physical memory of a system, more RAM is required on the system. In essence, this measures the amount of bytes currently in use and needed by all applications.

When attempting to optimize memory usage by NT server, one important service can be tweaked to provide NT Server with direction on how to autotune its own behavior. The Server Service can be configured to improve the use of memory by this service when fulfilling requests for server services by connected users. To access the Server dialog box, choose the Services tab in the Control Panel's Network application, select the Server service, and click on the Properties button.

By default, Windows NT Server is configured to work best as a file server for 64 or more users. Table 5.1 shows the optimum Server service settings.

TABLE 5.1   **SERVER SERVICE OPTIMIZATION**

Setting	Description
Minimize Memory Used	Up to 10 connections
Balance	Up to 64 connections
Maximize Throughput	64 or more connections, large file cache (best suited for file sharing and print servers)
Maximize Throughput for Network Application	64 or more connections, small file cache (best suited for PDCs, BDCs, and application servers)

8. Which of the following are valid Processor object counters? Select all that apply.

C. % Processor Time

D. Processor Queue Length

E. Interrupts/sec

8. CORRECT ANSWERS: C - D - E

% Processor Time, Processor Queue Length, and Interrupts/sec certainly are not the only counters associated with the Processor object. They are, however, the most prevalent in terms on monitoring. For more information see the next section, "Processor."

Pages/sec is a memory counter, and % Processing Time is not a valid counter.

9. A review of the Performance Monitor log reveals that unusual behavior has been occurring on your system. Which of the following Interrupts/sec profiles is an indication of a potential problem? Select all that apply.

   B. Consistently around 1200, with spikes up to 1800

   D. Consistently around 900, with spikes up to 2300

9. CORRECT ANSWERS: B - D

The Processor counter Interrupts/sec should consistently be between 100 to 1000 per second, with occasional spikes up to 2000. Any values not falling within these ranges should be considered an indication of a problem with the system.

10. You are deciding how to implement fault tolerance on your NT Server. You've heard that using hardware fault tolerance is better than using NT's software fault tolerance. Why is one better than the other? Select the best response.

    C. Hardware fault tolerance takes the parity calculation load off the processor.

10. CORRECT ANSWER: C

When using hardware-based fault tolerance, such as a hardware-based RAID drive array, parity information is calculated by the hardware, alleviating the processor from performing that task.

NT's software-based fault tolerance is not limited to SCSI drives. In general, software-based fault tolerance is considered slightly less reliable than hardware-based fault tolerance. The hardware abstraction layer does not limit Windows NT's capability to work with hardware-based fault tolerance.

11. Which Performance Monitor object and counter measure the amount of time the processor is busy? Select the best response.

    B. Processor: % Processor Time

11. CORRECT ANSWER: B

The % Processor Time counter of the Processor object indicates the amount of time the processor is busy processing tasks. If this value consistently is above 80 percent, the processor is considered to be underpowered for the system needs.

12. While monitoring system performance in Performance Monitor, you notice that the Interrupts/sec value has doubled. You haven't increased the number of users or added any new applications to the server. What does this sudden increase imply? Select the best response.

    B. It could mean you have a potential hardware problem—a piece of hardware is generating many more interrupts than normal.

12. CORRECT ANSWER: B

An increase in interrupts without an increase in users or applications to the server generally means a hardware device is acting improperly. This could be the result of a hardware failure or a device driver failing to communicate properly with the device. This can cause an unusual degree of spurious communication and interrupts to be generated in the confusion.

The Interrupts/sec counter should not increase gradually over time. This should remain a fairly consistent value within the range of 100 to 1000. The network card in a server is a device that contributes to the number of interrupts per second, however, it definitely is not the only device contributing to this value. Therefore, no direct relationship can be assumed. The processor is responsible for processing the interrupts; it actually is considered to be the consumer or recipient of the interrupts, not the generator. It should not be considered a bottleneck in the presence of a rapid increase of interrupts per second.

13. **You're trying to explain the System: Processor Queue Length counter in Performance Monitor to a coworker. Which of the following statements best describes the purpose of this counter?**

B. **It indicates the number of threads waiting for processor time.**

13. CORRECT ANSWER: B

A thread is the smallest unit of executing code. Applications can be written to be single-thread or multithreaded. A process in memory can be running multiple threads. For this reason, it is beneficial to be able to monitor the number of threads currently waiting to be executed. This is the purpose of the Processor Queue Length counter.

The Processor Queue Length can influence the amount of activity the processor currently is experiencing, or it can be an indirect indicator of its relative activity. It does not, however, report that value directly. The concepts of users and threads are distinctly different. One refers to executing code; the other refers to a conceptual object that collectively requests the users of numerous services on the server. All of these services, at the lowest level, involve thread execution. In most cases, however, it is involved indirectly.

Processor

This explanation supports questions 8–13.

When considering optimization procedures involving a processor, the following three key considerations should be addressed:

- the need for upgrading the speed of the processor

- The need and capability of adding another processor (for example, two Pentium processors on an SMP system)

- The options for upgrading the secondary cache

The following two additional optimization considerations should be taken into account concerning fault tolerance:

- If you are using software-based fault tolerance such as mirroring (RAID 1) or striping with parity (RAID 5), use a hardware-based solution instead of Windows NT fault tolerance for better performance.

- If your goal is the greatest availability of data, you should consider mirroring (using Windows NT fault-tolerant drivers) two hardware-based RAID 5 arrays.

▼ **NOTE**

The exam focuses on Performance Monitor-related questions when testing your understanding of processor-usage optimization. When looking at the processor, be sure to remember that high levels of processor activity can result from two situations other than handling a processor-intensive task:

- There is a severe memory shortage and the processor is busy managing virtual memory (swapping pages of memory to and from the disk).

- The system is busy handling a large number of interrupts.

The following generally are considered the most important counters for the processor object:

- % Processor Time. This counter measures the amount of time the processor spends executing nonidle threads. Threads currently waiting in the processing queue do not contribute to this value.

- Interrupts/sec. This counter measures the number of interrupts the processor handles per second from hardware devices.

- Processor Queue Length. This counter measures the number of threads waiting in the queue for an available processor. Generally, if the number of threads in the queue exceeds two, you have a problem with processor performance.

Part of the optimization process for a system should include a careful analysis of any software components that are not necessary to support the intended functionality of the server. Unused drivers, services, and software components running in memory take away from the processing cycles that otherwise could go to required components. In addition, unnecessary components can increase the odds of paging, which leads to increased processing needs. These software components fall into three categories: device drivers, network protocols, and services.

- Device drivers. Any drivers loaded into memory but not used should be removed.

- Network protocols. Remove any unnecessary network protocols. You can remove the bindings for a protocol selectively.

- Services. Any services this server does not need to provide should be disabled or configured to start manually.

Beyond simply removing unused services from your system, adjusting the applicable Registry entries to tweak the performance of used services helps to reduce any unnecessary processing needs by these services. Table 5.2 lists some common values for standard Windows NT services that are a good starting point for evaluation.

TABLE 5.2 COMMON REGISTRY VALUES FOR STANDARD WINDOWS NT SERVICES

Service	Value
Net Logon	Pulse, Pulse Concurrency, Pulse Maximum
Directory Replication	Interval, Guard Time
Computer Browser	Hidden, IsDomainMaster, MaintainServerList
Spooler	DefaultSpoolDirectory, PriorityClass

14. **For the past several months, you have been monitoring the disk-related counters on an intermittent basis. You suspect the current hard drive in your system could use a little performance boost. You have decided to add two more disk drives to your system, and you are trying to determine the relative merits, in terms of disk efficiency, of using a stripe set on the additional drives. Which of the following are disk efficiency benefits of using stripe sets?**

    B. Stripe sets enable Windows NT to perform simultaneous writes, thereby decreasing wait times while writing large amounts of data to a disk drive.

---

14. CORRECT ANSWER: B

By using a stripe set, Windows NT is able to write to multiple disks at the same time, thereby benefitting from the separate disk drive mechanisms.

Stripe sets do not provide any manner of redundant storage capability. Stripe sets do not generate parity information. Parity information requires the use of stripe sets with parity. Stripe sets do not guarantee that data will be written in contiguous locations.

---

15. **While installing NT Server on a new system with a large hard drive, you come to the part of the installation when you are asked to decide what file system you want. You are interested in file system allocation efficiency. Which file system should you use for the larger partitions? Select the best response.**

    A. NTFS

---

15. CORRECT ANSWER: A

NTFS is designed for partitions larger than 400MB. The method NTFS follows for data allocation is less efficient than other file systems for partitions smaller than 400MB. Any partition greater than 400MB benefits more from the NTFS file system than from FAT, HPFS, or FAT32.

Currently, Windows NT does not support FAT32.

---

16. **You decide to perform some system analysis on the new hard drive you just added to the system. You read that you need to use the `diskperf` command-line utility to enable the disk counters. You enter a `diskperf` command at the command prompt, but upon starting Performance Monitor, you still see no activity in the disk-related counters. What additional steps must you take? Select all that apply.**

    B. Rerun the `diskperf` command with the `-y` parameter.

    D. Restart the server.

---

16. CORRECT ANSWERS: B - D

The `diskperf` command requires the `-y` parameter. After running the `diskperf` command, the system must be restarted for the changes to take effect.

Starting Performance Monitor is not inherently necessary to start the disk counters. If the disk counters are not already started, starting Performance Monitor does not start them. The Network Monitor has no direct relationship to the functionality of the disk counters. The Disk Administrator also has no direct relationship to the disk counters.

17. What hardware implementations should you use to improve data-transfer performance? Select all that apply.

    A. Use only SCSI host adapters.

    B. Use host adapters capable of asynchronous I/O.

    C. Implement stripe sets with parity through either NT's Disk Administrator or hardware RAID solutions.

    D. Distribute data across several servers to accomplish load balancing.

17. CORRECT ANSWERS: A · B · C · D

Using only SCSI adapters and SCSI drives results in improved performance over the generally slower IDE drives. Using host adapters capable of asynchronous I/O significantly improves the capability of the disk drives to transfer data to memory faster. Implementation of stripe sets with parity improves data transfer performance by taking advantage of multiple disk drive controllers and drive read/write mechanisms. Distributing data across multiple servers provides multiple points of improvement.

Disk

This explanation supports questions 14–17.

When considering optimizing a system, the disk drive can be a significant source of bottlenecks. This is because so many of the system functions are affected by the speed at which data is moved from short-term or volatile memory (RAM) to long-term or durable memory (hard disk).

When considering optimization procedures involving the disk system, the following key considerations should be included:

- Replace slow disks with faster ones.

- Use NTFS for partitions larger than 400MB.

- Use a defragmentation tool if disks become fragmented.

- Upgrade from IDE to SCSI.

- Use a controller with the highest possible transfer rate and the best multitasking functionality.

- Isolate disk I/O-intensive tasks on separate physical disks or disk controllers.

- Create a stripe set to gain the advantage of simultaneous writes to multiple disks if your hardware supports it. Stripe sets write data to the drives in 64KB segments. Stripe sets without parity offer no fault-tolerance. Should a drive fail, all data on the stripe set is lost. You should use stripe sets with parity when they are available.

A primary focal point of system optimization often includes the page file settings. The configuration of the pagefile is a common concern of disk-related optimization. You configure the size of the paging file in the Virtual Memory dialog box. To open the Virtual Memory dialog box, click on the Change button in the Performance tab of the Control Panel's System application.

Regarding Virtual Memory settings, the following are some sound recommendations:

- Consider spreading the paging file across multiple physical disks if your hardware supports writing to those disks at the same time.

- Move the paging file to the disk with the lowest amount of total disk activity.

- If you plan to use Windows NT's Recovery feature, which writes out debugging information if a stop error occurs to disk, the swap file located on your system partition must be larger than the amount of physical RAM present on the system.

- Monitor the size of the paging file during peak usage and then set the minimum size to that value.

- To determine the amount of RAM that should be added to reduce paging activity, use a tool such as Performance Monitor to determine the amount of memory each application needs. Then remove applications (noting their working set sizes) until paging activity falls within acceptable limits.

EXAM TIP

The exam focuses on Performance Monitor-related questions when testing your understanding of disk optimization and monitoring concerns. Before you can use Performance Monitor to monitor disk activity, you must enable the disk performance counters. Otherwise, all values for the disk counters report zeros in Performance Monitor.

To turn on the disk performance counters, log on as a user with administrative privileges and type the following command:

```
diskperf -y
```

After the disk performance counters are enabled, you will notice that the counters are divided into two distinct camps: the logical disk and the physical disk. The main difference between the two is that the logical disk is used to measure performance at a higher level than the physical disk. The counters for the logical disk can be used to measure the performance of network connections mapped as drives, the performance of volume sets, or stripe sets that cross physical disk drives. Generally, disk-induced bottlenecks first are uncovered by analyzing logical disk counters. The source of the bottlenecks then is determined by the physical disk counters. The physical disk counters focus on real data transfers from actual disk drives.

The following counters should be reviewed for the exam:

- **PhysicalDisk: % Disk Time.** This counter reports the percentage of time that the physical disk is busy reading or writing data.

- **PhysicalDisk: Avg. Disk Queue Length.** The average disk queue length is the average number of requests for a physical disk (both read and write requests).

- **LogicalDisk: % Disk Time.** This counter reports the percentage of time that the logical disk (for example, C:) is busy.

- **LogicalDisk: Avg Disk Queue Length.** This counter measures the number of read and write requests waiting for the logical disk to become available.

18. To optimize the network components in an NT Workstation or Server, which one of the following should you do?

D. You should disable the server service for a workstation and disable the workstation service for a server.

18. CORRECT ANSWER: D

By disabling the Server service on a workstation and the Workstation service on a server, the overhead involved in network functionality can be reduced by avoiding loading unutilized services into memory.

Windows can perform a number of aspects of its functionality, but NT does not provide for all possible autotuning possibilities including optimizing the network components. Removing unused protocols and adapters can provide some degree of optimization. Not removing them does not contribute to the optimization goal. Installing additional protocols that are not used, such as TCP/IP and NWLink, increases network-related system overhead.

19. **Which of the following are considerations with regard to optimizing NT with network cards? Select all that apply.**

A. Get a network card with the widest data bus available.

D. Divide your network into multiple networks, attaching the server to each network with a different adapter.

19. CORRECT ANSWERS: A - D

Using a network card with the widest bus available provides additional bandwidth for moving data off the network and onto the system when existing as the target of the network packets. Dividing your network into multiple segments and attaching a server to each network by using additional network adapters reduces network traffic. Care should be taken, however, especially if the only protocol used on the network is not routable.

20. **You have a server that is receiving requests from users running only IPX/SPX, yet you have TCP/IP installed so you can browse IP resources from this machine. How can you configure bindings to improve performance on this server? Select the best response.**

B. Unbind IPX/SPX from the Workstation service and unbind TCP/IP from the server service.

20. CORRECT ANSWER: B

Because the server is providing only IPX/SPX packets for users' requests, unbinding IPX/SPX from the Workstation service does not produce a problem and lowers network activity overhead. A similar scenario exists if only TCP/IP is used for browsing. Unbinding TCP/IP from the Server service likewise reduces network activity overhead.

Removing TCP/IP also removes the capability to browse IP resources. Unbinding TCP/IP from the Workstation service or unbinding IPX/SPX from the Server service interrupts the listed network activities.

21. **What does the counter Network: Bytes Total/sec measure?**

C. Bytes sent to and from the network

21. CORRECT ANSWER: C

The Bytes Total/sec counter of the Network object is used to measure the number of bytes sent both to and from the network.

22. You are monitoring the counter Network: Bytes Total/sec in Performance Monitor. On each server, you tally the total amount; you realize that this amount is nearly the total amount of maximum throughput for your network medium. What does this mean you need to do to increase productivity?

B. You need to segment the network.

22. CORRECT ANSWER: B

By segmenting the network, the amount of traffic effectively is reduced for each network segment created. The entire LAN no longer carries all the packets over the entire network, reducing the overall load.

Simply installing faster network cards does not completely alleviate the problem because network hubs, and possibly improved cabling, also might need to be installed. Adding more memory does not address the issue of near-capacity traffic, and upgrading network drivers does not directly address network capacity issues.

IDENTIFYING PERFORMANCE BOTTLENECKS

1. After logging system performance to a log file during peak hours over the course of several days, you decide to analyze the resulting information log. You notice that the Available Bytes counter of the Memory object routinely fell to 3MB. What situation occurred on this server that indicates a performance concern? Select the best response.

   A. No disk paging occurred during the logging period.

   B. The system routinely experienced periods of excessive disk activity on the drive containing the pagefile.

   C. Windows NT increased the size of the pagefile several times.

   D. The pagefile was increased by 3MB.

   E. Nothing can be assumed.

2. Concerning the Committed Bytes counter of the Memory object, at what point should the user consider it necessary to add more RAM to the server? Select the best response.

   A. When the amount of committed memory exceeds twice the amount of physical memory available on the server

   B. When the amount of committed memory equals zero

   C. When the Committed Bytes counter exceeds the physical memory plus 11MB

   D. When the Committed Bytes counter exceeds the Available Bytes counter

   E. When the amount of committed bytes exceeds the physical memory available on the server

3. Which of the following symptoms generally are present when a server is suffering from a memory shortage, as confirmed by the appropriate Performance Monitor counters? Select all that apply.

   A. Busy processors

   B. Low disk space

   C. A high level of disk activity on the drive containing the pagefile

   D. Slow response times in applications

   E. Slow boot times

4. When viewing the Pages/sec counter of the memory object in Performance Monitor, you notice that, during times of fairly routine operation, the value of Pages/sec sometimes spikes above 3 but usually hovers around 2 Pages/sec? This indicates a problem that can be solved by which of the following steps? Select all that apply.

A. Stop using Performance Monitor.

B. Add more RAM.

C. Increase the size of the pagefile.

D. Add a pagefile segment to another drive.

E. Move the pagefile from off the boot drive.

5. **You recently have become aware that your NT Server's processor seems to be running at a significantly high level of activity. Although not consistently high, you do notice that it routinely spikes up to a high level (95 percent) for protracted periods of time. Which of the following might explain this behavior without implying that the processor is under-powered for this system? Select all that apply.**

A. Many interrupts are being handled by the processor during the suspected times of high activity.

B. A severe memory shortage with system.

C. A member of a software-based RAID level 5 hard drive array has failed.

D. The pagefile on the system is too small, causing constant pagefile increases.

E. A second processor should be added to the system.

6. **While using Performance Monitor to analyze the potential of the processor as a source of a future bottleneck, you watch the System: Processor Queue Length**

counter. **You happily notice that the counter appears to be steady on a reading of zero. What is a possible explanation for this reading? Select the best response.**

A. Your system is running smoothly; no problem currently exists.

B. You have not turned on the disk counters by running the `diskperf` command.

C. A thread-specific counter is not currently being monitored in Performance Monitor.

D. A processor-specific counter is not currently being monitored in Performance Monitor.

7. **A slow hard disk generally is considered one of the biggest potential bottlenecks in a system. This primarily is due to the fact that a slow hard drive could poten-tially affect which of the following system activities? Select all that apply.**

A. Swap file performance

B. Application loading

C. Booting

D. Data retrieval

E. Memory paging

8. **While using Performance Monitor, you track the performance of Physical Disk: Disk Queue Length. You suspect that the disk is a bottleneck. What setting indi-cates that this disk is beginning to be a bottleneck? Select the best response.**

A. A value exceeding 10.

B. A value exceeding 5.

C. A value exceeding 1.

D. A value exceeding 2.

E. This counter alone does not indicate that the hard drive is a bottleneck.

9. **While using Performance Monitor, you track the performance of Physical Disk: Disk Queue Length. You determine that** the disk is a bottleneck. What can you use to improve this? Select all that apply.

A. RAID

B. Memory

C. Faster disk interface

D. Asynchronous disk drivers

ANSWER KEY

1. B	4. B	7. A-B-C-D-E
2. E	5. A-B	8. D
3. A-C	6. C	9. A-C-D

ANSWERS & EXPLANATIONS

IDENTIFYING PERFORMANCE BOTTLENECKS

1. After logging system performance to a log file during peak hours over the course of several days, you decide to analyze the resulting information log. You notice that the Available Bytes counter of the Memory object routinely fell below 3MB. What situation occurred on this server that indicates a performance concern? Select the best response.

   B. The system routinely experienced periods of excessive disk activity on the drive containing the pagefile.

1. CORRECT ANSWER: B

The Available Bytes counter associated with the Memory object refers to the amount of physical memory still available. When this value drops below 4MB, excessive paging is said to occur. Excessive disk activity has occurred on the drive that holds the pagefile.

When Available Bytes approaches, the amount of paging increases more and more. Some degree of paging certainly occurred. No assumption can be made that the swap actually was increased by Windows NT during this time.

2. Concerning the Committed Bytes counter of the Memory object, at what point should the user consider it necessary to add more RAM to the server? Select the best response.

   E. When the amount of committed bytes exceeds the physical memory available on the server

2. CORRECT ANSWER: E

The Committed Bytes countermeasures the amount of virtual memory committed to physical RAM or to a pagefile space. At the point when Committed Bytes exceeds the physical memory (or RAM) on the system, more RAM should be added to the system.

If Committed Bytes exceeds either twice the physical memory or the physical memory plus 11, the system already has passed the point at which RAM should have been added. More RAM still should be added, but the initial point at which more RAM was needed has passed. If Committed Bytes equals zero, no data has been committed to pagefile and no additional RAM is required.

3. Which of the following symptoms generally are present when a server is suffering from a memory shortage, as confirmed by the appropriate Performance Monitor counters? Select all that apply.

   A. Busy processors
   C. A high level of disk activity on the drive containing the pagefile

3. CORRECT ANSWERS: A - C

When a system suffers from memory shortages, the processor becomes increasingly busy with requests to process paging memory in and to process out memory to disk. Consequently, the disk(s) containing the pagefiles experiences a high level of activity because the pagefile is almost constantly being written to and read from.

Low disk space can be an indirect result of a large pagefile, which itself can indicate a memory shortage or can be the result of a large amount of memory already in the system (hence, an equally large pagefile). Either way, this is not a direct result or a general occurrence in a memory-shortage situation. Slow response times can be the result of a memory shortage because application files are waiting to be loaded into memory while other data is paged out. Numerous other scenarios, however, can explain slow application boot times. Slow boot times also can be the result of a memory shortage severe enough to require virtual memory even before completely booting up. This certainly is not considered a general scenario.

4. When viewing the Pages/sec counter of the memory object in Performance Monitor, you notice that, during times of fairly routine operation, the value of Pages/sec sometimes spikes above 3 but usually hovers around 2 Pages/sec? This indicates a problem that can be solved by which of the following steps? Select the best response.

   B. Add more RAM

4. CORRECT ANSWER: B

A consistent value of 2 or higher in the Pages/sec counter of the memory object is a sure sign that more RAM should be added to the system.

Not using the Performance Monitor obviously is a Three Stooges approach to fixing the problem. This answer is provided only as a weak attempt at humor. Increasing the size of the pagefile provides more storage for these excessive pages, but the rate of paging (> 2/sec) still is not addressed. Moving the pagefile from the boot drive increases virtual memory performance. Once again, however, it does not address the rate at which virtual memory is utilized.

5. You recently have become aware that your NT Server's processor seems to be active at a significantly high level of activity for quite some time. Although not consistently high, you do notice that it routinely spikes up to a high level (95 percent) for protracted periods of time. Which of the following might explain this behavior without implying that the processor is under-powered for this system? Select all that apply.

5. CORRECT ANSWERS: A - B

When an unusually large number of hardware interrupts are requested by devices—the result of high activity or a hardware failure of some type—the processor can become especially busy trying to process those interrupts. This surfaces as spikes in processor activity. In addition, severe memory shortages in a system result in excessive paging, which correlates into a high degree of processor activity as the processor attempts to process the needs of the paging.

A. Many interrupts are being handled by the processor during the suspected times of high activity.

B. A severe memory shortage with system.

In a system that uses a software-based (NT-based) RAID level 5 disk array, failure of a member of the array results in higher levels of processor activity. This is because the system processor not only is responsible for generating the parity information, it is responsible for re-creating the inaccessible data from the parity information when requested. This increases processor activity but not for a protracted period of time. If a pagefile is too small for the needs of a system, this situation occasionally causes an increase in the size of the pagefile, but it does not result in protracted periods of high processor activity.

EXAM TIP

The option of adding a second processor eliminates, or severely reduces, high levels of processor activity. It is important to note, however, that the exam words questions in such a way to eliminate certain options. This question plainly requested an answer that did not imply insufficient processing power. The addition of a second processor certainly implies the current processor is underpowered.

6. While using Performance Monitor to analyze the potential of the processor as a source of a potential bottleneck, you watch the System: Processor Queue Length counter. You happily notice that the counter appears to be steady on a reading of zero. What is a possible explanation for this reading? Select the best response.

C. A thread-specific counter is not currently being monitored in Performance Monitor.

6. CORRECT ANSWER: C

The processor queue length cannot be monitored properly if the system is not actively monitoring a thread-related counter. Only when monitoring a thread counter can Performance Monitor access information to determine and to monitor how many threads currently are waiting for execution.

Monitoring the Processor Queue Length counter should indicate an occasional value above zero on most systems. A consistent value of zero generally implies that something is not completely correct. The `diskperf` program and the disk counters do not have any direct relationship to the proper functioning of the Processor Queue Length counter. The Processor Queue Length counter is a processor-specific counter. No other processor-specific counter is inherently required for proper function of this counter.

7. A slow hard disk generally is considered one of the biggest potential bottlenecks in a system. This primarily is due to the fact that a slow hard drive could potentially affect which of the following system activities? Select all that apply.

   A. Swap file performance

   B. Application loading

   C. Booting

   D. Data retrieval

   E. Memory paging

7. CORRECT ANSWERS: A - B - C - D - E

A slow hard drive in a system also can generate other issues with system performance. Swap file performance is affected by a slow hard drive because the pagefile involves writing information to the hard drive. Application loading is affected by a slower hard drive because the application files are read from the hard drive. System booting can be negatively affected because of system files being read from the hard drive into memory prior to loading. Memory paging, which inherently involves writing to the hard drive, also is affected by slow hard drives.

8. While using Performance Monitor, you track the performance of Physical Disk: Disk Queue Length. You suspect that the disk is a bottleneck. What setting indicates that this disk is beginning to be a bottleneck? Select the best response.

   D. A value exceeding 2

8. CORRECT ANSWER: D

Whenever the value of the Disk Queue Length counter exceeds 2, it should be considered a sign of a bottleneck on the system.

9. While using Performance Monitor, you track the performance of Physical Disk: Disk Queue Length. You determine that the disk is a bottleneck. What can you use to improve this? Select all that apply.

   A. RAID

   C. Faster disk interface

   D. Asynchronous disk drivers

9. CORRECT ANSWERS: A - C - D

Implementing a RAID disk array can provide numerous hard disk performance improvements. Faster controllers can help speed up disk access by increasing data processing. Asynchronous disk drivers boost performance.

Adding memory to the system cannot help improve excessive disk queuing.

CHAPTER SUMMARY

In addition to the numerous Performance Monitor issues of which you should be aware, a few additional concepts should be briefly mentioned. Although there is little to tune in NT itself, you still have several reasons to monitor system performance, as follows:

- To optimize specific tasks. If you want to optimize a particular application on your server, monitoring system performance can tell you whether changing your hardware will help your application run faster.

- To troubleshoot performance problems. One of the most difficult types of performance problems to troubleshoot is diagnosing transient network problems.

- To plan for future needs. Another reason to monitor performance is that it enables you to detect changes in the way the server is being used by users.

In addition to the Performance Monitor objects and counters already mentioned, you also should take notice of the Server object. The Server component itself is responsible for handling all SMB-based requests for sessions and for file and print services. If the Server service becomes the bottleneck, requests from clients are denied. This forces retries and creates slower response times and increased traffic. The following are the counters:

- Bytes Total/sec. This counter measures the number of bytes sent to and received from the network.

- Logon/sec. This counter measures logon activity to predict whether you need to add a BDC on the segment.

- Pool Nonpaged Failures. This counter measures the number of times a request from the server to allocate memory from the nonpaged pool failed. It generally is an indication that the computer's physical memory is not sufficient.

- Pool Paged Failures. This counter measures the number of times a request from the server to allocate memory from the paged pool failed. It generally is an indication that the computer's physical memory or pagefile size is not sufficient.

For a Performance Monitor counter value to be of use, baseline values must first be determined to compare against. Many of the counters Performance Monitor provides cannot be interpreted without some baseline data to which to compare it.

It is a good idea to regularly log performance from your servers at various times of the day so you have appropriate baselines with which to compare.

CHAPTER 6

Troubleshooting

The questions in this chapter address several major components of troubleshooting in a Windows NT server environment. You will examine the appropriate course of action to resolve issues ranging from installation failures to access permissions. You also will look at steps that can be taken to promote fault tolerance.

Troubleshooting a Windows NT environment usually is no different than daily life. Some people, for example, wake up every day to the soothing sound of an alarm clock. The night before, a simple routine is executed. You make sure the clock is plugged in, the proper time is set to wake you, and the selection is made for radio or buzzer. If you don't wake at the desired time for some reason, the troubleshooting begins. This might sound somewhat simplified compared to a Windows NT network, but these situations are the same in principle. Troubleshooting is simply a method for detecting what step of execution did not perform as expected.

Troubleshooting can be defined as recommending that certain steps be performed, such as checking to make sure an item is plugged in or double-checking that a printer is online. Troubleshooting procedure recommendations can be found on Web sites, in newsgroups, and in this book. The bottom line, however, is that the right method is the one that works best for you.

OBJECTIVES

This chapter helps prepare you for the exam by covering the following objectives:

Choose the appropriate course of action to take to resolve installation failures.

▶ Problems can occur during any installation, be it a computer program or your child's gift on Christmas Eve. You will examine the different elements involved in installation and how to address any hurdles that might arise.

Choose the appropriate course of action to take to resolve boot failures.

▶ Even after a successful installation, issues might surface involving the boot process. You will examine the steps involved in the boot process and the different methods to achieve success.

continues

Choose the appropriate course of action to take to resolve configuration errors.

▶ Configuration errors can be an ongoing issue. Every time you add new software or hardware, you increase the risk of a configuration error taking place. This chapter examines how to resolve these errors so you will be better prepared next time.

Choose the appropriate course of action to take to resolve printer problems.

▶ Every network environment has a printer or printing problem. Similar in nature to configuration errors, printer problems also can be an ongoing issue. Even after a successful installation of printers, they can get offline or run out of paper. You will examine the steps involved in reducing the amount of time spent finding and resolving the issues at hand.

Choose the appropriate course of action to take to resolve RAS problems.

▶ Remote Access Server (RAS) issues can vary widely, depending on the actual use of RAS. You will focus on the main issues surrounding RAS and how best to resolve them.

Choose the appropriate course of action to take to resolve connectivity problems.

▶ Connectivity problems, like RAS problems, can be as widespread as its use. You will focus on the Windows NT perspective, coupled with the connectivity of a Windows client.

Choose the appropriate course of action to take to resolve resource access problems and permission problems.

▶ So far, this chapter has discussed resolving issues surrounding installation, connectivity, and configuration. This objective focuses on the resources themselves and how to better manage and troubleshoot a user's access to those resources.

Choose the appropriate course of action to take to resolve fault-tolerance failures. Fault-tolerance methods include the following:

• **Tape backup**

• **Mirroring**

• **Stripe set with parity**

• **Disk duplexing**

▶ This final objective introduces fault tolerance. The current fabric of business society demands that information be available 24 hours a day, 7 days a week. This is a tremendous responsibility for the individual given this task. Making sure a Windows NT network is up and running on a continuous basis certainly provides a challenge. To help you meet this challenge, this objective explores the resolution of fault-tolerance methods. You will examine the available options including tape backups, mirroring, stripe set with parity (which should not be confused with just a stripe set), and disk duplexing.

RESOLVING INSTALLATION FAILURES

1. **You are installing NT Server from CD. During the installation phase, NT cannot recognize the CD-ROM. What can you do to install NT Server? Select the best response.**

   A. Choose another CD-ROM controller that the unsupported CD-ROM emulates during the installation phase.

   B. Boot to another operating system that supports the CD-ROM and run `winnt.exe` from the CD.

   C. Contact the manufacturer of the CD-ROM and install an updated driver.

   D. Contact Microsoft to obtain NT Server on floppies.

   E. You must install NT from a CD-ROM listed on the Hardware Compatibility List.

2. **When installing NT Server as a BDC, which of the following is *not* a requirement? Select all that apply.**

   A. The BDC must have a unique NetBIOS name.

   B. The PDC must be operational and accessible on the network.

   C. A logical drive must be formatted with NTFS that will contain the Domain account database.

   D. A computer account must be created in the Domain that matches the name of the new BDC.

   E. The Domain Administrator account must be used to install the BDC.

3. **You are installing NT Server to act as a standalone server. During the network installation process, you receive an error that indicates a dependency service has failed to start. What is most likely the problem? Select the best response.**

   A. The NetBEUI protocol was not installed. This protocol must be installed during setup, but it can be removed later.

   B. The network interface card driver you selected is not compatible with the NIC installed on the server.

   C. You accidentally selected the backup domain controller, and the PDC was not available.

   D. The computer or domain name you selected already is in use on the network.

   E. You selected IIS to be installed, but you did not install TCP/IP.

4. **You want to repair a damaged installation of NT. You have the Emergency Repair Disk and the installation CD, but you do not have the three installation floppies. What process should you use to create another set of installation floppies? Select the best response.**

   A. Run `winnt.exe /b` from the installation CD on an MS-DOS–based computer.

   B. Run `winnt32.exe` from the installation CD on an MS-DOS–based computer.

   C. Run `setup.exe` from the installation CD on an MS-DOS–based computer.

   D. Run `winnt.exe` from the installation CD on an NT-based computer.

   E. Run `setup.exe` from the installation CD on an NT-based computer.

5. **During the initial boot of NT after installing it for the first time, you receive the message The dependency service failed to start. Where should you look to troubleshoot the problem?**

   A. `Bootlog.txt`

   B. `Device.log`

   C. `Detect.log`

   D. The Services option in the Control Panel

   E. Event Viewer

ANSWER KEY

1. B	3. D	5. E
2. C-E	4. A	

RESOLVING INSTALLATION FAILURES

1. You are installing NT Server from CD. During the installation phase, NT cannot recognize the CD-ROM. What can you do to install NT Server? Select the best response.

B. Boot to another operating system that supports the CD-ROM and run winnt.exe **from the CD.**

1. CORRECT ANSWER: B

This popular question type has appeared on a couple different Microsoft Windows NT exams. Microsoft supports answer B because it is the most resourceful method when considering time and effort expensed during a setup. Windows NT has been tested with several hardware components, all of which are listed in the Hardware compatibility list. If Windows NT does not recognize the CD, the installation process from the CD-ROM cannot continue. Several other methods, however, can be employed to succeed. One such method involves installing from a network share; another is as simple as copying the source files to the local hard disk and running the installation using the Winnt.exe /b command. Windows NT can be installed by using a CD-ROM that is not on the HCL. Currently, Windows NT does not ship on floppy disks. Although an updated driver might work, it is not the best answer.

2. When installing NT Server as a BDC, which of the following is *not* a requirement? Select all that apply.

C. A logical drive must be formatted with NTFS that will contain the Domain account database.

E. The Domain Administrator account must be used to install the BDC.

2. CORRECT ANSWERS: C-E

All Windows machines must have a unique NetBIOS name, and the BDC must have access to the PDC. In addition to these requirements, a computer account must be created on the PDC. This can be accomplished during the configuration of the BDC or prior to installation. Neither a domain administrator account nor an NTFS partition is required to install a BDC.

3. You are installing NT Server to act as a standalone server. During the network installation process, you receive an error that indicates a dependency service has failed to start. What is most likely the problem? Select the best response.

3. CORRECT ANSWER: D

When configuring the network settings on a Windows NT machine, the computername must be unique to connect to the network with success. Although NetBEUI coupled with a bad Network Interface Card (NIC) can cause problems, this

D. The computer or domain name you selected already is in use on the network.

4. You want to repair a damaged installation of NT. You have the Emergency Repair Disk and the installation CD, but you do not have the three installation floppies. What process should you use to create another set of installation floppies? Select the best response.

A. Run `winnt.exe /b` from the installation CD on an MS-DOS–based computer.

5. During the initial boot of NT after installing it for the first time, you receive the message `The dependency service failed to start`. Where should you look to troubleshoot the problem?

E. Event Viewer

combination of protocol and NIC do not produce the service error outlined in the question. As for the inaccessibility of the PDC, an error message stating that it couldn't find the PDC displays. When installing Windows NT Server and selecting to include IIS, the TCP/IP option is grayed out. You are not allowed to uninstall.

4. CORRECT ANSWER: A

When faced with the troubleshooting issue in this question, you are armed with an option. Running `WINNT.exe /OX` enables you to create the three Windows NT boot disks without running the installation program. If you have access to the CD, however, running `winnt.exe /b` starts the installation of Windows NT without the three boot disks. This enables you to utilize your Emergency Repair Disk and to bring your system back to life. `Winnt32.exe` must be run from a Windows NT environment; `Winnt.exe` must be run from an MS-DOS environment. The `Setup` command is not an option when installing Windows NT.

5. CORRECT ANSWER: E

Windows NT has some wonderful utilities and tools to aid you in troubleshooting. One of these utilities is the Event Viewer. When rebooting a Windows NT machine, errors and information pertaining to applications, security, and the system are recorded in the Event Viewer. If auditing is enabled, additional information is written to the appropriate log in the Event Viewer. The additional log files created during the boot process have definite advantages when troubleshooting; however, the `dependency service failed to start` message can be directly referenced in Event Viewer.

FURTHER REVIEW

RESOLVING INSTALLATION FAILURES

Microsoft has identified the following common installation problems and solutions:

- Media errors. If there seems to be a problem with the Windows NT Installation CD-ROM or floppy disks, ask Microsoft Sales to replace the disk. Call 800-426-9400.

- Insufficient disk space. Delete unnecessary files and folders, compress NTFS partitions, reformat an existing partition, use Setup to create more space, or create a new partition with more space.

- Nonsupported SCSI adapter. Boot to a different operating system (one that can use the SCSI adapter) and run WINNT from the installation CD-ROM. Try a network installation and replace the unsupported adapter with a supported adapter on the Hardware Compatibility List.

- Failure of dependency service to start. Verify the protocol and adapter configuration in the Control Panel's Network application. Make sure the local computer has a unique name.

- Inability to connect to the domain controller. Verify the account's name and password, make sure the domain name is correct, make sure the primary domain controller is functioning properly, and verify protocol and adapter configuration settings in the Control Panel's Network application. If you just finished installing or upgrading, make sure the domain account for the computer has been reset (added to the network again).

- Error in assigning domain name. Make sure the domain name isn't identical to another domain or computer name on the network.

Server cannot be installed strictly from disks or floppies. To install Server 4.0 on a previous version of NT and keep all the settings, install it in the same directory as the old version. If you install into any other directory, you have not upgraded; you have created a dual-boot machine. Windows 95/98 cannot be upgraded to NT Server because of incompatibilities in the Registry, the drivers, and so on. You must install NT into a separate directory from Windows 95/98 and must reinstall all applications.

Three startup disks are made during installation. If you lose these disks, you can re-create them by running WINNT /OX. If you don't have the three startup disks and you need to install Windows NT, you can use the WINNT /b switch to run an installation and to bypass the boot floppies.

RESOLVING BOOT FAILURES

1. After doing routine maintenance on a backup domain controller, the server's video card fails. You want to take this opportunity to upgrade the video card, but you are worried about the compatibility of the old card's video drivers and the new video card you are about to install. What steps must you take after the new video card is installed? Select all that apply.

   A. Reinstall NT Server and perform an upgrade.

   B. When NT boots, select the [VGA Mode].

   C. Press the Spacebar to invoke the Last Known Good configuration.

   D. Boot off the Emergency Repair Disk and install the new video drivers.

   E. Install the new video drivers using the Display option in the Control Panel.

2. You install your boot partition on mirrored SCSI drives with the BIOS enabled. The primary drive of the mirror fails. Which of the following is the syntax in the BOOT.INI file that will allow NT to boot off the remaining portion of the mirror? Select the best response.

   A. multi(0)disk(0)rdisk(1)part(1)\winnt

   B. multi(0)disk(0)rdisk(0)part(2)\winnt

   C. multi(0)disk(1)rdisk(0)part(1)\winnt

   D. scsi(0)disk(1)rdisk(0)part(1)\winnt

   E. scsi(0)disk(0)rdisk(1)part(1)\winnt

3. Your NT server with a mirrored system and boot partition has lost the primary drive in the mirror. What steps must you take to get NT to boot as quickly as possible? Select the best response.

   A. Format a floppy with MS-DOS.

      Copy NTLDR, NTDETECT.COM, and BOOT.INI to the floppy.

      Make no changes to the files on the floppy.

   B. Format a floppy with MS-DOS.

      Copy NTLDR, NTDETECT.COM, and BOOT.INI to the floppy.

      Edit the BOOT.INI file on the floppy to point to the remaining HD containing the NT system files.

   C. Format a floppy on NT.

      Copy NTLDR, NTDETECT.COM, and BOOT.INI to the floppy.

      Make no changes to the files on the floppy.

   D. Format a floppy on NT.

      Copy NTLDR, NTDETECT.COM, and BOOT.INI to the floppy.

      Edit the BOOT.INI file on the floppy to point to the remaining HD containing the NT system files.

E. Boot from the Emergency Repair Disk.

Follow the online prompts and break the mirror.

4. **After installing a new UPS system on your NT server, you begin to experience problems with your mouse. You suspect there is a conflict with the serial mouse and the UPS interface. What parameter should you use in the `Boot.ini` file to correct the problem? Select the best response.**

   A. `/debug`

   B. `/SOS`

   C. `/noserialmice`

   D. `/crashdebug`

   E. `/debugport`

5. **After installing a new hard disk onto your NT server, you receive the following error:**

   ```
   Windows NT could not start because the
   following file is missing or corrupt:
   <winnt root>\system32\NTOSKRNL.EXE
   Please Reinstall a copy of the above
   file.
   ```

   What is most likely the cause of this problem? Select the best response.

   A. The System files were damaged when the new hard drive was powered on.

B. The configuration of the hard disks has changed, making the path in `boot.ini` invalid.

C. The `NTOSKRNL.EXE` file is corrupt.

D. The `NTLDR` file is corrupt.

E. There is no problem. NT always displays this message during the initial boot after the hard disk configurations have changed. Reboot NT and the problem will be solved.

6. **A user calls you and says he has somehow damaged his NT server. The user further states that he does not have an emergency repair disk for his computer. How can you create an ERD for the user's computer? Select the best response.**

   A. Run `RDISK.EXE` and create an ERD for the user.

   B. Run `RDISK.EXE`, connect to the user's server, and create an ERD remotely.

   C. Copy your ERD and modify `boot.ini` to reflect the user's NT server configuration.

   D. Format a floppy on NT and copy over all the NT boot files. The disk now can be used in place of the ERD for repair purposes.

   E. You cannot create an ERD from a machine that is intended to be used on another computer.

ANSWER KEY

1. B-E	3. D	5. B
2. A	4. C	6. E

ANSWERS & EXPLANATIONS

RESOLVING BOOT FAILURES

1. After doing routine maintenance on a backup domain controller, the server's video card fails. You want to take this opportunity to upgrade the video card, but you are worried about the compatibility of the old card's video drivers and the new video card you are about to install. What steps must you take after the new video card is installed? Select all that apply.

   B. When NT boots, select the [VGA Mode].

   E. Install the new video drivers using the Display option in the Control Panel.

1. CORRECT ANSWERS: B-E

During the Windows NT boot process, the user is presented with boot menu options. Selecting the [VGA Mode] option enables Windows NT to load the base video drivers, similar to safe mode in Windows 95. After the machine is up and running, the user can make the necessary modifications. Reinstalling Windows NT is extremely time-consuming; invoking the Last Known Good configuration loads the old video drivers. Meanwhile, the Emergency Repair Disk is not a bootable disk.

2. You install your boot partition on mirrored SCSI drives with the BIOS enabled. The primary drive of the mirror fails. Which of the following is the syntax in the BOOT.INI file that will allow NT to boot off the remaining portion of the mirror? Select the best response.

   A. multi(0)disk(0)rdisk(1)part(1)\winnt

2. CORRECT ANSWER: A

This question's wording is very important. The first sentence states that the mirror is on a SCSI controller with the BIOS enabled; thus, it is using the multi option. Answer A is correct because the rdisk value now points to the second disk indicated by rdisk(1). Answer B is incorrect because it points to the same failed disk, only the second partition is referenced. Answer C is incorrect because the disk value is used rather than the rdisk value. Answers D and E are incorrect because the SCSI value is used. SCSI should be used only in circumstances in which the BIOS is disabled. Answer E also can be eliminated as a possibility because it uses the rdisk value.

3. Your NT server with a mirrored system and boot partition has lost the primary drive in the mirror. What steps must you take to get NT to boot as quickly as possible? Select the best response.

   D. Format a floppy on NT.
      Copy NTLDR, NTDETECT.COM, and Boot.ini to the floppy.

3. CORRECT ANSWER: D

This is a fairly straightforward question. Answer A is incorrect for two reasons. First, the file was formatted in DOS; second, the boot.ini file was never updated. Answer B is incorrect because the floppy was formatted in DOS. C is incorrect because the boot.ini file was not updated. Answer E is

Edit the `boot.ini` file on the floppy to point to the remaining HD containing the NT system files.

4. **After installing a new UPS system on your NT server, you begin to experience problems with your mouse. You suspect there is a conflict with the serial mouse and the UPS interface. What parameter should you use in the Boot.ini file to correct the problem? Select the best response.**

   C. `/noserialmice`

5. **After installing a new hard disk onto your NT server, you receive the following error:**

   ```
   Windows NT could not start
   because the following file is
   missing or corrupt:

   <winnt
   root>\system32\NTOSKRNL.EXE

   Please Reinstall a copy of
   the above file.
   ```

   What is most likely the cause of this problem? Select the best response.

   B. The configuration of the hard disks has changed, making the path in `BOOT.INI` invalid.

6. **A user calls you and says he has somehow damaged his NT server. The user further states that he does not have an emergency repair disk for his computer. How can you create an ERD for the user's computer? Select the best response.**

   E. You cannot create an ERD from a machine that is intended to be used on another computer.

incorrect simply because the Emergency Repair Disk is not a bootable disk.

4. CORRECT ANSWER: C

Answer C is correct because it tells NT which serial ports not to scan for a mouse. Answer A is incorrect because it is used only to put NT in a debugging mode when programmers are testing code. Answer B is incorrect because it shows only the device drivers as they load. Answer D is incorrect because it is used to have NT automatically reboot in the event of a blue screen. Answer E is incorrect because it tells NT to which port to send the debug information when a crash occurs.

5. CORRECT ANSWER: B

Answer B is correct because the location of the physical hard disk configuration has possibly changed, requiring the update of the BOOT.INI file. Answer A is incorrect because the error typically has nothing to do with damaged files. The user most likely did not corrupt the files during the installation of the new disk. Answer C is incorrect because, most likely, the file is not referenced by the BOOT.INI file and is perfectly fine. Answer D is incorrect because, if NTLDR was corrupt, the error would have been displayed well before the NTOSKRNL.EXE file is accessed. Answer E is not correct because NT never fixes itself.

6. CORRECT ANSWER: E

Answer E is correct because each machine has its own Registry. A Registry reflects only its own system and cannot be used on another machine, even if the machines are similar in hardware and configuration. Answer A is incorrect because the ERD created won't work on the user's machine. Answer B is incorrect because connecting to another machine through the RDISK.EXE program is not supported. Answer C is not correct for the same reasons Answer A is not correct. Answer D is not correct because it describes the steps needed to create a boot disk. A boot disk is very different than an ERD.

RESOLVING BOOT FAILURES

The explanation in this section supports questions 1–6.

The boot process is one of the most common sources of problems in Windows NT. The following information not only will help you with the exam questions, it also will enable you to bolster your real-world troubleshooting confidence. When troubleshooting boot failures, the cause usually is a lost or corrupt boot file. Try booting from the Windows NT boot disk and performing an emergency repair (a process described later in this section) if necessary.

The boot process begins when your computer accesses the hard drive's Master Boot Record (MBR) to load Windows NT. If your system fails during the Power On Self Test (POST), the problem isn't NT-related; instead, it is a hardware issue. What happens after the MBR's program loads depends on the type of computer you are using.

If one of the important boot files is missing or corrupt, Windows NT can't boot correctly. If NTLDR, NTDTECT.COM, NTBootDD.sys (SCSI only), or NTOSKRNL.EXE fail, NT displays a message that tells you the name of the missing file. Use the Emergency Repair Process to restore the system.

If BOOT.INI is missing, NTLDR tries to start Windows NT without consulting BOOT.INI or the boot menu. This works as long as Windows NT is installed in the default \Winnt directory on the first partition of the first disk. If Windows NT is installed in a different directory, NTLDR cannot find

it and issues an error message stating that the file \<winntroot>\system32\ntoskrnl.exe is missing or corrupt.

If BOOT.INI contains an invalid path name or if a BOOT.INI path includes an invalid device, the boot fails. Verify all BOOT.INI paths. If possible, boot from a floppy and edit BOOT.INI to fix the problem. The Emergency Repair Process described later in this chapter can restore BOOT.INI if the error stems from a recent change.

The Intel Boot Sequence

On Intel x86-based computers, the boot sector of the active partition loads a file called NTLDR. Similar to IO.SYS for MS-DOS or Windows 95, NTLDR is a hidden, system, read-only file in the root of your system partition. It is responsible for loading the rest of the operating system, and it carries out the following steps:

1. NTLDR switches the processor to the 32-bit flat-memory model necessary to address 4GB of RAM.

2. NTLDR then starts the minifile system driver necessary for accessing the system and boot partitions. This minifile system driver contains just enough code to read files at boot time. The full file systems are loaded later.

3. NTLDR displays a Boot Loader menu that enables the user to choose which operating system to load and then waits for a response. The options for the Boot Loader

menu are stored in a hidden, read-only file in the root of your system partition named BOOT.INI.

4. If Windows NT is the selected system, NTLDR invokes the hardware-detection routine to determine the hardware required. NTDETECT.COM (the same program that detects the hardware during NTSETUP) performs the hardware detection. NTDETECT.COM builds the hardware list and returns it to NTLDR. NTDETECT.COM is a hidden, system, and read-only file in the root of the system partition.

5. NTLDR loads the kernel of the operating system. The kernel is called NTOSKRNL.EXE, and you can find it in the <winnt_root>\SYSTEM32 directory. At this point, the screen clears and displays OS Loader V4.xx.

6. NTLDR loads the Hardware Abstraction Layer (HAL). The HAL is a single file (HAL.DLL) that contains the code necessary to mask interrupts and exceptions from the kernel.

7. NTLDR loads SYSTEM, the HKEY_LOCAL_MACHINE\SYSTEM hive in the Registry. You can find the corresponding file in the <winnt_root>\SYSTEM32\CONFIG directory.

8. NTLDR loads the boot-time drivers. Boot-time drivers have a start value of 0. These values are loaded in the order in which they are listed in HKEY_LOCAL_MACHINE\SYSTEM\CurrentControlSet\ Control\ServiceGroupOrder. Each time a driver loads, a dot is added to the series following the OS Loader V4.00 at the top of the screen. If the /sos switch is used in

BOOT.INI, the name of each driver appears on a separate line as each is loaded. The drivers are not initialized yet.

9. NTLDR then passes control, along with the hardware list collected by NTDETECT.COM, to NTOSKRNL.EXE.

After NTOSKRNL.EXE takes control, the boot phase ends and the load phases begin.

The RISC Boot Sequence

On a RISC-based computer, the boot process is much simpler because the firmware does much of the work that NTLDR does on the Intel platform. RISC-based computers maintain hardware configuration in their firmware (also called non-volatile RAM), so they don't need NTDETECT.COM. Their firmware also contains a list of valid operating systems and their locations, so they don't need BOOT.INI either.

RISC-based machines don't look for the Intel-specific NTLDR to boot the operating system; instead, they always look for a file called OSLOADER.EXE. This file receives the hardware configuration data from the firmware. It then loads NTOSKRNL.EXE, HAL.DLL, and SYSTEM, and the boot process concludes.

Booting to Windows 95, MS-DOS, or OS/2

On Intel-based computers, you can install Windows NT with Windows 95 or MS-DOS. The boot loader screen offers the user a choice of Windows NT Workstation 4, Microsoft Windows, and MS-DOS. If the user chooses a non-Windows NT operating system, a file called BOOTSECT.DOS is loaded and executed. BOOTSECT.DOS is a hidden, system, read-only file in the root of the system partition. It contains the information that was present in the boot sector before Windows NT was installed. If a user chooses Windows 95 from the boot menu, for example, BOOTSECT.DOS loads IO.SYS and passes control to it.

BOOT.INI

To understand the BOOT.INI file, you must understand two things—the ARC syntax and the actual use of the file. Both topics are discussed in the sections that follow.

Because not all machines use MS-DOS–style paths (for example, c:\winnt) for referring to locations on a hard drive, Windows NT uses a cross-platform standard format called Advanced RISC Computer (ARC) within BOOT.INI. An ARC-compliant path consists of the following four parameters:

Parameter	Description
scsi(x) or multi(x)	Identifies the hardware adapter.
disk(y)	The SCSI bus number. Always is 0 if multi.
rdisk(z)	The physical drive number for multi. Is ignored for SCSI.
partition(a)	The logical partition number.

The first three parameters are zero-based; that is, the first physical IDE drive is rdisk(0), and the second is rdisk(1). The partition parameter, however, is one-based; the first partition on the drive is rdisk(0)partition(1).

All the parameters—even the ones that are ignored—must be present in the path. For instance, multi(0)disk(0)rdisk(0)partition(1) is a valid path even though disk(0) essentially is

unnecessary. The path multi(0)rdisk(0) partition(1), however, is not valid.

The first parameter almost always is multi, even for a SCSI controller. The only time you ever see SCSI in a BOOT.INI file is if the BIOS on the disk controller is turned off. When this is the case, don't worry; an additional hidden, system, read-only file, NTBOOTDD.SYS, is present in the root of the system partition. NTBOOTDD.SYS is a device driver necessary for accessing a SCSI controller that doesn't have an onboard BIOS or doesn't use INT 13 to identify hard disks. If this file is present, you probably see a scsi(x) entry in BOOT.INI. If you don't, you probably have upgraded from Windows NT 3.1 (where this setting is more common) without ever deleting the file.

The same holds true for a RISC-based computer. Look at the firmware entries for the operating system paths; you should see the same type of ARC-compliant paths.

NTLDR might invoke the Boot Loader menu, but BOOT.INI, an editable text file, controls it. (It is read-only, an attribute you must remove before editing it.) BOOT.INI is the only INI file that Windows NT uses—if indeed you can actually say NT uses it. After all, Windows NT is not loaded when this file is called on.

BOOT.INI has only two sections, [boot loader] and [operating systems], which are covered next.

[boot loader]

The [boot loader] section of BOOT.INI defines the operating system loaded if the user doesn't make a selection within a defined period of time. By default, you see something like the following:

```
[boot loader]
timeout=30
default=multi(0)disk(0)rdisk(0)
➥partition(1)\WINNT
```

The timeout parameter is the length of time (in seconds) that NTLDR has to wait for the user to make a decision. If timeout is set to 0, the default operating system loads immediately. If it is set to -1, the menu displays until the user makes a decision.

The default parameter defines the actual path to the directory that contains the files for the default operating system.

You can edit BOOT.INI directly, but remember that a mistyped character in NOTEPAD.EXE or EDIT.COM can result in your system not booting properly.

[operating systems]

The [operating systems] section contains a reference for every operating system available to the user from the Boot Loader menu as well as any special switches necessary to customize the Windows NT environment. One of these entries must match the default= entry in the [boot loader] section. Otherwise, you end up with two entries for the same OS onscreen, one of which has (default) following it.

Note that the paths are in ARC format with a label in quotation marks, which display as an on-screen selection. The following is an example of an [operating systems] section:

```
multi(0)disk(0)rdisk(0)partition(1)\WINNT=
➥Windows NT Workstation "Version 4.00"
```

Table 6.1 delineates several useful switches you can include in the [operating systems] section of BOOT.INI. The only way to include these switches is to manually edit the BOOT.INI file. (First remove the read-only attribute and then save the file as a text file.)

TABLE 6.1 SWITCHES UTILIZED IN [operating systems]

Switch	Description
/basevideo	Tells Windows NT to load the standard VGA driver rather than the optimized driver written for your video card. Selecting the VGA mode entry uses the standard VGA 640×480, 16-color driver that works with almost every video card.
/sos	Enumerates to the screen each driver as it loads during the kernel load phase. If Windows NT hangs during this phase, you can use the /sos switch to determine which driver caused the problem.
/noserialmice= ➥[COMx¦COMx,y,z_]	When Windows NT boots, NTDETECT.COM looks for the presence of serial mice (among other things). Sometimes this detection routine misfires and identifies modems or other devices as serial mice. When Windows NT loads and initializes, the serial port then is unavailable; the device is unusable because Windows NT is expecting a serial mouse. This switch tells NTDETECT.COM not to bother looking for serial mice. Used with a specific COM port(s), NTDETECT.COM still looks for serial mice but not on the port(s) specified.
/crashdebug	Turns on the Automatic Recovery and Restart capability, which you also can configure by using the Control Panel System application. In fact, when you configure this capability through Control Panel, you are adding this switch to the OS path in BOOT.INI.

continues

TABLE 6.1 Continued

Switch	Description
/nodebug	Programmers often use a special version of Windows NT that includes debugging symbols useful for tracking down problems with code. This version of Windows NT runs slowly compared to the retail version because of the extra overhead in tracking every piece of executing code. To turn off monitoring in this version of NT, add the /nodebug switch to the OS path in BOOT.INI.
/maxmem:n	Memory parity errors can be notoriously difficult to isolate. The /maxmem switch helps. When followed with a numeric value, this switch limits Windows NT's usable memory to the amount specified in the switch. This switch also is useful for developers using high-level workstations who want to simulate performance on a lower-level machine.
/scsiordinal:n	If your system has two identical SCSI controllers, you need a way to distinguish one from the other. The /scsiordinal switch is used to assign a value of 0 to the first controller and 1 to the second.

After all the initial drivers have loaded, the screen turns blue and the text height shrinks; the kernel initialization phase has begun. Now the kernel and all the drivers loaded in the previous phase are initialized. The Registry begins to flesh out. The CurrentControlSet is copied to the Clone set, and the volatile HARDWARE key is created. The system Registry hive is then scanned once more for higher-level drivers configured to start during system initialization.

Here the session manager scans the system hive for a list of programs that must run before Windows NT fully initializes. These programs can include AUTOCHK.EXE, the boot-time version of CHKDSK.EXE that examines and repairs any problems within a file system, or AUTOCONV.EXE, which converts a partition from FAT to NTFS. These boot-time programs are stored in the following:

```
HKEY_LOCAL_MACHINE\SYSTEM\CurrentControl
➥Set\Control\Session Manager\BootExecute
```

Following these programs, the page file(s) is created based on the locations specified in the following:

```
HKEY_LOCAL_MACHINE\SYSTEM\CurrentControl
➥Set\Control\Session Manager\Memory
➥Management
```

Next, the SOFTWARE hive loads from <winnt_root>\SYSTEM32\CONFIG. Session Manager then loads the CSR subsystem and any other required subsystems from the following:

```
HKEY_LOCAL_MACHINE\System\CurrentControl
➥Set\Control\Session Manager\SubSystems\
➥Required
```

Finally, drivers that have a start value of 2 (Automatic) load.

After the Win32 subsystem starts, the screen switches into GUI mode. The Winlogon process is invoked, and the Welcome dialog box opens. Although users can go ahead and log on at this point, the system might not respond for a few more moments while the Service Controller initializes automatic services.

The critical file at this point is SERVICES.EXE, which actually starts Alerter, Computer Browser, EventLog, Messenger, NetLogon, NT LM Security Support Provider, Server, TCP/IP NetBIOS

Helper, and Workstation. A missing or corrupt `SERVICES.EXE` cripples your Windows NT-based computer.

After a user successfully logs on to the system, the LastKnownGood control set is updated and the boot is considered good. Until a user logs on for the first time, however, the boot/load process technically remains unfinished. Therefore, a problem that Windows NT cannot detect but that a user can see (such as a video problem) can be resolved by falling back on the LastKnownGood configuration.

Control Sets and LastKnownGood

A *control set* is a collection of configuration information used during boot by Windows NT. A special control set, called *LastKnownGood*, plays a special role in troubleshooting the boot process.

After the system boots and a user logs on successfully, the current configuration settings are copied to the LastKnownGood control set in the Registry. These settings are preserved so that, if the system cannot boot successfully the next time a user attempts to log on, the system can fall back on the LastKnownGood configuration, which, as the name implies, is the last configuration known to facilitate a good boot. LastKnownGood is stored in the Registry under the following:

    HKEY_LOCAL_MACHINE\SYSTEM\CurrentControlSet

The key to understanding LastKnownGood is recognizing that it updates the first time a user logs on to Windows NT after a reboot.

To boot with the LastKnownGood configuration, press the Spacebar when prompted during the boot process. You are presented with the Hardware Profile/Configuration Recovery menu. Select a hardware profile and enter **L** for the LastKnownGood configuration.

Windows NT occasionally boots using LastKnownGood automatically, but this occurs only if the normal boot process produces severe or critical errors in loading device drivers.

LastKnownGood does not do you any good if files are corrupt or missing. You must use the Emergency Repair Process for aid with those problems.

The Emergency Repair Process

The installation process enables you to create an emergency repair directory and an emergency repair disk, both of which are backup copies of Registry information. (This comes in handy if you can't boot Windows NT because of missing or corrupt files.) This section examines ways in which the Emergency Repair Process can aid a troubled Windows NT installation.

Installation always creates the emergency repair directory. You can find it in `<winnt_root>\REPAIR`. You also can create an emergency repair disk.

Both the directory and the disk are computer-specific. Keep a separate emergency repair disk for each computer and tag it with the serial number of the computer.

Table 6.2 lists and describes the files on the emergency repair disk.

TABLE 6.2 FILES ON THE EMERGENCY REPAIR DISK

Files	Description
SETUP.LOG	A text file that contains the names of all the Windows NT installation files, along with the checksum values for each. If any files on your hard drive are missing or corrupt, the Emergency Repair Process should detect them with the aid of this hidden, system, read-only file.
SYSTEM._	A compressed copy of the Registry's SYSTEM hive. This is the Windows NT control set collection.
SAM._	A compressed copy of the Registry's SAM hive. This is the Windows NT user accounts database.
SECURITY.__	A compressed copy of the Registry's SECURITY hive. This is the Windows NT security information, which includes SAM and the security policies.
SOFTWARE._	A compressed copy of the Registry's SOFTWARE hive. This hive contains all Win32 software configuration information.
DEFAULT._	A compressed copy of the system default profile.
CONFIG.NT	The VDM version of the MS-DOS CONFIG.SYS file.
AUTOEXEC.NT	The VDM version of the MS-DOS AUTOEXEC.BAT file.
NTUSER.DA_	A copy of the file NTUSER.DAT (which contains user profile information) from the directory winnt_root\profiles\Defaultuser.

RDISK.EXE

Both the emergency repair disk and the directory are created during installation, but neither is updated automatically at any time thereafter. To update the emergency repair information, use the hidden utility RDISK.EXE (located in \<winnt_root>\SYSTEM32).

RDISK offers two options for administrators: Update Repair Info and Create Repair Disk.

Update Repair Info

The Update Repair Info button updates only the emergency repair directory, although it does prompt for the creation or update of an emergency repair disk immediately following successful completion of the directory update. Always update the directory before creating the disk because the disk is created by using the information in the directory.

Create Repair Disk

If the information in the repair directory is up-to-date, you can choose to create or update an emergency repair disk. You don't have to use a preformatted disk for the repair disk. RDISK formats the disk regardless.

A significant limitation of RDISK is that it will not update DEFAULT._, SECURITY., or SAM. in the repair directory (or disk). In other words, you can update your repair disk week-to-week, but none of your account changes are backed up. To do a complete emergency repair update, you must run RDISK.EXE using the /S switch.

Starting the Emergency Repair Process

Whether you use the emergency repair directory or the emergency repair disk, you need to recognize that you can't boot from either or use either from within Windows NT. To actually invoke the Emergency Repair Process, you must access the original three Windows NT setup disks. If you don't have the original disks handy, you can generate them from the CD by using the WINNT /OX command on a DOS-based machine.

The setup process offers the choice to either install Windows NT or repair an existing installation. Pressing **R** on this screen invokes the Emergency Repair Process.

After you select your repair options, setup attempts to locate your hard drive. After setup locates your hard drive, it asks whether you want to use an emergency repair disk or to have Setup search for your repair directory. You then encounter a series of restoration choices based on the repair options you selected and the problems setup uncovers as it analyzes your system.

RESOLVING CONFIGURATION ERRORS

1. **You have configured mandatory roaming profiles for your remote users. You want to schedule downtime for the server that contains the profiles. What will happen to the users while the server is down? Select the best response.**

   A. Users log on successfully and receive the default profile.

   B. Users log on successfully and receive their assigned profile, but they cannot save any changes to the profile while the server is down.

   C. Users cannot log on.

   D. Users can choose to log on to the domain and select a profile stored on a different server.

   E. Users can log on and receive their locally cached profile.

2. **You installed a new SCSI card on your NT Server. After configuring the SCSI driver, you realize that you installed the wrong SCSI driver. You want to boot by using the LastKnownGood configuration. What key(s) needs to be pressed to accomplish this? Select the best response.**

   A. Press F3 when the hardware profile screen appears.

   B. Press Ctrl+Alt+Delete when prompted during the boot process.

   C. Press the Escape key when prompted during the boot process.

   D. Press the Spacebar when prompted during the boot process.

   E. Press F8 when prompted during the boot process.

3. **After installing a new hard drive onto your Windows NT server, you open up the Disk Administrator utility to partition and format the new drive. Upon committing the changes, you are presented with a message to update your Emergency Repair Disk. By updating the ERD, you are providing an accurate reflection of the system configuration in case of disaster. During the update process, which files have been modified? Select all that apply.**

   A. `Default.log`

   B. `Config.NT`

   C. `SOFTWARE._`

   D. `NTUSER.DA_`

   E. `NTLDR`

4. **You are concerned that the hard disk on your server is beginning to fail. You begin to perform backups, but you want to take an additional precaution and back up the server's Registry. Which of the**

following are valid methods of backing up the Registry? Select all that apply.

A. `RDISK.EXE`

B. Server Manager

C. `Regedt32.exe`

D. Event Viewer

E. NT Backup

5. You are the administrator of a small NT network, and you recently obtained an updated SCSI driver for your SCSI controller. After installing the device driver and clicking the Restart button, you realize that you configured the controller with the wrong settings. You want to boot with the LastKnownGood configuration. At what point are you no longer able to boot by using the old configuration settings? Select the best response.

A. It already is too late. When the user logs out, the current configuration is considered to be the Last Known Good configuration.

B. After you choose to load NT from the `boot.ini` file.

C. After NT prompts you to log on.

D. After you log on.

E. After you successfully log on and then shut down or restart.

6. The developers in your company are trying to debug one of their new programs. You enable the debugging features of NT to better assist them. You receive a call from the programmers, and they ask you for the name of the file NT created with all the debugging information. What is the name of the file? Select the best response.

A. `Dump.hex`

B. `Dump.txt`

C. `Memory.dmp`

D. `Memory.txt`

E. `Debug.log`

7. During a routine inspection of the Event Viewer, you notice a lot of yellow alerts. What do these yellow alerts represent? Select the best response.

A. Informational event

B. Warning

C. Critical stop

D. Success

E. Failure

8. As the administrator of a large NT network, you are concerned about security. You have a share on a standalone NT server that contains highly sensitive data. You go to the Event Viewer to look at the security log and are surprised to see that no events have been logged. You know that users have accessed the shared directory and are curious whether any

unauthorized users have tried to access it. Why are no events showing in the security log? Select the best response.

A. The share is on a FAT partition.

B. No unauthorized users have tried to access the share.

C. The share must reside on a domain controller for logging to occur.

D. Auditing has not been enabled.

E. The Alerter service is not running.

ANSWER KEY

1. C
2. D
3. A-B-C

4. A-C-E
5. D
6. C

7. B
8. D

RESOLVING CONFIGURATION ERRORS

1. You have configured mandatory roaming profiles for your remote users. You want to schedule downtime for the server that contains the profiles. What will happen to the users while the server is down? Select the best response.

C. Users cannot log on.

1. CORRECT ANSWER: C

Answer C is correct because no mandatory profile is available to log in. During the logon process, the domain controller authenticates the user account. If mandatory profiles are established, the user is required to download the mandatory profile from the location configured in the User Manager for Domains utility. By selecting the properties of the account and clicking the Profiles button, you can configure the location of the mandatory profile. You can designate the actual computer and path to the mandatory profile. If the computer holding the mandatory profile is inaccessible, the logon process cannot continue; thus, the user cannot log on.

Answer A is incorrect because the server is down, and users won't be able to receive any profiles. The only time users receive the default profile is when mandatory profiles are not enabled and the user logs on for the first time. Answer B is incorrect because the server is down; users won't be able to access the profiles at all. The second portion of the answer is correct, however, regarding mandatory profiles in general. Answer D is not even a valid function. Users cannot ever select another server where their profiles are stored. Answer E occurs only if the server that contains the profiles is unavailable, and the profiles are not configured as mandatory.

2. You installed a new SCSI card on your NT Server. After configuring the SCSI driver, you realize that you installed the wrong SCSI driver. You want to boot using the LastKnownGood configuration. What key(s) needs to be pressed to accomplish this? Select the best response.

D. Press the Spacebar when prompted during the boot process.

2. CORRECT ANSWER: D

Answer D is correct because it is the key pressed to invoke the LastKnownGood configuration. Answer A is incorrect because it is used to boot to different hardware profiles. Answer B is incorrect because Ctrl+Alt+Delete cannot be invoked until after the boot process. Answer C is incorrect because the Esc key has nothing to do with anything in NT. Answer E is incorrect because the F8 key is used with DOS, Windows 95, and Windows 98.

3. After installing a new hard drive onto your Windows NT server, you open up the Disk Administrator utility to partition and format the new drive. Upon committing the changes, you are presented with a message to update your Emergency Repair Disk. By updating the ERD, you are providing an accurate reflection of the system configuration in case of disaster. During the update process, which files have been modified? Select all that apply.

A. Default.log

B. Config.NT

C. SOFTWARE

3. CORRECT ANSWERS: A-B-C

Answers A, B, and C are correct because they all are copied onto the ERD whenever it is created or updated. NTUSER.DA_ is the users portion of the Registry and is not copied. NTLDR also is not copied because the ERD is not a boot disk.

4. You are concerned that the hard disk on your server is beginning to fail. You begin to perform backups, but you want to take an additional precaution and back up the server's Registry. Which of the following are valid methods of backing up the Registry? Select all that apply.

A. RDISK.EXE

C. Regedt32.exe

E. NT Backup

4. CORRECT ANSWERS: A-C-E

You must know the methods used to back up the Registry. Answer A is correct because running the RDISK program enables you to back up the Registry and related files to the \winnt\sytem32\backup directory as well as to create an ERD. Answer B is incorrect because Server Manager does not support this feature. Answer C is correct because regedt32.exe enables you to back up a particular key or an entire hive. Answer D is incorrect because this is not a feature of Event Viewer. Answer E is correct because it has the capability to back up the registry directly.

Extra note: There actually is another way to back up the Registry. The NT resource kit provides two command-line utilities called REGBACK.EXE and REGREST.EXE.

5. You are the administrator of a small NT network, and you recently obtained an updated SCSI driver for your SCSI controller. After installing the device driver and clicking the Restart button, you realize that you configured the controller with the wrong settings. You want to boot with the LastKnownGood configuration. At what point are you no longer able to boot by using the old configuration settings? Select the best response.

D. After you log on.

5. CORRECT ANSWER: D

Answer D is correct because the Last Known Good configuration is not considered to be a successful boot until a user logs on. No matter how many times the server is powered on and off, as long as a user doesn't log on, the LastKnownGood configuration is not saved. Answers A, B, and C are incorrect and are misleading. Answer E is incorrect as well, but you might notice that, in reality, it is the same choice as answer A.

6. The developers in your company are trying to debug one of their new programs. You enable the debugging features of NT to better assist them. You receive a call from the programmers, and they ask you for the name of the file NT created with all the debugging information. What is the name of the file? Select the best response.

C. Memory.dmp

6. CORRECT ANSWER: C

The debugging option can be set through the System icon in the Control Panel. Answers A, B, D, and E are incorrect simply because of the names. Answer C is the correct name of the file. It is stored in a nonreadable hex format.

7. During a routine inspection of the Event Viewer, you notice a lot of yellow alerts. What do these yellow alerts represent? Select the best response.

B. Warning

7. CORRECT ANSWER: B

Answer B is the correct answer, not only because the entry in the log file is represented by a yellow icon, but because it is used to indicate some type of warning or potential problem. Answer A is incorrect because this is a blue icon that represents some type of significant information. Answer C is incorrect because it is represented by a red stop icon. This presents a critical stop notification. Stop messages typically are indicative of a failed service. Answers D and E are incorrect because they have to do only with the auditing feature of NT. Answer D is a successful audit represented by a Key; answer E is a failed audit represented by a lock.

8. As the administrator of a large NT network, you are concerned about security. You have a share on a standalone NT server that contains highly sensitive data. You go to the Event Viewer to look at the security log and are surprised to see that no events have been logged. You know that users have accessed the shared directory and are curious whether any unauthorized users have tried to access it. Why are no events showing in the security log? Select the best response.

D. Auditing has not been enabled.

8. CORRECT ANSWER: D

Auditing, by default, is not enabled on a Windows NT machine. To enable Auditing, you must open User Manager for Domains, select Policies from the menu bar, and then select Audit. Answer A is incorrect because shares can be configured for auditing. The directory itself cannot be audited but the shares can. Answer B is not correct because the question states that users have accessed the share; therefore, if logging was enabled, their access would show as successful events in the security log. Answers C and E are just incorrect and misleading.

FURTHER REVIEW

RESOLVING CONFIGURATION ERRORS

Common device problems include resource conflicts (such as interrupt conflicts) and SCSI problems. Use Windows NT diagnostics to check resource settings. If the error is the result of a recent configuration change, you can reboot the system and boot to the LastKnownGood configuration.

If a Windows NT service doesn't start, check the Event Viewer or check the Control Panel Services application to make sure the service is installed and configured to start. Windows NT includes the following important tools:

- Event Viewer

- Windows NT Diagnostics

- System Recovery

Event Viewer

If your Windows NT-based computer manages to boot successfully, yet it still isn't performing correctly, the first thing to check is the system event log. This log is where all critical system messages are stored.

Windows NT includes the Event Viewer application in the Administrative Tools program group for viewing the messages stored in the system, security, and application log files.

System Log

The system log, the default view in Event Viewer, is maintained by the operating system. It tracks the following three types of events:

- Errors. Symbolized by Stop signs, these events indicate the failure of a Windows NT component or device or perhaps its inability to start. These errors are common on notebook computers when Windows NT fails to start the network components because PCMCIA network cards are not present.

- Warnings. Symbolized by exclamation points, these events indicate an impending problem. Low disk space on a partition, for example, will trigger a warning.

- Information events. Symbolized by the traditional I in a blue circle, these events indicate an event that isn't at all bad but is still somehow significant. Browser elections often cause information events.

Security Log

The security log remains empty until you enable auditing through User Manager. After enabling auditing, the audited events reside here. The security log tracks the following two types of events:

- Success Audits. Symbolized by a key, these events indicate successful security access.

- Failure Audits. Symbolized by a padlock, these events indicate unsuccessful security access.

Application Log

The application log collects messages from native Windows NT applications. If you aren't using any Win32 applications, this log remains empty.

Securing Event Logs

Ordinarily, anyone can view event log information. Some administrators, however, might not want guests to have this sort of access. There is one restriction, enabled through the Registry, that you can place on Event Viewer—you can prohibit guests from accessing the system or application logs from the following Registry location, in which <log_name> is either System or Application:

```
HKEY_LOCAL_MACHINE\System\CurrentControl
➥Set\Services\EventLog\<log_name>
```

You need to add a value called RestrictGuestAccess of type REG_DWORD and set it equal to 1. To re-enable guest access to either log, set the appropriate RestrictGuestAccess value to 0 or just delete the value altogether.

Configuring Event Viewer

By default, log files can reach 512KB, and events are overwritten after seven days. You can change these settings in the Event Log Settings dialog box, which you can open by choosing Log Settings in the Event Viewer Log menu.

The Save As option in the Log menu enables you to save the log as an event log file (with an EVT extension), making it available for examination on another computer at a future time. You also can save it as a comma-separated value text file (with a TXT extension) for importing into a spreadsheet or database.

Using Event Viewer

At some point, every Windows NT user receives the following infamous message:

```
One or more services failed to start.
➥Please see the Event Viewer for
➥details.
```

This message appears when the first user logs on to the system after at least one Windows NT component fails to load successfully. As directed, you should immediately proceed to Event Viewer.

To find the source of the problem, look at the system log under the Event heading. Somewhere toward the top of the column, you should find an Event code of 6005. By default, the logs list the most recent events at the top. Start scanning at the top of the list, or you might not find the most recent 6005 event. Event 6005 means the EventLog service was successfully started.

To examine an event message, double-click on an event to open the Event Detail dialog box.

Note the following identifying information for the event:

- Date of the event
- Time of the event
- User account that generated the event, if applicable (usually found in the security log)
- Computer on which the event occurred
- Event ID (the Windows NT Event code)
- Source Windows NT component that generated the event
- Type of event (Error, Warning, and so on)
- Category of event (Logon/Logoff audit, for example)

- Description of the event
- Data in hexadecimal format, useful to a developer or a debugger

Windows NT Diagnostics

Windows NT Diagnostics provides a tidy front-end to much of the information in the HKEY_LOCAL_MACHINE Registry subtree. Like its ancestor, MSD from Windows 3.1, Windows NT Diagnostics can create incredibly detailed and valuable system configuration reports. One thing you cannot do with Windows NT Diagnostics, however, is edit the system configuration.

System Recovery

The Recovery utility is a tool you can use to record debugging information, to alert an administrator, to reboot the system in the event of a Stop error. (A Stop error causes Windows NT to stop all processes.) To configure the Recovery utility, start the Control Panel System application and click on the Startup/Shutdown tab.

The bottom frame of the Startup/Shutdown tab is devoted to Recovery options. The options are as follows:

- Write an event to the system log.
- Send an administrative alert.
- Write debugging information to (specify a filename). In the event of a Stop error, the Savedump.exe program dumps everything in memory to the pagefile and marks the location of the dump. When you restart your system, Windows NT copies the

memory dump from the pagefile to the file specified in the Startup/Shutdown tab. You then can use a program called Dumpexam.exe in the \Support directory of the Windows NT CD-ROM to study the contents of the memory dump and to determine the cause of the Stop error.

- Automatically reboot. You might not want to have your server sit idle after a Stop error. This option instructs Windows NT to reboot automatically after a Stop error.

Backing Up the Registry

Two files are associated with each hive. One file is named after the hive and has no extension, and the other is identically named with a LOG extension (with the exception of SYSTEM, which has a SYSTEM.ALT counterpart for reasons to be explained shortly). Both files reside in the \<winnt_root>\SYSTEM32\CONFIG directory. Most of the hives loaded at any given time are residents of HKEY_LOCAL_MACHINE, and the others belong to HKEY_USERS. The following is a list of the Registry hives:

HKEY_LOCAL_MACHINE\SAM (SAM, SAM.LOG)

HKEY_LOCAL_MACHINE\SECURITY (SECURITY, SECURITY.LOG)

HKEY_LOCAL_MACHINE\SOFTWARE (SOFTWARE, SOFTWARE.LOG)

HKEY_LOCAL_MACHINE\SYSTEM (SYSTEM, SYSTEM.ALT)

HKEY_USERS\.DEFAULT (DEFAULT, DEFAULT.LOG)

HKEY_USERS\<user_sid> (<user_profile>, <user_profile>.LOG)

The LOG files provide fault tolerance for the Registry. Whenever configuration data is changed, the changes are written to the LOG file first. Then the first sector of the actual hive is flagged to indicate that an update is taking place. The data is transferred from the log to the hive, and the update flag on the hive is then lowered. If the computer crashes after the flag has been raised but before it has been lowered, some (if not all) of the

data quite possibly is corrupted. If that happens, when Windows NT restarts, it detects the flag still raised on the hive, and it uses the log to redo the update.

Registry files almost always are in a state of flux and constantly are open for read/write access. The Windows NT Backup program usually skips over these files for that reason. Probably the best way to back up the SYSTEM and SOFTWARE files is to use the Repair Disk application, another hidden application in the \<winnt_root>\SYSTEM32 directory. The section "RDISK.EXE" earlier in this chapter discussed the Repair Disk utility, otherwise known as RDISK.EXE.

RESOLVING PRINTER PROBLEMS

1. **You are the administrator of an NT-based network. You recently purchased an HP LaserJet with a network interface. As you create the printer that eventually will be shared, you notice that the Hewlett-Packard Network Port is not an option when specifying a print destination. What is the reason the HP port does not appear? Select the best response.**

    A. The print device already is configured by another server.

    B. The print device is not properly configured to use the LaserJet's network interface port.

    C. The DLC protocol is not installed on the NT Server.

    D. You did not select an HP-compatible driver.

    E. You didn't map an LPT port to the LaserJet's network interface.

2. **A user reports that she is having printing problems. Upon inspection of the print queue, you notice a corrupt print job in the queue. You are unable to delete the print job through the print monitor; consequently, no new jobs are able to print. What must you do to delete the corrupt print job? Select the best response.**

    A. Start and stop the Spooler service.

    B. Pause the printer, access the spool directory by using NT Explorer, and manually delete the files.

    C. Remove the Printer and reinstall it.

    D. Log in as administrator. Access the property sheet of the printer and print a test page.

    E. Delete the corrupted document from the user's machine.

3. **You recently installed a new inkjet printer. As you configure the settings and drivers for the printer, you choose to print a test page. The test page does not print; instead, nearly a hundred pages are printed with just a few control characters on each sheet. What has gone wrong? Select the best response.**

    A. The printer is not on the Microsoft Hardware Compatibility List.

    B. The printer is not properly configured with the correct interrupt and port settings.

    C. The NT server is using RAW format to send data to the printer.

    D. The NT server is using the DLC protocol to send data to the printer.

    E. A PostScript driver was installed, and the printer is not PostScript.

4. **A printer has been created and shared on the network. Users are sending print jobs to the printer, but the jobs are being printed at two separate printers. What is the problem? Select the best response.**

   A. The printer is configured with two printer devices.

   B. The printer is configured to use printer pooling.

   C. The printing devices have been assigned equal priorities.

   D. Two servers have created a share with the same printer name.

   E. The user has enabled printer pooling on the networked printer.

5. **An HP printer has been installed on the network using a network interface card. DLC is installed on the NT server. With the network interface installed correctly and DLC installed on the NT server, the server is unable to print to the HP printer. What is possibly the problem? Select the best response.**

   A. The HP printer is configured to accept print jobs only from authorized users.

   B. The HP printer is out of paper.

   C. Another computer on the network has attached to the HP printer using continuous connection mode.

   D. The NT server is configured to print directly to the device, which is not supported by HP printers.

   E. The printer is configured to accept only TCP/IP connections.

6. **Users are complaining that they are not able to print documents consistently. Upon further inspection, you discover that the NT server controlling several printers is nearly out of disk space. You want to create additional disk space for the spool directory for the printers. How can you accomplish this? Select the best response.**

   A. Use NT Explorer to drag the spool directory to a new logical drive that contains more disk space.

   B. Change the properties on the server to specify a new location for the spool directory. Give the spool directory a new location that contains more disk space.

   C. Change the printer properties of each printer to specify a new location with more disk space.

   D. Use Disk Administrator to extend the system partition so it contains more free space.

   E. Change the properties for each printer to spool the printed documents on the client's hard drive rather than on the server's hard drive.

7. You are running out of disk space on the hard disk that contains the spool directory. You check the printer queues of all the printers, and all show that there are no current print jobs. Using NT Explorer, you access the spool directory. What types of files should you look to delete to free up disk space? Select all that apply.

A. TMP

B. SPL

C. PNT

D. SHD

E. RAW

ANSWER KEY

1. C	4. B	6. B
2. A	5. C	7. B-D
3. E		

ANSWERS & EXPLANATIONS

RESOLVING PRINTER PROBLEMS

1. You are the administrator of an NT-based network. You recently purchased an HP LaserJet with a network interface. As you create the printer that eventually will be shared, you notice that the Hewlett-Packard Network Port is not an option when specifying a print destination. What is the reason the HP port does not appear? Select the best response.

   C. The DLC protocol is not installed on the NT Server.

1. CORRECT ANSWER: C

After the DLC protocol is installed, the HP printer port becomes an available printer port option. Answer A is incorrect because the HP port still shows up, but the specific instance of the LaserJet's card MAC address does not. After you configure a LaserJet once, it no longer shows up under the available ports. The question doesn't ask why the printer won't show up; it asks why the HP option won't show up. Answer B is incorrect, but it actually could be a reason why the printer wouldn't show up. Again, the question doesn't ask why the printer won't show; it asks why the port won't show. Answer D is incorrect because the driver has nothing to do with the list of ports available. In addition, it doesn't necessarily have to be an HP printer installed on the port. It can be anything attached to the jetdirect network card. Answer E is incorrect because mapping a port has nothing to do with why the port won't show.

2. A user reports that she is having printing problems. Upon inspection of the print queue, you notice a corrupt print job in the queue. You are unable to delete the print job through the print monitor; consequently, no new jobs are able to print. What must you do to delete the corrupt print job? Select the best response.

   A. Start and stop the Spooler service.

2. CORRECT ANSWER: A

Stopping and starting the Spooler service in the Services dialog box is the only way to remove corrupted jobs. Answer B is not correct because, although the actual files that make up the document will be deleted, it does not remove the entries in the Print Monitor. Answer C is incorrect because this still does not remove the files from the spool directory. It does, however, enable you to start printing again. Answer D is incorrect because printing a test page (whether or not you are an administrator) does nothing except send another print job. Answer E is incorrect because, if the user could have deleted the job, he would have done so a long time ago. The user is able to delete the job.

3. You recently installed a new inkjet printer. As you configure the settings and drivers for the printer, you choose to print a test page. The test page does not print; instead, nearly a hundred pages are printed with just a few control characters on each sheet. What has gone wrong? Select the best response.

   E. A PostScript driver was installed, and the printer is not PostScript.

3. CORRECT ANSWER: E

This is a classic error that occurs when PostScript drivers are used on non-PostScript printers. Answer A is not correct because, if the printer has a parallel port, it typically will emulate some type of supported printer. In addition, just because the printer isn't on the HCL doesn't mean it won't work. Answer B is incorrect because printers do not have interrupts or port settings; they just receive input from a cable or network I/O. Answer C is incorrect because NT always uses the RAW language by default. RAW means nothing more then sending the data in the printer's native language, so no additional processing of the print job needs to take place. Answer D is incorrect because the DLC protocol deals only with sending data, not formatting data. In addition, DLC most likely would not be used with an inkjet because inkjets typically are parallel.

4. A printer has been created and shared on the network. Users are sending print jobs to the printer, but the jobs are being printed at two separate printers. What is the problem? Select the best response.

   B. The printer is configured to use printer pooling.

4. CORRECT ANSWER: B

A printer pool is easy to configure (just a simple check box). One problem, however, is that you never know where a print job will show up. Answer A is incorrect because, even though a printer can have two printing devices installed, only one can be active at a time. Answer C is incorrect because printer priorities have nothing to do with printing devices, just printers. Answer D is incorrect because the user needs to select two separate printers. The printers are referenced by two separate UNC names \\server1\printer and \\server2\printer. Answer E is just misleading; there is no such thing as printer pooling from the user side.

5. An HP printer has been installed on the network using a network interface card. DLC is installed on the NT server. With the network interface installed correctly and DLC installed on the NT server, the server is unable to print to the HP printer. What is possibly the problem? Select the best response.

   C. Another computer on the network has attached to the HP printer using continuous connection mode.

5. CORRECT ANSWER: C

Answer C is correct because a feature of DLC allows a node to connect to an HP printer and control it exclusively. This is called *continuous connection*. Answer A is incorrect because printers couldn't care less what user is printing to them; they simply print whatever is sent to them. Answer B is incorrect because the print monitor would indicate that there is a problem with the printer. Answer D also is incorrect because NT does not queue the printed document; it forces the client to send it directly to the printer. This has nothing to do with the type of printer. Answer E technically could be a correct answer, but you would have to go to great lengths to configure the HP's I/O card to accept only TCP/IP connections.

6. Users are complaining that they are not able to print documents consistently. Upon further inspection, you discover that the NT server controlling several printers is nearly out of disk space. You want to create additional disk space for the spool directory for the printers. How can you accomplish this? Select the best response.

    B. Change the properties on the server to specify a new location for the spool directory. Give the spool directory a new location that contains more disk space.

6. CORRECT ANSWER: B

Changing the server's properties for the location of the spool directory configures the information. This affects all the installed printers on the server. Answer A is incorrect because this choice does not inform the NT core services where the new location of the spool directory is going to be. This actually causes severe printing problems (namely, no printing). Answer C is incorrect because you cannot specify a different spool directory for an individual printer (at least not through the printer's properties sheet). Answer D is incorrect because this is not a valid feature of Disk Administrator. You cannot extend the system partition. Answer E is incorrect because this is not even a real function of NT printing.

7. You are running out of disk space on the hard disk that contains the spool directory. You check the printer queues of all the printers, and all show that there are no current print jobs. Using NT Explorer, you access the spool directory. What types of files should you look to delete to free up disk space? Select all that apply.

    B. SPL

    D. SHD

7. CORRECT ANSWERS: B-D

Answers A, C, and E are all incorrect. They are strictly distracters. Answer B is a correct answer because the SPL files are the actual spooled print jobs. They typically are stored in RAW format and already have been processed by the printer driver (directly from the client). Answer D also is correct. SHD files are called shadow files, and they contain only the information regarding the specifics of the print job such as time, user, node, and so on.

RESOLVING PRINTER PROBLEMS

This explanation in this section supports the answers for questions 1–7.

When you try to isolate printing problems, the following guidelines can be helpful:

- Check the cable connections and the printer port to verify that the printing device is on and that the cables all are securely fitted. This precaution might seem rather obvious, but the simplest of things can cause some of the most perplexing problems.

- To verify that the correct printer driver is installed and configured properly, establish the type of printing device (such as PCL, PostScript, and so on) and verify that the correct driver type has been installed. If necessary, reinstall the printer driver. If a printer driver needs updating, use the Printers folder to install and configure the new printer driver.

- Verify that the printer is selected, either explicitly in the application or as the default printer. Most Windows NT applications have a Printer Setup menu or a toolbar button. When printing by using OLE or another indirect means, you need to specify a default printer.

- Verify that enough hard disk space is available to generate the print job, especially on the partition that has the spooler directory specified. This, by default, is the boot partition (that is, the winnt_root partition).

- Run the simplest application possible (such as Notepad) to verify that printing can occur from other applications within Windows NT. If problems are encountered when printing from the application (other than a Win32-based application), check the appropriate application subsystem (such as DOS, Win16, POSIX, and OS/2).

- Print to a file (`FILE:`) and then copy the output file to a printer port. If this works, the problem is the spooler or is data-transmission related. If this doesn't work, the problem is application- or driver-related.

Spooling Problems

By default, spooled print jobs reside in the `\<winnt_root>\SYSTEM32\SPOOL\PRINTERS` directory until completely printed. If a Windows NT-based computer is acting as a print server for the network, make sure plenty of free disk space is available on the partition that contains the default spool directory. In addition, keeping this partition defragmented improves printing performance. Because Windows NT doesn't include a defrag utility, you need to use a third-party utility (or boot to MS-DOS if you are using the FAT file system).

If you have more room on another partition, you can change the default spool directory in the Advanced tab of the Server Properties dialog box. You also can change the spool directory in the Registry by adding a value called

`DefaultSpoolDirectory` of type REG_SZ to the following and by entering the path to the new spool directory:

```
HKEY_LOCAL_MACHINE\System\CurrentControl
➥Set\Control\Print\Printers
```

You need to restart the spooler service (or the computer itself) for the change to take effect.

You also can assign a separate spool directory for each individual printer. Enter the path to the new spool directory as the data for the value `SpoolDirectory` in the following, where `<Printer>` is the name of the printer you want to redirect:

```
HKEY_LOCAL_MACHINE\System\CurrentControl
➥Set\Control\Print\Printers\<Printer>
```

Again, you need to restart the spooler service for this change to take effect.

Printing from Non-Windows–Based Applications

Non-Windows–based applications—such as MS-DOS–based applications—need their own printer drivers if the application requires any type of formatted output other than plain ASCII text. WordPerfect for MS-DOS, for example, does not even allow the user to print a document unless there is a WordPerfect-specific and printer-specific driver installed. Non-Windows-based applications are not written to conform to or to take advantage of the Windows APIs. Also remember that you might need to use the `NET USE LPT1:` `\\servername\printername` command to enable the DOS-based application to print.

Handling the Computer Crashing

When a document prints, two files are created for the print job in the spool directory (by default,

`<winnt_root>\SYSTEM32\SPOOL\PRINTERS`). One of the files, which has an SPL extension, is the actual print job spool file. The other file, which has an SHD extension, is a shadow file that contains information about the job such as its owner and its priority. These files remain in the spool directory until the job finishes printing, at which point they are deleted.

In the event of a system crash, some spool and shadow files can be left over from jobs that were waiting to print. When the spooler service restarts (along with the rest of the system), the printer should process these files immediately. They are, however, sometimes corrupted during the crash and might get stuck. Be certain, therefore, to check the spool directory every so often. Delete any spool and shadow files with old date/time stamps. What is considered old depends on how long it takes to print a job on your printer. Certainly, anything from days, weeks, or months ago should be deleted.

If a print job gets stuck in the printer and you cannot delete it, stop the spooler service in Control Panel's Services applet and delete the SPL and SHD file for that job from the spool directory. (Match the date/time stamp on the files to the Print Manager to determine which files are causing the problem.)

Printing Too Slow or Workstation Too Sluggish

Windows NT Workstation assigns priority 7 to the spooler service, which puts printing on an equal footing with other background applications. Windows NT Server, which favors printing over background applications, assigns priority 9 to the spooler. This puts it neck-and-neck with the foreground applications.

If a Windows NT-based workstation moonlighting as a print server prints too slowly, consider raising the priority by one or two classes. If the workstation is responding sluggishly to the user while printing, consider lowering the priority by a class or two. Don't alter the priority by more than two levels under any circumstances without a full understanding of the performance consequences involved.

To change the priority class for the Spooler service, add a value called `PriorityClass` of type REG_DWORD to HKEY_LOCAL_MACHINE\ System\CurrentControlSet\Control\Print and set it equal to the priority class desired. If this value is set to `0` or isn't present, the default is used (7 for Windows NT Workstation or 9 for Windows NT Server).

RESOLVING RAS PROBLEMS

1. Your RAS server is configured with a proprietary card that allows for eight simultaneous connections through eight modems. Remote users are reporting that, when they dial into the RAS server, they are immediately disconnected. What is the best way to diagnose the problem? Select the best response.

   A. Use the Remote Access Admin utility to view port status.

   B. Use the Network Monitor Agent to view inbound connections.

   C. Use Regedt32.exe to edit the Registry to enable device logging.

   D. Use Performance Monitor to view logs generated by the RAS Server service.

   E. Use Server Manager to check to see whether the RAS Server service is running.

2. After recently installing RAS server, you are experiencing many intermittent problems. What two log files are available for use in troubleshooting?

   A. SLIP.log

   B. PPP.log

   C. PPTP.log

   D. Device.log

   E. Modem.log

3. You want to provide the best service to your remote customers using the RAS server. You implement callback security so the remote users do not have to pay for the long distance phone call. You also have configured eight separate modems so users can take advantage of the multilink feature of RAS. Users are reporting that, when they log on to the RAS server, they are able to use multiple modems. When the RAS server calls them back, however, it calls back using a single modem. What is the problem? Select the best response.

   A. The RAS server does not have multilink enabled.

   B. The modems installed on the RAS server are not compatible with multilink.

   C. Callback security allows users to be called back only at a single number. Thus, they can't take advantage of callback security using multilink.

   D. The clients are using a default installation of Windows 95 that does not support multilink.

   E. Multilink can be used only with ISDN modems.

4. Users are complaining that they receive busy signals when dialing in to the RAS server. What utility should be used to

check the status of the RAS ports? Select the best response.

   A. Remote Access Admin

   B. Dial-Up Networking

   C. Remote Access Service

   D. Server Manager

   E. Performance Monitor

5. **The network you are administering has both NT and NetWare servers. You have implemented RAS as a remote dial-in solution to allow your users to access your internal resources. Remote clients need to access the NetWare servers through the RAS server. Your Windows 95 clients are reporting that they are unable to access the NetWare servers, but they can access all other resources on the network. Which of the following are possible problems? Select all that apply.**

   A. The Windows 95 clients do not have the NetWare Client installed on their computers.

   B. The RAS Server does not have Gateway Services for NetWare installed.

   C. The RAS Server does not have the NWLink IPX/SPX protocol configured properly.

   D. The NetBIOS gateway has not been installed on the RAS server.

   E. The NetWare servers are configured to not allow inbound connections from remote clients.

6. **You are troubleshooting your RAS server. You want to view the log files that the RAS service has generated. What is the default location in which the RAS logs will be stored?**

   A. `\winnt\system\RAS`

   B. `\winnt\system32\RAS`

   C. `\winnt\system\logs`

   D. `\winnt\ssytem32\logs`

   E. `\winnt\RAS\logs`

ANSWER KEY

1. C	3. C	5. A-C
2. B-D	4. A	6. B

RESOLVING RAS PROBLEMS

1. Your RAS server is configured with a proprietary card that allows for eight simultaneous connections through eight modems. Remote users are reporting that, when they dial into the RAS server, they are immediately disconnected. What is the best way to diagnose the problem? Select the best response.

   C. Use `Regedt32.exe` to edit the Registry to enable device logging.

1. CORRECT ANSWER: C

Answer C is correct because it is the only way to enable logging for the RAS devices (modems). The logs then can be viewed in the `\winnt\system32\logs` directory. Answer A is incorrect because the Remote Admin utility is used only to view the status of the ports and to grant users the capability to log in. The network monitor agent has nothing to do with RAS; it has everything to do with the network card. Answer D is incorrect because Performance Monitor can monitor certain aspects of RAS but not the physical devices. Answer E is incorrect because it has nothing to do with the RAS server (other than what is stated in the choice).

2. After recently installing RAS server, you are experiencing many intermittent problems. What two log files are available for use in troubleshooting?

   B. `PPP.log`

   D. `Device.log`

2. CORRECT ANSWERS: B-D

PPP logging is available and must be enabled by editing the Registry. The device log is used to identify any problems with the RAS devices (X.25, modems, ISDN). It also can be enabled by editing the Registry. Answer A is incorrect because the RAS server cannot act as a SLIP server; therefore, it cannot log SLIP connections. Answer C is incorrect because there is no PPTP logging feature. Answer E is incorrect because it is a distracter—it just sounds good.

3. You want to provide the best service to your remote customers using the RAS server. You implement callback security so the remote users do not have to pay for the long distance phone call. You also have configured eight separate modems so users can take advantage of the multilink feature of RAS. Users are reporting that, when they log on to the RAS server, they are able to use multiple modems. When the RAS server calls them back,

3. CORRECT ANSWER: C

With callback security, the user can enter only one number to be called back. The initial connection takes advantage of multilink, but the callback does not. Answer A is incorrect because multilink does not need to be enabled at the RAS server. It is built into the core functionality of RAS. Answer B is incorrect because the modems have nothing to do with multilink. The modems simply transmit the data without respect to what the data is. Answer D is incorrect. The default Dial-Up

however, it calls back using a single modem. What is the problem? Select the best response.

C. Callback security allows users to be called back only at a single number. Thus, they can't take advantage of callback security by using multilink.

4. **Users are complaining that they receive busy signals when dialing in to the RAS server. What utility should be used to check the status of the RAS ports? Select the best response.**

A. Remote Access Admin

5. **The network you are administering has both NT and NetWare servers. You have implemented RAS as a remote dial-in solution to allow your users to access your internal resources. Remote clients need to access the NetWare servers through the RAS server. Your Windows 95 clients are reporting that they are unable to access the NetWare servers, but they can access all other resources on the network. Which of the following are possible problems? Select all that apply.**

A. The Windows 95 clients do not have the NetWare Client installed on their computers.

C. The RAS Service does not have the NWLink IPX/SPX protocol configured properly.

Networking client that comes with the default installation of Windows 95 does not support it. The DUN 1.2 upgrade does support multilink, as does Windows 98. Answer E is incorrect because it works with any type of devices that must initiate a phone call.

4. CORRECT ANSWER: A

Answer A is correct because Remote Access Admin is used to check the port status of the RAS devices and to grant users the dial-in right. Answer B is incorrect because DUN is used strictly for the client and for configuring entries to dial in to RAS, PPP, and SLIP servers. Answer C also is incorrect because the Remote Access Service is used to configure the security implemented on dial-in connections. This service is found through the Network Control Panel. Access the Services tab and double-click on the Remote Access Service. This service also enables you to configure what portions of the LAN the user can access. Answer D is incorrect because Server Manager has nothing to do with RAS other than just viewing the service. Answer E is incorrect because it also has nothing to do with configuring the RAS server. It is used strictly to monitor the load created by RAS.

5. CORRECT ANSWERS: A-C

Answer A is correct because both IPX and the NetWare client must be installed on the client. Answer B is not correct because the RAS server is not accessing the NetWare server. It is merely allowing the client to access the network remotely. Answer C also is correct. The RAS server needs to have NWLink IPX/SPX installed and configured to allow access to the entire network. Answer D, on the other hand, is not correct for two reasons. First, you do not have to install the NetBIOS Gateway. It is part of the core functionality of the RAS Service. Second, the Windows 95 client is not issuing NetBIOS calls when trying to access the NetWare server. It is issuing NetWare Core Protocol (NCP) commands. Answer E is not correct because the basic function of the RAS Server is to make it appear that the remote clients are not remote. This being the case, the NetWare servers cannot tell that the dial-up clients are trying to access the server remotely.

6. **You are troubleshooting your RAS server. You want to view the log files that the RAS service has generated. What is the default location in which the RAS logs will be stored?**

    B. \Winnt\System32\RAS

6. CORRECT ANSWER: B

\Winnt\System32\RAS is the folder to reference when viewing the log files generated by the RAS service. All other options provide incorrect locations and are nothing more than distracters.

FURTHER REVIEW

RESOLVING RAS PROBLEMS

If RAS isn't working, check the Event Viewer. Several RAS events appear in the system log. You also might check the Control Panel's Dial-Up Networking Monitor application. The Status tab of Dial-Up Networking Monitor displays statistics about current conditions, including connection statistics and device errors.

RAS supports TCP/IP, NWLink, and NetBEUI protocols for both dial-in and dial-out connections. TCP/IP benefits from being available on a number of different platforms, being easily routable, and being the compatibility choice of the Internet.

If you are having problems with PPP, you can log PPP debugging information to a file called PPP.Log in the \<winnt_root>\System32\Ras directory. To log PPP debugging information to PPP.Log, change the Registry value for the following subkey to 1:

```
\HKEY_LOCAL_MACHINE\System\CurrentControl
➥Set\Services\Rasman\PPP\Logging
```

Microsoft has identified the following common RAS problems and some possible solutions:

- Authentication. RAS authentication problems often stem from incompatible encryption methods. Try to connect using the Allow any authentication including clear text option. If you can connect using clear text and you can't connect using encryption, you know the client and server encryption methods are incompatible.

- Callback with multilink. If a client makes a connection using multilink over multiple phone lines with callback enabled, the server calls back using only a single phone line. (In other words, multilink functionality is lost.) RAS can use only one phone number for callback. If the multilink connection uses two channels over an ISDN line, the server can still use multilink on the callback.

- AutoDial at logon. At logon, when Explorer is initializing, it might reference a shortcut or another target that requires an AutoDial connection. This causes AutoDial to spontaneously dial a remote connection during logon. The only way to prevent this is to disable AutoDial or to eliminate the shortcut or other target causing AutoDial to occur.

RESOLVING CONNECTIVITY PROBLEMS

1. **A Windows 95 user connects to a shared printer on the primary domain controller. The user then tries to connect to a shared directory on the same server but is denied access. You look at the share permissions and notice that the user has not been granted access. You add the user to a group and contact the user to let her know that the problem has been resolved. The user tries to access the share again and is still denied access. What is the cause of the problem? Select the best response.**

   A. The changes you made do not take effect until the user logs off and then back on.

   B. The user is using the wrong password for the share.

   C. The user does not have an account in the domain.

   D. The change you made has not yet been replicated to all the backup domain controllers.

   E. The primary domain controller must be restarted.

2. **Your Windows NT Workstation clients are running NWLink IPX/SPX as well as the NT server. The clients are unable to connect. What is most likely the problem? Select the best response.**

   A. The clients' workstations are configured with the wrong Default Gateway.

   B. The server is configured with the wrong Default Gateway.

   C. The file permissions are set to No Access for all the NT Workstation user accounts.

   D. The frame types on the workstations are different than the servers.

   E. The NT server's Workstation service is not started.

3. **You are the administrator of a Windows NT network. Users are complaining that they cannot connect to certain servers. Investigating the problem further, you determine that the servers the clients cannot connect to are on a different subnet. The clients are using TCP/IP as their networking protocol. Which of the following are the most likely problems? Select all that apply.**

   A. The frame type used by the clients is different than the one configured on the server.

   B. The server is configured with the wrong subnet mask.

   C. The clients are configured with the wrong subnet mask.

D. The server is configured with the wrong default gateway.

E. The clients are configured with the wrong default gateway.

4. **You are planning to upgrade your network to Windows 95 clients accessing NT Servers. Your network will still contain several Novell servers that will act as file servers while the NT servers are upgraded. When implementing Gateway Services for NetWare, you are unable to configure the gateway from the NT server to the NetWare server. Which of the following are possible problems? Select all that apply.**

A. Your NT server does not have supervisor rights on the NetWare server.

B. The NetWare server does not have a user created and placed in the NTGATEWAY group.

C. The NetWare server does not have TCP/IP or NetBEUI installed.

D. Client Services for NetWare has not been installed on the NT Server.

E. The NT server does not have NWLink IPX/SPX installed.

5. **Your clients are complaining that the NT Server is not accessible from the network. From the NT server, you try to browse the network and are successful. You further test the NT server by accessing one of the client systems from the NT**

server. **You assure the clients that the NT server is up and running, but they still report that the server is inaccessible. What is the problem? Select the best response.**

A. The clients are running an incompatible version of NetBIOS.

B. The server is running an incompatible version of NetBIOS.

C. The server's Server service is not functioning properly.

D. The server is configured with the wrong subnet mask.

E. The server is configured with the wrong Default Gateway.

6. **Some of your Windows 95 clients are having intermittent problems connecting to a Windows NT Server across one of your wide area network links. What utility should you use to best diagnose whether the problem is related to the wide area link or the NT server itself? Select the best response.**

A. ARP

B. NETSTAT

C. NBTSTAT

D. PING

E. IPCONFIG

7. **After installing a new printer on your NT Server, NT reports that a service failed during boot. You check the appropriate**

log files and find that a series of services failed to load and initialize. The services are Server, Workstation, network card, and a few others. What is the most likely cause of all the errors? Select the best response.

A. The printer you just installed is conflicting with internal resources on the NT server.

B. The network interface card failed, causing all the other network services to fail.

C. The administrator account has become corrupt, and the service used the administrator account to initialize and access NT resources.

D. The printer cable is not properly seated into the back of the NT Server, causing a short that affects the network services.

E. There is probably nothing wrong because this is a typical error after installing a printer. Reboot and, if the problem persists, additional troubleshooting will be required.

ANSWER KEY

1. A
2. D
3. C-E

4. B-E
5. C

6. D
7. B

ANSWERS & EXPLANATIONS

RESOLVING CONNECTIVITY PROBLEMS

1. A Windows 95 user connects to a shared printer on the primary domain controller. The user then tries to connect to a shared directory on the same server but is denied access. You look at the share permissions and notice that the user has not been granted access. You add the user to a group and contact the user to let her know that the problem has been resolved. The user tries to access the share again and is still denied access. What is the cause of the problem? Select the best response.

   A. The changes you made do not take effect until the user logs off and then back on again.

1. CORRECT ANSWER: A

During the logon process, an access token is created and is issued to the user. This access token reflects the user and the groups of which the user is a member. When an administrator changes a user's group membership, the access token does not automatically regenerate. For the user to accurately reflect the changes, he must log on again to generate a new access token. Passwords assigned to shares are available only in the Windows 95 and 98 environments. Because the user has logged on to the PDC previously, you can conclude that the user account has been created and that BDC replication isn't an issue.

2. Your Windows NT Workstation clients are running NWLink IPX/SPX as well as the NT server. The clients are unable to connect. What is most likely the problem? Select the best response.

   D. The frame types on the workstations are different than the servers.

2. CORRECT ANSWER: D

The frame types most likely are set to 802.2 or 802.3. Answers A and B are incorrect because they only have to do with TCP/IP. Answer C is incorrect because the clients don't even have connectivity to the server; therefore, the file permissions have yet to even be checked. Answer E is incorrect because the Workstation server has nothing to do with users connecting, only with the NT server connecting to something else.

3. You are the administrator of a Windows NT network. Users are complaining that they cannot connect to certain servers. Investigating the problem further, you determine that the servers the clients cannot connect to are on a different subnet. The clients are using TCP/IP as their networking protocol. Which of the following are the most likely problems? Select all that apply.

3. CORRECT ANSWERS: C-E

Answer A definitely is incorrect because only NWLink uses frame types. Answer B also is incorrect because the clients aren't connecting at all. Answer C is a possible problem because, if the clients have an improperly configured subnet mask, they can't properly determine what was local and what was remote. Answer D is incorrect because the connectivity issues revolve around the client and not the server. Answer E also is a possible problem because, if the clients determine that

C. The clients are configured with the wrong subnet mask.

E. The clients are configured with the wrong default gateway.

4. You are planning to upgrade your network to Windows 95 clients accessing NT Servers. Your network will still contain several Novell servers that will act as file servers while the NT servers are upgraded. When implementing Gateway Services for NetWare, you are unable to configure the gateway from the NT server to the NetWare server. Which of the following are possible problems? Select all that apply.

B. The NetWare server does not have a user created and placed in the NTGATEWAY group.

E. The NT server does not have NWLink IPX/SPX installed.

the server is not on their local subnet, they need to know where to forward all the IP packets.

4. CORRECT ANSWERS: B-E

Answer B is a possible problem because it describes the process of creating the NetWare client and the corresponding group. Answer E also is a possible problem because you definitely need NWLink installed to connect to the NetWare server. In fact, NWLInk is installed automatically when GSNW is installed. Answer A is incorrect because the NT server does not need supervisor rights. It merely needs a valid NetWare account in the NTGATEWAY group. Answer C is incorrect because NT only accesses NetWare servers through the IPX/SPX protocol. Installing NetBEUI (which you can't) and TCP/IP on the NetWare server does nothing as far as NT is concerned. Answer D is not correct because Client Services for NetWare is an NT Workstation element. This is the trick part of the question.

5. Your clients are complaining that the NT Server is not accessible from the network. From the NT server, you try to browse the network and are successful. You further test the NT server by accessing one of the client systems from the NT server. You assure the clients that the NT server is up and running, but they still report that the server is inaccessible. What is the problem? Select the best response.

C. The server's Server service is not functioning properly.

5. CORRECT ANSWER: C

Answer C is correct strictly by process of elimination, yet the question itself gives clues that this is most likely the problem. Taking a step back, you can determine that the server has the capability for outgoing network connectivity but not incoming. By further analyzing the services provided by Windows NT, you can isolate the network connectivity. Outgoing is the responsibility of the Workstation service, and incoming is the responsibility of the Server service. By focusing on the server service, you can better troubleshoot the issue.

Answer A is incorrect because there is no such thing as incompatible versions of NetBIOS. This is further proven wrong because the server can connect to the Windows 95 machines. Answer B is incorrect for the same reason. Answers D and E are both incorrect because the server can connect to the client machines.

6. Some of your Windows 95 clients are having intermittent problems connecting to a Windows NT Server across one of your wide area network links. What utility should you use to best diagnose whether the problem is related to the wide area link or the NT server itself? Select the best response.

   D. PING

Answer D is correct because it checks to see whether something is up and accessible. Answer A is incorrect because it is used to resolve hardware address from IP addresses. Answer B is incorrect because it shows information only about the local machine and not links. Answer C is incorrect because it is used to troubleshoot and configure NetBIOS names over IP and is not used for connectivity. Answer E is incorrect because it merely reports on how the IP protocol stack is configured on the NT server.

7. After installing a new printer on your NT Server, NT reports that a service failed during boot. You check the appropriate log files and find that a series of services failed to load and initialize. The services are Server, Workstation, network card, and a few others. What is the most likely cause of all the errors? Select the best response.

   B. The network interface card failed, causing all the other network services to fail.

This question gauges whether you understand that, if the NIC fails, it typically causes several of the networking services to fail as well. Answer A is incorrect because the resources used by the parallel port have not changed (nor will they regardless of what printer is connected to it). Answer B is the correct answer. There's no telling why it would fail after a printer was installed. Given the context of the question, however, it is the logical and best answer. Answer C is incorrect because the network services log on as the local system and not as the administrator account. Answer D is incorrect because, even if only one pin is connected, it still does not cause the NIC to fail. Answer E is invalid simply because this certainly is not a typical error when installing a printer. Hopefully, there is no such thing as a typical error when installing a printer.

RESOLVING CONNECTIVITY PROBLEMS

Network problems often are caused by cables, adapters, IRQ conflicts, or problems with transmission media. Protocol problems also can disrupt the network. Use a diagnostics program to check the network adapter card. Use a cable analyzer to check the cabling. Use Network Monitor to check network traffic or use a network protocol analyzer.

Microsoft provides this objective for the Windows NT Server exam: Choose the appropriate course of action to take to resolve connectivity problems.

Pinging Other Computers

If you are using TCP/IP, the IP address and the subnet mask must be given when installed in a nonrouted environment. You often can isolate problems by pinging the other computers on your network. Pinging is a common diagnostic procedure, as follows:

1. Ping 127.0.0.1 (the loopback address).

2. Ping your own IP address.

3. Ping the address of another computer on your subnet.

4. Ping the default gateway.

5. Ping a computer beyond the default gateway.

Check the Control Panel Services application to make sure the Server service and the Workstation service (and any other vital services that might affect connectivity) are running properly. Check

the Bindings tab in the Control Panel's Network application to make sure the services are bound to applications and adapters.

Network Monitor

Windows NT Server 4 includes a tool called Network Monitor. Network Monitor captures and filters packets and analyzes network activity. The Network Monitor included with Windows NT Server can monitor only the specific system on which it is installed.

To install Windows NT Server's Network Monitor, execute the following steps:

1. Start the Network application in Control Panel and click on the Services tab.

2. Click on the Add button and select Network Monitor and Tools from the network services list.

After Network Monitor is installed, it appears in the Administrative Tools program group.

The Network Monitor window is divided into four sections, or panes. The Graph pane (in the upper-left corner) shows current network activity in a series of five bar charts. Note the scroll bar to the right of the Graph section. To view the bar charts, scroll down or drag the lower border down to expose the hidden charts. The five bar graphs are as follows:

- % Network Utilization

- Frames Per Second

- Bytes Per Second

- Broadcasts Per Second

- Multicasts Per Second

Below the Graph pane, you can see the Session Stats pane. The Session Stats pane indicates the exchange of information from two nodes on the network, the amount of data, and the direction of travel. This data is limited to a per-session basis.

On the right side of the display windows is the Total Stats pane, which reveals information relevant to the entire activity on the network. Whether statistics are supported depends on the network adapter. If a given network adapter isn't supported, Unsupported replaces the label.

At the bottom of the display window, you can see the Station Stats pane. The Station Stats pane displays information specific to a workstation's activity on the network. You can sort any category by right-clicking on the column label.

RESOLVING ACCESS AND PERMISSION PROBLEMS

1. **A user is trying to log on to the domain from his NT workstation. He calls the system administrator, informing her that he is unable to log in. The administrator checks the status of the account; it is not disabled and is not locked out. The user assures the administrator that he is properly typing in his account name and password. Which of the following are possible problems? Select all that apply.**

   A. The user has the Caps Lock enabled.

   B. The user is trying to log on to the NT Workstation's local account database and not the domain.

   C. The user is trying to log on to a trusted domain and not the domain where their account exists.

   D. The network media (wire) has been moved or possibly has become unplugged.

   E. A domain controller on the user's local subnet is not available.

2. **Your head developer has accepted a new job with another company. You log in as Administrator and are denied access when you try to read the data stored in his home directory. The user's home directory is stored on an NTFS partition. How can you read the data? Select the best response.**

   A. Boot off a DOS disk and access data through DOS. Copy the data to

   a directory to which the administrator has rights.

   B. Right-click on the user's home directory and add the Administrator as a valid user.

   C. Right-click on the user's home directory and take ownership.

   D. Use `Regedt32.exe` to remove the restrictions on the share.

   E. There is no way to retrieve the user's data.

3. **Your CFO has left the company to pursue other interests. Given the sensitivity of the data owned by the user, you quickly remove his account. Later that afternoon, you receive a call from the CEO. She tells you that the CFO has changed his mind and has been given his old job back. You quickly re-create the user's account and assign the user to the proper groups. Later that afternoon, the CFO informs you that he is unable to access the resources on his home directory. What is the problem? Select the best response.**

   A. The user has not changed his password on the initial login.

   B. The user account contains a new SID and is not able to access the files without the assistance of the administrator.

C. A new home directory was created for the user when the account was re-created.

D. One of the groups to which the user belongs has been denied access at the user's home directory.

E. The user's home directory automatically denies access to all users when the corresponding account is deleted. The administrator must manually grant the user access.

4. **A user calls you worried about the security of a certain file. He created and saved a file on his home directory, which is on an NTFS partition. The user set the security permissions so that his user account has full control and the Everyone group has read-only control. He copied the file to a floppy and handed it to one of his colleagues. He was shocked when he realized that the colleague also has full control over the file, not read-only control. How could this be? Select the best response.**

A. The colleague's user account is a member of the domain admins global group.

B. The colleague used the same account and password as the owner of the file.

C. The user accidentally granted the group Everyone full control.

D. The floppy's write protection was not engaged.

E. The floppy disk uses the FAT file system, which provides no security.

5. **During a routine inspection of the log files, you realize that a particular user is trying to access resources to which she does not have access. You load Server Manager and notice that the user currently is logged in. You want to disable the user from trying to access any other resources. Through User Manager for Domains, you disable the user's account. You return to Server Manager and notice that the user is still logged in and is trying to access the file. How is the user still able to be logged on and accessing files? Select the best response.**

A. The user is a member of the Local Administrators group.

B. The user is a member of the Domain Admins group.

C. The user has not logged off.

D. Server Manager gathers statistics on a five-minute delay. Simply wait five minutes and the information will show that the user has been removed from the system.

E. The user has logged in to the server twice with two separate accounts.

ANSWER KEY

1. A-B-C-D-E
2. C

3. B
4. E

5. C

ANSWERS & EXPLANATIONS

RESOLVING ACCESS AND PERMISSION PROBLEMS

1. A user is trying to log on to the domain from his NT workstation. He calls the system administrator, informing her that he is unable to log in. The administrator checks the status of the account; it is not disabled and is not locked out. The user assures the administrator that he is properly typing in his account name and password. Which of the following are possible problems? Select all that apply.

   A. The user has the Caps Lock enabled.

   B. The user is trying to log on to the NT Workstation's local account database and not the domain.

   C. The user is trying to log on to a trusted domain and not the domain where their account exists.

   D. The network media (wire) has been moved or possibly has become unplugged.

   E. A domain controller on the user's local subnet is not available.

1. CORRECT ANSWERS: A-B-C-D-E

All the answers are correct. The one to stress the most is Caps Lock. Do not be surprised to see questions about the Caps Lock problem on the exam. Answer B also is a valid error. The user could be trying to log in to the NT workstation using the domain account. Answer C is valid because it is nearly the exact same problem as answer B (except in this case a different domain). Answer D also is correct. It probably is not likely that this is an answer MS would ever pick, but it is a very common error. Answer E is a long shot, but it is still a valid option. If the NT Workstation can't forward the logon request to a valid DC, the workstation will not allow the user to log in.

2. Your head developer has accepted a new job with another company. You log in as Administrator and are denied access when you try to read the data stored in his home directory. The user's home directory is stored on an NTFS partition. How can you read the data? Select the best response.

   C. Right-click on the user's home directory and take ownership.

2. CORRECT ANSWER: C

All administrators have the capability to take ownership, regardless of the permissions set on the server. Answer A is incorrect because the home directory is stored on an NTFS partition, which cannot be accessed through DOS. Answer B is not correct because the administrator would not have rights to add himself as a valid user. Answer D is not correct because, by default, the administrator does not have access to the security portion of the Registry where this information is stored. Answer E is not correct because it is possible to retrieve to user's data.

3. Your CFO has left the company to pursue other interests. Given the sensitivity of the data owned by the user, you quickly remove his account. Later that afternoon, you receive a call from the CEO. She tells you that the CFO has changed his mind and has been given his old job back. You quickly re-create the user's account and assign the user to the proper groups. Later that afternoon, the CFO informs you that he is unable to access the resources on his home directory. What is the problem? Select the best response.

B. The user account contains a new SID and is not able to access the files without the assistance of the administrator.

3. CORRECT ANSWER: B

The old account and the new account have nothing to do with each other, even though the account names are the same. Answer A is incorrect because it has nothing to do with the real problem. When the administrator creates a new account, he has the option to force the client to change his password. Answer C is not correct because, if the user did have a home directory automatically created for him, he would be able to access the directory. NT, by default, doesn't create home directories automatically. Answer D is incorrect because groups typically are not denied access to home directories. Technically, it could potentially be a problem, but it is not the correct answer with respect to the question. Answer E is not a valid function of NT—it is nothing more than a distracter.

4. A user calls you worried about the security of a certain file. He created and saved a file on his home directory, which is on an NTFS partition. The user set the security permissions so that his user account has full control and the Everyone group has read-only control. He copied the file to a floppy and handed it to one of his colleagues. He was shocked when he realized that the colleague also has full control over the file, not read-only control. How could this be? Select the best response.

E. The floppy disk uses the FAT file system, which provides no security.

4. CORRECT ANSWER: E

Answer A is not correct because, even if the colleague had administrative rights, he would not be able to access the file. Answer B also is incorrect because, no matter how the user logged in, he still would be able to access the file because it is on a FAT partition. Keep in mind that FAT partitions offer nothing more than share-level permissions. To restrict access at the file and directory level, you must use NTFS. Answer C is not correct; it is just a distracter. Answer D is not correct because the write-protect feature has nothing to do with NTFS permissions. Answer E is correct because NTFS cannot be used to format a floppy. FAT must be used; therefore, there is no security.

5. During a routine inspection of the log files, you realize that a particular user is trying to access resources to which she does not have access. You load Server Manager and notice that the user currently is logged in. You want to disable the user from trying to access any other resources. Through User Manager for Domains, you disable the user's account. You return to Server

5. CORRECT ANSWER: C

Answers A and B are not correct because locking out the user's account has nothing to do with the groups to which he belongs. Answer C is the correct answer because, until the user logs on, he is an authenticated user and does not have to validate with NT until he ends the session. Answer D is incorrect because Server Manager does not work on a delay. Answer E is

Manager and notice that the user is still logged in and is trying to access the file. How is the user still able to be logged on and accessing files? Select the best response.

C. The user has not logged off.

incorrect as well because it is not possible to authenticate on an NT server with two separate accounts from the same machine. The error message states something to the effect of `The credentials you supplied conflict with the current credentials.`

RESOLVING ACCESS AND PERMISSION PROBLEMS

If you can't log on, you might be using an incorrect username or password. Also make sure the correct account database is selected in the drop-down list at the bottom of the dialog box. You can log on to the domain or to the local workstation account database. If you still can't log on, try logging on using another account. If other accounts are working normally, check the settings for your account in User Manager for Domains. If you can't log on from any account, repair the accounts database using the emergency repair process. One of the worst culprits for logon problems is the Caps Lock key. Also make sure the user isn't typing the password in all caps.

Microsoft lists this objective for the Windows NT Server exam: Choose the appropriate course of action to take to resolve resource access problems and permission problems.

If a user can't access a file, a share, a printer, or some other resource, check the resource permissions. Try connecting using a different account. Try accessing a similar resource to see whether the problem also appears there. Make sure the user has spelled the name of the resource correctly.

Check the Control Panel's Services application to make sure the NetLogon service, the Server service, and the Workstation service are running properly. Check the Bindings tab in the Control Panel's Network application to make sure the services are bound to applications and adapters.

You also can check User Manager for Domains to make sure that the user's group memberships haven't changed or that a change to a group rights setting hasn't inadvertently denied the user access to the resource. Finally, check System Policy Editor for restrictions on the user's access to computers or other resources.

RESOLVING FAULT-TOLERANCE FAILURES

1. **You have configured the hard disks on one of your application's servers as a stripe set. The stripe set is made up of three physical hard disks. What can you do to recover the data in the event that one of the hard disks fails? Select the best response.**

   A. Through Disk Administrator, break the stripe and recover the lost data onto a drive with free space.

   B. Replace the failed drive and choose the Regenerate command from the Fault Tolerance menu in Disk Administrator.

   C. Replace the failed drive and, from the properties sheet on the logical drive, run ScanDisk. ScanDisk recovers the data from the remaining disk in the stripe set.

   D. In the Check for Errors dialog box in Disk Administrator, select Fix File System Errors to recover the lost data.

   E. Restore the data from backup.

2. **You have installed NT server with a stripe set with parity. The stripe set is configured with eight physical disks. A power outage damages two of the physical disks. What do you need to do to recover the data from the failed stripe set? Select the best response.**

   A. Replace the failed drives. Choose Regenerate from Disk Manager.

   B. Replace the failed drives. NT automatically recovers the data from the remaining drives in the stripe set.

   C. Replace the failed drives. Restore the data from a current backup.

   D. Replace the failed drives. Run ScanDisk from the properties sheet of the logical drive.

   E. The data can be recovered by using the Emergency Repair Disk.

3. **You are concerned about not having a disaster recovery plan in case one of the disks on your NT server fails. You decide the best solution is to place the system and boot partitions on a stripe set with parity. After several attempts with Disk Administrator, you are unable to create the stripe set. What is the problem? Select the best response.**

   A. You cannot gain exclusive access to the physical drives.

   B. The current file system is FAT.

   C. The drives are not the same make and manufacturer.

   D. One drive is SCSI; the others are IDE.

   E. You cannot create a stripe set with parity on the boot and system partitions.

4. **Your NT server is configured with a single logical drive that resides on a disk duplex. The primary drive has failed, and you need to quickly correct the error to get back up and running as soon as possible. The duplex is made up of two SCSI drivers, and the controllers BIOSes are enabled. What modifications do you need to make to the Boot file to allow NT to boot? Select the best response.**

   A. multi(0)disk(0)rdisk(1)partition(1)\winnt

   B. multi(1)disk(0)rdisk(1)partition(1)\winnt

   C. multi(0)disk(1)rdisk(0)partition(1)\winnt

   D. scsi(1)disk(0)rdisk(1)partition(1)\winnt

   E. scsi(2)disk(0)rdisk(1)parition(1)\winnt

5. **What type of backup scheme copies only the files that have changed since the last backup and clears the archive bit?**

   A. Full

   B. Copy

   C. Differential

   D. Incremental

   E. Clone

ANSWER KEY

1. E	3. E	5. D
2. C	4. B	

RESOLVING FAULT-TOLERANCE FAILURES

1. You have configured the hard disks on one of your application's servers as a stripe set. The stripe set is made up of three physical hard disks. What can you do to recover the data in the event that one of the hard disks fails? Select the best response.

    E. Restore the data from backup.

1. CORRECT ANSWER: E

The wording of the question is very important. Notice that the question didn't say stripe set with parity; therefore, no fault tolerance options are available. Answers A–D all are incorrect because there is no fault tolerance. Answer E is the only valid answer.

2. You have installed NT server with a stripe set with parity. The stripe set is configured with eight physical disks. A power outage damages two of the physical disks. What do you need to do to recover the data from the failed stripe set? Select the best response.

    C. Replace the failed drives. Restore the data from a current backup.

2. CORRECT ANSWER: C

Answer A is incorrect because two drives in the stripe set failed. There is not enough parity on the remaining drives to recover the data. Answer B is incorrect because NT does not automatically recover a stripe set with parity, even if just one drive fails. Only answer C is correct. You need to replace the disks and re-create the stripe set. The data can be recovered from backup. Answer D is incorrect because this isn't even a function of ScanDisk. Basically, you cannot recover the data from a stripe set with parity if two disks fail. Answer E also is incorrect. The Emergency Repair Disk is capable of restoring only the Windows NT Registry information. The Emergency Repair Disk is not a bootable disk.

3. You are concerned about not having a disaster recovery plan in case one of the disks on your NT server fails. You decide the best solution is to place the system and boot partitions on a stripe set with parity. After several attempts with Disk Administrator, you are unable to create the stripe set. What is the problem? Select the best response.

    E. You cannot create a stripe set with parity on the boot and system partitions.

3. CORRECT ANSWER: E

This question is intended to test your knowledge of stripe sets. All the options are incorrect because this is not possible. Answer A is a typical error when you try to convert a file system from FAT to NTFS. Answer B is not valid because you cannot create a stripe set with parity on a FAT partition. Answers C and D wouldn't make a difference because the drives can be different makes, sizes, and interfaces. Answer E is the only valid option. Windows NT does not allow the system and boot partitions to reside on a stripe set with parity.

4. Your NT server is configured with a single logical drive that resides on a disk duplex. The primary drive has failed, and you need to quickly correct the error to get back up and running as soon as possible. The duplex is made up of two SCSI drivers, and the controller's BIOSes are enabled. What modifications do you need to make to the Boot file to allow NT to boot? Select the best response.

B. multi(1)disk(0)rdisk(1)partition(1)\ winnt

4. CORRECT ANSWER: B

Answer A is incorrect because it simply references the second disk off the primary controller. Answer B is the correct answer because the multi value is pointing to the second controller. Answer C is incorrect because it still points to the primary controller and uses the disk value. Answers D and E are incorrect because it uses the SCSI value and the RDISK value.

5. What type of backup scheme copies only the files that have changed since the last backup and clears the archive bit?

D. Incremental

5. CORRECT ANSWER: D

Answer A is incorrect because it backs up every file and clears the archive bit. Answer B is incorrect because Copy backs up all the files you have selected and does not copy the archive bit. Answer C is incorrect because it copies only the files that have changed since the last backup, but it does not clear the archive bit. Only answer D is a correct choice. Incremental backs up any file that has changed and clears the archive bit. Answer E also is incorrect because this is a distracter. There is no option called Clone.

RECOVERING FROM FAULT-TOLERANCE FAILURES

Even if you are employing a high-tech RAID fault-tolerance system, a well-planned backup routine still is your best defense against lost data. Windows NT includes a backup utility (NTBACKUP.EXE). Backup is part of the Administrative Tools group.

Microsoft lists this objective for the Windows NT Server exam: Choose the appropriate course of action to take to resolve fault-tolerance failures. Fault-tolerance methods include: tape backup, mirroring, stripe set with parity, and disk duplexing.

Backing Up Files and Directories

The Backup main window shows the disk drives presently accessible to the Backup utility. Double-click on a drive to see an Explorer-type directory tree. Note that every directory or file has a small box beside it. Click on the box to back up the file or directory and all child files and directories beneath it.

To start a backup, click on the Backup button in the toolbar or choose Operations, Backup. The Backup Information dialog box opens, offering a number of backup options. Note the Log Information frame at the bottom of the Backup Information dialog box. You can write a summary or a detailed description of the backup operation to a log file.

Restoring Files and Directories

To restore a file or directory using the Backup utility, open the Tapes window (if you don't see the Tapes window on your screen, pull down the Window menu and choose Tapes) and select the backup set you want to restore. Like the Drives window, the Tapes window enables you to expand directories and to select individual files for restoration.

Select the files and directories you want to restore and click on the Restore button in the toolbar (or choose Operations, Restore). The Restore Information dialog box opens. Select the desired restore options and click on OK to restore the files and directories.

You also can run the NTBACKUP utility from the command prompt. This enables you to automate the backup process through batch files so you can perform backups at regular intervals. You can back up only directories with the ntbackup command (not individual files). The syntax is as follows:

```
ntbackup operation path
```

operation is the name of the operation (backup, restore, and so on) and path is the path to the directory you're backing up. The NTBACKUP command includes a number of switches, including the following:

/a causes the backup set to be appended after the last backup set. (If you don't specify, /a overwrites existing backup sets on the tape.)

/v verifies the backup operation.

/d "text" enables you to add a description of the data in the backup set.

/t {option} enables you to specify the backup type (normal, incremental, daily, differential, copy).

Breaking a Mirror Set

A mirror set is the only fault-tolerant option capable of holding the system and boot partitions. When a partition in a mirror set fails, it becomes an orphan. To maintain service until the mirror is repaired, the fault-tolerant device directs all I/0 requests to the healthy partition. If the boot or system partitions are involved, a fault-tolerant boot disk is required to restart the system. To create a fault-tolerant boot disk, follow these steps:

1. Format a floppy disk using Windows NT.

2. If you are using an I386 system, copy NTLDR, NTDETECT.COM, NTBOOTDD.SYS (for SCSI disks not using SCSI BIOS), and BOOT.INI to the disk.

   If you're using a RISC-based computer, copy OSLOADER.EXE and HAL.DLL.

3. Modify the BOOT.INI file so it points to the mirrored copy of the boot partition.

To fix a mirror set, you must first break it by choosing Fault Tolerance, Break Mirror. This action exposes the remaining partition as a separate volume. The healthy partition is given the drive letter previously assigned to it in the set. The orphaned partition is given the next logical drive letter or one that you manually selected for it.

After the mirror (RAID level 1) has been re-established as a primary partition, selecting

additional free space and restarting the process of creating a mirror set can form a new relationship.

Regenerating a Stripe Set with Parity

Like a mirror set, the partition that fails in a stripe set with parity (RAID level 5) becomes an orphan. In addition, the fault-tolerant device redirects I/O requests to the remaining partitions in the set to enable reconstruction. So this can be done, the data is stored in RAM using the parity bits (which can affect the system's performance).

To regenerate a stripe set with parity, follow these steps:

1. Select the stripe set with parity by clicking on it.

2. Select an area of free space at least as large as the stripe set. The size of the stripe set becomes the size of the smallest amount of free space on any drive multiplied by the number of drives.

3. Choose Fault Tolerance, Regenerate.

You must close the Disk Administrator and restart the system before the process can begin. After the system restarts, the information from the existing partitions in the stripe set is read into memory and is re-created on the new member. This process completes in the background. The stripe set with parity isn't active in the Disk Administrator until it finishes.

Troubleshooting Partitions and Disks

When you install Windows NT, your initial disk configuration is saved on the emergency repair disk and in the directory \<winnt_root>\Repair. The RDISK utility updates the disk configuration information stored on the repair disk and in the Repair directory. You also can save or restore the disk configuration by using Disk Administrator.

You periodically should update emergency configuration information in case you ever need to use the Emergency Repair Process or you ever want to upgrade to a newer version of Windows NT. Otherwise, NT restores the original configuration that was saved when you first installed Windows NT.

CHAPTER SUMMARY

Windows NT provides several tools to help the troubleshooting efforts of a network administrator. From the installation process to fault tolerance, Windows NT aids in troubleshooting through utilities such as Event Viewer, log files, and Performance Monitor.

For the exam, it is important to know how to troubleshoot the BOOT.INI file by modifying its properties and by understanding the Advanced RISC Computing (ARC) naming convention. You also would benefit from becoming comfortable with the different methods of fault tolerance and how to recover from system or component failures.

Combining these skills with the steps outlined during the boot process will increase your ability to successfully navigate the troubleshooting area of the Microsoft exam.

Microsoft 070-067—Implementing and Supporting Microsoft Windows NT Server 4 exam instructions:

You are given 90 minutes to complete 55 questions. The exam requires a passing score of 764, which allows approximately 13 questions out of 55 to be missed. The exam pool consists of two types of multiple-choice questions:

- Select the correct answer.
- Select all answers that are correct.

It is highly recommended that, when taking the practice exam, you strive to match normal exam-taking conditions as much as possible. This requires that you use a timer or a watch to limit the amount of time you take to complete the practice exam.

Practice Exam 1

EXAM QUESTIONS

1. **Your network uses TCP/IP and NWLink. You want to remotely generate TCP/IP performance-analysis information from an NT Server. You start Performance Monitor on your NT Workstation, but the desired counters are not available for the NT Server to be monitored. What must be done to make them available? Select the best response.**

   A. Install TCP/IP on all network BDCs.

   B. Install SNMP Service on your workstation.

   C. Uninstall NWLink from the NT Server being monitored.

   D. Install SNMP Service on the NT Server being monitored.

   E. Install SNMP Service on the PDC.

2. **Your network consists of three main servers—Marketing1, Marketing2, and Sales. Employees in the marketing department often need to send multiple large files (200MB and larger) to the sales department on Thursdays and Fridays. When this happens, traffic on the network slows considerably. Which of the following is the best solution?**

   A. Add a second network card to the Marketing1 and Marketing2 servers, enable IP forwarding, and configure a second physical subnet consisting of the Sales server and the second NICs on the Marketing1 and Marketing2 servers.

   B. Bind a second IP address to the NIC on the Sales server and have the marketing servers use that IP number.

   C. Add a second network card to the Sales server, enable IP forwarding, and configure a second physical subnet consisting of Marketing1, Marketing2, and the second NIC on the Sales server.

D. Use the AT command to schedule network traffic relating to the desired file transfers to expected times of lower network utilization.

E. Replace the 10MB ethernet network card in the Sales server with a 100MB ethernet NIC.

3. **To help prevent users from making undesired changes to their user profiles, you decide to implement mandatory user profiles. After a few weeks, you get several phone calls from users who cannot log on to the network. What might be the reason? Select the best response.**

A. The users changed their profiles back to roaming profiles, but they left the file named NTUSER.MAN and now it cannot be found.

B. The mandatory user profile expired, and the users forgot to change the expiration date.

C. The server that holds the mandatory profile file is down; thus, the network logon was not successful.

D. NTUSER.DAT is corrupted and cannot be read by the users trying to log on.

E. The users had a conflict between their roaming and mandatory profiles.

4. **Your LAN just inherited 10 DOS systems from another small company's liquidation sale. After upgrading the systems to meet the minimum hardware**

requirements for NT Server, you proceed to boot to DOS. What manual steps must be taken to begin installation of NT Server from CD-ROM? Select all that apply.

A. Install or load into memory the necessary real-mode CD-ROM drivers.

B. Run winnt.exe from the \i386 directory on the NT Server installation CD and choose the option to create a setup disk set.

C. Run winnt32.exe from the \i386 directory on the NT Server installation CD.

D. Enter the location of the installation files when prompted.

E. Reboot the computer from the NT Server setup boot disk, which already is in the floppy drive.

5. **Your collection of 14 NT Workstations currently are configured in a workgroup. After careful consideration, you decide to purchase and install an NT Server on your LAN to provide better services. What procedures can be followed to add the workstations to the resulting domain created? Select all that apply.**

A. Use Server Manager on each workstation to add the computer to the domain.

B. Reinstall NT Workstation on each workstation computer and choose the domain membership option.

C. Have the Domain Admin add each computer account to the domain using the Server Manager on the NT Server.

D. Use the Network applet in the Control Panel to join the domain.

E. Use User Manager for Domains on the server to add each workstation to the domain.

6. **You have set up a mirror disk set on your NT Server computer using a FAT file system. Your primary disk fails. Which of the following steps must be taken to create a fault-tolerance boot disk for disaster-recovery purposes? Select all that apply.**

A. Copy NTLDR to the floppy disk.

B. Copy NTDETECT.COM to the floppy disk.

C. Copy BOOTSECT.DOS to the floppy disk.

D. Copy original BOOT.INI to the floppy disk.

E. Copy NTBOOTD.COM to the floppy disk.

7. **The LAN in your small business currently exists as 68 NT Workstations, four member servers, and one server configured as the primary domain controller. Users are reporting that, after the recent LAN expansion, network logon speed has deteriorated. What can be done to improve logon times? Select the best response.**

A. Segment the network into two logical networks by using member servers to validate network logons.

B. Reinstall one of the member servers as a new primary domain controller.

C. Upgrade one of the NT Workstations to an NT Server and configure it as a member server.

D. Reinstall one of the member servers as a BDC.

E. Reinstall the PDC as a BDC.

8. **Which tool can be used to create a network share from a remote client for server resources? Select the best response.**

A. Windows Explorer

B. Server Manager

C. User Manager for Domains

D. Resource Manager for NT Server

E. Control Panel

9. **You just installed seven Windows NT version 4 Workstations on your network. They are installed with only the NWLink protocol, and you can see all seven NT Workstations. To support an older application that runs only on Windows NT 3.51, you installed NT Workstation version 3.51. From this system, you cannot see the first seven added servers. What is most likely the cause of this problem? Select all that apply.**

A. There is a frame-type value mismatch.

B. There is a mismatch in Windows NT Workstation build numbers.

C. NWLink was not installed on the NT 3.51 workstation.

D. NT Workstation 3.51 must be rebooted one more time.

E. Windows NT 3.51 and NT 4 workstations cannot communicate using NWLink.

10. **Your network is configured with TCP/IP and NetBEUI on all the workstations. An analysis of your network traffic indicates that 80 percent is NetBEUI in origin; only 20 percent is TCP/IP. What can be done to improve performance? Select the best response.**

A. Add a second network card to each system to segment TCP/IP traffic.

B. Make sure NetBEUI is bound to the NIC first, followed by TCP/IP.

C. Restrict bandwidth to the TCP/IP protocol.

D. Uninstall TCP/IP from the network adapters.

E. Add a second network card for use only by NetBEUI.

11. **Your system is configured with a mirror disk set. The mirror disk in the set fails. After getting a replacement disk, but before creating a new mirror set, what is the first action that must be performed?**

A. Install Windows NT on the replacement mirror disk.

B. Break the original mirror set.

C. Create a new mirror set.

D. Format the replacement drive.

E. Create a new volume on the replacement drive.

12. **To assign a home directory to a domain user account, the network administrator should do which of the following? Select the best response.**

A. Create a local drive-letter mapping to the network share for the location of the user's home directory.

B. Use User Manager for Domains and provide the UNC name for the network location of the home directory.

C. Use User Manager for Domains and provide the locally mapped drive letter for the home directory.

D. Use the Network applet in Control Panel and provide the UNC location for the home directory.

E. Use the Passwords applet in Control Panel and enter the UNC name in the user's home directory box in the Network properties tab.

13. **Which of the following statements accurately indicate minimum-hardware requirements for the given disk-drive configurations? Select all that apply.**

A. The minimum requirements for a stripe set are one controller and two disks.

B. The minimum requirements for a stripe set with parity are two controllers with three disks.

C. The minimum requirements for a stripe set with parity are one controller with three disks.

D. The minimum requirements for disk duplexing are two controllers with two disks.

E. The minimum requirements for disk mirroring are one disk with two controllers.

14. **You have just integrated a legacy NetWare 4.11 server into your NT Domain LAN. You do not plan to install Client Services for NetWare on any NT Workstations. You need to configure your NT Server to support access to NetWare file and print resources. You also want to support NT long filenames. What must you do to provide this access in this environment? Select all that apply.**

A. Install CSNW on the desired workstations.

B. Install CSNW on an NT Server.

C. Install GSNW on an NT Server.

D. Create a group named NTGATEWAY on the NetWare volumes.

E. Configure the OS/2 namespace on the NetWare server.

15. **You have just integrated a NetWare 3.x server into your NT Domain LAN. You plan to install Client Services for NetWare on some of your NT**

Workstations. You need to configure your NT Server to support access to NetWare file and print resources. You also want to support NT long filenames. What must you do to provide this access in this environment? Select all that apply.

A. Install GSNW on an NT Server.

B. Install CSNW on the desired NT Workstations.

C. Create a group named NWGATEWAY on the NT Server.

D. Create a group named NTGateway on the NetWare Server.

E. Configure the OS/2 namespace on the NetWare volumes.

16. **An NT Server is configured with one SCSI adapter and two SCSI hard drives. If your budget allows you to add either one more adapter or one more hard drive, and if the system requires a fault-tolerant disk configuration, which of the following are possible configurations? Select all that apply.**

A. Disk duplexing with parity

B. Mirror disk set

C. Stripe set

D. Stripe set with parity

E. Disk duplexing

17. **While installing NT Server, the installation program does not properly detect your CD-ROM. What must do you to continue installing NT Server? Select all that apply.**

A. Restart the server setup by using Ctrl+Alt+Delete and let the setup redetect the CD-ROM.

B. Restart the server setup from the beginning and choose the option to manually select CD-ROM drivers.

C. Choose Ignore and continue with the installation. The installation will use a generic CD-ROM driver until the 32-bit environment is loaded.

D. Load real-mode drivers provided by the CD-ROM manufacturer and copy the installation files to the disk. Run the setup from the disk.

E. Install NT Server from the floppy disk set.

18. **Concurrent performance monitoring of multiple servers is being performed from a single workstation for comparison analysis. This has a profoundly negative effect on workstation performance. What action can be taken to decrease the workstation load while monitoring performance real-time? Select the best response.**

A. Increase the sampling interval.

B. Log to a file instead of monitoring real-time.

C. Alternate server monitoring at different time frames.

D. Decrease the sampling interval.

E. Increase memory on the workstation.

19. **After adding a new hard drive to a workstation, you create a new partition on the drive in Disk Administrator. You now want to format the partition. What additional step must be taken prior to formatting the partition? Select the best response.**

A. Save changes to disk.

B. Click Apply Changes Now.

C. Reboot the server.

D. Click Commit Changes Now.

E. Do nothing.

20. **A backup schedule recently was implemented for your network. The department head asks about the verification of the backup procedures. To make sure your backup procedures and restore processes are fully completed and accurate, which of the following options should you use to make sure a backup/restore was successful? Select the best response.**

A. Perform a backup once a month.

B. Select Verify when performing a complete backup.

C. Restore files to a different path option from your backup procedure and compare the restore files with the original files.

D. Select Verify when performing a complete restore.

E. Perform a backup of a single file to a tape device and verify that the file exists on the tape. Restore the file to the hard drive to verify the backup and restore process.

21. **What is the desired method for renaming an NT domain? Select the best response.**

A. Reinstall NT Server on the PDC.

B. Use the Network applet in the Control Panel to change the name of the domain.

C. Use the Domain Manager to change the domain name and then choose Replicate Changes.

D. You cannot change a domain name.

E. Use the Server Manager to change the name of the domain.

22. **After the MIS department spent the weekend tweaking the configuration of multiple NT Servers, you return to work to find that the NT Server in your office fails to start up. The screen provides an error message indicating something might be wrong with the boot files. What action can be taken to correct the problem? Select the best response.**

A. Format the boot partition and reinstall startup files from the NT startup disk.

B. Boot to an MS-DOS boot disk and run sys.com.

C. Reinstall NT Server.

D. Boot from an NT startup disk previously made on this system and choose the Repair option.

E. Boot to an NT startup disk and choose Restore system files.

23. **To help avoid insufficient server storage space, you want to be notified when available disk space on the servers drops below 10 percent. What tool should you use? Select the best response.**

A. Server Manager

B. Performance Monitor

C. Network Monitor

D. Resource Manager

E. System Tracker

24. **What configuration steps must be taken for an NT Server to act as an IP router? Select all that apply.**

A. Move TCP/IP protocol binding to the top of the bindings order.

B. Install at least two network cards on the server.

C. Manually assign a unique IP to each NIC card.

D. Enable IP forwarding.

E. Set Router Service to automatic startup in the Services applet of Control Panel.

25. **User Manager for Domains can be used to administer which types of user accounts? Select the best response.**

A. Only local user accounts

B. Only domain accounts

C. Domain accounts and local accounts simultaneously

D. Domain accounts or local accounts independently

E. Local accounts but only on a PDC

26. **A UPS has been added to your system. You want to receive notification when the power goes out. What services must be**

running on the server for this to be accomplished? Select all that apply.

A. Alerter

B. Spooler

C. UPS

D. Site Server Message Builder

E. Messenger

27. **Several home directories have been created for users on the NT Server. Three of the users are on NT Workstation; two users are on Windows for Workgroups. After attempting to log on to the network, the Windows for Workgroup users do not have access to their home directories. What last step must be taken for the Windows for Workgroup users? Select the best response.**

A. There is no last step. WFW cannot connect to NT Server–based home directories.

B. Map a drive on each WFW system to the appropriate home directory on the server.

C. Configure the home directories to allow access permission by 16-bit clients.

D. Create a share on the home directories for the WFW clients, allowing Full Control access by the Everyone group.

E. Add share permission on the directories for each home drive, allowing Full Control access by each user to his or her own home directory.

28. **Members of the Account Operators group can perform many administrative operations. These operations include which of the following? Select all that apply.**

A. Creating a user account

B. Assigning user rights

C. Modifying user accounts or groups

D. Logging on or shutting down an NT Server

E. Administering existing user rights

29. **When using the Disk Administrator, what happens if you attempt to delete the partition on which the NT system files are found? Select the best response.**

A. An error message occurs when you attempt to exit the Disk Administrator.

B. NT immediately presents an error message.

C. Nothing. NT does not allow this operation.

D. An error message occurs when you click Commit Changes.

E. The change does not occur until the next server reboot.

30. **After using DISKPERF -Y to enable the disk performance counters on your system, you decide you no longer want to incur the additional overhead of the statistics collections required for the disk counters. What steps must be taken to disable the disk counters in Performance Monitor? Select all that apply.**

A. Use `DISKPERF -U` and then log on to the server again.

B. Start Performance Monitor and choose Disable disk counters.

C. Use the `DISKPERF -N` command.

D. Use the `DISKPERF -U` command.

E. Restart your computer.

31. **You are creating a share for a UNIX-connected printer running TCP/IP. Your server has TCP/IP, and NWLink is installed and bound to the NIC. You have a second NIC installed in the server with TCP/IP bound to it, GSNW installed, and IP forwarding enabled. What additional network protocols must be installed on NetBEUI clients to access the printer share created by the NT Server? Select the best response.**

A. No additional protocols are required if NetBEUI is installed on the NT Server.

B. NWLink

C. NetBEUI

D. NWLink and TCP/IP

E. NetBEUI and NWLink

32. **When changes to the disk configuration are requested in the Disk Administrator, when are the requested changes actually enforced? Select the best response.**

A. Upon the next server restart

B. Upon exiting the Disk Administrator

C. Immediately upon request

D. Only after clicking Commit Changes Now

E. After clicking Apply Changes

33. **What action is required to install a different keyboard in NT Server by using a different layout than the current keyboard? Select all that apply.**

A. Run NT setup and choose the correct style of keyboard.

B. Use the Keyboard applet in Control Panel.

C. No action is required. NT automatically adjusts to the different keyboard.

D. Reboot the server twice with the new keyboard attached.

E. Reinstall NT Server.

34. **You notice that your hard drive is making excessive disk noises, and the noises coincide with periods of degraded system performance. What action should be performed to confirm an excessive paging problem? Select the best response.**

A. In Performance Monitor, check the Committed Bytes counter of the Memory object.

B. In Performance Monitor, check the Pages/sec counter of the Disk Access object.

C. In Performance Monitor, check the Available Bytes counter of the Memory object.

D. In Performance Monitor, check the Pages/sec counter of the Memory object.

E. Enable the Performance Monitor disk counters by running the `DISKPERF` command and then checking the disk performance counters.

35. **While in the process of installing NT Server onto a number of MS-DOS systems, you realize the current system does not have a functional CD-ROM. Time is critical in getting these systems up and running. What steps can be taken to quickly install NT on this system? Select all that apply.**

   A. Boot MS-DOS.

   B. Copy the installation files to a network share.

   C. Connect to a network share.

   D. Copy `winnt.exe` from the network share.

   E. Run `winnt.exe` from the shared folder.

36. **If a user accidentally deletes a file that he needs to recover, who can restore the file from tape? Select all that apply.**

   A. Backup Operators

   B. Server Operators

   C. Administrators

   D. Anyone given Restore File rights

   E. Any member of the Everyone group

37. **Windows NT Directory Services is the directory database residing on the domain's primary domain controller. Which features does NT Directory Services provide? Select all that apply.**

   A. Universal access to resources

   B. Automated backup operations

   C. Distributed account administration

   D. Single-user logon

   E. Centralized account administration

38. **You have just added two more hard drives to a system, increasing the number of drives to five disks, each with two partitions. The first disk is the boot and system partition. What should be done to optimize the pagefile? Select the best response.**

   A. Place a pagefile on each disk.

   B. Place a pagefile on each partition.

   C. Place a pagefile on each disk except the first.

   D. Place a pagefile on one disk.

   E. Create two different hard drive partitions on the same drive.

39. **Your office has one NetWare server and one NT Server. The network has both Windows 95 clients and MS-DOS clients. Clients have NWLink-compatible protocols loaded on their computers. They are configured for Microsoft Network. Clients must have access to data on both the NT server and the NetWare Server. What should you load on the NT Server? Select the best response.**

   A. Enable NWLink-compatible transport on the server

   B. File Services for NetWare

   C. Gateway Services for NetWare

D. RIP

E. SAP

40. **You need a fault-tolerant drive configuration for one controller and three drives with a total of one partition per drive. One drive has NT Server boot and system files. What is the best method?**

A. Stripe set with parity

B. Stripe set without parity

C. Mirror

D. Duplex

E. Duplex with parity

41. **After partying hard all night long, you wake up the morning of January 1, 2000, and begin your day. You start to install a new video card, but it's not working and seems to have a few problems. The system will boot up but not to acceptable video. What should you do? Select the best response.**

A. The video card is not Y2K-compliant; replace it.

B. Boot to VGA, install the correct driver in Control Panel, and display.

C. Make sure the current video drive is Y2K-compliant.

D. Reseat the video card in the slot.

E. Reboot the system one more time.

42. **You need to view dependency services that have failed to start properly on your Windows NT Server. Where can you do this? Select the best response.**

A. Event Viewer

B. Device Manager

C. The Registry

D. Both A and C

E. The Services applet in Control Panel

43. **Windows NT Server provides the capability to modify the Registry of another NT system remotely. What is the first step to take when preparing to perform this function? Select the best response.**

A. Start the Registry Editor on the local computer.

B. Make sure Server services is running.

C. Start the Registry Editor on the remote Windows NT computer.

D. Make sure the remote NT computer is using the NetBEUI protocol.

E. Start Network Monitor on the remote NT system.

44. **You have a single accounts domain and a single resource domain on your LAN. If the Marketing domain (the resource domain) trusts the Accounting domain (the accounts domain), how can you grant members of the Accounting domain dial-in access to resources of the Marketing domain? Select the best response.**

A. Use the Remote Access Admin application and grant dial-in permission to each user in the Accounting domain.

B. Use the User Manager for Domains, select User Rights, and then select each user who will be given dial-in rights. Check the Dial-In Permission check box.

   C. Use the User Manager, select User Rights, and then select each user who will be given dial-in rights. Check the dial-in permission check box.

   D. Use the Remote Access Admin application and grant dial-in permission to each user in the Marketing domain.

   E. Install the dial-up adapter and grant permission to the Marketing domain users dialing in through the dial-up adapter.

45. **When tweaking the behavior of the Server service in terms of memory allocation, an NT Server can be configured to Maximize Throughput for Network Applications. Under what scenario would this setting best be employed? Select the best response.**

   A. When the server is expected to have up to 64 concurrent users

   B. When the server is a member server in a workgroup

   C. When network throughput is critical

   D. When the server is going to function as a file and print server

   E. When an NT Server is designed to function as an application server or as part of a domain server with just one domain controller

46. **After careful analysis, you determine that your processor is underpowered on your server. Your original system is capable of**

moving to a multiprocessor system, and now is the time to do it. After installing the second processor onto your system, what step should be performed next? Select the best response.**

   A. Install the processor, run `Uptomp.exe`, and then reinstall NT Server.

   B. Run the `uptomp.exe` utility to upgrade NT Server to multiprocessor code.

   C. Install the processor, run `uptomp.exe`, and then reset user permissions.

   D. Install the processor and then restart the server.

   E. Rerun the NT setup, choosing the multiprocessor configuration option.

47. **Your field engineers dial in to a RAS server on your network to access a database on another server on your network. Other remote clients use third-party PPP software to dial in to the RAS server. You want the field engineers to use encrypted security when connecting, but you still want the other clients to be able to access information on your RAS server. What should you do? Select the best response.**

   A. Encrypt the data being transferred between the two servers by allowing any authentication method but requiring the engineers to use MS-CHAP.

   B. Configure encryption for connections from NT Workstations only.

   C. Configure encryption to work through COM ports and set up workstations to dial in to those ports.

D. Support MS-CHAP only for dial-in connections.

E. This option is not supported because dial-in access is not supported for third-party PPP software.

48. **You are upgrading a Windows NT 3.51 machine to Windows NT 4. You have spent a lot of time customizing the system to your liking, and you want to keep all the same settings and migrate them into your profile. How should you perform the upgrade to make sure your system settings are preserved as much as possible? Select the best response.**

   A. Boot to DOS and run `winnt.exe` from the NT 4 CD-ROM. Install Windows NT 4 into the same directory in which Windows NT 3.5x was installed.

   B. From the Windows 3.51 machine, run `winnt32.exe` from the NT 4 CD-ROM. Install NT Server 4 into the same directory in which Windows NT 3.5x was installed.

   C. Run `setup.exe` from the NT 4 CD-ROM. You will be prompted to upgrade or begin a new installation.

   D. Boot to DOS and run `winnt32.exe` from the Windows NT 4 CD-ROM. Choose migrate current system settings when prompted for upgrade options.

   E. Run `winnt.exe` using the `/U Preserve` command-line parameter.

49. **After setting up a Remote Access Server for dial-in access by several company** executives, you are informed that several of the RAS clients are having modem-initialization problems. What step should you take to help diagnose the problem? Select the best response.

   A. Enable logging in the Registry (`device.log`).

   B. Restart the RAS server.

   C. Run Network Monitor and track dial-in session communication.

   D. Enable logging by checking the audit dial-in access check box in the Remote Access Admin.

   E. Use the Modem applet in the Control Panel to analyze active dial-in connections.

50. **Which of the following RAID levels are software supported by Windows NT Server 4? Select all that apply.**

   A. RAID Level 0 (disk duplexing)

   B. RAID Level 1 (disk mirroring)

   C. RAID Level 5 (disk striping with parity)

   D. RAID Level 1 (disk mirroring with parity)

   E. RAID Level 0 (disk basic disk striping)

51. **Your users are trying to print to a print server, but they can't print or clear the print queue. How can you make the print jobs print? Select all that apply.**

   A. The printer queue must be rebuilt.

   B. The printer must be turned off for 15 seconds and then restarted.

C. Stop the spooler service and then restart it.

D. All of the above.

E. Stop the spooler service, rebuild the queue, and choose to reprint each of the documents in the queue.

52. **Due to recent disk-drive failure, you opt to install a backup drive onto your NT Server. This new tape backup drive uses a SCSI controller card. What steps should be taken to install this tape backup unit? Select the best response.**

A. Install the drive and the controller, install the driver for the SCSI controller, and then restart the computer.

B. Install the driver for the SCSI controller, install the drive and the controller, and then restart the computer.

C. Install the driver for the SCSI controller, install the drive and the controller, restart the computer, go to Add New Hardware, and then add the tape drive.

D. Install the drive and the controller, install the driver for the SCSI controller, restart the computer, go to Add New Hardware, and then add the tape drive.

E. Use Add New Hardware to install the driver and then shut down, install the drive, and then restart the system.

53. **When using a fault-tolerant disk configuration such as RAID level 5 (disk striping with parity), what steps must be taken**

when an error in one of the member disks is detected? Select the best response.

A. After seeing the Disk Sector Error Detected dialog box, use Disk Administrator to regenerate the damaged data areas.

B. After seeing the Disk Sector Error Detected dialog box, shut down the server, replace the appropriate disk, and then reboot.

C. After seeing the Disk Sector Error Detected dialog box, use the Disk Administrator to orphan the affected member and then shut down and replace the drive. Reboot and use the Disk Administrator to rebuild the appropriate member of the fault-tolerant volume.

D. After receiving a message indicating the inaccessibility of a member of a fault-tolerant volume, shut down and replace the disk. Reboot and use Disk Administrator to acknowledge the new drive, add its area to the volume, and then regenerate the volume's set fault-tolerance status.

E. Do nothing. NT automatically orphans the drive and repairs the information on-the-fly. The drive should be replaced only when an error develops that affects NT's capability to regenerate the information.

54. **Which of the following are tabs found in the Networking applet in the Control Panel?**

A. Adapters

B. Services

C. Drivers

D. Shares

E. Identification

55. **You are preparing to set up a number of new servers in each of several departments. You have only one copy of your NT Server installation CD currently available, although you have purchased the necessary licenses. How can you create a network boot floppy that will attach to your file server so you can install Windows NT Server from a network location to speed up the installation of these new servers as much as possible? Select the best response.**

A. Use the Network Client Administrator and make a Network Installation Startup disk.

B. Boot by using the first disk in the three-disk NT installation set and choose the Make Network Install disk option.

C. Boot to an NT recovery disk and choose the Make Network Install disk option.

D. Use the Network Client Administrator and make an Installation Startup disk.

E. Use the winnt32.exe program in the \i386 directory of the NT 4 installation CD and choose the Make Network Install Startup disk option.

ANSWERS & EXPLANATIONS

1. **D.** The Performance Monitor counters for TCP/IP become available for monitoring TCP/IP performance on a given system only when the SNMP Service is installed on the machine you're trying to monitor. If this service is not installed, the statistical information regarding TCP/IP activity on the system being monitored is not gathered and, therefore, is not available.

   In a TCP/IP network, it is assumed that TCP/IP already is properly installed on all BDCs. In the event that this is not true, unless the system wanting to be monitored is a BDC, the monitoring of TCP/IP performance on a given server is not directly impacted. Because the source of the data for the counters is not the workstation on which Performance Monitor is being run, the SNMP Service should be installed on the NT Server being monitored—not on the workstation from which the monitoring is taking place. Uninstalling NWLink from the NT Server is not directly related to the question under consideration and could possibly result in network communication failure, depending on the protocol needs. Installing the SNMP Service on the primary domain controller (PDC) does not have any direct impact on the capability to monitor TCP/IP activity on an NT Server in the domain.

2. **C.** Adding a second network card to the Sales server (thus creating a separate physical subnet) allows isolation of the network traffic generated by the large file transfers originating from the marketing servers. This effectively reduces the total network traffic on each resulting network segment.

   Adding second network cards to the two marketing servers either switches only the NICs used by the marketing servers for the LAN (if no change is made on the NIC for the Sales server) or results in completely isolating the rest of the LAN from the Sales server. Binding a second IP address to the NIC on the Sales server does not clearly perform the desired task. Additional steps would have to be taken for this to result in the desired effect. Using the AT command clearly does not apply to this situation. The AT utility does not directly affect network traffic in any way.

3. **C.** If the server that holds the mandatory profile for a user when logging in to the network is down, the user will not have the capability to log on to the network. The user can use a local profile to log in to the NT Server locally, but logging in to the network will not succeed.

   Users do not have the ability to change their own mandatory profile; thus, any steps involving user interaction or modification of a mandatory profile are incorrect. A mandatory profile does not maintain any sort of configurable expiration date attribute. In addition, a user theoretically would not have access to this attribute. Because the question refers to a mandatory profile, any corruption of the `NTUSER.DAT` (not the `NTUSER.MAN`) file would have no impact. If a user is subject to a mandatory profile, he does not have the option to use a different roaming profile other than the roaming status of the mandatory profile itself.

4. **A - B.** Real-mode CD-ROM drivers are necessary for access to the CD-ROM. The `winnt.exe` file is located in the `\i386` subdirectory of the installation and is used to start the installation process. The first disk of the three-disk set created by `winnt.exe` is still in the floppy drive after the disks are finished. Rebooting the server is an automatic option when creation of the three-disk boot set is completed.

The `winnt32.exe` installation program is for a 32-bit environment and does not work for non-32-bit operating systems. When installing, it is not necessary to provide the location of the installation files by manually typing the path. The location of the installation files already is provided by the installation program when it is run from the same location as the remainder of the setup files. This is the case when installing from the CD-ROM.

5. **B - C - D.** The question asks what procedures can be followed to add the workstations to the domain. Reinstalling NT Workstation is an option, although it is not the preferred option. The Server Manager on the NT Server is used to add the computer account to the domain. The Network applet in the Control Panel of the workstation to be added is the preferred method of joining a domain. Server Manager on the workstation is applicable. The User

Manager for Domains utility applies to user accounts.

6. **A - B.** To create a bootable NT startup floppy disk to boot to the mirror drive in a mirror set, you must copy several files to the disk, including `NTLDR` and `NTDETECT.COM`.

The file `BOOTSECT.COM` is an optional file required when dual-booting to another OS. The file `BOOT.INI` must be altered to reflect the location of the mirror partition. The file `NTBOOTD.COM` does not exist.

7. **D.** Reinstalling one of the member servers as a BDC provides a second server capable of validating logons. This creates an added resource to decrease the amount of time required to log on to the network.

Member servers cannot be used to validate network logons. You cannot have more than one primary domain controller; hence, upgrading a member server to a PDC creates a new domain. Adding another member server does not alleviate network logon validation resources, because member servers do not validate domain logins. Reinstalling the PDC as a BDC is not possible without altering the current domain setup; certainly, this would not decrease logon times.

8. **B.** Server Manager enables you to manage shared directories on a server remotely from a client system. By choosing Computer-Shared Directories, a user can create, stop, and manage a share remotely.

The Windows Explorer can be used for creating shares on a local computer but not remotely. The User Manager for Domains utility does not work with sharing network resources. There currently is no Resource Manager for NT Server utility. The Control Panel consists of numerous applets; by itself, however, the Control Panel is just a host window.

9. **A - C.** If the NT 3.51 workstation uses a different frame type for the IPX header structure, that workstation is not able to detect frames built to a different header structure as defined by the frame type. This effectively hides frames from one another. If the workstation is not even using a compatible protocol at all, as in the case of NWLink not being installed, it is not able to see the NT 4 workstations.

A difference in NT build numbers has no direct relationship to this scenario. Rebooting the NT 3.51 workstation has no additional effect on this scenario. No immediate factor causes NT 4 and NT 3.51 workstations to not be able to communicate by using NWLink.

10. **B.** Whenever a majority of the network traffic generated on a system is attributable to a specific protocol, listing that protocol first in the bindings list improves performance. This performance boost is derived from quicker recognition of the packets from that protocol.

Adding a second network card creates a second physical network but does not guarantee a performance boost. There is no way to restrict traffic on a protocol basis. Uninstalling TCP/IP eliminates the TCP/IP traffic altogether.

11. **B.** Before anything can be done to re-create or repair a mirror set, the original mirror set must be broken. Although a member of a mirror set might be unavailable, the mirror set relationship still must be broken prior to repairing the individual members.

There is no need to install an independent operating system on the replacement mirror drive. Creating a new mirror set is unnecessary because this already was done in the question. Formatting the replacement drive is unnecessary, as is creating a volume.

12. **B.** User Manager for Domains is used to specify the location of a user's home directory by providing the Universal Naming Convention (UNC) path to the directory share.

Creating a local drive-letter mapping does no good, because the home directory path must be not be limited to a local mapping. The Network applet in the Control Panel has no provision for specifying home directories. Likewise, the Passwords applet in Control Panel does not provide such functionality.

13. **A - C - D.** A minimum of two disks is required to stripe data writes. To provide disk striping with parity, a minimum of three disks is required to both stripe data writes and parity information writes. To perform disk duplexing, two controllers and two drives are required to duplex across controller/drive pairs.

Disk striping with parity does not inherently require two controllers. Disk mirroring cannot be performed with only one disk drive.

14. **B - C - D.**   Because the question mentions that installing CSNW on any workstation is not desired, installation of Gateway Service for NetWare is required on the NT Server. Installation of CSNW on the server also is required. Access on the NetWare server is handled by creating an NT user; this user will be a member of a group on the NetWare server named NTGATEWAY.

    The question indicates that installing CSNW on *any* workstation is not desired. Because the NetWare server is 4.11, configuration of the OS/2 namespace on the NetWare volumes is not required.

15. **A - B - D - E.**   Installation of GSNW is required on the NT Server because not all workstations have CSNW installed for direct communication with the NetWare server. For those desired, CSNW can be installed to provide better performance in accessing a NetWare server. Because the NetWare server is earlier than NetWare 4.11, configuration of the OS/2 namespace on the NetWare volumes is required to support long filenames.

    No groups need to be created directly on the NT Server to support access to a NetWare server.

16. **B - D - E.**   A mirror set can be created without adding another adapter or another disk drive. A stripe set with parity requires a minimum of three disks, which can be accomplished by adding just one more hard drive to the disk configuration. Disk duplexing requires a minimum of two disk controllers, which can be accomplished by adding one more adapter to the disk configuration.

The concept of disk duplexing with parity is an imaginary mix of disk fault-tolerance concepts. Disk striping alone does not provide fault tolerance; hence, it does not satisfy the requirements of the question.

17. **B - D.**   If the NT installation program fails to automatically determine the existence of a CD-ROM, the primary option left is to restart the installation and choose the manual CD-ROM option. Loading real-mode drivers (if available) followed by copying the files to the hard drive would work, although it should be noted that this definitely is not the desired alternative.

    Restarting the server will not cause the setup program to consistently detect the CD-ROM if it failed to do so on previous boots. It is not possible to ignore the failure to recognize a CD-ROM and to continue with installation of NT from a CD-ROM. The installation will not reach loading of the 32-bit environment.

18. **A.**   Increasing the sampling interval results in performance counter data being checked on a less frequent basis, which reduces the processing overhead.

    Logging to a file rather than monitoring real-time does not alleviate the resources required nor the processing requirements; it merely delays the capability to review the data immediately. Alternating the time frames during which the servers are monitored does not allow for concurrent monitoring of the servers, as is currently being performed. Decreasing the sampling interval increases the processing requirements, which decreases workstation performance even further. Increasing the amount of memory on the workstation can improve performance during times of monitoring, but this option cannot be considered a convenient option (as the question requires).

19. **D.** To format a newly created partition, a user must either exit the Disk Administrator to enforce the changes and then reopen it to perform the format, or, more conveniently, click the Commit Changes Now command button.

Disk Administrator does not have a Save Changes to Disk option or an Apply Changes Now option. Rebooting the server involves exiting Disk Administrator, which commits the changes. This option, however, is not required. Doing nothing is not an option, because the partition information will not have been written to the drive.

20. **C.** Restoring files to a different path and then comparing the restored files to the originals is the only way to guarantee complete success of restoration procedures.

Backups performed at a given frequency do not test for success of the processes. Any methods of verification short of a full cycle of backup, restore, and compare do not guarantee successful backup procedures.

21. **B.** By using the Network applet in the Control Panel on the PDC, the domain name served by the primary domain controller can effectively be changed to a different name. This is the most popular method of changing a domain name.

Reinstalling NT Server on a PDC can result in the domain name being changed, although this method certainly is not the desired method. Reinstallation can generate many more changes in the network than simply changing the domain name. In NT Server, no utility or applet is referred to as the Domain Manager; therefore, a Replicate Changes option does not exist. Certainly, changing a domain name is a valid administrative option. The Server Manager cannot currently be used to change a domain's name.

22. **D.** The Repair option provides a mechanism for restoring boot files in cases when corruption to one or more files might have occurred.

Formatting the boot partition is not a desired action in this scenario, because it wipes out the NT installation. Likewise, running sys.com damages NT further. In addition, installing NT is not a desired option. A simpler action, such as choosing the Repair option, might correct the problem.

23. **B.** The Performance Monitor monitors a number of system states, as provided by the available counters. One of these values is the available disk space.

Server Manager and Network Monitor do not provide similar functionality. Resource Manager and System Tracker are nonexistent utilities.

24. **B - C - D.** To configure or enable an NT Server to function as an IP router—or to simply provide IP routing functionality—three primary steps must be taken. The NT Server must be provided with at least two network cards. The two network cards represent the two individual subnets that will have their traffic routed. Each NIC must be

assigned a unique IP to the card. Finally, IP forwarding must be enabled on the TCP/IP protocol as bound to the network cards.

Moving the TCP/IP protocol binding to the top of the protocols binding list is not a requirement. No service exists by the name of Router.

25. **D.**   User Manager for Domains can administer either domain accounts from the domain accounts database or local accounts from the local accounts database (but not at the same time).

User Manager for Domains is not limited to administering local accounts, nor is it limited to domain accounts as the name implies. Domain accounts and local accounts cannot be administered simultaneously. Account administration of local accounts is not limited to the PDC.

26. **A - C - E.**   To receive notification of power failure (and, hence, the startup of an attached UPS), NT Server must be configured with the Alerter, Messenger, and UPS services running.

The Spooler service supports print functionality in NT Server, and the Site Server Message Builder service is one of many services that supports Microsoft Site Server.

27. **B.**   Windows for Workgroups 16-bit clients require an additional drive-letter mapping to make home directories available to the user.

Windows for Workgroups clients are not denied the capability to connect to NT Server–based home directories. Access permissions are not granted or denied based on

whether a client is 16- or 32-bit. Creating a network share for a home directory intended for a WFW client is an unnecessary action.

28. **A - C - D.**   Members of the Account Operators group can perform many tasks. Some of these capabilities include account administration functions such as creating or modifying user accounts or modifying groups. Account Operators also can perform actions not directly related to user accounts, such as logging on or shutting down an NT Server.

Account Operators cannot assign rights relating to users, such as modifying existing rights.

29. **B.**   Deleting a partition that contains a system file results in the loss of that file, potentially causing catastrophic problems. For this reason, NT Server does not allow any partition deletion requests to be honored.

Exiting Disk Administrator results in partition changes being enforced. Because partitions containing system files cannot be deleted, the request is inverted when made, not when attempting to be enforced. This also is the case with the Commit Changes button.

30. **C - E.**   Disabling the disk performance counters requires the same command-line utilities used to enable the counters. Therefore, disabling the counters requires the DISKPERF utility with the -N command. After issuing this command, restarting the computer is required to stop the counters.

31. **A.** Although binding TCP/IP to the client might provide access directly to the printer, access to the printer share can be accomplished only by installing NetBEUI on the NT Server.

32. **B.** Exiting Disk Administrator causes requested changes to be enforced, although this is not the only way to enforce changes. Clicking Commit Changes Now is another method.

    A server restart is not required to enforce changes made in Disk Administrator. On the other hand, requested changes do not take effect immediately upon request. Clicking Commit Changes Now is not the only way to enforce the changes. Apply Changes is not an available option.

33. **A - B.** Changing to a different style keyboard requires running NT setup to make the necessary driver changes. The same driver changes can be made by using the General tab in the Keyboard applet of the Control Panel.

    NT does not have the capability to automatically recognize when new keyboards are switched out. Similarly, reinstalling or simply rebooting NT Server does not make the proper adjustments for new keyboards.

34. **D.** The Pages/sec counter of the Memory object can reveal when excessive paging is occurring on a system. This typically is a sign of insufficient RAM installed on the system.

    The Committed Bytes and Available Bytes counters of the Memory object do not address paging issues. The Pages/sec counter is from the Memory object, not the Disk

Access object. Disk counters are not necessary for monitoring paging issues.

35. **A - B - C - E.** If a CD-ROM does not exist on the MS-DOS system, running `winnt.exe` from a connected network share after copying the installation files to the share can allow installation of NT.

36. **A - B - C - D.** Restoring a file from a tape backup can be performed by members of Backup Operators, Server Operators, or Administrators. In addition, the Restore File right can be explicitly granted to a user.

37. **A - D - E.** With NT Directory Services, users are provided a method of single-user logon to the NT domain model. This provides automatic access to any resource assigned to an account through an access token provided to a user by NT Directory Services. Account administration also is centralized for ease and convenience.

38. **C.** By placing a pagefile on each drive, you can take advantage of the individual read/write drive mechanisms on each drive, improving the total efficiency of the paging process. By avoiding the first disk, contention with the drive hosting the system files can be avoided.

    Placing a pagefile on each drive (including the first) is good for optimizing, but the first partition should not be used. Placing a pagefile segment on each partition is not necessary. Two different hard drive partitions on the same physical hard drive do not further optimize the pagefile; therefore, it is unnecessary. Placing a pagefile on one disk does not optimize the pagefile.

39. **C.**   Loading Gateway Services for NetWare (GSNW) opens up access to resources on the NetWare server by way of the NT Server. Use of this service replaces use of the Client for NetWare Services (CSNW) on each client.

   Simply enabling NWLink on the server does not open up access to the NetWare server. File Services for NetWare addresses access by NetWare clients to files on the NT Server, not vice versa. RIP and SAP do not address NT client-to-NetWare server communications; therefore, they do not apply to this question.

40. **C.**   Creating a mirror set is your only option. By using the two non-boot-partition drives, you can set up a mirror set that provides fault tolerance.

   A stripe set with parity requires the use of at least two drives, but a drive containing the boot and system files cannot be one of those drives. Therefore, this system does not have enough drives to set up a stripe set with parity. Using a stripe set without parity does not provide any fault tolerance, which was one condition of the question. Duplexing your disk drives certainly provides fault tolerance, but it also requires that a second controller be added to this system.

41. **B.**   Booting the system to VGA mode and then installing the correct video driver (provided by the manufacturer of the video card) should work. As long as the video card is on the hardware compatibility list, it should work properly.

Any video cards bought at this point should have no Y2K issues, especially because the function of a video card is controlled primarily by onboard chips. It is conceivable that a video driver could be written by using some type of time-based function, but it is safe to assume that video cards will not be victims of the Y2K issue. Reseating the video card usually is used to fix a complete lack of video; thus, the system would not be able to boot at all. Under most circumstances, simply rebooting the system does not induce the system to work, especially when the system boots but has incorrect video.

42. **A.**   The Windows Event Viewer is the primary tool used to check for system, application, or security messages regarding the operation of Windows NT and for any software components running on it.

   The Device Manager is a Windows 95/98 system properties tab. It is not available in Windows NT. The Registry is not designed for users to view common or repetitive data, configuration values, or notifications.

43. **B.**   Before the Registry of an NT Server can be configured remotely, the first step is to make sure Server services is running on the remote NT system.

   Starting the Registry Editor on the local computer is not the first step; it is, however, a necessary step to remotely configure a Registry. Starting the Registry Editor on the remote computer is not a required step. Use of the NetBEUI protocol by the remote NT computer being configured also is not a required step. In fact, it is not directly related to the process at all.

44. **A.** The Remote Access Permissions windows of the Remote Access Admin program are used to grant, to revoke, to grant all, or to revoke all dial-in permissions to and from users of the server. Because the accounts domain is the Accounting domain, and the Marketing domain (the resource domain) trusts the Accounting domain, giving dial-in permission to those users enables the desired access.

The User Manager for Domains utility does not allow the assignment of dial-in permissions. Many different user rights can be assigned, but dial-in permissions are not one of those user rights. Granting dial-in permissions to members of the Marketing domain does not do any good because that domain was listed as the resource domain that users wanted to access.

45. **E.** When a server is destined to perform the functions of a primary domain controller or to act as an application server, requesting the Server service to retain enough memory resources to effectively and efficiently serve the numerous user logon requests, application file requests, and so on can improve server performance. In addition, this setting should be used for servers functioning as backup domain controllers (in a multi-domain controller environment).

A server that expects no more than 64 users should be configured with the Balance setting. Being a member of a workgroup has no direct impact on the expected type of usage; therefore, without explicit indications of user count, the server should be set to Balance. Generic network throughput is not directly related to the server setting Maximize Throughput for Network Applications. A server expected to function as a file and print server should be set to Maximize Throughput for File Sharing.

46. **B.** The `uptomp.exe` utility is found in the NT resource kit. This utility is used to upgrade certain portions of NT Server system code to fully support a multi-processor system. This utility, whose name is short for Upgrade to Multi-Processor, is necessary because portions of NT code are left optimized for single-processor systems. It is this code that `uptomp.exe` upgrades.

After running `uptomp.exe`, reinstalling NT Server is not a necessary or recommended step. Along with the use of `uptomp.exe`, no permissions need to be reassigned. In addition, restarting the server is not necessary after running this utility.

47. **A.** By allowing any authentication including clear text but requiring the engineers to use MS-CHAP, the data being transferred over the RAS connection will be encrypted. Third-party PPP clients, however, can still connect.

48. **B.** `winnt32.exe` is the Windows NT 4 installation program designed to be run from a Windows 32-bit environment. Running `winnt32` from Windows NT 3.5x results in most of your system settings and customizations being preserved during the migration, as long as Windows NT 4 is installed into the same directory as the original system installation directory for Windows NT 3.5x.

Running `winnt.exe` from DOS and installing Windows NT 4 does not preserve your system settings, even if you install into the same directory as Windows NT 3.5x. Windows NT does not use a `setup.exe` application to install. `winnt32` cannot be run from DOS because it is designed to be run from a 32-bit environment.

49. **A.** To audit RAS client dial-in information, logging in to the `device.log` file can be enabled in the Registry.

Restarting the RAS server does not reveal any information about the nature of the initialization problems. Network Monitor does not capture or display any information regarding dial-in access attempts. The Remote Access Admin utility does not have an option to enable auditing of dial-in access.

50. **B - C - E.** RAID Level 1 (disk mirroring) is a RAID implementation supported by NT, creating duplicate concurrent copies of a chosen hard disk. RAID Level 5 (disk striping with parity) also is supported by NT, where the parity information generation of a software process is handled by the operating system NT. RAID Level 0 (basic disk striping) is supported by NT, although it is not highly recommended because of its lack of fault tolerance.

RAID Level 0 does not refer to disk duplexing. RAID Level 1, as implemented by NT, encompasses both disk mirroring and disk duplexing. Furthermore, RAID Level 0 does not refer to disk striping with parity, which is more aptly described as RAID level 5.

51. **C.** When users have difficulty printing to a network printer or print server, the problem may be corrected by stopping and restarting the spooler service. This service is responsible for spooling the print jobs to the disk and when a print job can not be deleted or restarted, the spooler service must be stopped and restarted to correct the problem.

The printer queue can not actually be rebuilt, except by resending the existing print jobs to the printer. Print jobs will not work if print jobs can not also be deleted from the queue. Turning the printer off for 15 seconds may occasionally correct some network problems, but it is not considered a standard fix, and does not properly address the issue.

52. **A.** The proper order for installing the tape backup unit first involves physically installing the tape drive and controller into the system. After this is completed, the driver for the SCSI controller should be installed. This is followed by restarting the NT Server for the driver to load into memory.

Installing the SCSI driver first might keep the controller from being recognized upon reboot.

53. **D.** NT's support for RAID Level 5 (disk striping with parity) includes the capability to regenerate lost information from the saved parity information. Regenerating this information on-the-fly is a core functionality of proper implementation of RAID Level 5. After being notified that a disk member of the fault-tolerant volume no longer is accessible, the disk immediately

should be replaced. Shut the system down, replace the drive, and then reboot. The Disk Administrator then should be used to set up the new drive and to add the storage area to the volume set (including the final step of regenerating the stripe set).

There is no error message indicating `Disk Sector Error Detected`. NT notifies the user that the entire disk is not accessible. Furthermore, Disk Administrator is not used to regenerate lost data directly. Replacing the disk is required, although the Disk Administrator must initiate the regeneration of the entire volume set in one process. Although NT automatically recognizes the failed member, replacing the disk is required because of the overhead necessary to generate the lost information on-the-fly and the loss of fault tolerance in this situation.

54. **A - B - E.** The Network applet in Control Panel contains five tabs: Identification, Services, Protocols, Adapters, and Bindings. The Adapters tab provides the capability to change the properties of the installed adapters. The Services tab provides the capability to remove or install additional services concerning network functionality. The Identification tab handles the server name and domain or workgroup membership information.

The Networking applet in Control Panel does not provide a Drivers tab or a Shares tab. Shares are handled either in the Server Control Panel applet or by NT Explorer.

55. **A.** The Network Client Administrator can be used to make a Network Installation Startup disk. This creates a single, unique floppy disk for each client on which you want to install NT Server. Booting to this floppy automatically installs all the necessary client software directly from the server without any user intervention. This requires a unique floppy for each system, but the additional effort required to do this usually is less than the time needed to answer the installation questions when using a generic Installation Disk Set.

The three-disk set created initially during NT Server setup does not have an option to make a network install disk. Furthermore, until NT Server installation is initiated on one of the new servers, a set of disks must already be available. An NT recovery disk does not have a Make Network Install Disk option. The `winnt32.exe` program is not used to create a disk capable of installing NT over the network.

The Network Client Administrator has the capability to create two kinds of installation disk sets. The Make Installation Disk option creates a generic set of installation disks that still require the user to input information during the installation process. This is slightly slower when installing a small number of clients and generally is reserved for situations involving many clients.

NT Server exam instructions:

You have 90 minutes to complete 55 questions. The passing score is 764 out of 1,000. Each correctly answered question is worth 18 points. There are two types of questions:

Multiple Choice: Select the correct answer.

Multiple Multiple Choice: You must select all correct answers to receive the 18 points. If there are three correct answers and you mark only two, that question does not count for any points.

The answers and explanations follow the actual test. We suggest you set a timer to track your progress while taking the practice exam; the time-constraint on the test often is a big obstacle to overcome. Begin after you set your time.

EXAM QUESTIONS

1. **Which statements about NTFS are true? Select all that apply.**

    A. NTFS is the only file system for NT that can support filenames over 8.3.

    B. NTFS easily can be converted to FAT.

    C. NTFS provides file-system security.

    D. NTFS has less overhead than FAT.

2. **Which of the following are true for Point-to-Point Tunneling Protocol? Select all that apply.**

    A. It uses the Internet for connections.

    B. It has lower hardware costs than other network solutions.

Practice Exam 2

    C. It provides security.

    D. It has high transmission costs.

3. **Which protocols can be used by Windows NT Server for Remote Access Service? Select all that apply.**

    A. TCP/IP

    B. NetBEUI

    C. IPX

    D. SNMP

4. **Jim, who is currently a member of the support group, calls to request access to the Accounting Group share. You add him to the Accounting Group, which currently has Change access to this share. Jim calls back an hour later complaining that he still cannot access the Accounting share. Which option might fix the problem? Select the best response.**

    A. Wait until synchronization has occurred.

    B. Have Jim log off and then log back on.

C. The next time the PDC is rebooted, the access permission will be correct.

D. Wait until directory replication occurs.

5. **Your company has purchased several 4GB drives for setting up servers throughout your building. The Marketing department needs fault-tolerant data storage of at least 12GB. What is the minimum number of drives the Marketing department must have in its server to set up Windows NT RAID 5 and still meet the 12GB minimum requirement and boot requirements? Select the best response.**

   A. 2

   B. 3

   C. 4

   D. 5

6. **You've created a page file on each physical disk. How does this affect the system? Select the best response.**

   A. It improves overall performance because more than one disk I/O can be performed simultaneously.

   B. You are able to use less disk space for the paging file.

   C. It makes it easier to convert to RAID 5 if you need to do so later.

   D. It degrades overall performance.

7. **Which of the following cannot be implemented by using a DHCP server? Select all that apply.**

   A. IP addresses

   B. DNS server address

   C. WINS server address

   D. Profile path

8. **The administrator of the domain XYZ has noticed problems with the application server's performance. The administrator suspects that the processor needs to be upgraded. Using Performance Monitor, which counter values can prove the suspicions about processor activity being too high? Select the two best responses.**

   A. System Object processor Queue length < 2

   B. System Object processor Queue length > 2

   C. % Processor Time = 1%

   D. % Processor Time = 99%

9. **You have a NetWare 4.x network to which you want to add a Windows NT server to utilize as an application server. To do this, what must you install to enable your NetWare clients to access applications on your server? Select the best response.**

   A. TCP/IP protocol

   B. NWLink protocol

   C. IPX Service

   D. Gateway Services for NetWare

10. You are considering converting all your existing NetWare clients to NT. If you decide not to convert them, what must be done to each NetWare client PC so it can connect to the NT servers? Select the best response.

    A. Install Gateway Services for NetWare on the NT Server.

    B. Install Gateway and Client Services for NetWare on the NT Server.

    C. Install File and Print Services for NetWare on each client.

    D. Install a Microsoft Redirector on each client.

11. You want Windows DHCP clients on two subnets to receive IP addresses from a Windows NT DHCP server on a third subnet. Which service is required on a local Windows NT server to accomplish this? Select the best response.

    A. Gateway Services for DHCP

    B. DHCP Relay Agent

    C. RIP for TCP/IP

    D. BOOTP

12. You want to migrate all your NetWare clients to Windows NT by using the Migration Tool for NetWare. What needs to be loaded on the NT server to complete the migration? Select the best response.

    A. File and Print Services for NetWare

    B. Directory Replicator for NetWare

    C. Gateway Services for NetWare

    D. RIP for NetWare

13. You want to upgrade NT Server from 3.51 to 4.0 from a distribution share on the network. Which command line should you execute to perform a floppyless upgrade while running NT 3.51? Select the best response.

    A. `winnt.exe /F`

    B. `setup.exe`

    C. `winnt32.exe /F`

    D. `winnt32.exe /B`

14. You currently have 1,000 domain users complaining about logons being too slow. You notice that the Logons/sec counter in Performance Monitor is high. What can be done to speed up the time it takes to log on to the domain? Select the best response.

    A. Add another PDC.

    B. Increase the Logon Concurrency entry in the Registry.

    C. Increase the Pulse Concurrency entry in the Registry.

    D. Add another BDC.

15. You have an NT server with two physical drives. Currently, the system and boot files are on the first drive, and the page file is on the second. You decide to add another page file to the first disk, equal in size to the amount of RAM installed on the server. By splitting the page file between the two drives, what benefits will you receive? Select all that apply.

A. You will get better performance.

B. You will get a crash dump file if the system fails.

C. You will get fault tolerance.

D. You will decrease page swapping.

16. **You are attempting to figure out the best time to schedule your weekly backups for the NT servers on your network. How can you gather this information? Select the best response.**

    A. Review the Event Log.

    B. Use the Chart option in Performance Monitor.

    C. Use the Log option in Performance Monitor.

    D. Review the System Load log.

17. **When repairing a damaged Windows NT installation, the repair option Verify Windows NT System Files does what? Select the best response.**

    A. It prompts for replacement of each Registry file.

    B. It verifies that NT is an option in `boot.ini`.

    C. It replaces files such as `NTLDR` and `NTOSKRNL.EXE`.

    D. It verifies and/or fixes the boot sector and `NTLDR`.

18. **Using the NTBackup utility, which of the following options must be selected to perform a successful backup of the local Registry on an NT server? Select all that apply.**

A. Select the local drive containing the Registry as part of the backup.

B. Select the Backup Local Registry check box.

C. Select the Registry check box.

D. Select the directory that contains the Registry.

19. **You currently have an NT server running virus-scan software that automatically detects and cleans viruses. You accidentally leave a floppy in the server while rebooting it. After the server comes back up, a virus alert notifies you that the server was infected with a boot sector virus and the contents of the boot sector have been cleaned to remove the virus. The next time the server restarts, the server does not boot successfully because it cannot find the operating system. What steps need to be taken to fix the problem? Select the best response.**

    A. Boot from the emergency repair disk and restore the boot partition.

    B. Boot the server with the Windows NT installation disks and use Server Manager to restore the boot partition.

    C. Boot the server with the Windows NT installation disks and use the emergency repair disk to restore the boot partition.

    D. Boot the system by using an NT boot disk and use the emergency repair disk to restore the boot partition.

20. **You have a total of five hard disks on your NT server. The first disk contains**

the boot and system partitions. The remaining four disks are configured as a stripe set with parity containing user data files. The first disk fails and needs to be replaced. What step must you take to recover from this failure? Select the best response.

   A. Reinstall NT Server to disk one.

   B. You need to recover all five disks from tape backup.

   C. Reinstall NT Server to disk one and then restore the other four disks from tape backup.

   D. Reinstall NT Server to disk one and then restore the Registry information from tape backup.

21. You have installed a new video card in your NT server because the old one has failed. The new video card is from a different vendor. What must be done to get the NT server working with the new video card? Select the best response.

   A. Boot with the three NT Installation disks and then load the driver for the new video card.

   B. Boot with the three NT Installation disks and then perform an emergency repair to change the video driver to Standard VGA.

   C. Choose the VGA option for Windows NT Server during the boot process. After the system comes up, install the driver for the new video card.

   D. Install the new driver.

22. The system partition on your server has just failed. Fortunately, the system partition was part of a mirror set. Now all you have to do is create a fault-tolerant boot disk so you can boot the system into Windows NT from the mirrored partition. The computer only has the two disks that make up the mirrored set. Both the physical disks are SCSI without the SCSI BIOS enabled. They both are connected to the same SCSI controller card. Which ARC name should be used in the boot.ini file on the boot disk to make sure the disk boots the server successfully into Windows NT? Select the best response.

   A. scsi(0)disk(0)rdisk(0)partition(1)

   B. multi(0)disk(1) rdisk(0)partition(1)

   C. scsi(0)disk(1)rdisk(0)partition(1)

   D. multi(0)disk(0) rdisk(0)partition(1)

23. Which of the following statements are true about disk striping with parity? Select all that apply.

   A. Striping requires less disk overhead than mirroring.

   B. Striping has better read performance than mirroring.

   C. Striping supports up to 32 hard disks.

   D. Striping requires two hard disks.

24. You have the memory.dmp file your NT server created after a system failure. What utility can you use to decode the data in that file? Select the best response.

A. `dumpexam.exe`

B. `rdisk.exe`

C. `dumpflop.exe`

D. `dumpchk.exe`

25. **Steve is logged in as the administrator on his NT workstation computer, and he wants to join a domain called HEAD-QUARTERS. What is the best way to accomplish this? Select the best response.**

    A. The domain administrator for HEAD-QUARTERS can add Steve's work-station on the PDC. Steve then can join the domain in the Network option of Control Panel.

    B. Steve can add his computer to the domain by using Server Manager and his administrator password.

    C. The domain administrator can add Steve to the domain HEAD-QUARTERS by using the Network option on the PDC.

    D. The administrator of the HEAD-QUARTERS domain can add Steve's machine to the domain by using the Network option in Control Panel on Steve's machine after supplying the domain administrator username and password.

26. **You want to change a member server on your domain to a BDC. What is the correct procedure to do so? Select the best response.**

    A. Promote the member server to a BDC.

    B. Copy the user accounts database to the member server so it can validate users.

    C. Reinstall the member server as a BDC.

    D. Use the Services option in the Control Panel to start the BDC service for the member server.

27. **Increasing the Pulse Registry entry on the PDC does what? Select the best response.**

    A. Frees memory on the PDC for use by other processes

    B. Decreases the frequency at which BDCs are synchronized, freeing processor time on the PDC

    C. Increases communication with the BDCs, causing domain information to be updated more frequently

    D. Increases the number of BDCs allowed on the domain

28. **The developers department has hired a new user named Mary. You want to add a user account for Mary with the same attributes as an existing worker in the department. Using User Manager for Domains, what procedure should you follow? Select the best response.**

    A. Select the existing user and choose New User from the user pull-down menu.

    B. Create a new user for Mary and then copy the existing user's profile to Mary's account.

    C. Create a new user and then use Edit, Copy Permissions to copy the existing user's permissions.

    D. Select the existing user's account and choose User, Copy.

29. You have created roaming profiles for users in your domain. Your coworkers suggest that you rename `NTUser.dat` to `NTUser.man`. What will this accomplish? Select the best response.

    A. This enables users to choose whether to run the profile at login.

    B. This has no effect on the profile.

    C. This enables the user to change the profile.

    D. This keeps the user from saving any changes to the profile.

30. The users in your domain want to be able to log in at any workstation while retaining desktop attributes specific to each user. How do you implement this? Select the best response.

    A. As long as the users are logging on to the domain at each workstation, their individual profiles will be used by default.

    B. Use the User Manager for Domains to specify the full UNC profile path for each user.

    C. A copy of each user's profile must be placed on the NETLOGON share.

    D. Set up replication to copy all user profiles to each machine.

31. Where would you look to find out why many different users' RAS connections to your NT server are being dropped after users have been connected for various amounts of time? Select the best response.

    A. The `device.log`

    B. The administrative tools Event Viewer on the RAS Server

    C. The `ras.log`

    D. The remote machine's Event Viewer

32. Which of the following statements are true about the Point-to-Point Protocol (PPP)? Select all that apply.

    A. Uses built-in error correction

    B. Uses built-in password encryption

    C. Is used by RAS clients only

    D. Supports secure authentication

33. The development department in your company shares a single new server with one large-capacity hard drive. This department is divided into five groups. The managers of these groups have asked you to create separate locations on the hard drive with controlled access for each group. Which of the following methods can you use? Select the best response.

    A. Create a single primary partition with directories for each group. Share the directories with appropriate permissions for each group.

    B. Create five separate extended partitions, one for each group. Share each partition with the appropriate permissions.

C. Create five separate primary partitions shared with the appropriate permissions for each group. Also create one primary partition for the operating system.

D. Create a single primary partition and subdivide it into five smaller, logical drives.

34. **Which statements are true about a FAT file system under Windows NT? Select all that apply.**

    A. You can use filenames of up to 255 characters.

    B. FAT generally is slower than NTFS.

    C. The maximum file, directory, or partition size under FAT is 2GB.

    D. FAT does not offer the security features offered by NTFS.

35. **Your company needs to implement a fault-tolerance method for the PDC that currently contains one 4GB hard drive. You have decided that 8GB of data storage is necessary. Your coworker suggests that you implement RAID Level 5 (disk striping with parity.) Which of the following statements about this plan are true? Select all that apply.**

    A. This will be more efficient in I/O performance than in disk mirroring (RAID Level 1).

    B. The more disks you use, the more efficient RAID Level 5 becomes in disk-space usage.

C. A minimum of three partitions are needed to implement this plan.

D. If a disk failure occurs, this plan will recover lost data faster than RAID Level 1.

36. **Which of the following statements are true about TCP/IP? Select all that apply.**

    A. It is routable.

    B. It is a widely accepted standard.

    C. It provides compatibility with Novell NetWare IPX/SPX networks.

    D. It was designed for Microsoft Networks.

37. **Which of the following are not one of the eight default Windows NT domain local groups? Select all that apply.**

    A. Administrators

    B. Users

    C. Backup Operators

    D. Power Users

38. **Which of the following statements are true about the Guest account? Select all that apply.**

    A. It is permanent.

    B. Its group memberships can be changed.

    C. It can be disabled.

    D. It inherently has restricted permissions.

39. **Your company has hired some temporary employees. You want to allow them some access to the domain, yet you want them**

to log on only at a single machine. How do you accomplish this? Select the best response.

A. Using User Manager for Domains, add a new user. Use the Logon To option to specify the computer.

B. Add the user locally to the workstation on which you want them to log.

C. Under User Manager for Domains, add a new user and then use the permission pull-down menu to restrict access to a single machine.

D. Add the user locally to the workstation on which you want them to log. Then add this user to the domain's Guest group.

40. Which of the following statements are not true about Access Control Lists (ACLs) in an NTFS file or folder? Select all that apply.

A. They are retained after being backed up or restored to any NTFS volume.

B. They are retained when moved to the same volume.

C. They are retained when copied to any other NTFS folder or volume.

D. They are retained when moved to another NTFS volume.

41. Martha wants to know whether she can access the share "info" from your server. Martha is a member of the global Software group and the global Software Engineers group. Software is a member of your local Reviewers group. Software Engineers is a member of your local Testers group.

The "info" share on your server grants the Reviewers group Read access and the Testers group Change access. The NTFS permissions in this share grant the Testers group Read access and the Reviewers group Full Control access. What access does Martha have to this share? Select the best response.

A. Read and Change

B. Read and Full Control

C. Read

D. Full Control

42. The clients on your Windows NT network use DHCP. None of the computers on one subnet can access any resources on the Internet or on any machines on any other subnet. Which DHCP option most likely is configured wrong? Select the best response.

A. Default gateway

B. WINS server address

C. WINS node type

D. DNS server address

43. Which of the following attributes are true about NetBEUI? Select all that apply.

A. Fast for small networks

B. Easy to administer

C. Routable

D. Frequent broadcasts

44. You have a group of NT workstations that need to access files on a NetWare server. You want to set up a gateway via

an NT server. Which of the following steps are necessary on the NetWare server? Select all that apply.

A. Create a user account for the NT server's gateway service.

B. Put the user account in a group called NTGateway on the NetWare server.

C. Assign Trustee Rights to the previously mentioned accounts.

D. Put the Gateway Service Account in a group called NWLink.

45. Your company's support department has 10 users. It has a computer running NT Server that has been optimized for its current workload. The department is adding 25 users over the next month. What server setting should you configure to keep the machine optimized for the new number of users? Select the best response.

A. Virtual Memory

B. Foreground and Background Task Balance

C. Workstation service

D. Server service

46. Which of the following sentences are true about a hardware-based security host? Select all that apply.

A. It sits between the RAS server and the modem.

B. It provides encryption.

C. It adds a layer of password protection.

D. It requires two or more data lines.

47. You have an RAS server that will be used by employees using a PPP client. This client supports CHAP encryption for logon authentication only. You want to provide the highest level of security possible. What type of authentication should you use? Select the best response.

A. Clear text

B. Microsoft Encrypted Authentication

C. Data encryption

D. PAP encryption

48. You want to use DHCP to configure TCP/IP settings on your remote clients. Which of the following configuration settings cannot be set on remote clients using RAS to connect? Select all that apply.

A. DNS server address

B. Default gateway address

C. WINS server address

D. Default WWW server address

49. At what location should you place your system policy, config.pol, and logon scripts on your Windows NT workstation to have them replicated to your Windows NT server machine? Select the best response.

A. The NT workstation cannot be used as an export replication machine.

B. The files must be placed in the Replication share on your NT workstation computer.

C. The files should be placed in the
`%systemroot%\system32\repl\`
`export` directory.

D. The files should be placed in the
`%systemrrot%\system32\repl\`
`exports\scripts` directory.

50. **Your software department has just purchased a new computer. The department wants to use it to store source code and wants to make it fault-tolerant. What are the minimum disk requirements? Select the best answer.**

    A. Two disk drives with one controller

    B. Two disk drives with two controllers

    C. Three disk drives with one controller

    D. Three disk drives with three controllers

51. **What fault-tolerance levels of RAID are standard with Windows NT Server? Select all that apply.**

    A. 5

    B. 2

    C. 4

    D. 1

52. **Your company has four servers (one PDC and three BDCs). You also have NT Workstation 3.51, NT Workstation 4.0, and Windows 95 clients. You plan to configure one of the servers as a print server. On which machines do you need to load the appropriate drivers? Select the best response.**

A. The print server and the Windows 95 clients

B. The PDC only

C. The print server only

D. The PDCs and the BDCs

E. The PDC and the print server (if they are not the same machine)

53. **To establish a printer pool, what must you do? Select all that apply.**

    A. Configure the printers with the appropriate driver.

    B. Select Enable Print Pooling.

    C. Configure all printers in the pool with the same name.

    D. Add a Pooled port.

    E. Connect all the printers to the same port.

54. **Which of the following clients cannot download print drivers from an NT 4.0 print server? Select all that apply.**

    A. Windows for Workgroups

    B. Windows 95

    C. Windows NT 3.51 Server

    D. Windows NT 4.0 Workstation

    E. Windows NT 4.0 Server

55. **Your support department has just purchased a new machine to use as an application server. The department will use the hard drive from the old server for the system and boot drive, and it has budgeted to purchase some additional hardware. How would you suggest the**

department spend its money to configure the server for maximum performance in disk I/O? Select the best response.

A. Buy as many drives as necessary to support the department's needs and to set up a stripe set.

B. Set up as many mirrored sets (with one controller per set) as necessary to meet the department's requirements.

C. Buy as many drives as necessary and set up a stripe set with parity.

D. Purchase multiple drives, each with its own controller, to set up a stripe set.

ANSWERS & EXPLANATIONS

1. **C.** FAT file systems under NT can support long filenames. NTFS cannot be converted to FAT. NTFS is usable only by Windows NT, and it uses more overhead than FAT.

2. **A - B - C.** PPTP uses the Internet for connections, is less expensive when compared to other network solutions (such as leasing your own T1 line), and encrypts transmissions for security.

3. **A - B - C.** The following protocols can be used with RAS: NetBEUI, TCP/IP, and IPX.

4. **B.** Permissions are contained in the user's access token. This token is generated when the user logs on. The permissions are not checked again until the user logs off and then back on. Jim will have access to the Accounting share the next time he logs on.

5. **D.** Each disk has 4GB of space. In RAID 5, however, one disk of available storage is used up in parity checking. We need to use four disks, or 16GB, to end up with 12GB of actual storage. The system and boot partitions cannot be on a stripe set because NT must load to run the software to mount the stripe set.

6. **A.** When a page file is split between physical disks, performance is improved because disk I/O is shared between the separate disks.

7. **D.** The other answers can be configured by using the Defaults, Global, and Scope options on the DHCP server.

8. **B - D.** The System Object processor Queue length always should be two or less. The 99% Processor time shows that the processor is so loaded it has no free time while tasks are waiting.

9. **B.** The NWLink protocol must be loaded on the NT server for NetWare Clients to access it.

10. **D.** Microsoft Redirector (Client Services for Microsoft Networks) is all the client PCs need to communicate with the NT server.

11. **B.** DHCP Relay Agent allows DHCP to broadcast over multiple subnets.

12. **C.** Gateway Services for NetWare is the NT service that allows for migration by providing the connectivity to the NetWare server and by installing the Migration tool (nwconv.exe).

13. **D.** winnt32.exe is the 32-bit installation program for NT. The /B parameter invokes a floppyless install.

14. **D.** One way to speed up the logon process is to add another BDC. When the PDC is busy, logons can be validated by any available BDC. (Note: Another method is to make sure the PDC Server service is optimized for network applications. This increases logons from 6–7 per second to around 20 per second.)

15. **A - B.** Performance will increase because you can do concurrent reads from the page file. When any part of the page file exists on

the system drive, a system failure will generate a crash dump file.

16. **C.** The Log option in the Performance Monitor saves information over long periods of time. This information can be reviewed later.

17. **C.** All the other answers are tasks performed by other valid installation repair options. C is the task performed by Verify Windows NT System Files for repairing the NT system boot files.

18. **A - B - D.** The local drive and directory that contain the Registry must be selected along with the Backup Local Registry check box. If you do not select all of these, the Registry backup will fail.

19. **C.** The Windows NT installation disks must be loaded first to repair anything from the emergency repair disk.

20. **D.** NT Server needs to be installed to disk one, and the Registry needs to be recovered to get back the shares on the user data files that reside on the remaining four disks.

21. **C.** The VGA option for Windows NT is added by default to the boot.ini file during NT installation. This option is used to troubleshoot video problems with NT.

22. **C.** SCSI represents a disk on which SCSI BIOS is not enabled. MULTI represents a disk other than SCSI or a SCSI accessed by the SCSI BIOS. DISK indicates the hard drive of the controller you are using. RDISK is ignored for SCSI controllers and represents the ordinal number of the disk you are using. PARTITION refers to the partition number, which always is assigned

beginning with the number 1. SCSI/ MULTI, DISK, and RDISK all begin with the number 0.

23. **A - B - C.** If you have four hard drives, mirroring utilizes only 50 percent of disk space. Striping would utilize at least 67 percent. With disk striping, data is split over multiple drives and can be read simultaneously. Disk striping supports 3–32 hard disks.

24. **A.** DUMPEXAM.EXE writes information from the dump file to a text file so you can find out what caused the system failure.

25. **A - D.** Only domain administrators have the capability to add a computer to a domain. After this has been done, a local administrator can join a machine to the domain, as in answer A. In answer D, the machine is added and joined in a single step.

26. **C.** The only way to create a BDC is during the installation of NT Server. A member server never can be promoted to a BDC.

27. **B.** The Pulse Registry entry controls the amount of time between synchronization of the BDCs and the PDC on the domain. Increasing this time decreases the workload on the PDC.

28. **D.** Copying an existing account enables the creation of a new user with identical attributes.

29. **D.** The .man extension on a profile makes it unchangeable by the user. This also is known as a mandatory profile.

30. **B.** The profile path can be set only in the User Manager for Domains, and it must be a full UNC path to be accessed from any machine.

31. **A.** Device errors, such as modem errors, are written to the `device.log` file. Because multiple users are having the same problem, the problem is likely to be on the server end.

32. **A - B - D.** PPP can be used by RAS clients and servers. PPP is not limited to Microsoft, NT, and RAS; it is a universal protocol for dial-in access. UNIX or NetWare computers also can use it.

33. **A.** One partition works because the shared folder permissions can be set individually. B is incorrect because only one extended partition can reside on a hard drive. C is incorrect because a hard drive can contain only four primary partitions. D is incorrect because primary partitions cannot be divided into logical drives.

34. **A - B - D.** The maximum file, directory, or partition size under FAT is 4GB.

35. **A - B.** C is incorrect because you need at least three physical disks not partitions. You also need an additional partition for the boot and system partition. D is incorrect because RAID Level 5 needs to regenerate missing data, whereas RAID Level 1 has a complete copy of missing data.

36. **A - B.** NWLink is required for Novell compatibility, and NetBEUI was designed for Microsoft Networks.

37. **D.** The default NT domain local groups are Administrators, Users, Guests, Backup Operators, Replicator, Print Operators, Server Operators.

38. **A - B - C.** The Guest account has no inherent power or lack of power. Group membership for the account establishes its scope.

39. **A.** By default, a domain user has the capability to log on to all domain machines. The Logon To option in User Manager for Domains gives you the capability to restrict user accounts to certain machines.

40. **C - D.** In both cases, the ACLs are inherited from the destination folder.

41. **C.** The files have Full Control privilege on NTFS because multiple privileges result in the least restrictive privileges. The share has Change privileges for the same reason. When calculating the result between share and file privileges, the most restrictive privilege is used (in this case, Read).

42. **A.** The default gateway setting shows TCP/IP where to send packets destined for remote networks.

43. **A - B - D.** NetBEUI is not routable.

44. **A - B - C.** These are the only three steps that need to be performed on the NetWare server to set up a gateway via an NT Server.

45. **D.** The Server services can be set to Balance, which is optimal for up to 64 connections.

46. **A - C.** A hardware-based security host requires only the normal communication lines set up for RAS communication, and it does not supply encryption.

47. **B.** This is the most secure encryption.

48. **D.** The following addresses can be assigned through DHCP to RAS clients: IP address, default gateway address, WINS server address, WINS node type, DNS server address, and DNS domain names.

49. **A.** Only NT Server can be used as an export replication machine.

50. **A.** Disk mirroring (RAID 1) requires only two drives and a single controller.

51. **A - D.** The following levels of RAID are options under NT: RAID 0 (striping), RAID 1 (mirroring/duplexing), and RAID 5 (striping with parity).

52. **C.** Each machine loads the appropriate drivers from the print server as needed.

53. **A - B.** All printers in a printer pool must be able to utilize the same printer driver. Enable Print Pooling must be selected on the print server.

54. **A.** All Microsoft clients, except WFW clients, can download drivers from 4.0 print servers. The drivers must be installed locally on the WFW computer.

55. **D.** Stripe sets with multiple controllers allow concurrent I/O requests, dramatically improving performance.

Exam Strategies

You must pass rigorous certification exams to become a Microsoft Certified Professional. These closed-book exams provide a valid and reliable measure of your technical proficiency and expertise. Developed in consultation with computer industry professionals who have on-the-job experience with Microsoft products in the workplace, the exams are conducted by two independent organizations. Sylvan Prometric offers the exams at more than 1,400 Authorized Prometric Testing Centers around the world. Virtual University Enterprises (VUE) testing centers offer exams as well.

To schedule an exam, call Sylvan Prometric Testing Centers at 800-755-EXAM (3926) or VUE at 888-837-8616.

This appendix is divided into two main sections. First, it describes the different certification options provided by Microsoft, and how you can achieve those certifications. The second portion highlights the different kinds of examinations and the best ways to prepare for those different exam and question styles.

TYPES OF CERTIFICATION

Currently Microsoft offers seven types of certification, based on specific areas of expertise:

- **Microsoft Certified Professional (MCP).** Qualified to provide installation, configuration, and support for users of at least one Microsoft desktop operating system, such as Windows NT Workstation. Candidates can take elective exams to develop areas of specialization. MCP is the base level of expertise.

- **Microsoft Certified Professional+Internet (MCP+Internet).** Qualified to plan security, install and configure server products, manage server resources, extend service to run CGI scripts or ISAPI scripts, monitor and analyze performance, and troubleshoot problems. Expertise is similar to that of an MCP, but with a focus on the Internet.

- **Microsoft Certified Professional+Site Building (MCP+Site Building).** Qualified to plan, build, maintain, and manage Web sites by using Microsoft technologies and products. The credential is appropriate for people who manage sophisticated, interactive Web sites that include database connectivity, multimedia, and searchable content.

- **Microsoft Certified Systems Engineer (MCSE).** Qualified to effectively plan, implement, maintain, and support information systems with Microsoft Windows NT and other Microsoft advanced systems and workgroup products, such as Microsoft Office and Microsoft BackOffice. MCSE is a second level of expertise.

- **Microsoft Certified Systems Engineer+ Internet (MCSE+Internet).** Qualified in the core MCSE areas, and also qualified to enhance, deploy, and manage sophisticated intranet and Internet solutions that include a browser, proxy server, host servers, database, and messaging and commerce components. An MCSE+Internet–certified professional is able to manage and analyze Web sites.

- **Microsoft Certified Solution Developer (MCSD).** Qualified to design and develop custom business solutions by using Microsoft development tools, technologies, and platforms, including Microsoft Office and Microsoft BackOffice. MCSD is a second level of expertise, with a focus on software development.

- **Microsoft Certified Trainer (MCT).** Instructionally and technically qualified by Microsoft to deliver Microsoft Education Courses at Microsoft-authorized sites. An MCT must be employed by a Microsoft Solution Provider Authorized Technical Education Center or a Microsoft Authorized Academic Training site.

▼ **NOTE**

For the most up-to-date information about each type of certification, visit the Microsoft Training and Certification Web site at http://www.microsoft.com/train_cert. You also can call or email the following sources:

- Microsoft Certified Professional Program: 800-636-7544

- mcp@msprograms.com

- Microsoft Online Institute (MOLI): 800-449-9333

CERTIFICATION REQUIREMENTS

The requirements for certification in each of the seven areas are detailed below. An asterisk after an exam indicates that the exam is slated for retirement.

How to Become a Microsoft Certified Professional

Passing any Microsoft exam (with the exception of Networking Essentials) is all you need to do to become certified as an MCP.

How to Become a Microsoft Certified Professional+Internet

You must pass the following exams to become an MCP specializing in Internet technology:

- Internetworking Microsoft TCP/IP on Microsoft Windows NT 4.0, #70-059

- Implementing and Supporting Microsoft Windows NT Server 4.0, #70-067

- Implementing and Supporting Microsoft Internet Information Server 3.0 and Microsoft Index Server 1.1, #70-077

  OR Implementing and Supporting Microsoft Internet Information Server 4.0, #70-087

How to Become a Microsoft Certified Professional+Site Building

You need to pass two of the following exams in order to be certified as an MCP+Site Building:

- Designing and Implementing Web Sites with Microsoft FrontPage 98, #70-055

- Designing and Implementing Commerce Solutions with Microsoft Site Server 3.0, Commerce Edition, #70-057

- Designing and Implementing Web Solutions with Microsoft Visual InterDev 6.0, #70-152

How to Become a Microsoft Certified Systems Engineer

You must pass four operating system exams and two elective exams to become an MCSE. The MCSE certification path is divided into two tracks: the Windows NT 3.51 track and the Windows NT 4.0 track.

The following lists show the core requirements (four operating system exams) for both the Windows NT 3.51 and 4.0 tracks, and the elective courses (two exams) you can take for either track.

The four Windows NT 3.51 Track Core Requirements for MCSE certification are as follows:

- Implementing and Supporting Microsoft Windows NT Server 3.51, #70-043*

- Implementing and Supporting Microsoft Windows NT Workstation 3.51, #70-042*

- Microsoft Windows 3.1, #70-030*

  OR Microsoft Windows for Workgroups 3.11, #70-048*

  OR Implementing and Supporting Microsoft Windows 95, #70-064

  OR Implementing and Supporting Microsoft Windows 98, #70-098

- Networking Essentials, #70-058

The four Windows NT 4.0 Track Core Requirements for MCSE certification are as follows:

- Implementing and Supporting Microsoft Windows NT Server 4.0, #70-067

- Implementing and Supporting Microsoft Windows NT Server 4.0 in the Enterprise, #70-068

- Microsoft Windows 3.1, #70-030*

  OR Microsoft Windows for Workgroups 3.11, #70-048*

  OR Implementing and Supporting Microsoft Windows 95, #70-064

  OR Implementing and Supporting Microsoft Windows NT Workstation 4.0, #70-073

  OR Implementing and Supporting Microsoft Windows 98, #70-098

- Networking Essentials, #70-058

For both the Windows NT 3.51 and the 4.0 tracks, you must pass two of the following elective exams for MCSE certification:

- Implementing and Supporting Microsoft SNA Server 3.0, #70-013

  OR Implementing and Supporting Microsoft SNA Server 4.0, #70-085

- Implementing and Supporting Microsoft Systems Management Server 1.0, #70-014*

  OR Implementing and Supporting Microsoft Systems Management Server 1.2, #70-018

  OR Implementing and Supporting Microsoft Systems Management Server 2.0, #70-086

- Microsoft SQL Server 4.2 Database Implementation, #70-021

  OR Implementing a Database Design on Microsoft SQL Server 6.5, #70-027

  OR Implementing a Database Design on Microsoft SQL Server 7.0, #70-029

- Microsoft SQL Server 4.2 Database Administration for Microsoft Windows NT, #70-022

  OR System Administration for Microsoft SQL Server 6.5 (or 6.0), #70-026

  OR System Administration for Microsoft SQL Server 7.0, #70-028

- Microsoft Mail for PC Networks 3.2-Enterprise, #70-037

- Internetworking with Microsoft TCP/IP on Microsoft Windows NT (3.5-3.51), #70-053

  OR Internetworking with Microsoft TCP/IP on Microsoft Windows NT 4.0, #70-059

- Implementing and Supporting Microsoft Exchange Server 4.0, #70-075*

  OR Implementing and Supporting Microsoft Exchange Server 5.0, #70-076

  OR Implementing and Supporting Microsoft Exchange Server 5.5, #70-081

- Implementing and Supporting Microsoft Internet Information Server 3.0 and Microsoft Index Server 1.1, #70-077

  OR Implementing and Supporting Microsoft Internet Information Server 4.0, #70-087

- Implementing and Supporting Microsoft Proxy Server 1.0, #70-078

  OR Implementing and Supporting Microsoft Proxy Server 2.0, #70-088

- Implementing and Supporting Microsoft Internet Explorer 4.0 by Using the Internet Explorer Resource Kit, #70-079

How to Become a Microsoft Certified Systems Engineer+ Internet

You must pass seven operating system exams and two elective exams to become an MCSE specializing in Internet technology.

The seven MCSE+Internet core exams required for certification are as follows:

- Networking Essentials, #70-058

- Internetworking with Microsoft TCP/IP on Microsoft Windows NT 4.0, #70-059

- Implementing and Supporting Microsoft Windows 95, #70-064

  OR Implementing and Supporting Microsoft Windows NT Workstation 4.0, #70-073

  OR Implementing and Supporting Microsoft Windows 98, #70-098

- Implementing and Supporting Microsoft Windows NT Server 4.0, #70-067

- Implementing and Supporting Microsoft Windows NT Server 4.0 in the Enterprise, #70-068

- Implementing and Supporting Microsoft Internet Information Server 3.0 and Microsoft Index Server 1.1, #70-077

  OR Implementing and Supporting Microsoft Internet Information Server 4.0, #70-087

- Implementing and Supporting Microsoft Internet Explorer 4.0 by Using the Internet Explorer Resource Kit, #70-079

You must also pass two of the following elective exams for MCSE+Internet certification:

- System Administration for Microsoft SQL Server 6.5, #70-026

- Implementing a Database Design on Microsoft SQL Server 6.5, #70-027

- Implementing and Supporting Web Sites Using Microsoft Site Server 3.0, # 70-056

- Implementing and Supporting Microsoft Exchange Server 5.0, #70-076

    OR Implementing and Supporting Microsoft Exchange Server 5.5, #70-081

- Implementing and Supporting Microsoft Proxy Server 1.0, #70-078

    OR Implementing and Supporting Microsoft Proxy Server 2.0, #70-088

- Implementing and Supporting Microsoft SNA Server 4.0, #70-085

How to Become a Microsoft Certified Solution Developer

The MCSD certification is undergoing substantial revision. Listed next are the requirements for the new track (available fourth quarter 1998), as well as the old.

For the new track, you must pass three core exams and one elective exam.

The core exams include the following:

Desktop Applications Development (1 required)

- Designing and Implementing Desktop Applications with Microsoft Visual C++ 6.0, #70-016

    OR Designing and Implementing Desktop Applications with Microsoft Visual Basic 6.0, #70-176

Distributed Applications Development (1 required)

- Designing and Implementing Distributed Applications with Microsoft Visual C++ 6.0, #70-015

    OR Designing and Implementing Distributed Applications with Microsoft Visual Basic 6.0, #70-175

Solution Architecture (required)

- Analyzing Requirements and Defining Solution Architectures, #70-100

Elective Exams

You must also pass one of the following elective exams:

- Designing and Implementing Distributed Applications with Microsoft Visual C++ 6.0, #70-015

    OR Designing and Implementing Desktop Applications with Microsoft Visual C++ 6.0, #70-016

    OR Microsoft SQL Server 4.2 Database Implementation, #70-021*

- Implementing a Database Design on Microsoft SQL Server 6.5, #70-027

  OR Implementing a Database Design on Microsoft SQL Server 7.0, #70-029

- Developing Applications with C++ Using the Microsoft Foundation Class Library, #70-024

- Implementing OLE in Microsoft Foundation Class Applications, #70-025

- Designing and Implementing Web Sites with Microsoft FrontPage 98, #70-055

- Designing and Implementing Commerce Solutions with Microsoft Site Server 3.0, Commerce Edition, #70-057

- Programming with Microsoft Visual Basic 4.0, #70-065

  OR Developing Applications with Microsoft Visual Basic 5.0, #70-165

  OR Designing and Implementing Distributed Applications with Microsoft Visual Basic 6.0, #70-175

  OR Designing and Implementing Desktop Applications with Microsoft Visual Basic 6.0, #70-176

- Microsoft Access for Windows 95 and the Microsoft Access Development Toolkit, #70-069

- Designing and Implementing Solutions with Microsoft Office (Code-named Office 9) and Microsoft Visual Basic for Applications, #70-091

- Designing and Implementing Web Solutions with Microsoft Visual InterDev 6.0, #70-152

Former MCSD Track

For the old track, you must pass two core technology exams and two elective exams for MCSD certification. The following lists show the required technology exams and elective exams needed to become an MCSD.

You must pass the following two core technology exams to qualify for MCSD certification:

- Microsoft Windows Architecture I, #70-160*

- Microsoft Windows Architecture II, #70-161*

You must also pass two of the following elective exams to become an MSCD:

- Designing and Implementing Distributed Applications with Microsoft Visual C++ 6.0, #70-015

- Designing and Implementing Desktop Applications with Microsoft Visual C++ 6.0, #70-016

- Microsoft SQL Server 4.2 Database Implementation, #70-021*

  OR Implementing a Database Design on Microsoft SQL Server 6.5, #70-027

  OR Implementing a Database Design on Microsoft SQL Server 7.0, #70-029

- Developing Applications with C++ Using the Microsoft Foundation Class Library, #70-024

- Implementing OLE in Microsoft Foundation Class Applications, #70-025

- Programming with Microsoft Visual Basic 4.0, #70-065

OR Developing Applications with Microsoft Visual Basic 5.0, #70-165

OR Designing and Implementing Distributed Applications with Microsoft Visual Basic 6.0, #70-175

OR Designing and Implementing Desktop Applications with Microsoft Visual Basic 6.0, #70-176

- Microsoft Access 2.0 for Windows-Application Development, #70-051

OR Microsoft Access for Windows 95 and the Microsoft Access Development Toolkit, #70-069

- Developing Applications with Microsoft Excel 5.0 Using Visual Basic for Applications, #70-052

- Programming in Microsoft Visual FoxPro 3.0 for Windows, #70-054

- Designing and Implementing Web Sites with Microsoft FrontPage 98, #70-055

- Designing and Implementing Commerce Solutions with Microsoft Site Server 3.0, Commerce Edition, #70-057

- Designing and Implementing Solutions with Microsoft Office (Code-named Office 9) and Microsoft Visual Basic for Applications, #70-091

- Designing and Implementing Web Solutions with Microsoft Visual InterDev 6.0, #70-152

Becoming a Microsoft Certified Trainer

To understand the requirements and process for becoming an MCT, you need to obtain the Microsoft Certified Trainer Guide document from the following site:

http://www.microsoft.com/train_cert/mct/

At this site, you can read the document as Web pages or display and download it as a Word file. The MCT Guide explains the four-step process of becoming an MCT. The general steps for the MCT certification are as follows:

1. Complete and mail a Microsoft Certified Trainer application to Microsoft. You must include proof of your skills for presenting instructional material. The options for doing so are described in the MCT Guide.

2. Obtain and study the Microsoft Trainer Kit for the Microsoft Official Curricula (MOC) courses for which you want to be certified. Microsoft Trainer Kits can be ordered by calling 800-688-0496 in North America. Interested parties in other regions should review the MCT Guide for information on how to order a Trainer Kit.

3. Take the Microsoft certification exam for the product about which you want to be certified to teach.

4. Attend the MOC course for the course for which you want to be certified. This is done so you can understand how the course is structured, how labs are completed, and how the course flows.

◆ **WARNING**

You should consider the preceding steps a general overview of the MCT certification process. The precise steps that you need to take are described in detail on the Web site mentioned earlier. Do not misinterpret the preceding steps as the exact process you need to undergo.

If you are interested in becoming an MCT, you can receive more information by visiting the Microsoft Certified Training Web site at `http://www.microsoft.com/train_cert/mct/` or by calling 800-688-0496.

STUDY AND EXAM PREPARATION TIPS

This part of the appendix provides you with some general guidelines for preparing for the exam. It is organized into three sections. The first section, "Study Tips," addresses your pre-exam preparation activities, covering general study tips. This is followed by "Exam Prep Tips," an extended look at the Microsoft Certification exams, including a number of specific tips that apply to the Microsoft exam formats. Finally, "Putting It All Together" discusses changes in Microsoft's testing policies and how they might affect you.

To better understand the nature of preparation for the test, it is important to understand learning as a process. You probably are aware of how you best learn new material. You may find that outlining works best for you, or you may need to see things as a visual learner. Whatever your learning style, test preparation takes place over time. Although it is obvious that you can't start studying for these exams the night before you take them, it is very important to understand that learning is a developmental process. Understanding it as a process helps you focus on what you know and what you have yet to learn.

Thinking about how you learn should help you to recognize that learning takes place when you are able to match new information to old. You have some previous experience with computers and networking, and now you are preparing for this certification exam. Using this book, software, and supplementary materials will not just add incrementally to what you know. As you study, you actually change the organization of your knowledge as you integrate this new information into your existing knowledge base. This will lead you to a more comprehensive understanding of the tasks and concepts outlined in the objectives and of computing in general. Again, this happens as an iterative process rather than a singular event. Keep this model of learning in mind as you prepare for the exam, and you will make better decisions about what to study and how much more studying you need to do.

Study Tips

There are many ways to approach studying, just as there are many different types of material to study. However, the tips that follow should prepare you well for the type of material covered on the certification exams.

Study Strategies

Individuals vary in the ways they learn information. Some basic principles of learning apply to everyone, however; you should adopt some study strategies that take advantage of these principles. One of these principles is that learning can be broken into various depths. Recognition (of terms, for example) exemplifies a more surface level of learning—you rely on a prompt of some sort to elicit recall. Comprehension or understanding (of the concepts behind the terms, for instance) represents a deeper level of learning. The ability to analyze a concept and apply your understanding of it in a new way or novel setting represents an even further depth of learning.

Your learning strategy should enable you to understand the material at a level or two deeper than mere recognition. This will help you to do well on the exam(s). You will know the material so thoroughly that you can easily handle the recognition-level types of questions used in multiple-choice testing. You will also be able to apply your knowledge to solve novel problems.

Macro and Micro Study Strategies

One strategy that can lead to this deeper learning includes preparing an outline that covers all the objectives and subobjectives for the particular exam you are working on. You should delve a bit further into the material and include a level or two of detail beyond the stated objectives and subobjectives for the exam. Then flesh out the outline by coming up with a statement of definition or a summary for each point in the outline.

This outline provides two approaches to studying. First, you can study the outline by focusing on the organization of the material. Work your way through the points and subpoints of your outline with the goal of learning how they relate to one another. For example, be sure you understand how each of the main objective areas is similar to and different from another. Then do the same thing with the subobjectives; be sure you know which subobjectives pertain to each objective area and how they relate to one another.

Next, you can work through the outline, focusing on learning the details. Memorize and understand terms and their definitions, facts, rules and strategies, advantages and disadvantages, and so on. In this pass through the outline, attempt to learn detail rather than the big picture (the organizational information that you worked on in the first pass through the outline).

Research has shown that attempting to assimilate both types of information at the same time seems to interfere with the overall learning process. Separate your studying into these two approaches, and you will perform better on the exam than if you attempt to study the material in a more conventional manner.

Active Study Strategies

In addition, the process of writing down and defining the objectives, subobjectives, terms, facts, and definitions promotes a more active learning strategy than merely reading the material. In human information-processing terms, writing forces you to engage in more active encoding of the information. Simply reading over it constitutes more passive processing.

Next, determine whether you can apply the information you have learned by attempting to create examples and scenarios of your own. Think about how or where you could apply the concepts you are learning. Again, write down this information to process the facts and concepts in a more active fashion.

The hands-on nature of the step-by-step tutorials and exercises at the ends of the chapters provide further active learning opportunities that will reinforce concepts as well.

Common-sense Strategies

Finally, you should follow common-sense practices in studying. Study when you are alert, reduce or eliminate distractions, take breaks when you become fatigued, and so on.

Pre-testing Yourself

Pre-testing allows you to assess how well you are learning. One of the most important aspects of learning is what has been called meta-learning. *Meta-learning* has to do with realizing when you know something well or when you need to study more. In other words, you recognize how well or how poorly you have learned the material you are studying. For most people, this can be difficult to assess objectively on their own. Practice tests are useful in that they reveal more objectively what you have learned and what you have not learned. You should use this information to guide review and further studying. Developmental learning takes place as you cycle through studying, assessing how well you have learned, reviewing, assessing again, until you feel you are ready to take the exam.

You may have noticed the practice exams included in this book. Use them as part of this process.

Exam Prep Tips

Having mastered the subject matter, your final preparatory step is to understand how the exam will be presented. Make no mistake about it—a Microsoft Certified Professional (MCP) exam will challenge both your knowledge and test-taking skills! This section starts with the basics of exam design, reviews a new type of exam format, and concludes with hints that are targeted to each of the exam formats.

The MCP Exams

Every MCP exam is released in one of two basic formats. What's being called exam format here is really little more than a combination of the overall exam structure and the presentation method for exam questions.

Each exam format utilizes the same types of questions. These types or styles of questions include multiple-rating (or scenario-based) questions, traditional multiple-choice questions, and simulation-based questions. It's important to understand the types of questions you will be presented with and the actions required to properly answer them.

Understanding the exam formats is key to good preparation because the format determines the number of questions presented, the difficulty of those questions, and the amount of time allowed to complete the exam.

Exam Formats

There are two basic formats for the MCP exams: the traditional fixed-form exam and the adaptive form. As its name implies, the fixed-form exam presents a fixed set of questions during the exam session. The adaptive format, however, uses only a subset of questions drawn from a larger pool during any given exam session.

Fixed-form

A fixed-form, computerized exam is based on a fixed set of exam questions. The individual questions are presented in random order during a test session. If you take the same exam more than once, you won't necessarily see the exact same questions. This is because two to three final forms are typically assembled for every fixed-form exam Microsoft releases. These are usually labeled Forms A, B, and C.

The final forms of a fixed-form exam are identical in terms of content coverage, number of questions, and allotted time, but the questions themselves are different. You may have noticed, however, that some of the same questions appear on, or rather are shared across, different final forms. When questions are shared across multiple final forms of an exam, the percentage of sharing is generally small. Many final forms share no questions, but some older exams may have a ten to fifteen percent duplication of exam questions on the final exam forms.

Fixed-form exams also have a fixed time limit in which you must complete the exam.

Finally, the score you achieve on a fixed-form exam, which is always reported for MCP exams on a scale of 0 to 1000, is based on the number of questions you answer correctly. The exam passing score is the same for all final forms of a given fixed-form exam.

The typical format for the fixed-form exam is as follows:

- 50–60 questions

- 75–90 minute testing time

- Question review allowed, including the opportunity to change your answers

Adaptive Form

An adaptive form exam has the same appearance as a fixed-form exam, but differs in both how questions are selected for presentation and how many questions actually are presented. Although the statistics of adaptive testing are fairly complex, the process is concerned with determining your level of skill or ability with the exam subject matter. This ability assessment begins by presenting questions of varying levels of difficulty and ascertaining at what difficulty level you can reliably answer them. Finally, the ability assessment determines if that ability level is above or below the level required to pass that exam.

Examinees at different levels of ability will then see quite different sets of questions. Those who demonstrate little expertise with the subject matter will continue to be presented with relatively easy questions. Examinees who demonstrate a higher level of expertise will be presented progressively more difficult questions. Both individuals may answer the same number of questions correctly, but because the exam-taker with the higher level of expertise can correctly answer more difficult questions, he or she will receive a higher score, and is more likely to pass the exam.

The typical design for the adaptive form exam is as follows:

- 20–25 questions

- 90-minute testing time, although this is likely to be reduced to 45–60 minutes in the near future

- Question review not allowed, providing no opportunity to change your answers

Your first adaptive exam will be unlike any other testing experience you have had. In fact, many examinees have difficulty accepting the adaptive testing process because they feel that they are not provided the opportunity to adequately demonstrate their full expertise.

You can take consolation in the fact that adaptive exams are painstakingly put together after months of data gathering and analysis and are just as valid as a fixed-form exam. The rigor introduced through the adaptive testing methodology means that there is nothing arbitrary about what you'll see! It is also a more efficient means of testing, requiring less time to conduct and complete.

As you can see from Figure A.1, there are a number of statistical measures that drive the adaptive examination process. The most immediately relevant to you is the ability estimate. Accompanying this test statistic are the standard error of measurement, the item characteristic curve, and the test information curve.

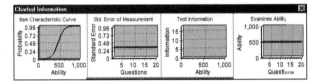

FIGURE A.1
Microsoft's Adaptive Testing Demonstration Program.

The standard error, which is the key factor in determining when an adaptive exam will terminate, reflects the degree of error in the exam ability estimate. The item characteristic curve reflects the probability of a correct response relative to examinee ability. Finally, the test information statistic provides a measure of the information contained in the set of questions the examinee has answered, again relative to the ability level of the individual examinee.

When you begin an adaptive exam, the standard error has already been assigned a target value below which it must drop for the exam to conclude. This target value reflects a particular level of statistical confidence in the process. The examinee ability is initially set to the mean possible exam score: 500 for MCP exams.

As the adaptive exam progresses, questions of varying difficulty are presented. Based on your

pattern of responses to these questions, the ability estimate is recalculated. Simultaneously, the standard error estimate is refined from its first estimated value of one toward the target value. When the standard error reaches its target value, the exam terminates. Thus, the more consistently you answer questions of the same degree of difficulty, the more quickly the standard error estimate drops, and the fewer questions you will end up seeing during the exam session. This situation is depicted in Figure A.2.

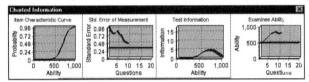

FIGURE A.2
The changing statistics in an adaptive exam.

As you might suspect, one good piece of advice for taking an adaptive exam is to treat every exam question as if it were the most important. The adaptive scoring algorithm is attempting to discover a pattern of responses that reflects some level of proficiency with the subject matter. Incorrect responses almost guarantee that additional questions must be answered (unless, of course, you get every question wrong). This is because the scoring algorithm must adjust to information that is not consistent with the emerging pattern.

New Question Types

A variety of question types can appear on MCP exams. Examples of multiple-choice questions and scenario-based questions appear throughout this book. They appear in the Top Score software as well. Simulation-based questions are new to the MCP exam series.

Simulation Questions

Simulation-based questions reproduce the look and feel of key Microsoft product features for the purpose of testing. The simulation software used in MCP exams has been designed to look and act, as much as possible, just like the actual product. Consequently, answering simulation questions in an MCP exam entails completing one or more tasks just as if you were using the product itself.

The format of a typical Microsoft simulation question is straightforward. It presents a brief scenario or problem statement along with one or more tasks that must be completed to solve the problem. An example of a simulation question for MCP exams is shown in the following section.

A Typical Simulation Question

It sounds obvious, but the first step when you encounter a simulation is to carefully read the question (see Figure A.3). Do not go straight to the simulation application! Assess the problem being presented and identify the conditions that make up the problem scenario. Note the tasks that must be performed or outcomes that must be achieved to answer the question, and review any instructions about how to proceed.

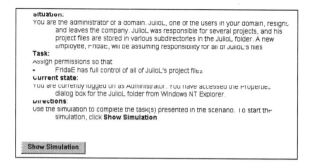

FIGURE A.3
Typical MCP exam simulation question with directions.

The next step is to launch the simulator. Click the Show Simulation button to see a feature of the product, such as the dialog box shown in Figure A.4. The simulation application partially covers the question text on many test center machines. Feel free to reposition the simulation or to move between the question text screen and the simulation using hot keys, point-and-click navigation, or even by clicking the simulation launch button again.

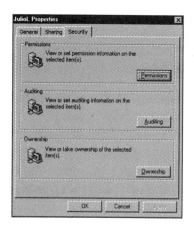

FIGURE A.4
Launching the simulation application.

It is important to understand that your answer to the simulation question is not recorded until you move on to the next exam question. This gives you the added capability to close and reopen the simulation application (using the launch button) on the same question without losing any partial answer you may have made.

The third step is to use the simulator as you would the actual product to solve the problem or perform the defined tasks. Again, the simulation software is designed to function, within reason, just as the product does. But don't expect the simulation to reproduce product behavior perfectly.

Most importantly, do not allow yourself to become flustered if the simulation does not look or act exactly like the product. Figure A.5 shows the solution to the example simulation problem.

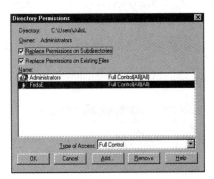

FIGURE A.5
The solution to the simulation example.

There are two final points that will help you tackle simulation questions. First, respond only to what is being asked in the question. Do not solve problems that you are not asked to solve. Second, accept what is being asked of you. You may not entirely agree with conditions in the problem statement, the quality of the desired solution, or the sufficiency of defined tasks to adequately solve the problem. Always remember that you are being tested on your ability to solve the problem as it has been presented.

The solution to the simulation problem shown in Figure A.5 perfectly illustrates both of these points. As you'll recall from the question scenario (refer to Figure A.3), you were asked to assign appropriate permissions to a new user, FridaE. You were not instructed to make any other changes in permissions. Thus, if you had modified or removed Administrators permissions, this item would have been scored as incorrect on an MCP exam.

Putting It All Together

Given all these different pieces of information, the task is now to assemble a set of tips that will help you successfully tackle the different types of MCP exams.

More Pre-exam Preparation Tips

Generic exam preparation advice is always useful. Tips include the following:

- Become familiar with the product. Hands-on experience is one of the keys to success on any MCP exam. Review the exercises and the step-by-step activities in the book.

- Review the current exam preparation guide on the Microsoft MCP Web site. The documentation Microsoft makes publicly available over the Web identifies the skills every exam is intended to test.

- Memorize foundational technical detail as appropriate. Remember that MCP exams are generally heavy on problem solving and application of knowledge rather than just questions that only require rote memorization.

- Take any of the available practice tests. We recommend the ones included in this book and the ones you can create using New Riders' exclusive Top Score Test Simulation software suite, available through your local bookstore or software distributor. Although these are fixed-format exams, they provide practice that is valuable for preparing for an adaptive exam. Because of the interactive nature of adaptive testing, it is not possible to provide examples of the adaptive format in the included practice exams. However, fixed-format exams do provide the same types of questions as found on adaptive exams and are the most effective way to prepare for either type of exam. As a supplement to the material bound with this book, also try the free practice tests available on the Microsoft MCP Web site.

- Look on the Microsoft MCP Web site for samples and demonstration items. These tend to be particularly valuable for one significant reason: They allow you to become familiar with any new testing technologies before you encounter them on an MCP exam.

During the Exam Session

Similarly, the generic exam-taking advice you've heard for years applies when taking an MCP exam:

- Take a deep breath and try to relax when you first sit down for your exam session. It is very important to control the pressure you may (naturally) feel when taking exams.

- You will be provided scratch paper. Take a moment to write down any factual information and technical detail that you've committed to short-term memory.

- Carefully read all information and instruction screens. These displays have been put together to give you information relevant to the exam you are taking.

- Accept the Non-Disclosure Agreement and preliminary survey as part of the examination process. Complete them accurately and quickly move on.

- Read the exam questions carefully. Reread each question to identify all relevant detail.

- Tackle the questions in the order they are presented. Skipping around won't build your confidence; the clock is always counting down.

- Don't rush, but similarly, don't linger on difficult questions. The questions vary in degree of difficulty. Don't let yourself be flustered by a particularly difficult or verbose question.

Fixed-form Exams

Building from this basic preparation and test-taking advice, you also need to consider the challenges presented by the different exam designs. Because a fixed-form exam is composed of a fixed, finite set of questions, add these tips to your strategy for taking a fixed-form exam:

- Note the time allotted and the number of questions appearing on the exam you are taking. Make a rough calculation of how many minutes you can spend on each question and use this to pace yourself through the exam.

- Take advantage of the fact that you can return to and review skipped or previously answered questions. Mark the questions you can't answer confidently, noting the relative difficulty of each question on the scratch paper provided. When you reach the end of the exam, return to the more difficult questions.

- If there is session time remaining after you have completed all questions (and you aren't too fatigued!), review your answers. Pay particular attention to questions that seem to have a lot of detail or that required graphics.

- As for changing your answers, the rule of thumb here is *don't*! If you read the question carefully and completely, and you felt like you knew the right answer, you probably did. Don't second-guess yourself. If, as you check your answers, one stands out as clearly marked incorrectly, however, you should change it in that instance. If you are at all unsure, go with your first impression.

Adaptive Exams

If you are planning to take an adaptive exam, keep these additional tips in mind:

- Read and answer every question with great care. When reading a question, identify every relevant detail, requirement, or task that must be performed and double-check your answer to be sure you have addressed every one of them.

- If you cannot answer a question, use the process of elimination to reduce the set of potential answers, then take your best guess. Stupid mistakes invariably mean additional questions will be presented.

- Forget about reviewing questions and changing your answers. After you leave a question, whether you've answered it or not, you cannot return to it. Do not skip a question, either; if you do, it's counted as incorrect!

Simulation Questions

You may encounter simulation questions on either the fixed-form or adaptive form exam. If you do, keep these tips in mind:

- Avoid changing any simulation settings that don't pertain directly to the problem solution. Solve the problem you are being asked to solve, and nothing more.

- Assume default settings when related information has not been provided. If something has not been mentioned or defined, it is a non-critical detail that does not factor in to the correct solution.

- Be sure your entries are syntactically correct, paying particular attention to your spelling. Enter relevant information just as the product would require it.

- Close all simulation application windows after completing the simulation tasks. The testing system software is designed to trap errors that could result when using the simulation application, but trust yourself over the testing software.

- If simulations are part of a fixed-form exam, you can return to skipped or previously answered questions and review your answers. However, if you choose to change your answer to a simulation question, or even attempt to review the settings you've made in the simulation application, your previous response to that simulation question will be deleted. If simulations are part of an adaptive exam, you cannot return to previous questions.

FINAL CONSIDERATIONS

There are a number of changes in the MCP program that will impact how frequently you can repeat an exam and what you will see when you do.

- Microsoft has instituted a new exam retake policy. This new rule is "two and two, then one and two." That is, you can attempt any exam two times with no restrictions on the time between attempts. But after the second attempt, you must wait two weeks before you can attempt that exam again. After that, you will be required to wait two weeks between any subsequent attempts. Plan to pass the exam in two attempts, or plan to increase your time horizon for receiving an MCP credential.

- New questions are being seeded into the MCP exams. After performance data has been gathered on new questions, they will replace older questions on all exam forms. This means that the questions appearing on exams are regularly changing.

- Many of the current MCP exams will be republished in adaptive format in the coming months. Prepare yourself for this significant change in testing format; it is entirely likely that this will become the new preferred MCP exam format.

These changes mean that the brute-force strategies for passing MCP exams may soon completely lose their viability. So if you don't pass an exam on the first or second attempt, it is entirely possible that the exam will change significantly in form. It could be updated to adaptive form from fixed-form or have a different set of questions or question types.

The intention of Microsoft is clearly not to make the exams more difficult by introducing unwanted change. Their intent is to create and maintain valid measures of the technical skills and knowledge associated with the different MCP credentials. Preparing for an MCP exam has always involved not only studying the subject matter, but also planning for the testing experience itself. With these changes, this is now more true than ever.

Glossary

A

access token   A Windows NT object describing a user account and group memberships. This object is provided by the Local Security Authority when logon and validation are successful, and it is attached to all user processes.

account lockout   A Windows NT Server security feature that locks a user account if a certain number of failed logon attempts occur within a specified amount of time (based on account policy lockout settings). Locked accounts cannot log on.

account policy   Controls the way passwords must be used by all user accounts of a domain or of an individual computer. Specific settings include minimum password length, how often a user must change his or her password, and how often users can reuse old passwords. Account policy can be set for all user accounts in a domain when administering a domain and for all user accounts of a single workstation or member server when administering a computer.

active partition   The disk partition that has been designated as being bootable. Although up to four partitions on an NT system can be capable of booting, only one can be active at any one time.

administrative share   A network share that is created and maintained by the Windows NT operating systems. Administrative shares are hidden and are accessible only by users in the local Administrators account. All disk partitions have administrative shares associated with them (such as C$ for drive C).

Alert View   A Performance Monitor view in which thresholds for counters are set and then actions are taken when those thresholds are crossed.

application log   A Server log that's accessible from the Event Viewer. This log records messages, warnings, and errors generated by applications running on your NT Server or Workstation.

ARC-path   The Advanced RISC Computing path is an industry standard method for identifying the physical location of a partition on a hard drive. ARC-paths are used in the BOOT.INI file to identify the location of NT boot files.

B

backup browser   A computer chosen by an election process to maintain a list of resources on a network. A master browser directs clients' requests for resources on a network to the backup browser.

backup domain controller (BDC) In a Windows NT Server domain, this is a computer running Windows NT Server that receives a copy of the domain's directory database, which contains all account and security policy information for the domain. The copy is synchronized periodically and automatically with the master copy on the primary domain controller (PDC). BDCs also authenticate user logons and can be promoted to function as PDCs as needed. Multiple BDCs can exist on a domain. *See also* member server; primary domain controller (PDC).

binding A process that establishes the communication channel between a protocol driver (such as TCP/IP) and a network card.

boot partition The volume, formatted for either an NTFS or FAT file system, that contains the Windows NT operating system and its support files. The boot partition can be (but does not have to be) the same as the system partition. *See also* partition; FAT; NTFS.

BOOT.INI A file located on the system partition of an NT Server or Workstation that is responsible for pointing the boot process to the correct boot files for the operating system chosen in the boot menu.

BOOTSECT.DOS A file located on the system partition that contains information required to boot an NT System to MS-DOS if a user requests it.

bottleneck The system resource that is the limiting factor in speed of processing. All systems have a bottleneck of some sort; the question is whether the bottleneck is significant in the context in which a Server finds it.

browser Called the Computer Browser service, the browser maintains an up-to-date list of computers and provides that list to applications when requested. This list is kept up-to-date through consultation with a master browser or backup browser on the network. It provides the computer lists displayed in the Network Neighborhood, Select Computer, and Select Domain dialog boxes and (for Windows NT Server only) in the Server Manager window.

C

call back A security feature enabled in the configuration of a RAS server, which requires that a RAS server call a client at a specific phone number (system- or user-configured) after a client initiates a RAS connection to the server. This feature is used either to transfer the bulk of long distance charges to the server instead of the user or to ensure that a user is authentic by confirming that he is at a specific location (and thus verifying that he's not a hacker trying to gain unauthorized access to a network via RAS).

Chart View A view in the Performance Monitor in which a dynamically updated line graph or histogram displays data for the counters selected in the view configuration.

Client Access License A license that's required by all users connecting to an NT server, which provides legal access to NT Server resources.

Client Administration Tools   A set of applications that allow for the administration of an NT Domain Controller from a Windows 95 or Windows NT Workstation, or Windows NT Server computer. The Client Administration Tools provide the most commonly used administration tools but do not provide complete administrative functionality.

Client Services for NetWare (CSNW)   Included with Windows NT Workstation, enabling workstations to make direct connections to file and printer resources at NetWare servers running NetWare 2.x or later.

COMPACT.EXE   A command line utility used to compress files on NTFS volumes. To see command line options, type `compact /?` at the command prompt. You can also access this utility by right-clicking any file or directory on an NTFS volume in Windows NT Explorer, clicking Properties, and changing the compression attribute for the files.

Control Panel   A folder containing a number of applets (applications) with which you configure and monitor your system running Windows NT. This includes configuring hardware, software, network configurations, service startup parameters, and system properties.

CONVERT.EXE   A command line utility used to convert an NT volume from FAT to NTFS. The command syntax is `CONVERT <drive letter>: /fs:NTFS` (for example, `CONVERT C: /fs:NTFS` to convert drive C).

counter   A specific component of a Performance Monitor object that has a displayable value. For example, for the Memory object, one counter is Available Bytes.

D

default gateway   In TCP/IP, the intermediate network device on the local network that has knowledge of the network IDs of the other networks in the Internet so it can forward packets to other gateways until the packet is eventually delivered to a gateway connected to the specified destination.

DETECT   A troubleshooting acronym indicating a recommended method for approaching NT problems. The DETECT acronym stands for Discover, Explore, Track, Execute, Check, Tie-Up.

differential backup   A backup method that backs up all files whose archive attributes are not set and but does not set the archive attribute of the files it backs up.

directory replication   The process of copying a master set of directories from a server (called an export computer) to specified servers or workstations (called import computers) in the same or other domains. Replication simplifies the task of maintaining identical sets of directories and files on multiple computers because only a single master copy of the data must be maintained. Files are first replicated when they are added to an exported directory and then every time a change is saved to the file.

Directory Service Manager for NetWare (DSMN)   An NT add-on that provides directory synchronization between an NT Network and a NetWare network.

Disk Administrator   An administration program that allows an NT administrator to create, format, and maintain hard drive partitions, volumes, and fault-tolerant mechanisms.

disk duplexing   A mirror set created with two hard drives controlled by separate disk controller cards. Disk duplexing provides more fault tolerance than standard mirror sets do because it ensures that a controller card failure will not bring down the mirror set.

disk mirroring   A fault-tolerance method that provides a fully redundant, or shadow, copy of data (a mirror set). Mirror sets provide an identical twin for a selected disk; all data written to the primary disk is also written to the shadow or mirror disk. This enables you to have instant access to another disk with a redundant copy of the information on a failed disk.

disk striping with parity   A method of data protection in which data is striped in large blocks across all the disks in an array. Data redundancy is provided by the parity information.

domain   In Windows NT, a collection of computers defined by the administrator of a Windows NT Server network that share a common directory database. A domain provides access to the centralized user accounts and group accounts maintained by the domain administrator. Each domain has a unique name.

domain master browser   A kind of network name server that keeps a browse list of all the servers and domains on the network. The domain master browser for a domain is always the primary domain controller.

Domain Name System (DNS)   DNS offers a static hierarchical name service for TCP/IP hosts. The network administrator configures the DNS with a list of hostnames and IP addresses, allowing users of workstations configured to query the DNS to specify remote systems by hostname instead of by IP address. For example, a workstation configured to use DNS name resolution could use the command ping *remotehost* instead of ping 1.2.3.4 if the mapping for the system named *remotehost* was contained in the DNS database.

Dynamic Host Configuration Protocol (DHCP)   A protocol that offers dynamic configuration of IP addresses and related information through the DHCP Server service running on an NT Server. DHCP provides safe, reliable, and simple TCP/IP network configuration, prevents address conflicts, and helps conserve the use of IP addresses through centralized management of address allocation.

E

Emergency Repair Disk   A floppy disk containing configuration information for a specific NT Server or Workstation. This disk is created and updated by using the RDISK utility and can be used in conjunction with the three NT setup disks to recover from many NT system failures resulting from file and/or Registry corruption.

Event Viewer   An administrative utility used to look at event logs. The event viewer provides three logs: system, security, and application.

export computer   In directory replication, a server from which a master set of directories is exported to specified servers or workstations (called import computers) in the same or other domains.

extended partition   Created from free space on a hard disk, an extended partition can be subpartitioned into zero or more logical drives. Only one of the four partitions allowed per physical disk can be an extended partition, and no primary partition needs to be present to create an extended partition.

F

FAT (File Allocation Table)   A table or list maintained by some operating systems to keep track of the status of various segments of disk space used for file storage. Also referred to as the FAT file system, this method is used to format hard drives in DOS, Windows 95, and OS/2, and it can be used in Windows NT.

FAT32   A variation of FAT that provides for more efficient file storage. This FAT variation is available only on Windows 95 and Windows 98 and is not readable by Windows NT.

fault tolerance   System of ensuring data integrity when hardware failures occur. In Windows NT, the FTDISK.SYS driver provides fault tolerance. In Disk Administrator, fault tolerance is implemented through the use of mirror sets, stripe sets with parity, and volume sets.

File and Print Services for NetWare (FPNW)   A service installed on an NT server that provides NetWare clients the ability to access an NT server for the purposes of reading files and printing to NT-controlled printers. In order for this to work, the NT Server must have NWLink installed on it.

filename alias   An 8.3-compatible short filename given to a long filename that's created on an NT computer so that MS-DOS and Windows 3.x clients can read the file.

frame type   The type of network package generated on a network. In NT configuration, this refers to the type of network packages sent by a NetWare server that an NT client is configured to accept.

G

Gateway Services for NetWare (GSNW)   Included with Windows NT Server, this service enables a computer running Windows NT Server to connect to NetWare servers. Creating a gateway enables computers running only Microsoft client software to access NetWare resources through the gateway.

global group   For Windows NT Server, a group that can be used in its own domain, member servers and workstations of its domain, and trusting domains. In all those places, it can be granted rights and permissions and can become a member of local groups. However, it can contain user accounts only from its own domain. Global groups offer a means of grouping users from inside the domain to give them rights both in and out of the domain.

Global groups cannot be created or maintained on computers running Windows NT Workstation. However, for Windows NT Workstation computers that participate in a domain, domain global groups can be granted rights and permissions at those workstations, and they can become members of local groups at those workstations.

group account   A collection of user accounts. Giving a user account membership in a group gives that user all the rights and permissions granted to the group.

H

Hardware Compatibility List (HCL)   The Windows NT Hardware Compatibility List lists all devices supported by Windows NT. The latest version of the HCL can be downloaded from the Microsoft Web Page (`microsoft.com`) on the Internet.

hidden share   A network share that is configured not to show up in browse lists but that a user can connect to explicitly if he knows the share name. You create a hidden share by appending a dollar sign ($) to the end of a share name, (as in SECRET$). All administrative shares are hidden shares.

hive   A section of the Registry that appears as a file on your hard disk. The Registry subtree is divided into hives (named for their resemblance to the cellular structure of a beehive). A hive is a discrete body of keys, subkeys, and values that is rooted at the top of the Registry hierarchy. A hive is backed by a single file and a .log file, which are in either the %SystemRoot%\system32\config folder or the %SystemRoot%\profiles\username folder. By default, most hive files (Default, SAM, Security, and System) are stored in the %SystemRoot%\system32\config folder. The %SystemRoot%\ profiles folder contains the user profile for each user of the computer. Because a hive is a file, it can be moved from one system to another, but it can be edited only by using Registry Editor.

Hkey_Local_Machine   A Registry subtree that maintains all the configuration information for the local machine, including hardware settings and settings for installed software.

I-K

import computer   In directory replication, the server or workstation that receives copies of the master set of directories from an export server.

incremental backup   A backup method that backs up all files whose archive attributes are not set and that sets the archive attribute of the files it backs up.

installation disk set   A set of floppy disks that contain a minimal configuration of NT used to initiate NT installation and repair.

IP address   Used to identify a node on a network and to specify routing information. Each node on the network must be assigned a unique IP address (usually the network ID) plus a unique host ID assigned by the network administrator. This address is typically represented in dotted-decimal notation, with the decimal values of the octets separated by periods (for example, 138.57.7.27).

In Windows NT, the IP address can be configured statically on the client or configured dynamically through DHCP.

IPCONFIG   A command line utility that is used to determine the current TCP/IP configuration of a local computer. It is also used to request a new TCP/IP address from a DHCP server through the use of the /RELEASE and /RENEW switches. The /ALL switch shows a complete list of TCP/IP configurations.

IPX/SPX   Transport protocols used in Novell NetWare networks. Windows NT implements IPX through NWLink.

L

LastKnownGood configuration   A set of Registry settings that records the hardware configuration of an NT computer during each successful login. LastKnownGood can be used to recover from an incorrect hardware setup as long as logon does not occur between the time the configuration was changed and the time the LastKnownGood was invoked.

License Manager   An administrative utility that allows you to track the purchase of client access licenses for an NT Server and/or Domain.

licensing mode   An indicator of what kind of licensing is being used on an NT Server. The choices are Per Server and Per Seat.

local group   For Windows NT Workstation, a group that can be granted permissions and rights only for its own workstation. However, it can contain user accounts from its own computer and (if the workstation participates in a domain) user accounts and global groups both from its own domain and from trusted domains.

For Windows NT Server, a group that can be granted permissions and rights only for the domain controllers of its own domain. However, it can contain user accounts and global groups both from its own domain and from trusted domains.

Local groups provide a means of grouping users from both inside and outside the domain to be used only at domain controllers of the domain.

local profile   A profile stored on a local machine, and which is accessible only to users who log onto the NT computer locally.

Local Security Authority (LSA)   The NT process responsible for directing logon requests to the local Security Accounts Manager (SAM) or to the SAM of a domain controller via the NetLogon service. The LSA is responsible for generating an access token when a user logon is validated.

Log View   A Performance Monitor view in which the configuration of a log is determined. Logs have no dynamic information; however, the resulting file can be analyzed by using any of the other Performance Monitor views.

logical drive   A subpartition of an extended partition on a hard disk.

M

mandatory profile   A profile that is downloaded to the user's desktop each time he or she logs on. A mandatory user profile is created by an administrator and assigned to one or more users to create consistent or job-specific user profiles. They cannot be changed by the user and remain the same from one logon session to the next.

Master Boot Record (MBR)   The place on the disk that the initial computer startup is directed to go to initiate operating system boot. The MBR is located on the primary partition.

master browser   A kind of network name server that keeps a browse list of all the servers and domains on the network. Also referred to as a browse master.

member server   A computer that runs Windows NT Server but is not a primary domain controller (PDC) or backup domain controller (BDC) of a Windows NT domain. Member servers do not receive copies of the directory database.

Migration Tool for NetWare   A tool included with Windows NT, enabling you to easily transfer user and group accounts, volumes, folders, and files from a NetWare server to a computer running Windows NT Server.

multi-boot   A computer that runs two or more operating systems. For example, Windows 95, MS-DOS, and Windows NT operating systems can be installed on the same computer. When the computer is started, any one of the operating systems can be selected. Also known as dual boot.

multilink protocol   Multilink combines multiple physical links into a logical "bundle." This aggregate link increases your bandwidth.

N

NetBEUI   A network protocol usually used in small department-sized local area networks of 1 to 200 clients. It is nonroutable and is, therefore, not a preferred WAN protocol.

NetLogon   For Windows NT Server, this process performs authentication of domain logons and keeps the domain's directory database synchronized between the primary domain controller and the other backup domain controllers of the domain.

network adapter   An expansion card or other device used to connect a computer to a local area network (LAN). Also called a network card, network adapter card, adapter card, or network interface card (NIC).

network monitor   An administrative utility installed on an NT computer when the Network Monitor Tools and Agent service is installed. The network monitor provided with NT allows you to capture and analyze network traffic coming into and going out of the local network card. The SMS version of network monitor runs in promiscuous mode, which allows monitoring of traffic on the local network.

network protocols   Communication "languages" that allow networked computer and devices to communicate with one another. Common network protocols are TCP/IP, NetBEUI, NWLink, and DLC (used for communicating with networked printers such as HP DirectJet).

network service   A process that performs a specific network system function and often provides an application programming interface (API) for other processes to call. Windows NT services are RPC-enabled, meaning that their API routines can be called from remote computers.

nonbrowser   A computer that is configured to never participate in browser elections and that, therefore, can never become a master browser or backup browser.

normal backup   Sometimes referred to as a full backup, this method backs up all files and then sets the archive attribute of those files it backs up.

NTBOOTDD.SYS   The driver for a SCSI boot device that does not have its BIOS enabled. NTBOOTDD.SYS is found on an NT system partition and is required for creation of a fault-tolerant boot disk.

NTCONFIG.POL   A file that defines an NT system policy.

NTDETECT.COM   The program in the NT boot process that's responsible for generating a list of hardware devices. This list is later used to populate part of the HKEY_LOCAL_MACHINE subtree in the Registry.

NTFS   An advanced file system designed for use specifically within the Windows NT operating system. It supports file system recovery, extremely large storage media, long filenames, and various features for compatibility with the POSIX subsystem. It also supports object-oriented applications by treating all files as objects with user-defined and system-defined attributes.

NTFS compression   A compression type supported only on an NTFS volume. This supports file-level compression and is dynamic.

NTFS permissions   Local permissions on NTFS volumes, which allow for the restriction of both local and network access to files and folders.

NTHQ   A program that executes from a floppy disk and that allows you to automatically check the hardware on a computer against the HCL for NT compatibility.

NTLDR   The program responsible for booting an NT system. It is invoked when an NT computer is started, and it is responsible for displaying the boot menu (from the BOOT.INI file) and starting the NTDETECT.COM program.

NTOSKRNL.EXE   The program responsible for maintaining the core of the NT operating system. When NTLDR completes the boot process, control of NT is handed over to the NTOSKRNL.

NWLink   A standard network protocol that supports routing and can support NetWare client/server applications, where NetWare-aware Sockets-based applications communicate with IPX/SPX Sockets-based applications.

O-Q

object   A specific system category for which counters can be observed in Performance Monitor. Objects whose counters are frequently monitored are Memory, Processor, Network, and PhysicalDisk.

OSLOADER.EXE   The program on a RISC-based machine that's responsible for the function of the NTLDR on an Intel-based machine.

partition   A portion of a physical disk that functions as though it were a physically separate unit.

per-client licensing mode   An NT licensing mode that allocates server access on a per-person basis (not on a per-connection basis). Using a per-client license, a user can connect to many NT servers simultaneously.

Performance Monitor   An administrative application used to monitor object counters on an NT computer in order to determine bottlenecks in the system and to increase overall efficiency.

per-server licensing mode   An NT licensing mode that allocates server access on a per-connection basis. This licensing mode allocates a certain number of simultaneous connections to a server, and when that number of connections is reached, no more users are allowed to access the server.

persistent connection   A network connection from a client to a server, which is automatically reestablished when disconnected.

ping   A command used to verify connections to one or more remote hosts. The PING utility uses the ICMP echo request and echo reply packets to determine whether a particular IP system on a network is functional. The PING utility is useful for diagnosing IP network or router failures.

Point to Point Protocol (PPP)   A set of industry-standard framing and authentication protocols that is part of Windows NT RAS and ensures interoperability with third-party remote access software. PPP negotiates configuration parameters for multiple layers of the OSI model.

Point to Point Tunneling Protocol (PPTP)   PPTP is a new networking technology that supports multiprotocol virtual private networks (VPNs), enabling remote users to access corporate networks securely across the Internet by dialing into an Internet service provider (ISP) or by connecting to the Internet directly.

potential browser   A computer that is not currently functioning as a browser on a network but which could become one if necessary.

primary domain controller (PDC)   In a Windows NT Server domain, the computer running Windows NT Server that authenticates domain logons and maintains the directory database for a domain. The PDC tracks changes made to accounts of all computers on a domain. It is the only computer to receive these changes directly. A domain has only one PDC.

primary partition   A partition is a portion of a physical disk that can be marked for use by an operating system. There can be up to four primary partitions (or up to three if there is an extended partition) per physical disk. A primary partition cannot be subpartitioned.

print device   Refers to the actual hardware device that produces printed output.

printer   Refers to the software interface between the operating system and the print device. The printer defines where the document will go before it reaches the print device (to a local port, to a file, or to a remote print share, for example), when it will go, and various other aspects of the printing process.

printer driver   A program that converts graphics commands into a specific printer language, such as PostScript or PCL.

printer pool   A group of two or more identical print devices associated with one printer.

protocol   *See* network protocols.

R

RDISK.EXE   A program used to create and update Emergency Repair Disks and the /REPAIR folder on an NT system.

recovery disk   A floppy disk that contains the files required by NT to begin the boot process and to point to the boot partition. The files required for an INTEL system are: BOOT.INI, NTDETECT.COM, NTLDR, and NTBOOTDD.SYS (if the hard drive is SCSI with BIOS disabled).

REGEDIT.EXE   One of two Registry editors available in NT. This one has the same interface as the Registry Editor available in Windows 95 and provides key value searching.

REGEDT32.EXE   One of two Registry editors available in NT. This one has a cascaded subtree interface and allows you to set Registry security.

regenerate   The process of rebuilding a replaced hard drive in a stripe set with parity after hard drive failure. This process can be initiated from the Disk Administrator.

Registry   The Windows NT Registry is a database repository for information about a computer's configuration. It is organized in a hierarchical structure and is comprised of subtrees and their keys, hives, and value entries.

Registry key   A specific Registry entry that has a configurable value.

Registry tree   A collection of similar Registry keys. HKEY_LOCAL_MACHINE is an example of a Registry tree.

Remote Access Service (RAS)   A service that provides remote networking for telecommuters, mobile workers, and system administrators who monitor and manage servers at multiple branch offices. Users with RAS on a Windows NT computer can dial in to remotely access their networks for services such as file and printer sharing, electronic mail, scheduling, and SQL database access.

Report View   A view in the Performance Monitor that displays data in a single-page format of current counter values.

reporting interval   In Performance Monitor, the interval at which a new set of statistical information is processed and delivered to the view or views currently operating.

roaming profile   The profile that is enabled when an administrator enters a user profile path into the user account. The first time the user logs off, the local user profile is copied to that location. Thereafter, the server copy of the user profile is downloaded each time the user logs on if it is more current than the local copy, and it is updated each time the user logs off.

S

SCSI adapter   SCSI is an acronym for small computer system interface, a standard high-speed parallel interface defined by the American National Standards Institute (ANSI). A SCSI adapter is used to connect microcomputers to peripheral devices, such as hard disks and printers, and to other computers and local area networks.

Security Accounts Manager (SAM)   The NT process that's responsible for querying the directory database to locate a specific username and password combination when a user attempts to log on.

security log   Records security events and can be viewed through the Event Viewer. This helps track changes to the security system and identify any possible breaches of security. For example, depending on the Audit settings in User Manager or User Manager for Domains, any attempts to log on the local computer may be recorded in the security log. The security log contains both valid and invalid logon attempts, as well as events related to resource use (such as creating, opening, and deleting files).

Serial Line Interface Protocol (SLIP)   An older industry standard that is part of Windows NT RAS and that ensures interoperability with third-party remote access software. Windows NT supports SLIP as a client but not as a server; in other words, an NT machine can connect to a SLIP server but cannot itself be a SLIP server.

Server Message Block (SMB)   A file-sharing protocol designed to allow systems to transparently access files that reside on remote systems.

service   A process that performs a specific system function and often provides an application programming interface (API) for other processes to call. Windows NT services are RPC-enabled, meaning that their API routines can be called from remote computers.

share permissions   A set of permissions controlling access to a network share when users attempt to access the share from over the network. Share permissions do not apply to local users of a system and can be applied only at the folder level.

sharing   The process of making a resource available on the network. This resource could be a drive, a folder, or a printer.

/SOS   A BOOT.INI switch indicating that during boot of NT Server or Workstation, the list of loading drivers should be displayed. This switch is used for troubleshooting and is normally configured as part of the [VGA] boot option.

spooler   Software that accepts documents sent by a user to be printed and then stores those documents and sends them, one-by-one, to available printer(s).

standalone server   An NT server that participates as part of a workgroup and not as a part of a domain.

stripe set   A method for saving data across identical partitions on different drives. A stripe set does not provide fault tolerance.

subnet mask   A 32-bit value that allows the recipient of IP packets to distinguish the network ID portion of the IP address from the host ID.

system groups   One or more groups maintained by NT for special purposes. The Everyone group is an example of a system group; it cannot be changed because its membership is defined and maintained by NT.

system log   The system log contains events logged by the Windows NT components and can be looked at through Event Viewer. For example, the failure of a driver or other system component to load during startup is recorded in the system log.

system partition   The volume that contains the hardware-specific files needed to load Windows NT.

system policy   Settings created with the System Policy Editor to control user work environments and actions and to enforce system configuration for Windows NT clients. System policies can be implemented for specific users, groups, or computers or for all users. A system policy for users overwrites settings in the current user area of the Registry, and a system policy for computers overwrites the current local machine area of the Registry. If you have clients who are using Windows 95, separate system policies need to be created for them on a Windows 95 system because NT system policies are not compatible with 95.

T

take ownership   The user right that enables the ownership of a resource to be transferred from one user to another. By default, Administrators have the ability to take ownership of any NT resource.

TCP/IP   An acronym for Transmission Control Protocol/Internet Protocol, TCP/IP is a set of networking protocols that enable communication across interconnected networks made up of computers with diverse hardware architectures and various operating systems. TCP/IP includes standards for how computers communicate and conventions for connecting networks and routing traffic.

Telephony API (TAPI)   A system used by certain programs to make data, fax, and voice calls. Those programs include the Windows NT applets HyperTerminal, Dial-Up Networking, Phone Dialer, and other Win32 communications applications written for Windows NT.

TRACERT   A TCP/IP troubleshooting utility that traces the route from one host to another. This utility can locate the source of transmission breakdown between TCP/IP hosts.

U

UNC (Universal Naming Convention) name
A full Windows NT name of a resource on a network. It conforms to the format *servername*\ *sharename*, where *servername* is the name of the server and *sharename* is the name of the shared resource. UNC names of directories or files can also include the directory path under the share name, in which case they adhere to the following syntax:

```
\\servername\sharename\directory\filename
```

UPS (Uninterruptible Power Supply)   A battery-operated power supply connected to a computer to keep the system running during a power failure.

user account   An account that contains all the information that defines a user to Windows NT. This includes such things as the username and password required for the user to log on, the groups in which the user account has membership, and the rights and permissions the user has for using the system and accessing its resources. For Windows NT Workstation, user accounts are managed with User Manager. For Windows NT Server, user accounts are managed with User Manager for Domains.

User Manager for Domains   A Windows NT Server tool used to manage security for a domain or an individual computer. This tool enables an administrator to maintain user accounts, groups, and security policies.

user profile   Configuration information that is retained on a user-by-user basis is saved in a user profile. This information includes all the user-specific settings of the Windows NT environment, such as the desktop arrangement, personal program groups and the program items in those groups, screen colors, screen savers, network connections, printer connections, mouse settings, window size and position, and more. When a user logs on, the user's profile is loaded, and the user's Windows NT environment is configured according to that profile.

V-Z

volume set   A combination of partitions on a physical disk that appear as one logical drive.

Windows Internet Name Service (WINS) A name resolution service that resolves Windows NT networking computer names to IP addresses in a routed environment. A WINS server handles name registrations, queries, and releases.

WinLogon   The NT process that initiates login by presenting the logon dialog box to the user.

WINNT.EXE   The program used to install Windows NT from a non-NT platform.

WINNT32.EXE   The program used to install or upgrade Windows NT from an NT platform.

workgroup   For Windows NT, a workgroup is a collection of computers that are grouped for viewing purposes. Each workgroup is identified by a unique name.

Fast Facts

Now that you have thoroughly read through this book, worked through the exercises, and gotten as much hands on exposure to NT Server as you could, you've now booked your exam. This chapter is designed as a last-minute cram for you as you walk out the door on your way to the exam. You can't reread the whole book in an hour, but you will be able to read this chapter in that time.

This chapter is organized by objective category, giving you not just a summary, but a rehash of the most important point form facts that you need to know. Remember that this is meant to be a review of concepts and a trigger for you to remember wider definitions. In addition to what is in this chapter, make sure you know what is in the glossary because this chapter does not define terms. If you know what is in here and the concepts that stand behind it, chances are the exam will be a snap.

PLANNING

Remember: Here are the elements that Microsoft says they test on for the "Planning" section of the exam.

- Plan the disk drive configuration for various requirements. Requirements include: choosing a file system and fault tolerance method.

- Choose a protocol for various situations. Protocols include TCP/IP, NWLink IPX/SPX-Compatible Transport, and NetBEUI.

Minimum requirements for installing NT Server on an Intel machine are 486DX/33, 16MB of RAM, and 130MB of free disk space.

The login process on an NT Domain is as follows:

1. WinLogon sends the user name and password to the Local Security Authority (LSA).

2. The LSA passes the request to the local NetLogon service.

3. The local NetLogon service sends the logon information to the NetLogon service on the domain controller.

4. The NetLogon service on the domain controller passes the information to the domain controller's Security Accounts Manager (SAM).

5. The SAM asks the domain directory database for approval of the user name and password.

6. The SAM passes the result of the approval request to the domain controller's NetLogon service.

7. The domain controller's NetLogon service passes the result of the approval request to the client's NetLogon service.

8. The client's NetLogon service passes the result of the approval request to the LSA.

9. If the logon is approved, the LSA creates an access token and passes it to the WinLogon process.

10. WinLogon completes the logon, thus creating a new process for the user and attaching the access token to the new process.

The system partition is where your computer boots and it must be on an active partition.

The boot partition is where the WINNT folder is found and it contains the NT program files. It can be on any partition (not on a volume set, though).

NT supports two forms of software-based fault tolerance: Disk Mirroring (RAID 1) and Stripe Sets with Paritiy (RAID 5).

Disk Mirroring uses 2 hard drives and provides 50% disk space utilization.

Stripe sets with Parity use between 3 and 32 hard drives and provide an (n-1)/n*100% utilization (n = number of disks in the set).

Disk duplexing provides better tolerance than mirroring because it does mirroring with separate controllers on each disk.

NT Supports 3 file systems: NTFS, FAT, and CDFS (it no longer supports HPFS, the OS/2 file system; nor does it support FAT32, a file system used by Windows 95).

Table 1 shows a quick summary of the differences between file systems:

TABLE 1   FAT VERSUS NTFS COMPARISON

Feature	FAT	NTFS
Filename length	255	255
8.3 filename compatibility	Yes	Yes
File size	4GB	16EB
Partition size	4GB	16EB
Directory structure	Linked list	B-tree
Local security	No	Yes
Transaction tracking	No	Yes
Hot fixing	No	Yes
Overhead	1MB	>4MB
Required on system partition for RISC-based computers	Yes	No
Accessible from MS-DOS/ Windows 95	Yes	No
Accessible from OS/2	Yes	No
Case-sensitive	No	POSIX only
Case preserving	Yes	Yes
Compression	No	Yes
Efficiency	200MB	400MB
Windows NT formattable	Yes	Yes
Fragmentation level	High	Low
Floppy disk formattable	Yes	No

Table 2 summarizes the protocols commonly used by NT for network communication:

TABLE 2 PRIMARY PROTOCOL USES

Protocol	Primary Use
TCP/IP	Internet and WAN connectivity
NWLink	Interoperability with NetWare
NetBEUI	Interoperability with old Lan Man networks

The main points regarding TCP/IP are as follows:

- Requires IP Address and Subnet Mask to function (default Gateway if being routed)
- Can be configured manually or automatically using DHCP server running on NT
- Common address resolution methods are WINS and DNS

INSTALLATION AND CONFIGURATION

Remember: Here are the elements that Microsoft says they test on for the "Installation and Configuration" section of the exam.

- Install Windows NT Server on Intel-based platforms.
- Install Windows NT Server to perform various server roles. Server roles include Primary domain controller, Backup domain controller, and Member server.
- Install Windows NT Server by using various methods. Installation methods include CD-ROM, Over-the-network, Network Client Administrator, and Express versus custom.
- Configure protocols and protocol bindings. Protocols include TCP/IP, NWLink, IPX/SPX-Compatible Transport, and NetBEUI.
- Configure network adapters. Considerations include changing IRQ, IObase, and memory addresses and configuring multiple adapters.
- Configure Windows NT server core services. Services include Directory Replicator, License Manager, and Other services.
- Configure peripherals and devices. Peripherals and devices include communication devices, SCSI devices, tape devices drivers, UPS devices and UPS service, mouse drivers, display drivers, and keyboard drivers.
- Configure hard disks to meet various requirements. Requirements include allocating disk space capacity, providing redundancy, improving security, and formatting.
- Configure printers. Tasks include adding and configuring a printer, implementing a printer pool, and setting print priorities.
- Configure a Windows NT Server computer for various types of client computers. Client computer types include Windows NT Workstation, Microsoft Windows 95, and Microsoft MS-DOS-based.

The Hardware Compatibility list is used to ensure that NT supports all computer components.

NT can be installed in three different configurations in a domain: Primary Domain Controller, Backup Domain Controller, and Member Server.

Two sources can be used for installation files: CD-ROM or network share (which is the hardware-specific files from the CD copied onto a server and shared).

Three Setup disks are required for all installations when a CD-ROM is not supported by the operating system present on the computer at installation time (or if no operating system exists and the computer will not boot from the CD-ROM).

WINNT and WINNT32 are used for network installation; WINNT32 for installations when NT is currently present on the machine you are installing to and WINNT when it is not.

Table 3 is a summary of the WINNT and WINNT32 switches:

TABLE 3   WINNT AND WINNT32 SWITCH FUNCTIONS

Switch	Function
/B	Prevents creation of the three setup disks during the installation process
/S	Indicates the location of the source files for NT installation (for example, /S:D:\NTFiles)
/U	Indicates the script file to use for an unattended installation (for example, /U:C:\Answer.txt)
/UDF	Indicates the location of the uniqueness database file which defines unique configuration for each NT machine being installed (for example, /UDF:D:\Answer.UDF)
/T	Indicates the place to put the temporary installation files
/OX	Initiates only the creation of the three setup disks
/F	Indicates not to verify the files copied to the setup disks
/C	Indicates not to check for free space on the setup disks before creating them

To remove NT from a computer, you must do the following:

1. Remove all the NTFS partitions from within Windows NT and reformat them with FAT (this ensures that these disk areas will be accessible by non-NT operating systems).

2. Boot to another operating system, such as Windows 95 or MS-DOS.

3. Delete the Windows NT installation directory tree (usually WINNT).

4. Delete pagefile.sys.

5. Turn off the hidden, system, and read-only attributes for NTBOOTDD.SYS, BOOT.INI, NTLDR, and NTDETECT.COM and then delete them. You might not have all of these on your computer, but if so, you can find them all in the root directory of your drive C.

6. Make the hard drive bootable by placing another operating system on it (or SYS it with DOS or Windows 95).

The Client Administrator allows you to do the following:

• Make Network Installation Startup disk: shares files and creates a bootable disk for initiating client installation

• Make Installation Disk Set: copies installation files to disk for installing simple clients such as MS-DOS network client 3.0

• Copy Client-Based Network Administration Tools: creates a folder that can be attached to from Windows NT

Workstation and Windows 95 clients to install tools for administering an NT Server from a workstation

MANAGING RESOURCES

Remember: Here are the elements that Microsoft says it tests on for the "Managing Resources" section of the exam.

- Manage user and group accounts. Considerations include managing Windows NT groups, managing Windows NT user rights, administering account policies, and auditing changes to the user account database.

- Create and manage policies and profiles for various situations. Policies and profiles include local user profiles, roaming user profiles, and system policies.

- Administer remote servers from various types of client computers. Client computer types include Windows 95 and Windows NT Workstation.

- Manage disk resources. Tasks include copying and moving files between file systems, creating and sharing resources, implementing permissions and security, and establishing file auditing.

Network properties dialog box lets you install and configure the following:

- Computer and Domain names
- Services
- Protocols

- Adapters
- Bindings

When configuring NWLink, ensure that if more than one frame type exists on your network, you don't use AutoDetect or only the first frame type encountered will be detected from then on.

Table 4 shows you three TCP/IP command line diagnostic tools and what they do:

TABLE 4 TCP/IP COMMAND LINE DIAGNOSTIC TOOLS

Tool	Function
IPConfig	Displays the basic TCP/IP configuration of each adapter card on a computer (with /all displays detailed configuration information)
Ping	Determines connectivity with another TCP/IP host by sending a message that is echoed by the recipient if received
Tracert	Traces each hop on the way to a TCP/IP host and indicates points of failure if they exist

Network adapter card configuration of IRQ and I/O port address may or may not be configurable from the Network Properties dialog box; it depends on the card.

To allow NT computers to participate in a domain, a computer account must be created for each one.

Windows 95 clients need special profiles and policies created on a Windows 95 machine and then copied onto an NT Server to participate in domain profile and policy configuration.

Windows 95 clients need printer drivers installed on an NT Server acting as a print controller to print to an NT controller printer.

Typical services tested for NT Server are listed and described in Table 5:

TABLE 5   NT SERVER SERVICES AND THEIR FUNCTIONS

Service	Function
DNS	Provides TCP/IP address resolution using a static table and can be used for non-Microsoft hosts.
WINS	Provides TCP/IP address resolution using a dynamic table and can be used for Microsoft hosts.
DHCP	Provides automatic configuration of TCP/IP clients for Microsoft clients.
Browser	Provides a list of domain resources to Network Neighborhood and Server Manager.
Replicator	Provides import and export services for automated file distribution between NT computers (Servers can be export and import, Workstations can only be import).

REGEDT32.EXE and REGEDIT are used to view and modify registry settings in NT.

The five registry subtrees are

- **HKEY_LOCAL_MACHINE.** Stores all the computer-specific configuration data.

- **HKEY_USERS.** Stores all the user-specific configuration data.

- **HKEY_CURRENT_USER.** Stores all configuration data for the currently logged on user.

- **HKEY_CLASSES_ROOT.** Stores all OLE and file association information.

- **HKEY_CURRENT_CONFIG.** Stores information about the hardware profile specified at startup.

REGEDT32.EXE allows you to see and set security on the registry and allows you to open the registry in read-only mode, but does not allow you to search by key value.

NT checking for serial mice at boot may disable a UPS. To disable that check, place the /noserialmice in the boot line in the BOOT.INI file.

The SCSI adapters icon in the Control Panel lets you add and configure SCSI devices as well as CD-ROM drives.

Many changes made in the disk administrator require that you choose the menu Partition, Commit Changes for them to take effect.

Although you can set drive letters manually, the following is how NT assigns letters to partitions and volumes:

1. Beginning from the letter C:, assigns consecutive letters to the first primary partition on each physical disk.

2. Assigns consecutive letters to each logical drive, completing all on one physical disk before moving on to the next.

3. Assigns consecutive letters to the additional primary partitions, completing all on one physical disk before moving on to the next.

Disk Administrator allows for the creation of two kinds of partitions (primary and extended) and four kinds of volumes (volume set, stripe set, mirror set, and stripe set with parity). The following table (Table 6) is a summary of their characteristics:

TABLE 6   PARTITION CHARACTERISTICS

Object	Characteristics
Primary partition	Nondivisible disk unit which can be marked active and can be made bootable.
	Can have up to four on a physical drive.
	NT system partition must be on a primary.
Extended partition	Divisible disk unit which must be divided into logical disks (or have free space used in a volume) in order to function as space storage tool.
	Can have only one on a physical drive.
	Logical drive within can be the NT boot partition.
Volume Set	Made up of 2-32 portions of free space which do not have to be the same size and which can be spread out over between 1 and 32 disks of many types (IDE, SCSI, and so on).
	Can be added to if formatted NTFS.
	Cannot contain NT boot or system partition.
	Removing one portion of the set destroys the volume and the data is lost.
	Is not fault tolerant.
Stripe Set	Made up of 2-32 portions of free space which have to be the same size and which can be spread out over between 2 and 32 disks of many types (IDE, SCSI, and so on).
	Cannot be added to and removing one portion of the set destroys the volume and the data is lost.
	Is not fault tolerant.
Mirror Set	Made up of 2 portions of free space which have to be the same size and which must be on 2 physical disks.
	Identical data is written to both mirror partitions and they are treated as one disk.
	If one disk stops functioning, the other will continue to operate.
	The NT Boot and System partitions can be held on a mirror set.
	Has a 50% disk utilization rate.
	Is fault tolerant.
Stripe Set with Parity	Made up of 3-32 portions of free space which have to be the same size and must be spread out over the same number of physical disks.
	Maintains fault tolerance by creating parity information across a stripe.
	If one disk fails, the stripe set will continue to function, albeit with a loss of performance.
	The NT Boot and System partitions cannot be held on a Stripe Set with Parity.
	Is fault tolerant.

Disk Administrator can be used to format partitions and volumes either FAT or NTFS.

If you have any clients who access a shared printer that are not using NT or are not using the same hardware platform as your printer server, then you must install those drivers when you share the printer.

By assigning different priorities for printers associated with the same print device, you can create a hierarchy among users' print jobs, thus ensuring that the print jobs of some users print sooner than others.

By adjusting the printer schedule, you can ensure that jobs sent to particular printers are printed only at certain hours of the day.

A printer has permissions assigned to it. The following is a list of the permissions for printers.

- **No Access.** Completely restricts access to the printer.

- **Print.** Allows a user or group to submit a print job, and to control the settings and print status for that job.

- **Manage Documents.** Allows a user or group to submit a print job, and to control the settings and print status for all print jobs.

- **Full Control.** Allows a user to submit a print job, and to control the settings and print status for all documents as well as for the printer itself. In addition, the user or group may share, stop sharing, change permissions for, and even delete the printer.

Printer pools consist of one or more print devices that can use the same print driver controlled by a single printer.

MS-DOS users must have print drivers installed locally on their computers.

The assignment of permissions to resources should use the following procedure:

1. Create user accounts.

2. Create global groups for the domain and populate the groups with user accounts.

3. Create local groups and assign them rights and permissions to resources and programs in the domain.

4. Place global groups into the local groups you have created, thereby giving the users who are members of the global groups access to the system and its resources.

The built-in local groups in a Windows NT Domain are as follows:

- Administrators

- Users

- Guests

- Backup Operators

- Replicator

- Print Operators

- Server Operators

- Account Operators

The built-in global groups in an NT Domain are as follows:

- Domain Admins

- Domain Users

- Domain Guests

The system groups on an NT server are as follows:

- Everyone

- Creator Owner

- Network

- Interactive

The built-in users on an NT server are as follows:

- Administrator

- Guest

The following table describes the buttons on the User Properties dialog box and their functions:

TABLE 7 BUTTONS ON THE USER PROPERTIES DIALOG BOX

Button	Function
Groups	Enables you to add and remove group memberships for the account. The easiest way to grant rights to a user account is to add it to a group that possesses those rights.
Profile	Enables you to add a user profile path, a logon script name, and a home directory path to the user's environment profile. You learn more about the Profile button in the following section.
Hours	Enables you to define specific times when the users can access the account. (The default is always.)
Logon To	Enables you to specify up to 8 workstations from which the user can log on. (The default is all workstations.)
Account	Enables you to provide an expiration date for the account. (The default is never.) You also can specify the account as global (for regular users in this domain) or domain local.

The following table is a summary of the account policy fields:

TABLE 8 ACCOUNT POLICY FIELDS

Button	Function
Maximum Password Age	The maximum number of days a password can be in effect until it must be changed.
Minimum Password Age	The minimum number of days a password must stay in effect before it can be changed.
Minimum Password Length	The minimum number of characters a password must include.
Password Uniqueness	The number of passwords that NT remembers for a user; these passwords cannot be reused until they are no longer remembered.
Account Lockout	The number of incorrect passwords that can be input by a user before the account becomes locked. Reset will automatically set the count back to 0

after a specified length of time. In addition, the duration of lockout is either a number of minutes or forever (until an administrator unlocks it).

Forcibly disconnect remote users from server when logon hours expire.

In conjunction with logon hours, this check box enables forcible disconnection of a user when authorized hours come to a close.

Users must log on in order to change password.

Ensures that a user whose password has expired cannot change his or her password but has to have it reset by an administrator.

Account SIDs are unique and therefore, if an account is deleted, the permissions cannot be restored by re-creating an account with the same name.

Local profiles are available only from the machine on which they were created, whereas roaming profiles can be accessed from any machine on the network.

A mandatory profile is a roaming profile that users cannot change. They have the extension .MAN.

Hardware profiles can be used with machines that have more than one hardware configuration (such as laptops).

The System Policy editor (POLEDIT) has two modes, Policy File mode and Registry Mode.

The application of system policies is as follows:

1. When you log in, the NTConfig.pol is checked. If there is an entry for the specific user, then any registry settings indicated will

be merged with, and overwrite if necessary, the user's registry.

2. If there is no specific user entry, any settings for groups that the user is a member of will be applied to the user.

3. If the user is not present in any groups and not listed explicitly, then the Default settings will be applied.

4. If the computer that the user is logging in on has an entry, then the computer settings are applied.

5. If there is no computer entry for the user, then the default computer policy is applied.

Windows 95 policies are not compatible with NT and therefore Windows 95 users must access a Windows 95 policy created on a Windows 95 machine and copied to an NT machine and named Config.Pol.

The Net Use command line can be used to map a drive letter to a network share; using the /persistent switch ensures that it is reconnected at next logon.

FAT long filenames under NT have 8.3 aliases created to ensure backward compatibility. The following is an example of how aliases are generated from five files that all have the same initial characters:

Team meeting Report #3.doc
TEAMME~1.DOC

Team meeting Report #4.doc
TEAMME~2.DOC

Team meeting Report #5.doc
TEAMME~3.DOC

Team meeting Report #6.doc
TEAMME~4.DOC

Team meeting Report #7.doc
TE12B4~1.DOC

A long filename on a FAT partition uses one filename for the 8.3 alias and then one more FAT entry for every 13 characters in the name.

A FAT partition can be converted to NTFS without loss of data through the command line

CONVERT <drive>: /FS:NTFS

NTFS supports compression as a file attribute that can be set in the file properties.

Compression can be applied to a folder or a drive, and the effect is that the files within are compressed and any file copied into it will also become compressed.

Compression can be applied through the use of the COMPACT.EXE program through the syntax

COMPACT <file or directory path> [/switch]

The available switches for COMPACT are as follows:

TABLE 9 COMPACT Switches

Switch	Function
/C	Compress
/U	Uncompress
/S	Compress an entire directory tree
/A	Compress hidden and system files
/I	Ignore errors and continue compressing
/F	Force compression even if the objects are already compressed
/Q	Display only summary information

Share-level permissions apply only when users access a resource over the network, not locally. The share-level permissions are

- **No Access.** Users with No Access to a share can still connect to the share, but nothing appears in File Manager except the message `You do not have permission to access this directory`.

- **Read.** Allows you to display folder and file-names, display file content and attributes, run programs, open folders inside the shared folder.

- **Change.** Allows you to create folders and files, change file content, change file attributes, delete files and folders, do everything READ permission allows.

- **Full Control.** Allows you to change file permissions and do everything change allows for.

Share-level permissions apply to the folder that is shared and apply equally to all the contents of that share.

Share-level permissions apply to any shared folder, whether on FAT or NTFS.

NTFS permissions can be applied only to any file or folder on an NTFS partition.

The actions that can be performed against an NTFS object are as follows:

- Read (R)
- Write (W)
- Execute (X)
- Delete (D)
- Change Permissions (P)
- Take Ownership (O)

The NTFS permissions available for folders are summarized in the following table:

TABLE 10   NTFS FOLDER PERMISSIONS

Permission	Action permitted
No Access	none
List	RX
Read	RX
Add	WX
Add & Read	RXWD
Change	RXWD
Full Control	RXWDPO

The NTFS permissions available for files are summarized in the following table:

TABLE 11   NTFS FILE PERMISSIONS

Permission	Action permitted
No Access	none
Read	RX
Add & Read	RX
Change	RXWD
Full Control	RXWDPO

If a user is given permission to a resource and a group or groups of which the user is a member is also given access, then the effective permission the user has is the cumulation of all of the user permissions. This applies unless any of the permissions is No Access, in which case the user has no access to the resource.

If a user is given permission to a shared resource, and is also given permission to that resource through NTFS permissions, then the effective permission is the most restrictive permission.

The File Child Delete scenario manifests itself when someone has full control of a folder but is granted a permission which does not enable deletion (Read or No Access, for example). The effect is that a user will be able to delete files inside the folder even though sufficient access does not appear to be present.

To close the File Child Delete loophole, do not grant a user Full Control access to a folder but instead, use special Directory permissions to assign RXWDPO access; this eliminates the File Child Delete permission.

Access Tokens do not refresh and a user needs to log off and log back on if changed permissions are to take effect.

MONITORING AND OPTIMIZATION

Remember: Here are the elements that Microsoft says it tests on for the "Monitoring and Optimization" section of the exam.

- Monitor performance of various functions by using Performance Monitor. Functions include processor, memory, disk, and network.
- Identify performance bottlenecks.

Performance monitor has four views: chart, alert, log, and report.

The subsystems that are routinely monitored are Memory, Disk, Network, and Processor.

Disk counters can be enabled through the command line:

Diskperf -y

or

Diskperf -ye (for RAID disks and volumes)

TROUBLESHOOTING

Remember: Here are the elements that Microsoft says it tests on for the "Troubleshooting" section of the exam.

- Choose the appropriate course of action to take to resolve installation failures.
- Choose the appropriate course of action to take to resolve boot failures.
- Choose the appropriate course of action to take to resolve configuration errors.
- Choose the appropriate course of action to take to resolve printer problems.
- Choose the appropriate course of action to take to resolve RAS problems.
- Choose the appropriate course of action to take to resolve connectivity problems.
- Choose the appropriate course of action to take to resolve fault-tolerance problems. Fault-tolerance methods include tape backup, mirroring, stripe set with parity, and disk duplexing.

The acronym DETECT can be used to define the troubleshooting process and stands for:

- Discover the problem
- Explore the boundaries
- Track the possible approaches
- Execute an Approach
- Check for success
- Tie up loose ends

An NTHQ disk can test a computer to ensure that NT will successfully install on it.

The following list identifies possible sources of installation problems:

- Media errors
- Insufficient disk space
- Nonsupported SCSI adapter
- Failure of dependency service to start
- Inability to connect to the domain controller
- Error in assigning domain name

The files involved in the boot process are identified in the following table for both Intel and RISC machines:

TABLE 12 FILES INVOLVED IN THE BOOT PROCESS

Intel	RISC
NTLDR	OSLOADER.EXE
BOOT.INI	NTOSKRNL.EXE
NTDETECT.COM	
NTOSKRNL.EXE	

In the NT boot process (in BOOT.INI), ARC paths define the physical position of the NT operating system files and come in two forms:

Scsi(0)disk(0)rdisk(0)partition(1)\WINNT

Multi(0)disk(0)rdisk(0)partition(1)\WINNT

SCSI ARC paths define hard drives which are SCSI and which have their BIOS disabled. The relevant parameters are

- SCSI: the SCSI controller starting from 0
- DISK: the physical disk starting from 0
- PARTITION: the partition on the disk starting from 1
- \folder: the folder in which the NT files are located

MULTI ARC paths define hard drives which are non-SCSI or SCSI with their BIOS enabled. The relevant parameters are

- MULTI: the controller starting from 0
- RDISK: the physical disk starting from 0
- PARTITION: the partition on the disk starting from 1
- \folder: the folder in which the NT files are located

Partitions are numbered as follows:

1. The first primary partition on each disk gets the number 0.

2. Each additional primary partition then is given a number, incrementing up from 0.

3. Each logical drive is then given a number in the order they appear in the Disk Administrator.

Switches on boot lines in the boot.ini file define additional boot parameters. The following table lists the switches you need to know about and their functions:

TABLE 13   BOOT.INI FILE SWITCHES

Switch	Function
/basevideo	Loads standard VGA video driver (640x480, 16-color)
/sos	Displays each driver as it is loaded
/noserialmice	Prevents autodetection of serial mice on COM ports which may disable a UPS connected to the port

A recovery disk can be used to bypass problems with system partition. Such a disk contains the following files (broken down by hardware platform):

TABLE 14   FILES ON A FAULT-TOLERANT BOOT DISK

Intel	RISC
NTLDR	OSLOADER.EXE
NTDETECT.COM	HAL.DLL
BOOT.INI	*.PAL (for Alpha machines)
BOOTSECT.DOS (allows you to boot to DOS)	
NTBOOTDD.SYS (the SCSI driver for a hard drive with SCSI BIOS not enabled)	

An emergency repair disk can be used to recover an NT system if the registry becomes corrupted and must be used in conjunction with the three setup disks used to install NT.

The RDISK programs allow you to update the \REPAIR folder which, in turn, is used to update your repair disk.

The Event Viewer allows you to see three log files: System Log, Security Log, and Application Log.

The Windows NT Diagnostics program allows you to see (but not modify) configuration settings for much of your hardware and environment.

The course of action to take when a stop error occurs (blue screen) can be configured from the System Properties dialog box (in the Control Panel) on the Startup/Shutdown tab.

To move the spool file from one partition to another, use the Advanced Tab on the server properties dialog box; this can be located from the File, Server Properties menu in the printers dialog box.

Common RAS problems include the following:

- User Permission: User not enabled to use RAS in User Manager for Domains

- Authentication: Often caused by incompatible encryption methods (client using different encryption than server is configured to receive)

- Callback with Multilink: Client configured for callback but is using multilink; server will only call back to a single number, thereby removing multilink functionality

- Autodial at Logon: Shortcuts on desktop referencing server-based applications or files cause autodial to kick in when logon is complete

User can't log in may be caused by a number of factors including:

- Incorrect user name or password

- Incorrect domain name

- Incorrect user rights (inability to log on locally to an NT machine, for example)

- Netlogon service on server is stopped or paused

- Domain controllers are down

- User is restricted in system policies from logging on at a specific computer

The right to create backups and restore from backups using NT Backup is granted to the groups Administrators, Backup Operators, and Server Operators by default.

NT Backup will back up files only to tape; no other media is supported.

The following table summarizes the backup types available in NT backup:

TABLE 15   BACKUP TYPES AVAILABLE IN NT BACKUP

Type	*Backs Up*	*Marks?*
Normal	All selected files and folders	Yes
Copy	All selected files and folders	No
Incremental	Selected files and folders not marked as backed up	Yes
Differential	Selected files and folders not marked as backed up	No
Daily Copy	Selected files and folders changed that day	No

The local registry of a computer can be backed up by selecting the Backup Local Registry check box in the Backup Information dialog box.

Data from tape can be restored to the original location or to an alternate location and NTFS permissions can be restored or not, however, you cannot change the names of the objects being restored until the restore is complete.

Backup can be run from a command line by using the NTBACKUP command in the syntax:

Ntbackup backup path [switches]

Some command line backup switches are shown in the following table:

TABLE 16   NTBACKUP COMMAND LINE SWITCHES

Switch	*Function*
/a	Append the current backup to the backup already on the tape.
/v	Verify the backed-up files when complete.
/d "text"	Add an identifying description to the backup tape.
/t option	Specify the backup type. Valid options are normal, copy, incremental, differential, and daily.

To recover from a failed mirror set, you must do the following:

1. Shut down your NT server and physically replace the failed drive.

2. If required, boot NT by using a recovery disk.

3. Start the Disk Administrator by using the menu Start, Programs, Administrative Tools (Common), Disk Administrator.

4. Select the mirror set by clicking on it.

5. From the Fault Tolerance menu, choose Break Mirror. This action exposes the remaining partition as a volume separate from the failed one.

6. Reestablish the mirror set if desired by selecting the partition you desire to mirror and a portion of free space equal in size and choosing the menu Fault Tolerance, Establish Mirror.

To regenerate a stripe set with parity, do the following:

1. Shut down your NT server and physically replace the failed drive.

2. Start the Disk Administrator by using the menu Start, Programs, Administrative Tools (Common), Disk Administrator.

3. Select the stripe set with parity by clicking on it.

4. Select an area of free space as large or larger than the portion of the stripe set that was lost when the disk failed.

5. Choose Fault Tolerance, Regenerate.

Hopefully, this has been a helpful tool in your final review before the exam. You might find after reading this that there are some places in the book you need to revisit. Just remember to stay focused and answer all the questions. You can always go back and check the answers for the questions you are unsure of. Good luck!

Index

E

Q-R

TRAINING GUIDES

Complete, Innovative, Accurate, Thorough

Our next generation *Training Guides* have been developed to help you study and retain the essential knowledge that you need to pass the MCSE exams. We know your study time is valuable, and we have made every effort to make the most of it by presenting clear, accurate, and thorough information.

In creating this series, our goal was to raise the bar on how MCSE content is written, developed, and presented. From the two-color design that gives you easy access to content, to the new software simulator that allows you to perform tasks in a simulated operating system environment, we are confident that you will be well-prepared for exam success.

Our New Riders Top Score Software Suite is a custom-developed set of full-functioning software applications that work in conjunction with the Training Guide by providing you with the following:

Exam Simulator tests your hands-on knowledge with over 150 fact-based and situational-based questions.
Electronic Study Cards really test your knowledge with explanations that are linked to an electronic version of the Training Guide.
Electronic Flash Cards help you retain the facts in a time-tested method.
An Electronic Version of the Book provides quick searches and compact, mobile study.
Customizable Software adapts to the way you want to learn.

MCSE Training Guide: Networking Essentials, Second Edition

1-56205-919-X, $49.99, 9/98

MCSE Training Guide: TCP/IP, Second Edition

1-56205-920-3, $49.99, 10/98

MCSE Training Guide: Windows NT Server 4, Second Edition

1-56205-916-5, $49.99, 9/98

MCSE Training Guide: SQL Server 7 Administration

0-7357-0003-6, $49.99, Q1/99

MCSE Training Guide: Windows NT Server 4 Enterprise, Second Edition

1-56205-917-3, $49.99, 9/98

MCSE Training Guide: SQL Server 7 Design and Implementation

0-7357-0004-4, $49.99, Q1/99

MCSE Training Guide: Windows NT Workstation 4, Second Edition

1-56205-918-1, $49.99, 9/98

MCSD Training Guide: Solution Architectures

0-7357-0026-5, $49.99, Q1/99

MCSE Training Guide: Windows 98

1-56205-890-8, $49.99, Q4/98

MCSD Training Guide: Visual Basic 6, Exam 70-175

0-7357-0002-8, $49.99, Q1/99

MCSD Training Guide: Microsoft Visual Basic 6, Exam 70-176

0-7357-0031-1, $49.99, Q1/99

TRAINING GUIDES

FIRST EDITIONS

Your Quality Elective Solution

MCSE Training Guide: Systems Management Server 1.2, 1-56205-748-0

MCSE Training Guide: SQL Server 6.5 Administration, 1-56205-726-X

MCSE Training Guide: SQL Server 6.5 Design and Implementation, 1-56205-830-4

MCSE Training Guide: Windows 95, 70-064 Exam, 1-56205-880-0

MCSE Training Guide: Exchange Server 5, 1-56205-824-X

MCSE Training Guide: Internet Explorer 4, 1-56205-889-4

MCSE Training Guide: Microsoft Exchange Server 5.5, 1-56205-899-1

MCSE Training Guide: IIS 4, 1-56205-823-1

MCSD Training Guide: Visual Basic 5, 1-56205-850-9

MCSD Training Guide: Microsoft Access, 1-56205-771-5

TESTPREPS

MCSE TestPrep: Networking Essentials, Second Edition

0-7357-0010-9, $19.99, 11/98

MCSE TestPrep: Windows 95, Second Edition

0-7357-0011-7, $19.99, 11/98

MCSE TestPrep: Windows NT Server 4, Second Edition

0-7357-0012-5, $19.99, 12/98

MCSE TestPrep: Windows NT Server 4 Enterprise, Second Edition

0-7357-0009-5, $19.99, 11/98

MCSE TestPrep: Windows NT Workstation 4, Second Edition

0-7357-0008-7, $19.99, 11/98

MCSE TestPrep: TCP/IP, Second Edition

0-7357-0025-7, $19.99, 12/98

MCSE TestPrep: Windows 98

1-56205-922-X, $19.99, Q4/98

TESTPREPS

FIRST EDITIONS

Your Quality Elective Solution

MCSE TestPrep: SQL Server 6.5 Administration, 0-7897-1597-X

MCSE TestPrep: SQL Server 6.5 Design and Implementation, 1-56205-915-7

MCSE TestPrep: Windows 95 70-64 Exam, 0-7897-1609-7

MCSE TestPrep: Internet Explorer 4, 0-7897-1654-2

MCSE TestPrep: Exchange Server 5.5, 0-7897-1611-9

MCSE TestPrep: IIS 4.0, 0-7897-1610-0

FAST TRACK SERIES

The Accelerated Path to Certification Success

Fast Tracks provide an easy way to review the key elements of each certification technology without being bogged down with elementary-level information.

These guides are perfect for when you already have real-world, hands-on experience. They're the ideal enhancement to training courses, test simulators, and comprehensive training guides. *No fluff, simply what you really need to pass the exam!*

LEARN IT FAST

Part I contains only the essential information you need to pass the test. With over 200 pages of information, it is a concise review for the more experienced MCSE candidate.

REVIEW IT EVEN FASTER

Part II averages 50–75 pages, and takes you through the test and into the real-world use of the technology, with chapters on:

1) Fast Facts Review Section
2) The Insider's Spin (on taking the exam)
3) Sample Test Questions
4) Hotlists of Exam-Critical Concepts
5) Did You Know? (real-world applications for the technology covered in the exam)

MCSE Fast Track: Networking Essentials

1-56205-939-4, $19.99, 9/98

MCSE Fast Track: TCP/IP

1-56205-937-8, $19.99, 9/98

MCSE Fast Track: Windows 98

0-7357-0016-8, $19.99, Q4/98

MCSE Fast Track: Internet Information Server 4

1-56205-936-X, $19.99, 9/98

MCSE Fast Track: Windows NT Server 4

1-56205-935-1, $19.99, 9/98

MCSD Fast Track: Solution Architectures

0-7357-0029-X, $19.99, Q1/99

MCSE Fast Track: Windows NT Server 4 Enterprise

1-56205-940-8, $19.99, 9/98

MCSD Fast Track: Visual Basic 6, Exam 70-175

0-7357-0018-4, $19.99, Q4/98

MCSE Fast Track: Windows NT Workstation 4

1-56205-938-6, $19.99, 9/98

MCSD Fast Track: Visual Basic 6, Exam 70-176

0-7357-0019-2, $19.99, Q4/98

How to Contact Us

IF YOU NEED THE LATEST UPDATES ON A TITLE THAT YOU'VE PURCHASED:

1) Visit our Web site at www.newriders.com.

2) Click on the DOWNLOADS link, and enter your book's ISBN number, which is located on the back cover in the bottom right-hand corner.

3) In the DOWNLOADS section, you'll find available updates that are linked to the book page.

IF YOU ARE HAVING TECHNICAL PROBLEMS WITH THE BOOK OR THE CD THAT IS INCLUDED:

1) Check the book's information page on our Web site according to the instructions listed above, or

2) Email us at support@mcp.com, or

3) Fax us at (317) 817-7488 attn: Tech Support.

IF YOU HAVE COMMENTS ABOUT ANY OF OUR CERTIFICATION PRODUCTS THAT ARE NON-SUPPORT RELATED:

1) Email us at certification@mcp.com, or

2) Write to us at New Riders, 201 W. 103rd St., Indianapolis, IN 46290-1097, or

3) Fax us at (317) 581-4663.

IF YOU ARE OUTSIDE THE UNITED STATES AND NEED TO FIND A DISTRIBUTOR IN YOUR AREA:

Please contact our international department at international@mcp.com.

IF YOU WISH TO PREVIEW ANY OF OUR CERTIFICATION BOOKS FOR CLASSROOM USE:

Email us at pr@mcp.com. Your message should include your name, title, training company or school, department, address, phone number, office days/hours, text in use, and enrollment. Send these details along with your request for desk/examination copies and/or additional information.

WE WANT TO KNOW WHAT YOU THINK

To better serve you, we would like your opinion on the content and quality of this book. Please complete this card and mail it to us or fax it to 317-581-4663.

Name _____

Address _____

City _____ State _____ Zip _____

Phone _____ Email Address _____

Occupation _____

Which certification exams have you already passed? _____
_____
_____
_____

Which certification exams do you plan to take? _____
_____
_____
_____

What influenced your purchase of this book?
❑ Recommendation   ❑ Cover Design
❑ Table of Contents   ❑ Index
❑ Magazine Review   ❑ Advertisement
❑ Reputation of New Riders ❑ Author Name

How would you rate the contents of this book?
❑ Excellent   ❑ Very Good
❑ Good   ❑ Fair
❑ Below Average ❑ Poor

What other types of certification products will you buy/have you bought to help you prepare for the exam?
❑ Quick reference books   ❑ Testing software
❑ Study guides   ❑ Other

What do you like most about this book? Check all that apply.
❑ Content   ❑ Writing Style
❑ Accuracy   ❑ Examples
❑ Listings   ❑ Design
❑ Index   ❑ Page Count
❑ Price   ❑ Illustrations

What do you like least about this book? Check all that apply.
❑ Content   ❑ Writing Style
❑ Accuracy   ❑ Examples
❑ Listings   ❑ Design
❑ Index   ❑ Page Count
❑ Price   ❑ Illustrations

What would be a useful follow-up book to this one for you?_____
Where did you purchase this book? _____
Can you name a similar book that you like better than this one, or one that is as good? Why?_____
_____
_____

How many New Riders books do you own? _____
What are your favorite certification or general computer book titles? _____
_____

What other titles would you like to see New Riders develop? _____
_____

Any comments? _____
_____
_____
_____

Place
Stamp
Here

New Riders
201 W. 103rd St.
Indianapolis, IN 46290